OBEDIENT SONS

Obedient Sons

THE DISCOURSE OF YOUTH
AND GENERATIONS
IN AMERICAN
CULTURE,
1630–1860

Glenn Wallach

University of Massachusetts Press

AMHERST

Copyright © 1997 by
The University of Massachusetts Press
All rights reserved
Printed in the United States of America
LC 96-18193
ISBN 1-55849-057-4
Set in Sabon by dix!
Printed and bound by Thomson-Shore, Inc.

Library of Congress Cataloging-in-Publication Data
Wallach, Glenn, 1959–
Obedient sons : the discourse of youth and generations in
American culture, 1630–1860 / Glenn Wallach.
        p.   cm.
Includes bibliographical references (p.   ) and index.
ISBN 1-55849-057-4 (cloth: alk. paper)
  1. Intergenerational relations—United States—History.
  2. Youth—United States—Popular opinion—History.
3. Young men—United States—Popular opinion—History.
        4. Popular culture—United States—History.
        5. Discourse analysis—United States. I. Title.
        HN90.I58W35   1997
    305.2′35—dc20   96-18193
                        CIP

British Library Cataloguing in Publication data
are available.

CONTENTS

FIVE

Young America

116

EPILOGUE

The Discourse of Youth and Generations since 1860: A Sketch

151

NOTES

163

BIBLIOGRAPHY

215

INDEX

259

Illustrations follow page 110

ACKNOWLEDGMENTS

When I wrote a graduate school paper in the spring of 1986 on antebellum young men's groups, I had an inkling of a potential dissertation topic. I never imagined this would be the result ten years later. In the intervening decade I have had the help, support, and cooperation of many friends, colleagues, and institutions.

For permission to quote from unpublished manuscripts in their collections, my thanks to the American Antiquarian Society and the Historical Society of Pennsylvania.

For permission to reprint paintings from their collections, thanks to: the Walters Art Gallery, Baltimore; the New-York Historical Society; the Saint Louis Art Museum; Hirschl & Adler Galleries, New York; the Manoogian Foundation.

I had the support of a Yale University Robert M. Leylan Fellowship during the year I wrote a majority of the dissertation. I thank the Frederick W. Hilles Publication Fund at Yale for a generous subvention to assist in the production of this book.

My thanks to these libraries and archives, and to their librarians: Sterling Memorial Library (particularly its reference and interlibrary loan staffs), Beinecke Rare Book and Manuscript Library, Manuscripts and Archives, Yale University; the Boston Public Library; the American Antiquarian Society; the New York Public Library; the New-York Historical Society; Butler Library, Rare Book and Manuscript Library, Columbia University; the Historical Society of Pennsylvania; Lauinger Library, Georgetown University; the Library of Congress; South Caroliniana

Library, University of South Carolina. I want to recognize in particular James Green of the Library Company of Philadelphia, for his help and hospitality during a research trip to Philadelphia.

My gratitude to individuals begins and ends at Yale University. David Brion Davis has supported this work since I wrote that paper in his research seminar during my first year in graduate school. As dissertation director he offered incisive readings and urged me to give the project the scope it deserved. Jean-Christophe Agnew has been an adviser and friend since my undergraduate days; he and John Demos, the rest of the dissertation committee, patiently tested my ideas and challenged me to explore this topic fully. My appreciation to professors Bryan Jay Wolf, Harry S. Stout, Jon Butler, Nancy F. Cott, Ann Fabian, and Jonathan Rieder for their comments on earlier versions of this work and discussions I've had with them about it.

Like the young men of the nineteenth-century city, both graduate students and professors in the early stages of their career spend years in a liminal state. I owe special thanks to those who were graduate students when this thing started: Christopher Shannon and Daniel Wickberg have each read and commented on several versions of this work. Both are models of scholarly excellence and commitment to the study of ideas. I have benefited greatly from conversations with Jacqueline Dirks that helped me to refine several key concepts in this work. Carol Sheriff took time out from her research in central New York to obtain photocopies from the New York State Historical Association in Cooperstown. Thanks to them and to these friends and colleagues who have shared ideas and references and offered support: Mary Anne Case, Scott Casper, Leah Dilworth, James T. Fisher, Laura King, Hillel Levine, Christopher Lowe, Kathryn Oberdeck, Dinah PoKempner, Stephen Rice, Kristin Robinson, Carlo Rotella, Margaret Sabin, Karen Sawislak, David Waldstreicher, James Wooten.

At Georgetown University, thanks to my colleagues in the history department, Aviel Roshwald, Richard Stites, and Tamara Giles-Vernick, for their comments on parts of the manuscript and their encouragement.

Back at Yale, again, thanks to the dean of Yale College Richard Brodhead. Morse College resident fellows Michael Thurston and Kathleen Pfeiffer made valuable comments on the introduction. My fellow residential college dean Stephen Lassonde has been hearing harangues on the subject of youth and generations since we were in graduate school. He has discussed this work and offered comments in its various stages. Thanks to him and his entire family.

At the University of Massachusetts Press, Clark Dougan believed in this project from the beginning. I am grateful to him for his stalwart support and to the entire staff of the press for their labors.

My family has been critical to this whole endeavor. My East Coast cousins and their families—Adele Pressman and Bob Gardner in Cambridge, Kate Stith and José Cabranes in New Haven—have provided havens on holidays and countless other occasions. Meanwhile, my mother, Vera Wallach, and my brothers Joel and Donald have watched this process with curiosity from the West Coast, not always exactly sure what I was up to in the mysterious East. This work is the best I can do for an explanation.

OBEDIENT SONS

INTRODUCTION

Thinking about Generations
in American Culture

The words seem simple, essential, and inextricably linked: youth and
generations. So many popular phrases in the twentieth century depend
on them to capture the spirit of an era and the responsibilities of America:
Lost Generation, Beat Generation, generation gap, Generation X. The
recent popularity of the label "Generation X" reveals some dimensions
of the story I describe in this book. Douglas Coupland's 1991 novel
Generation X unleashed a stampede of books and articles that used the
title as shorthand for diagnoses of the lives and futures of Americans
in their twenties.[1] Even before the advent of "Generation X," media
trend-spotters were already scouting for tag lines to label contemporary
youth. They began making ominous predictions about an emerging "Indifferent Generation." In 1990 *Time* magazine called them "twentysome-
thing." The words on the cover read: "Overshadowed by the baby
boomers, America's next generation has a hard act to follow." The fea-
ture article observed:

> Down deep, what frustrates today's young people—*and those who observe
> them*—is their failure to create an original youth culture. The 1920s had
> jazz and the Lost Generation, the 1950s created the Beats, the 1960s
> brought everything embodied in the Summer of Love. But the twentysome-
> thing generation has yet to make a substantial cultural statement.[2]

A few years later, this article was hailed as the harbinger of Generation
X's arrival.

By 1995, the phrase was in decline. "I have been a traitor to my
generation by labeling my friends and striving to define my classmates,"

wrote one journalist. Others attacked "hucksters" seeking profit from their cohort's experience. Alternatively, the editor of the *New Republic* grumbled, "This Generation X thing is entirely constructed by people in their forties who became addicted to the idea of a generation. . . . And I hope it dies with them."[3] The term lives on in the realms of organized knowledge. Since 1994 "Generation X" has been a subject heading at the Library of Congress.[4] Wherever it appeared, and whoever responded to it—from "authentic" youth spokespeople to skeptics pronouncing it unfair, unrepresentative, or a result of savvy marketing strategy—an underlying belief pervaded this coverage that young people must always be organized into a particular category called a generation. It seemed equally clear that generations mattered.

Most popular thought about youth and generations is either literally *Time*less, treating them as universal concepts, or wrapped up in contemporary history—assuming talk about generations is a recent trend. In fact, pundits and forecasters had dipped into one of the oldest streams in American thought. For more than three hundred years, there has been enduring public concern with the idea of a generation.

This book does not explore the nature of today's young people or compare them to youth of the past. It is not a study of generational rifts, or attitudes toward the young. I am interested less in particular attributes of youth in any historical era and much more in the way they have been imagined and explained over time. While this approach may omit individual experience, it offers a new perspective on a set of concerns most recently articulated in the modern obsession with naming and monitoring generations. The thousands of recent articles that dissected the prospects of the young and attached national significance to who they were, what they cared about, or whether they cared at all are not the first instance of this cultural theme; they will not be the last.

From the colonial era to the eve of the Civil War, specific crises and conditions in America produced a language that invested a "younger" generation with responsibilities for maintaining community ideals. As young people gathered in early nineteenth-century cities they formed their own responses to this rhetoric and used their youth to explain their growing involvement in public life. Antebellum young men's organizations claimed a particular connection to their fathers, both actual parents and metaphorical ancestors. This language migrated beyond the confines of youth and influenced the development of political and cultural nationalism. In the 1840s and 1850s a very distant ancestor to Generation X appeared; youth for the first time became part of a national catchphrase —Young America. The history of this discourse's development and its influence on American culture has never been told.

The expansion of the popular press and a new audience of readers shaped the language of generations. The New England Puritans who published sermons and pamphlets meant for popular instruction were the vanguard in the spread of print culture from the seventeenth to the nineteenth centuries. The broad availability of print allowed for the diffusion of a discourse that might be employed by different speakers in addresses delivered in rural western Connecticut as well as cosmopolitan Boston, New York, or Philadelphia. Such speakers did not offer identical messages, but the similarities in imagery and figurative language were much more than mere cliché or commonplace; they illustrate the enduring power of the ideas.

The creation of a literate American public that could *imagine* a community, in Benedict Anderson's phrase, made it easier to see individuals as representative members of groups, or groups as characteristic of something larger in society. Anderson has described how the overthrow of King Louis XVI of France in 1789 was transformed into "a 'thing' . . . with its own name: The French Revolution. . . . [an] experience . . . shaped by millions of printed words into a 'concept' on the printed page."[5]

Readers who could imagine a community formed a public that could imagine a generation. The significance of print culture in the preservation of memory is well known. The language of youth and generations was closely linked to the printed recording of memory; ministers quoted the words of those who had published years before them, and their own words formed the basis for later printed exhortations. The rise of a widely circulated popular press provided the circumstances for the language to become truly national.

This study, then, focuses not on individual psychology but on social discourse. It uncovers a powerful language of continuity shaping ideas about youth and generations. I reject the notion that there is any self-evident quality to "generations" or to "youth." I analyze these cultural concepts, as one historian suggests, by examining the "idioms, rhetorics, or paradigms in which such a discourse has been conducted." As another scholar puts it, this approach allows us to see "the extent to which those features of our own arrangements which we may be disposed to accept as traditional or even 'timeless' truths may in fact be the merest contingencies of our peculiar history and social structure."[6]

This book investigates the meaning of ideas about youth and generations in American culture. The very words *youth* and *generations* are more than simple "reflections, refractions or indices of some other 'real' thing"; they are "elements of a cultural reality themselves."[7] They are ideas constructed in public discourse about community and the transmission of values. These discourses emerged and took on particular meanings that helped to shape the way people saw, described, and understood the world.

It may seem anachronistic to study language and discourse in the face of a growing mountain of scholarship on the social-historical experience of young people.[8] A historian of youth in medieval times argues, for example, that "the most consistent issue is the struggle between adults and youth; it cuts across national, class, gender and time lines."[9] Whether this is, indeed, the central social relationship is beside the point.

My emphasis on discourse is much more than a casual choice of a convenient methodology. Most scholarly works, whatever their disciplinary grounding, treat youth or generations as almost natural phenomena. Some impose modern psychological concepts on their subjects and concentrate on aspects that seem most familiar to recent history: conflicts between children and parents, the protest activity of students.[10]

Because historians often assume an implicit character to these terms and then simply choose an approach appropriate to a specific question—community study, psychohistory, or whatever—the history of *the terms themselves* remains unexamined. I do not deny the existence of conflict between individual parents and children, even between youth and age more broadly. Nevertheless, did public, political, and cultural discourse imagine youth and generations *solely* in these terms? The cultural significance *assigned* to social experience has not remained consistent in every era. Either we can assume that a discourse of conflict is authentic, because it is what we expect to find, and dismiss continuity as mere rhetoric, or we can try to figure out the relationship between them.

The problem here is not determining the experience of youth in a particular era in American history, or finding the alchemical formula that will identify a supposedly authentic generation. Rather, youth and generations are "cultural ideals" and we must discover the "vocabulary of symbols, or metaphors" in them.[11] Unless we understand the roots, nature, and quality of the discourse about youth and generations, we cannot understand its various uses. The key lies in how youth and generations were defined in earlier times and the relationship between discourses produced by both adults and young people.[12]

At first glance, these issues seem familiar to some historical traditions. Certainly cultural historians have studied the political imagery of family or fathers, or analyzed the statements made by and about sons in connection with national issues.[13] But that scholarship produces a curious paradox. Separate studies of Puritan sermons, college students in the early national period, the image of the American Revolution, and leading antebellum political figures find sons struggling to pull themselves out of the shadow cast by imposing fathers. These figures are either literal or metaphorical founders.[14] Given the span of time encompassed by these studies, they cannot describe responses to the same fathers. By focusing on the broad discourse that provides the vocabulary for these various relationships, I suggest a different interpretation of these recurring performances of concern.

Ideas about youth and generations developed in the colonial era; they coalesced during the 1820s to the 1850s. The Revolutionary War marked a second national founding, and the first half of the nineteenth century established a new significance for generations in national life. As the men who had run the Revolution began to die, leaders increasingly expressed a sense of obligation to the passing Founding Fathers. Historians argue that an obsessive anxiety developed about the nation's ability to fulfill the vision and example set by the founders.[15] This anxiety, they suggest, was felt most intensely by the sons of the founders.

Forging continuity with the past and finding ideals that could unify an increasingly differentiated population represented an essential cultural dilemma in antebellum America. In the decades before the Civil War this growing separation coincided with a general cultural climate described by John Higham as the "Age of Boundlessness," when "most Americans conceived of theirs as a young, new country, still bathed in the morning light of the American Revolution." The forward march of "boundlessness" was overshadowed by a movement for "consolidation," exemplified by impulses to preserve the past.[16]

This historiographical tradition promotes the conclusion that any positive statement in the late eighteenth or early nineteenth century about the past or the founding fathers is simple "filiopietism." It is perhaps appropriate that Charles Francis Adams, Jr.'s attack in the last century on the "self-satisfied complacency" of Massachusetts historians helped popularize the notion that references to the founders represented a form of ancestor worship. Since then, the actual content of that language is rarely investigated. Loyalty to parents or founders becomes just another example of the psychological demands placed on those who succeeded them.[17]

An influential interpretation in this tradition has termed the antebellum period a "post-heroic" age and suggested that the new generation following the giants of the Revolution could feel only inadequate by comparison. Antebellum public speakers often referred to themselves as sons of the Founding Fathers. This has been interpreted as a conservative "holding action against the force of time," in which "the founders would assume the role of the fathers" who had to be obeyed according to the conservatives' directions. Sons would preserve the founders' wisdom and pass it on to future generations. Ultimately, "conservatives used the heroic model of the fathers to prepare children for nonheroic lives . . . to remain obedient children forever." [18]

This Freudian-influenced reading of the era suggests that the sons needed desperately to supersede their own fathers and other "heroic" founding figures to achieve their own identity. They sought to commit rhetorical patricide without appearing to do so. Evidence that many post-heroic sons did *not* rebel against their past is dismissed; boundlessness allegedly created "the illusion that the past was gone . . . thus obviating any desire to rebel against it." In this interpretation, "past" and "father" are the same. While the 1840s had been a time of challenge to the past, the 1850s repressed patricidal impulses and promoted veneration.[19] The generational assertions in this sophisticated and challenging appraisal of the sources of the Civil War cannot be accepted at face value.

"Obedience," for example, manifested several meanings. Young men's organizations, given scant attention in most historical works, were the most significant antebellum purveyors of the rhetoric of fathers and sons, but they did not deploy this language in an undifferentiated conservative stream. They developed a public rhetoric in which they claimed a particular connection to actual parents and metaphorical ancestors whose founding energies held great significance for the national future. Proclamations by youth organizations used the stuff of generational discourse to describe a more active and innovative future than seemed possible in an "unheroic" preservationist age.

The patricide image has captured later authors' imaginations.[20] It is true that some public rhetoric questioned the control imposed on the present by the past, but many other groups embraced the founders and identified their own activity in public in terms of the fathers' legacy. Why does a lack of open rebellion necessarily suggest an illusion? Were those who celebrated their obedience protesting *too* much?

An American rhetoric of youth and generations unfolded from 1630 to 1860 amid contradictory patterns of persistence and change. A language of continuity and generational obligation was established by Puritans and revolutionaries who themselves had repudiated tradition and thrown off the constraints of the past. The language of generations was corporate, national, civic. It yoked conservative motivations—follow in the footsteps of glorious founders, stay the course, transmit a heritage unimpaired to those who follow—to an activist vision of responsibility for building a new society. The language of youth, meanwhile, balanced the fear of disruption and the promise of growth. In one respect, it emphasized personal issues and spoke directly to individual family life. But it also addressed parents' concerns about their children's prospects and the progressive aspirations of young people who sought fulfillment of their personal goals in the future of America. These discourses mingled in a wide variety of literature and oratory, separating and intertwining. This book untangles those strands.

The first two chapters examine the composition and use of the terms *generation* and *youth* from the time of the first New England colonial settlement until the early nineteenth century. The Bible, classical literature, and Renaissance works were filled with references to generations. New England Puritans broke a timeless cycle by identifying a specific group of young people *as a generation* who had special significance in a particular time and place. The Puritans faced a crisis of institutional continuity during the controversy over church membership resolved in the Half-Way Covenant. They believed their colony's future rested on the shoulders of people they called the rising generation. That is a long way from associating that group *with* their time—"the Synod of 1662 Generation," let us say, or young people speaking of themselves as, perhaps, "the Halfwayers." The Puritans took an enduring form—"the rising generation"—and situated it in one group at one time. After that, later groups could be similarly identified and assigned their own responsibilities; generational language became associated with secular ideas about tradition and the past.

The first chapter explores the development of this new conception of generations, while the second examines the idea of "youth." Chapter 3 presents young people speaking for themselves and reveals the significant contribution of young men's organizations to this developing American language. The language of youthful duty and generational responsibility was transformed as it migrated into a wider nationalist discourse. The fourth chapter then explores the impact of this language on the movement for a unique American art and in commemorative and artistic representation: institutions and people struggling to reconcile the past and the future. Finally, I show how these themes culminate in the varieties of youth portrayed in the much-cited and rarely discussed phrase "Young America."[21] This was a slogan employed by a contradictory cast of persons; some thundered explicit and unrepressed patricidal rhetoric, while others sought a path toward the new based on notions of continuity with the past.

The purveyors of generational discourse, literate and mostly middle-class people, were primarily white men. National significance can be observed in the need felt by some free African Americans to situate themselves in relation to notions of youth and generations. The crucial role of Puritan thought in the discourse's formation, as well as the location of centers for print production, made this primarily an urban and Northern phenomenon. I consider variations to this discourse by region and race.

The concepts "generation" and "youth," while usually presented as universal, had powerful gender implications. Throughout this book I show that both terms have been male discourses and have been integral to the definition of manhood in society. Moreover, women's roles and responsibilities were often shaped by those assigned to the younger, male, generation. The male language of youth and generations affected ideas of education, participation in political life, and the rhetoric of national expansion.

Since elites—ministers, political leaders, and other cultural authorities —shaped this discourse, much of this study focuses on elite productions: sermons, pamphlets, newspapers, and other publications. While I devote some attention to renowned literary and political works, few of the items studied here are remembered today as major; some may seem second-rate. In some cases they were far more popular when originally published; in others they were equally as obscure then as now. But, for a variety of reasons, they had great impact despite their obscurity. It has been noted that "the great texts are almost invariably the worst guide to conventional wisdom" precisely because "they challenge the common-places of the period."[22] We often remember "classic" works today for their ability to step outside their own time and evoke notions more familiar to our own. Works lodged firmly in their time offer a stronger sense of the prevailing discourse that existed then and the long-range changes that emerged.

Many contemporary concepts about the social and psychological experience of young people are based on ideas developed in the late nineteenth and early twentieth century.[23] These insights reveal much about individual conflicts between parents and children and how the family relationship has been conceived throughout history, yet they tell only part of the story. We need to understand an earlier way of seeing the world that such approaches obscure. By unraveling the mess of meanings in the discourse of youth and generations we will see how an older language illuminates the concern for youth in society today and persists under the surface of the contradictory expectations that surround them. More than any insights that we may glean about the contemporary situation, the history of this discourse tells a new story about the past as it suggests different lessons for the present and the future.

CHAPTER ONE

Up and Doing:
The Past and Generations,
1630–1800

A Puritan read from his Book: "One Generation passeth away, and another Generation cometh: but the Earth abideth forever." "The Text is very plain," Cotton Mather explained, "It needs no *Commentary: We our selves* are the commentary. All that is wanting is a serious and useful Application of it."[1] Mather's appeal to the Massachusetts General Assembly in 1715 followed familiar rhetorical paths; it seemed that it could have been delivered at almost any time in the Bay Colony's existence. "We are to take notice of one Generation passing off; and this, the case of Every Generation. We Live in a Dying World," said Mather, as he described an unending process that seemed to include his own temporal location: "One Generation should make way for another. . . . Let them in the Generation that is passing off, be willing to pass. Let them in the Generation that is coming on, be willing to be likewise passing."[2]

Then Mather swept aside the image of ceaseless cycles and offered a plea to a particular class of people: "O Children, Beware of Degenerating from the Godliness of your Ancestors. . . . Ah, New-England, we fear, we fear, there is apace fulfilling on thee that word. . . . 'there arose another Generation after them, which knew not the Lord.' " His audience, "successors to a Generation Famous for their Piety," must protect "the Noble Vine once planted here" lest it become "a Degenerate Plant." He called on God to "save New-England from a Sett of Degenerate Grand-Children." It was clear to Mather that "the Affairs of the Country are very much come into the Hands of Another Generation from what had the Management of them some Years ago." He exhorted the "Generation coming on" to "Hearken to the Demands which the former Generation makes upon you." At the same time he claimed a special place for "The Generation, whose Glories, and Sentiments and Actions are handed down to you in an History that must be a standing Testimony against you, if you Apostatize. Being Dead, they yet speak."[3]

This seemingly timeless jeremiad was not the average minister's topic in 1715. The speech, and Cotton Mather himself, represented an increasingly moribund tradition in Massachusetts. The General Assembly, not ministers, controlled the colony's business—they were the "Managers of the Day." Even as Mather acknowledged their distance from the colony's founding in his reference to "Grand-Children," his rhetoric linked the legislators to an older heritage as he described "another Generation . . . which knew not the Lord." Even if "Puritan" power had faded, a discourse developed by Puritan divines endured that related timeless human change to contingent social processes. As Mather suggested, in order to find its application, his audience need only look at themselves. Puritans had regularly practiced self-examination before their arrival in the New World. They emphasized the unchanging character of tradition passed from father to son. In America, their response to demographic realities became a catalyst for the popular idea that particular young people had essential responsibility for society's very existence. "Generations" became the basis for a public vocabulary used to describe and explain changes in New England society. By the time Mather spoke, that language was no longer the sole possession of ministers. It had undergone a series of transformations.

The Puritans' interpretation of the word *generation* emerged from the Old Testament. Each reference seemed to resonate with a different aspect of the New England experience in the seventeenth century, from Puritans' identification as an exiled people to their obsessive concern with transmitting the founders' values to those who followed them. By the eighteenth century, generational language had become an essential part of a fabric of feeling about the future and the past, of survival and continuity with essential principles.

The Hebrew word for generation, *dor*, appears throughout the Old Testament. Its etymological meaning comes from the image of a circle, which has been interpreted to mean a community. More generally the term suggests a period or age, or a particular group of people living at a particular time.[4] The word implied an individual's community, "which for him extends only over his lifetime, but which continues in the same succession of identifiable and yet different assemblies in succeeding years."[5]

In its biblical usage the concept associated "the new generation of Israel" with the tradition of Moses. Mather's quotation from the Book of Judges, "there arose another Generation," had a double meaning. The legislators of 1715 had no direct experience of the founders Mather invoked, just as the next generation after Joshua had not personally experienced the moment on Mount Sinai or the years of wandering in the desert. Also, like the biblical predecessors, they did not know in the sense that they no longer observed the practices of the founders.[6] Through memory, though, one could "bridge the gap of time and form a solidarity with the fathers."[7] Puritan ministers applied their extensive knowledge of the Old Testament and Hebrew learning to local conditions by "associating the experience of New England with literal, historical movements in the past record of ancient Israel."[8] In addition to describing a person and his contemporaries, *generation* might be used simply as an evocative synonym for the current times.[9] As Increase Mather put it, "A Generation is sometimes taken for the Age of one man, as well as for the men of one Age."[10]

Generation had always been linked to *fathers*. The Hebrew word for generation was a masculine noun, and its roots derived from acts assumed to be a male prerogative: being "generative," literally bringing into being. The biblical uses of the word were linked initially to the kinship relationship. A generation described persons produced by the seed and from the loins of the biblical patriarchs, and all the subsequent generations from their children. The word *son* was related to *seed*, coming from a verb *to beget*. The word *gender*, in fact, derived from the same word for generation. Early grammars and etymologies emphasized masculine action and feminine passivity.[11] To be a father was to be a generator. Thus, Cotton Mather's uncle Eleazar described fathers as "All Superiors, and Ancestors. . . . In a word, all progenitors . . . Fathers by age . . . Fathers by office, in a civil sense and in a spiritual sense."[12] The language of fathers and sons would dominate the language of generations.

The wave of interest in generations crested during an era of sermons assailing the people for degeneration from the founders' ways. In this season of declension, from the 1660s to 1690s, Puritan sermons moved from describing a generation as the specific issue from parents or as a synonym for all contemporaries to identifying one special generation. What began as a concern about literal fathers became a powerful metaphor when actual progenitors had passed on. Two pleas intertwined so as to be sometimes indistinguishable: a generational responsibility to the nation/covenant, and the individual responsibility of children, or parents, to one another, and for their own salvation. While seemingly personal and otherworldly, the second could, in a wink of an eye, become part of the first. The complex quality of this rhetoric makes it especially unwise to imagine either that these references simply represent the Puritans' reliance on "the past" or that their invocation of founders, fathers, or generations was purely personal. The generational issue became the bridge between concern for the salvation of the individual soul and Puritan society.

Jeremiad and Generation

Scholars since Perry Miller have argued that with the return of the English monarchy in 1660 the Bay Puritans refigured their errand.[13] The Restoration was only one of the simultaneous crises that seemed to conspire against New England. A demographic transition took on particular significance. New England's founders, long-lived by seventeenth-century standards, were dying; the passage of time was separating the colony from its initial energies. Plagues and droughts that seemed all too familiar to the Bible-reading Puritans, Indian wars, and other domestic disturbances left the future of the founders' dream in grave doubt. It was at this moment that the concept of generation took on "a concrete reality, a precision of meaning that magnified the ministers' hortatory use of the term."[14]

The "second generation" of ministers—either the literal sons of founders or a new group mounting established pulpits—are said to have constructed an ideal image of monumental founders whose achievements could never be matched by their lesser successors. They spoke of the past as a "golden age" and instituted an excessive veneration for the founders and the past. As Robert Middlekauff put it, "The fathers may have founded the colonies, but the sons invented New England."[15]

The jeremiad, a rhetorical assault on the people for falling from the ways of the fathers, became the vehicle to articulate this special past.[16] Jeremiads during the Protestant Reformation and in English Puritan pulpits had upbraided congregations for a lack of faith. The New England jeremiad had a special quality as "a ritual of continuity through generational rededication." It increasingly came to be about the founders' successors "telling and retelling their inherited story." They tried to "reconcile, by proclaiming them one, the intent and the achievement of their fathers," according to one literary analyst.[17]

Puritan ministers generally avoided contemporary topics in the sermons on biblical texts that they regularly preached and rarely published. The extraordinarily high percentage of published "occasional" sermons for election or days of fasting and humiliation form the bulk of public Puritan thought. These were exceptional works by definition; nonetheless they were the recognized vehicle for "pulpit commentary on social and political themes." Reading them reveals "a process whereby a community could constitute itself by publication," a community shaped by the idea of generations. Print ensured that the dead would speak to those who followed them. It also guaranteed, of course, that subsequent appeals to the founders' memory would similarly endure. These addresses drew power and authority not only from the particular event that demanded recognition, but from the "intertextual connections from one ritual occasion to the next."[18] Precisely because they addressed the colony's past, present, and future, the special sermons often made the most explicit statements on generational themes. One kind of fast sermon existed solely to improve the lot of the rising generation. Much of the evidence in this chapter comes from prefaces, dedications, and introductions to sermons, suggesting that the generational concern was integral to their framing, context, and construction.[19]

Many historians have proposed that the decline described in the jeremiad was more mythological than actual, representing inner stresses rather than literal declension. Some authors, however, confuse the language of generations with interpersonal relationships as they propound a theory about "the psychological needs of the second-and-third generation Puritans that arose from the generational conflict between the founders and their sons."[20] Emory Elliott, for example, argued that the "founders" sought "to create a myth about themselves even before their own passing and to repress their sons in society and in the family." The "fathers" offered as evidence, however, were such founders' sons as Thomas Shepard, Jr., and Increase Mather. Werner Sollors defended Elliott's practice, arguing that "generational numbering is always a metaphoric enterprise."[21] Sollors claimed that something inherent in "American family symbolism seems more drawn to the quasi-typological sequence of grandparent (foundation, type), parent (declension), and grandchild-Ego (fulfillment, antitype)."[22] Evidently, metaphors were created and histories constructed. But why, then, did Increase Mather use biblical precedents to prove that "that most corrupt Generation were the *grand-children* of those that were first embodyed as a peculiar people"?[23] Rhetoric can move in contrary directions; the evidence resists being cloaked in overarching typology.

The second generation did not simply "create" their fathers. They devised a complex way of seeing the world that *began* with their holy and heroic forebears but quickly shifted to the succession and transmission of values from father to son. This was first done in sermons describing the current state of New England—"there arose another Generation"—but it was not solely a conservative plea to remember the fathers and obey. It was an activist vision of responsibility to the community. Sermons relied heavily on the image of David preparing the way for Solomon. The message was the same: the "rising generation" had work to do. The language of generations developed into a general reference to posterity. Ultimately the notion of posterity became so generalized that it could be transported out of a religious context and persist as a powerful image for secular society.[24]

Generation in Exile

The seeds of generational rhetoric were planted in the intellectual ferment of Renaissance and Reformation Europe and appear in the earliest words that we consider part of the Puritan sojourn in America. The early seventeenth-century debate over the inevitable decay of the world from an earlier golden age, with roots in writings by thinkers from Ovid to Boethius, showed that one did not have to be a Puritan to believe that one lived in "an age too late." Humanist philosophers promoted the image of decay by comparing changes in the world with human aging and the lives of nations with the natural life cycle.[25] Puritan ministers, in turn, raised the possibility of errant children even before the errand to the wilderness had begun.

John Cotton's sermon to departing Massachusetts Bay colonists used biblical portents of declension popular in Puritan thought: "Your Ancestors were of a noble and divine spirit, but if they suffer their children to degenerate, to take loose courses, then God will surely pluck you up." He warned them to "look well to the plants that spring from you, that is to your children, that they do not degenerate as the Israelites did."[26] Cotton's analysis of Ecclesiastes published shortly after his death in the 1650s described this "use" of the line "one generation passeth away, and another cometh": "To teach the younger sort . . . to make some benefit of their ancestors' going before, observing whatsoever was commendable

in them and imitating it."[27] Both elements in Cotton's interpretation—
that the founders were descended of noble ancestors and that the settlers
must ensure that the children planted in new soil grow properly—received further elaboration.

The first years of settlement saw few hints of trouble in the transmission of founding ideals to a new generation.[28] Inevitably, though, there
were darker shadows on the sunny prospect of generational comity. John
Cotton was already expressing dismay at the actions of those coming of
age in the 1640s.[29] William Bradford had written a private account of
cooperation between old and young but also penned these words around
1654:

> When I think on what I have often read
> How when the Elders and Joshua were dead;
> Who had seen those great works and them could tell,
> What God had done and wrought for Israel
> Yet they did soon forget and turn aside
> And in his truth and ways did not abide
> But in the next age did degenerate
> I wish this may not be New England's fate.[30]

The New England dilemma seemed to match the Bible again. If the
founders were like Moses' followers—doomed to wander—what would
protect the ones who would grow up in a new world free of the taint of
the old, but also lacking its binding traditions?

New England in the 1650s retained its sense that the world was watching to see whether it could accomplish its errand. There was still great
concern about what others might say. Thomas Cobbett of Lynn, Massachusetts, looked beyond the colonies as he considered "the honour due
from Children to Parents, and the duty of parents towards their children." He reminded the children of godly parents that despite their many
advantages disaster was certain if they strayed. Such decline would allow
those who opposed Puritanism's worldwide advance "to say of you; Yea,
these are your younger generation of the Church. . . . these are the brood
of such Puritan Ministers . . . and the like blasphemous sarcasmes."
Disobedience further ensured that "your posterity and the succeeding
generations become profane, irreligious."[31]

Increasingly, ministers directed their pleas to the young people of the
congregation, "the rising generation." Sermons also made a general diagnosis of the relations between generations, and addressed those of older
generations: the "standing" generation and those "passing from the

stage." The concern with Puritanism's opponents would be transferred to New England's Fathers and relations with their straying sons.

The Bible prophesied danger, and the founding ministers strove to halt seemingly inevitable decay. John Norton emphasized the utility of generational rhetoric: "The experiences of generations foregoing, are the instruction of generations following. . . . The woes of Ancestors, ought to be the warning of successors." He affirmed the importance of leaving a message to posterity after he and his fellows were dust.[32] Charles Chauncey's preface to Richard Mather's *Farewell Exhortation* reminded parents to "lay up from their Children and leave such an estate behind them, that their posterity after them may comfortably be provided for." It was especially important that such an estate be left by "Spiritual Fathers," and that the "Lord's living witnesses" provide testimony.[33]

Perhaps Cotton had sent the Bay Colony settlers on an unexceptional errand. Many historians now question whether the Puritan founders ever claimed that New England was the New Jerusalem. Indeed, in those first decades some argued the southern colonies in the West Indies and South America held the true destination God had charted for His chosen ones. Puritan England's designs on the West Indies included a disastrous expedition on Spanish lands. A Puritan in New England wrote Cromwell that perhaps the mission failed because "this generation" must "die in the wilderness."[34] While revolutionary England's grand "Western Design" faded, New England remained. Ministers recognized the intersection of a "genealogical watershed," the passing of the founders, with the disruption in the Puritan revolution.[35] They developed a language based on generational continuity to specify the colony's unique importance.

The Puritans knew that new people would rise to replace the founders. But what would the ones rising up be like? Sermons spared little detail in describing the consequences of broken generational continuity. "When Joseph or Joshua are unknown, or forgotten . . . how fearfully ominous to Israel must it needs be!" said Samuel Danforth in the preface to his sermon on New England's errand into the wilderness.[36] It became the community's responsibility to prevent the Lord's displeasure at the apostasy of the present and succeeding generation.[37]

David and Solomon — Generational Responsibility

"There is no little Expectation concerning you. . . . your predecessors those that have been before you, all of their expectations under God

himself, are in you: they hope you will stand up in their stead," said
Eleazar Mather.[38] The assertion that every generation had a responsibility
hovered in the background of any discussion of generations. David was
a central figure in defining notions of generation and service. Several
ministers titled sermons "David Serving His Generation."[39]

David had special significance because he bestowed on Solomon the
duty to build the Temple. "David when there was a Great Work to be
done for God, by his Young Son, thought it no Excuse for him to say My
Son is Young and Tender," Cotton Mather said once. "Be any of you
never so Young and Tender, yet I am to tell you, that you have a Great
Work . . . incumbent on you; Oh! Be up, and be Doing."[40] This challenge
to be up and doing—for sons to follow fathers in the building of a
hierarchical structure—the Temple, the Puritan mission—became a common part of the rhetoric of generations. As one minister noted, "Our
Fathers did like David, He Prepared materials for the Temple, and then
left it to his Sons to goe on with the Building."[41]

The special task left in the hands of a new generation touched the
entire community: "our own good is wrapped up in the good of our
Generation: the better it fares with our Generation, the better will it fare
with us." Christians serving their generation, therefore, "should be men
of publick spirits. . . . Publick persons are under a Special obligation and
Bond of Service." Eleazar Mather said it is "part of the Generation-work
of every Christian, to do his utmost that the Lords Name and Honour
may be held up to the succeeding Generation."[42] The call to serve rang
out in different registers, with varying emphases, in ministerial appeals
to all segments of the congregation as they exhorted the elders, diagnosed
present conditions, and looked to the children to save the day.

As the earliest New England rhetoric showed, the Puritans exalted and
exhorted a group it called "fathers." At times they were a category being
described, at others the group being addressed. Fathers were "those of
old, but especially . . . those in the former Generations," according to
James Allen. The word could also mean old men deserving respect.[43] The
"fathers" were invoked most often to describe the purposes that had
brought the original colonists to North America. They served as a major
point of comparison in the charges of declension and degeneracy made
in jeremiads and other sermons. Although degeneracy had plagued the
people of the Bible, it was a more serious offense in New England, "for
we . . . have been brought up under greater and more glorious Light than
they." The sentiment that it "was Another and Better Thing that we
followed the Lord into the Wilderness for" began early in the declension

era. Early jeremiads reminded listeners "alwayes to remember" that New England was "a *Plantation Religious,* not a plantation of Trade." Many sermons repeated the view that the "Interest" of New England was changing. "How many such are there in New-England that are not of their Fathers principles," Increase Mather asked.[44]

Ministers called on those who remembered the early days to confirm the truth of their charges. "O how excellent was it, as those of the first generation yet remaining knows and many also of the rising generation can Remember," said Thomas Shepard, Jr. Increase Mather's device was more extreme and played on the past of both Old England and New England. In a "Discourse Concerning the Danger of Apostasy" (1677) he said, "You old men that are here before the Lord this day, what say you to this Question, did you know such judgments upon New-England formerly. . . . In former times we heard of little besides settlement of plantations and gathering of Churches." In "Pray for the Rising Generation," the following year, he said, "In the last age, in the days of our Fathers, in other parts of the world, scarce a sermon preached but some evidently converted . . . which of us can say we have seen the like?"[45] A more general sentiment was expressed by the Bible text chosen for the 1679 election sermon, "The Lord our God be with us, as he was with our Fathers, let him not leave us, nor forsake us."[46] Even as they were being addressed, those fathers were being metaphorically entombed and memorialized.

A related term gained currency: "fore-fathers." The word first referred to the Puritans' predecessors in Old England, as in a 1679 colonial proclamation of a fast day calling on the Lord to "remember his people in Europe, more especially in the Land of our Fore-Fathers Sepulchres." The tombs of the fathers requiring remembrance became another flexible metaphor in the New World.[47] The 1697 publication *Remembrance of Former Times* asked, "Have we not too much forgotten the Design and Ends of our Fore-fathers coming into this Wilderness, viz. Religion and Godliness."[48] This last comment suggests that by 1697 both "fathers" and "fore-fathers" had come to mean the first progenitors on American soil. Rhetoric originally directed at a new generation had become "engrafted onto the history of the founders."[49]

The ministers raised the specter of angry, departed ancestors. They began biblically: "If Abraham, or Israel, were now alive again, they would not know, or own us to be their Posterity," said Thomas Cobbett in 1654. Thomas Shepard, Jr., spoke generally about more recent ancestors: "Should some of our Fathers that are now asleep in Jesus . . . arise out of their Graves, and hear. . . . would they not even rend their garments and weep over this Generation?" Increase Mather made the allusion more concrete. "Certainly . . . if your blessed Fathers, and predecessors were alive, and in place, it would not be so; If Winthrop, Dudley, Endicot were upon the Bench, such profaneness as this would soon be suppressed." The young Cotton Mather turned the image around: "What? Shall the Grandchildren of Moses turn Idolators? and shall the Children of Samuel become the Children of Belial? Shall we forget the Hope of our Fathers. . . . The very Graves of those blessed men, every Post, every Stone upon their Graves, is a witness against us, if we do."[50]

Posterity demanded details if memory were to survive the founders. Published opinions and remembrances by older colonists began appearing during the 1690s. A renowned example was entitled *Old Mens Tears for Their Own Declensions* (1691). The author hoped to rouse the "first and old Generation . . . out of our drowsie Lethargy," and move the young "to be the followers of their Fathers."[51] Old men's testimonies were only one aspect of the wider Puritan imperative to promote memory. Writing history became one approved means for such remembrance. John Higginson and Thomas Thacher hoped for a comprehensive history; failing that, "while sundry of the Elder Planters are yet living, that their records be preserved for future histories." They endorsed the publication of Nathaniel Morton's *New England's Memoriall*, (1669). Morton recognized "the weight of Duty that lieth upon us, to Commemorize to future Generations the memorable passages" of the founders. He concluded his chronicle with "a word of advice to the Rising generation" that echoed the general tenor of the era in its concern that the successors might yet degenerate.[52]

Election sermons regularly called for histories. Increase Mather called it "a duty incumbent upon present Generations to take care that there be a Record of the great works of God towards them, for the benefit of the Generations that shall follow." His son Cotton sometimes used the same words, and then combined them with his own images and interests: "I pray, go find if you can, the Tomb-stones of some Venerable persons to whom New-England owes an Everlasting Remembrance."[53]

Cotton Mather would publish many founders' biographies before making them part of his massive *Magnalia*. His father applauded this "special act of Obedience to the Fifth Commandment, to Endeavor the Preservation of the Names and Honour of them, who have been Fathers in Israel." The author's own introduction to one volume explained that these lives were "Offered unto the Contemplation and Imitation, Especially of the Generation which are now Rising up, After the Death of COTTON, and the Elders that out-Lived him." The biographies, he explained, were his way of showing readers "the Graves of their Dead Fathers."[54]

Even as they called on the fathers to leave posterity their testimony, ministers reminded them: "You must die and go off the Stage of Action shortly, but it should be your concern that Religion may not die with you." Theater provided the most popular metaphor; "your eyes behold this day, that another Generation is risen up and begin to stand thick upon the stage." The warning was clear—the fathers' responsibilities did not end with recollection. As Increase Mather put it, "Nor will it be for your honour, if the next Generation shall say, once such and such Worthies and Patriots had the management of affairs in New-England, and in their dayes things went well . . . but after they were gone, the work fell into other hands."[55]

As literal fathers died, rhetorical appeals to fathers continued. They were usually addressed or described in wide-ranging diagnoses of the current times: "A solemn and serious pondering and weighing of the fate of our Generation. . . . Let us consider one another." It was this accounting that provided most of the strident rhetoric associated with the jeremiad. The description of current times was usually accompanied by the conclusion that it was finally true that "the present standing Generation . . . is for the greater part another Generation, than what was in New England fourty years agoe." A large reservoir of biblical opprobrium served this purpose: "a stubborn and rebellious generation . . . an adulterous generation . . . A generation of vipers . . . a faithless and perverse generation . . . a generation of God's wrath." A theme particularly favored by Increase Mather and used by others was that "This generation is far short of the former."[56]

What was said of the present generation was felt more strongly by those who described the rising generation. "You are so strangely metamorphozed from any likeness to your good parents or Ancestors," Thomas Cobbett had said. Increase Mather asked, "do we not see that the Young Generation as to the greatest part of them is a poor unconverted, perishing Generation?" Significantly Mather referred to the Young Generation. The oft-mentioned "rising generation" did not necessarily include the young exclusively. In some instances, depending on who made the characterization, the phrase referred to all those following the founding generation, including the present and rising generation. It is a mistake to assume "rising" means young. What was surely true, the ministers said, was that the rising generation ignored the lessons of their predecessors.[57]

Children of Godly Parents and Spokesmen for Their Generation

The children of godly parents felt, if not the wrath of God, then that of His ministers. In fact, Edmund Morgan has suggested that the children of church members and no others comprised the rising generation. Certainly numerous sermons emphasized the special place of these children and suggested that the Fathers had gone into the wilderness for the lofty purpose of their children's future.[58] Yet, one would think that this modest sentiment would be the dominant Puritan view on the significance of one's birth:

> To be descended well, doth that commend?
> Can Sons their Fathers Glory call their own?
> Our Shepard justly might to this pretend
> (His Blessed Father was of high Renown,
> Both Englands speak him great, admire his Name)
> But his own personal worth is a better claim.[59]

"It must be such a generation that must save New-England's All. Don't boast it of being Abraham's children," warned William Stoughton. Their birth could not guarantee their salvation; special privilege only imposed greater obligations. The great number of children of godly parents represented the one encouraging sign to otherwise pessimistic speakers. But the eminent nature of their parents also made the consequences of any potential declension much more serious.[60] Morgan argues that Puritans did not seek to create new converts but "intensified the campaign to win the children," and that this was a prime cause of Puritanism's failure. Other scholars suggest that "the rhetoric of tribalism necessarily became less divisive . . . as the 'tribe' expanded to encompass the whole community."[61]

The passage of time forced the arch-ideologist of the original progenitors' significance to create ever more attenuated lines of descent in order to support his belief in the importance of the children of godly parents. By 1703 Increase Mather had added classical examples to the array of biblical and New England cases he had used in the previous decades as he noted that in Roman times an individual was honored if born into a famous family, "but it is a greater and better thing, when children can say, we are descended from Fathers, and from Grandfathers, and from Great Grandfathers who were Eminent Servants of God."[62] Although the pleas to children of the godly faded, the language of generations persisted.

In the regular life of individual congregations, concern with the rising generation was a concrete, daily issue, involving those "children" of the church baptized under the Half-Way Covenant but not full members. Thus, many sermons sought to speed their religious conversion.[63] Ministers did not merely bemoan their flock's fallen state but created institutions to enhance the few bright signs they saw. They tried above all to retain continuity with the past, to recreate the spirit that their fathers had felt.[64] Between 1660 and 1689 there were 258 days of "fast and humiliation" called to remind congregations of their many duties.[65] One innovation was the use of such days for the special purpose of improving the lot of the rising generation. Increase Mather predicted improvement "if there were more prayers poured forth before the Lord, for the conversion of the rising Generation." He preached "Pray for the Rising Generation" on just such a special day in 1678 when, as he remembered decades later, "all the churches in New England as one man" prayed in the same cause.[66] Fasts for the rising generation occurred outside the Mathers' congregation; many of the sermons mentioned here happened on those occasions.

The ministers thundering at the young might themselves be only in their early twenties. Some claimed contemporaneity with members of a generation and sought to express its view as their spokesmen. "Unto those who are the Generation risen and rising up. . . . suffer me, my Brethren and companions, who am one of you," said William Stoughton in *New England's True Interest.* The spokesmen for their own generation reminded their contemporaries of the responsibility they shared. "It is we that begin now to be the Body and Bulk of this people. . . . It is high time for us to stand up, solemnly to receive the charge" of those departing. If there were "some *first Ripe Grapes* to be found amongst us . . . why should we frustrate the Lord of that *full vintage* which he justly expects from *our* Generation." Stoughton and others often emphasized the pitiful nature of the rising generation: "*we,* poor *we,* alas what are we!" Nonetheless, the fundamental point remained that the future of New England "must stand or fall in our hands . . . it is now devolved upon us of the present Generation."[67]

Cotton Mather, not surprisingly, embraced the role of spokesman for his generation. Despite the "Decay of Piety" he saw, "yet even among us of the Third Generation" there were "such a number of Serious, Gracious, Fruitful Christians, as encourages our Hopes." Mather sought to "bespeak and beseech my own Generation, to begin the Doing of their part." As self-appointed generational spokesman, he could speak about youth's responsibilities to the society as a whole but could combine that with the pleas for their personal salvation. As he had when he called on young people to be up and doing, he noted the biblical precedents for "one Young Man calling upon another to do Service for God and their Generation."[68]

Generations of Mathers

The Mather family—Richard, Increase, Eleazar, and Cotton—drove the development of Puritan generational language. Increase and Cotton Mather dominated the Boston publishing scene as patrons of early printers and preeminent producers of material for the local press.[69] But particular facts about their family life need to be examined, without using this evidence to dismiss or excuse the implications for generational rhetoric. The Mathers' first published interest in generations emerged in the great controversy concerning the Half-Way Covenant.

The Synod of 1662 had resolved questions about admitting the founders' children into congregations by creating a new class of church members "capable of transmitting baptism, recognized as members and subject to church discipline, but barred from the Lord's Supper and from voting in church affairs," as one historian explained.[70] In the conflict over the covenant Richard Mather was one of the few founders supporting the new "halfway" members. Increase Mather, twenty-three years old in 1662, and his brother Eleazar joined the minority, composed primarily of "survivors of the first generation," in opposing the synod and the halfway measures. According to historians, Eleazar never renounced his opposition to the covenant.[71] Eleazar and Richard Mather both died in 1669, leaving Increase to tell their story. First he published a compilation of his brother's last sermons. His preface said:

> especially I was inclined to Publish what is here presented to you, because the dying counsel of my Reverend Father . . . left with me was, that I should seriously endeavor the good of the Rising Generation in this Country. What my Father said in the particulars and circumstances of it, I communicated to my Brother . . . which occasioned him to Preach these Sermons.

The most recent biographer of Increase Mather writes that "it is impossible to tell which words were Increase's and which were Eleazar's." Eleazar combined the many meanings of generation: "It is not one, or two, or a few, but a Generation that I plead for; and it is not onely a

Generation, but your Generation: now I come near indeed, a Generation that proceeds from your own loyns, and from your own bowels." He continued in the same vein, commenting that "I know men are apt to complain against the Rising Generation . . . but I beseech you to consider whether you give not too much occasion thereunto: Do they not see *your* pride, *your* worldliness." [72] Significantly, this language focuses not on the faults of either parents or children, but on the common responsibilities shared by both to take care of the future. Increase and Cotton Mather would later use similar sentiments to demand that parents remember their own responsibilities. [73]

After bringing his brother's last words to light and writing a biography of his father, Increase reversed his earlier position. He published a *defense* of the synod, "that I might please God in obeying the fifth commandment by vindicating the honour of my Fathers." Indeed, the volume, *First Principles of New England,* was largely composed of the words of his father, Richard Mather, and father-in-law, John Cotton. In the preface to an early sermon he spoke "of the Rising Generation in New England for whose sakes I am most willing, not only to Preach and to write, but to dy, if I may but thereby promote their conversion and salvation." Increase returned repeatedly to his father's dying words, and in some cases invoked his brother's loss as well, or combined the losses as he celebrated the significance of "the last words" of God's "eminent servants." [74]

Many of his generational writings occurred between 1669 and 1679, the decade of Increase Mather's thirties. In these years "he became easily the most important spokesman in print" of his time. [75] As he aged he would measure his career by the years that had passed since his first sermons on the theme. As president of Harvard (he was fifty-six), he began one treatise by greeting "the Young Generation in New England," and explained that "When I was (as you are) a young man, it pleased God to put into my heart an earnest desire to seek the Welfare of that Generation who are now past their Youth . . . God having lengthened my days to see many of the third Generation standing thick upon the stage. As my beloved sons let me warn you." Perry Miller remarked ironically that "by 1700 Increase, being one of the few survivors of even the second generation, virtually put himself in the posture of an ancestor." Mather's themes remained consistent as he extended the reach of the founders' influence. [76]

At the same time, however, the few rays of hope that occasionally shone in sermons were replaced by a uniformly dark perspective that demanded resistance to "Innovation" as the best service to the "Principles

and Spirit of their Fathers and Grandfathers." Earlier in his career he had
suggested that degeneration might come to pass without due care; in his
old age he concluded that it had arrived. In 1721 a group of ministers
led by Cotton Mather preached a series of sermons on early piety. They
asked Increase to write a preface and contribute a sermon. The ministers
lauded "their Venerable Father" whose contribution was "of most un-
common circumstances; Being of one who is in the Eighty Third Year of
his Age. . . . And at this very Great Age the Servant of God Preaches
(which he has done all his Days) without Using any Notes." The sermons
preached by the younger ministers concentrated on the personal crises of
sin and the need for early reformation. Increase's contribution, "Advice
to the Children of Godly Ancestors," shared the converting sentiment at
the outset, but moved without warning into the New England theme:
why did "our Fathers come into this Wilderness?"[77] As the eighteenth
century began, the Mathers' resistance to the gradual dissolution of the
Puritan errand revealed alternative approaches to generations.

Every seventeenth-century sermon had not preached strict adherence
to the past as a perfect model for behavior. Even during the years obsessed with declension, Thomas Shepard, Jr., had observed that "Ancestors are sometimes left to do that in their day, which the succeeding
generation payes the sad score of. . . . O may it be the portion of the
Rising Generation that they may not inherit any of the mistakes . . . of
such as have gone before them."[78] The Mathers, however, had little
patience for anything other than reverence for the past. They fired one
shot in a skirmish over adherence to certain principles of baptism by
reprinting in 1700 an English minister's work, *The Young Man's claim
unto the Sacrament of the Lords Supper.* In a lengthy preface they attacked other views which "can be only to fill the Mouths of a Revolting
Generation with cavils. . . . If a backsliding Generation do thus, while
we are yet Alive, what will they do a few years hence?" Their description
posed a marked contrast to the gentle treatment of "the Rising Generation, our hopeful Youth" in the English text. "Novelties" proposed by
Solomon Stoddard, who had been in the pulpit at Northampton since he
had succeeded Eleazar Mather, led to private and bitter reactions by
Cotton Mather, who "noted sorrowfully that hardly any but himself and
his father dared" defend the old ways, according to a recent biographer.[79]

The conflict simmered; it was renewed more than fifteen years later in
sermons by Stoddard and Benjamin Colman, minister at Brattle Street
Church. Stoddard echoed Thomas Shepard, Jr., when he said: "The mis-

takes of one Generation many times become the calamity of succeeding Generations. The present Generation are not only unhappy by reason of the darkness of their own minds, but the errors of those who have gone before them." He urged his audience to be wary of blind support for those who claimed to protect the colony's founding principles: "The first Planters drew up a platform of church disciplines . . . and some of their Posterity are mightily devoted to it, as if the platform were the Pattern in the Mount." [80]

Colman preached a fast-day sermon around the same time in which he argued for an even-handed treatment of the past: "a People in confessing their own Iniquity should confess also the sins of their Fathers." He was quick to emphasize: "I have no accusation to bring against the Fathers of my Country, whose memory is blessed with us; and with whom we may not compare our selves, being risen up a sinful Generation in their place. . . . Yet They were far from pretending to Perfection. . . . And while we Venerate their Devotion . . . we should take care not to be misled by their Example." The demand for too-strict obedience to church practices mirrored the assaults on faith that had originally driven the ancestors from England. Even as he sought to free himself from the impositions of memory, he sounded like a Mather: "Our Fathers would be ready to disown us" on account of contemporary profanity and hypocrisy. "Hear this, Ye old Men, and give ear all Inhabitants . . . hath this been in your days? Or even in the days of your Fathers?" [81]

Almost fifty years later, in 1763, Jonathan Mayhew published a series of sermons for young men. The minister said that he used no earlier sermons as a model for his discourse, seemingly rejecting the long-standing practice of alluding to or quoting from classics of the Puritan sermon literature. "It is said by some, that these times are very corrupt and degenerate in comparison with those of our fore-fathers; and particularly that the Youth of these days are remarkably light and vain." He agreed there was "always room . . . for reformation. I am not certain, however, that the above-mentioned charge is strictly just." Instead, "the most likely way to produce a reformation, is not to rail at the times, or to make such invidious comparisons betwixt the age present, and those which are past. I have, therefore, wholly declined this kind of rhetoric." [82] A century after the declension crisis, the language of generational respect and responsibility no longer described a specific group. Yet its influence endured.

In the eighteenth century, pleas to a generation as representative of the community's future became increasingly separated from the appeal to young people and their personal salvation. Election sermons began to change focus. Many of the traditional themes that spoke to generational consciousness—responsibility to posterity, the importance of continuity, and the Fathers' legacy—remained. But the charges of declension faded. The indictment of the rising generation occasionally surfaced, but only at the expense of a strident, labored telescoping of the original language: "What a melancholy Prospect wou'd lie before us—were we to draw the Parallel between the First and present Generation! . . . When their Heads were laid in the Grave there arose another Generation after them, which did not so much know the Lord . . . So the following Generation had still declined further: And now We are risen up in our Fathers stead."[83]

The heroic age of pious ancestors associated with the first decades of settlement collapsed into an undifferentiated, dusty, distant past. Thomas Prince's 1730 election sermon brimmed with references to earlier election-day speakers, but they were not stylistic inspirations. The appeal to the fathers settled into staid repetitions of increasingly vague formulae. Thus Daniel Lewis's election sermon in 1748, on the theme that rulers should be fathers to their people, concluded that "so many eminent Pens have gone before in this Way, as have left it very difficult for those who come after, either to say any Thing which they *have not* said, or not to say, that much worse, which they have."[84] The traditional acknowledgment that such words came from a proud tradition now seemed an admission of the emptiness of the election sermon form. The notion of "Generation-work" and responsibility had similarly come to describe more than upholding God's law. In a 1710 manual for constables, an imaginary dialogue between an old and new officer explained how to serve warrants, collect assessments, and so on. The old officer reassured his young colleague, "you must not mind the trouble; but consider the Publick Interest, and that every one ought to Serve his Generation."[85]

While the traditional saving sermon endured, ministers recognized the rising secular trend. Even "heathen" classical texts gave greater recognition to heroes "for their Publick Acts of Service, as the Fathers of their People" than did the religious community, one minister complained. It was "a deep stain," he suggested, "if with our superior Light . . . we be found strangers to that Publick Spirit that breathed in the Worthies of Greece and Rome." A negative comparison to the classical world was often as close as many eighteenth-century sermons came to recalling figures from the founding era.[86]

Commemoration and Revolution

If ancestors were not venerated so much in election and saving sermons in the mid-eighteenth century, they still found a place of honor at ceremonies remembering the acts of the original founders, beginning in the 1730s with the anniversaries and centennials of the founding of New England towns. A sermon on the hundredth anniversary of Dedham, Massachusetts, showed how secular society incorporated the language of the declension era into a celebration of secular, civic continuity. The sermon was intended for the "Edification of the Present and the Instruction and Admonition of Future Generations," and was supposed to provide suitable models for emulation in "the Example of our Venerable ForeFathers." Although descent from literal founding fathers might not be possible for all citizens, Samuel Dexter explained how *he* stood in the genealogy of the *town's* ministers. Dexter asked the now figurative question, "Our Fathers where are they?" and arrived at a familiar answer: "we are risen up in the Room of our Fathers, a Generation which do not know, love, fear, and obey the blessed God, with that Fervancy and Life, and strictness as they did." But the formula now admitted more members to the generational circle: "Our Care must be for Posterity in general, and not only for our own Posterity." The Puritan past now shared the stage with classical allusions; both church and the Roman republic demonstrated how values were "not . . . a Business of one Age," but should "be kept up, from one Generation to another."[87] Commemoration could thus be based on wholly secular principles, but retain a significance forged by religious conceptions. The celebration of the founders at Plymouth revealed the shared language of commemoration put to different purposes.

Plymouth enjoyed clear historical primacy, yet no ceremony honoring the Pilgrims was held until 1769, when the Old Colony Club, a group of local young men, began celebrating the landing. The "first oration ever delivered in memory of the Forefathers," according to the club, was given by a twenty-four-year-old member who recalled the Pilgrims' search for freedom. "If we their sons act from the same principles, and conduct with the same firmness and resolution when our holy religion or civil liberties are invaded, we may expect a reward proportionate." When a local minister suggested a special sermon "for the entertainment and instruction of the rising generation more especially," members responded with a clubman's perspective tinged by a familiar sentiment:

> Considering further that the assembling of a number of persons of different ages for the purpose of commemoration . . . would have a natural and direct tendency to introduce subjects for conversation relative to our illustrious progenitors. . . . the aged upon those days would with freedom communicate to the youth those circumstances. . . . by these means many pleasing and curious anecdotes of our pious forefathers. . . . would be snatched from oblivion and descend to posterity.

In 1772, "to show our gratitude to the Creator and Preserver of our ancestors and ourselves, and as a mark of respect most justly due to the memories of these heroic Christians," the minister delivered a sermon on Psalm 78—one of the most popular generation texts, and the same text Samuel Dexter had preached at the Dedham century sermon—"he commanded our fathers, that they should make them known to their children: that the generation to come might know them." [88]

Since the first address emphasized the forefathers' thirst for liberty, it might seem logical to assume the celebrations' proto-revolutionary content. In fact, the ceremonies became patriotic displays only after most of the Old Colony Club's membership fled to Canada or other Loyalist strongholds. A *Boston Gazette* article on a 1775 patriot celebration illustrates the transformation in the discourse:

> We the Posterity of those illustrious Heroes are now suffering under the galling pressure of that power, an emancipation from which, was one grand object they had in view, in the settlement of this Western World. . . . a pitiful number, who bear the names, and descendants from the loins of these ever to-be-revered Patriots. . . . have involved their native country, enriched with the blood of their Fathers, in accumulated Calamities and Distresses.

Nothing Britain could do would surpass the sufferings "those distinguished patrons of religion and freedom . . . patiently endured." [89] The revolutionary crisis infused the seemingly tired language with new life and new enduring images, particularly the blood of the Fathers.

Published sermons revealed strong links between the Revolution and traditional generational themes. Connecticut minister Judah Champion recounted the entire history of New England in a 1770 fast sermon. "The rising generation in particular are very much unacquainted with the distresses their ancestors encounter'd." The fathers' "difficulties and distresses" placed their descendants "under peculiar obligations to know and serve the Lord as we live in a land of liberty, civil and religious." Because of the "privileges . . . handed down to us, through the blood of our forefathers," all would be "inexcusably and aggravatedly guilty . . . if they refuse or neglect to know and serve the Lord God of their fathers." [90]

The Revolution's civic rhetoric also used the language of paternal obligation. Samuel Adams often wrote of "those precious rights and privileges for which our renowned forefathers expended so much Treasure and Blood." The Boston Committee of Correspondence appealed to providence and posterity as it demanded that citizens "save the present and future generations from . . . (we think we may with seriousness say) eternal destruction."[91]

After the Revolution, the boundaries of generational rhetoric expanded as Enlightenment ideas and impulses toward gentility crept into the discourse. For example, a 1792 sermon celebrating the centenary of Newton, Massachusetts, *The Succession of Generations,* observed that "numerous generations have trodden this earthly stage before us"; it made no special claims for particular actors. Then the speaker computed the duration of a modern generation compared to the generations of the Bible. Such calculations were rarely part of the old tradition. This tinkering, "Enlightenment" spirit persisted; do not complain about the brevity of life, he said, work to improve it "as becomes rational, social, and immortal beings." The minister alluded to the notion that the Lord might brand residents a "wicked" generation, but he preferred quiet satisfaction in "the well informed tradition of our fathers . . . which has left an instructive lesson as a legacy to their children, through following generations." This was history as legend; no more chronicles of particular hardships, but relative complacence with accomplishments and progress. The first settlers merged with a biblical time: "the many generations, that were once actors on the same stage, which we now occupy, and have gone before us. . . . Successive generations have appeared and disappeared in this infant country. The two first are entirely swept away . . . the great majority of the inhabitants consists of the fifth and sixth generations." The responsibilities of generations were not based in the town that celebrated its centennial but in an eternal "city, which has no need of the sun or moon to shine in it." The centennial of a Dorchester young person's religious society introduced a theme that would grow more popular: "it may pass for an assumption that the next age will look back on this as we review the past. At that time . . . your piety and zeal will be recollected and acknowledged with a gratitude and joy like that we feel for your predecessors."[92] No longer did the Lord on Judgment Day read the register of past lives, but a future generation read a history book.

In the nation's new magazines, republicanism balanced uneasily with a European-influenced gentility. In the Philadelphia-based *American Mu-*

seum, a journal that published patriotic tracts and debates on the new Constitution, an article entitled "Directions for the improvement of the rising generation" offered neither moral exhortations nor a connection between youth and the future of the new republic. Rather it sounded like an ersatz Lord Chesterfield as it urged readers to summarize stock phrases on constitutional rights "and thus be known as a patriot."[93]

Older forms persisted as some young men still wanted to speak *for* their generation. One minister, twenty-six years old in 1799, told his fellows: "I feel a trembling anxiety for the youth of the present genera- tion. . . . I feel myself your companion in years, and deeply interested both in your present and future welfare." He suggested the growing importance of the young: "The hopes of a family, or nation must ever lean upon the rising generation. Family respectability, and national pros- perity depend on them. . . . Young men are the strength and defense of a nation." He called on his fellows to "Love the country which gave you birth, be ready, ye sons, to support, and rally round the standard of our government, and yourselves worthy of that liberty, for which our fathers so gloriously fought and bled."[94]

The language of declension also continued, although now occasionally in partisan attire. A newspaper comment on a postwar anniversary cele- bration at Plymouth described ministers doing "real honor to the mem- ory of their departed worthies. The doings of some Federalists of the *modern* stamp *after* Dinner, is a melancholy discovery that in Plymouth as well as Boston, there are too many of their Posterity who dishonor them . . . indeed the Degenerate Plants of a Noble Vine."[95] If genera- tional responsibility touched anything beyond mere commemoration, the impulse to be up and doing rested with the young.

CHAPTER TWO

Youth Imagined in Revival and Revolution

The discourse of generational responsibility developed by Puritan ministers and cultivated by secular authorities stressed transmitting community values from founders to those who followed them. These inheritors, the "rising generation," became equated with "the young." Most historical interpretations of key events in early America that involved the idea of youth emphasize interpersonal or psychological conflicts. Thus the Great Awakening and the American Revolution have both been linked to literal and metaphorical struggles of fathers and sons. This argument fits modern preconceptions; it misses some historical realities. Certainly authorities had constructed youth in terms of family life and social relations. But that personal rhetoric mingled with the civic language of generations both in institutions that organized young people's lives and in social upheavals that invoked their experience and spirit. As with the discourse of generations, print culture also shaped ideas of youth. This chapter examines these complex relationships in the seventeenth and eighteenth centuries.

Ever since Philippe Ariès's *Centuries of Childhood* (1962), scholars have noted how medieval and Renaissance law, society, and art recognized young people's importance. Whether the Ages of Man were numbered as three or twelve, four or seven, there was always a place for youth.[1] Throughout the early-modern era, youth was defined less by cognitive or age-graded stages than by particular responsibilities. A man's youth often began when he was dubbed a knight (in medieval nobility) or confirmed in the church (in the early-modern period) and ended with marriage and establishing an independent household. By the early seventeenth century, a parents' advice manual said youth began around age fourteen and ended at twenty-eight, which was also, not coincidentally, about the mean marriage age for males.[2]

In the family, the father held supreme power based on his "natural" right to rule the household. Authority itself was linked to age and seniority.[3] Celebrations of patriarchal authority reflected the fact that while the number of young people grew, there were few places in society for them to fill. Renaissance Venice and Florence were exceptional in creating organizations to manage youth's initiation into political culture. In England, tradition restricted young people's political and occupational opportunities.[4] Young English men and women responded by leaving their birthplaces for the cities. Religious and civil authorities in turn designed services specifically for "youth," the apprentices, craft workers, and laborers crowding into London.[5]

From the days of roaming knights-errant to the era of urban apprentices, prescriptive literature consistently equated youth with disruption and disorder. Sermons reflected the Bible's recognition of youth as a significant stage in life, even if the Old Testament prophets did not apply the sophisticated shadings of modern adolescent psychology. "Rejoice, O young man in thy youth . . . but know thou, that for all these things God will bring thee to judgment. . . . Childhood and youth are vanity. . . . Remember now thy Creator in the days of thy youth," said the Book of Ecclesiastes in three successive verses that formed a crucial source for ministers' rhetoric.

John Cotton, while he lived in England's Boston, catalogued youth's caravan of follies, including "High conceit, of their own sufficiency and worth . . . Inordinate and excessive love of liberty . . . Wantonness . . . Impatience of counsels and reproofs . . . prodigality . . . Impudency."[6] Cotton's interpretation seemed an apt, if negative, appraisal of urban youth's participation in public activities and disorders.

A popular literary genre constructed an old concern as a new social problem: ungoverned youth. Books popular in the seventeenth and eighteenth centuries were written as direct counsel to children from concerned parents. "Courtesy books" usually offered practical advice from a wise father to a son setting out in the world on the best way to conduct a good and moral life.[7] Books for young English gentlemen guided readers through their first visit to London. In *The Young Gallants Whirligigg*, a young man went to the city, fell in with bad company, ate too much, attended the theater and read suspect books when he should have been working, and ultimately came to ruin. The author, a poet in Charles I's court, hoped that vulnerable youths would "know themselves before it be too late."[8]

While this literature targeted an audience of young people, recent scholarship demonstrates that little of it implied that they were thought to possess particular universal or ideal characteristics of "youth." The young urban masses themselves did little that resembled modern descriptions of unique youth subcultures. Nor were their values particularly different from those of adults.[9] Nonetheless, moral guardians still labored to save them.

"Gallants" were not the only young people tempted by the city's snares. A group of Dissenting London ministers developed a didactic genre that combined traditional salvation themes with the courtesy books' hints on correct conduct and getting along in the city, summarized in one title, "The Young Man's Guide Through the Wilderness of This World." They preached moderation and sobriety and called on apprentices and students to avoid profanity and dissolute companions.[10]

Puritans in Old and New England faced similar ideological conditions when the Stuart Restoration ended the English Revolution. Most English sermons, however, did not make the links between youth and a special generation drawn by New England ministers.[11] But a few clergymen who had been leaders in the revolution and in the writing of the new works for youth added this special plea to traditional Puritan warnings.[12] "It was no small mercy to you that God should make you to be the Seed of the Righteous. . . . Perhaps besides your immediate Parents, your Forefathers and Ancestors were such as walked with God in their several Generations. . . . Now what a dreadful thing would it be, if any of you should cut off the intail of Godliness," said one. Two ministers, John Howe and Vincent Alsop, asked "you that are young . . . seriously to consider, how much the stress of a Religious Interest for future time in England depends upon you." The Lord "hath long been England's God, your God, and your Forefathers." It was the people's responsibility to decide if they "shall continue the God of England," or if they would be revealed "a generation of Vipers."[13] This appeal does not appear to be typical English discourse: perhaps something about these particular ministers led to the striking similarities to New England sermons.

Howe, for example, had a special connection across the Atlantic. One year in the 1650s, when he was an official in Cromwell's government, he had a New England visitor substitute in his pulpit, the young Increase Mather. Mather had retained his links to English ministers, "acting as a broker" in "a common network," according to one study. The ministers exchanged their published works, helping to "insure that Puritans in both countries marched in cadence into the eighteenth century." [14] Works by the English ministers are among the books listed in the Mather library. Invoices of imports to a Boston bookseller reveal that multiple copies of at least eight different English titles on youth arrived in one year and sold in quantity. [15] Enduring English traditions, transformed by specific New World circumstances, fed a transatlantic dialogue. Shared Puritan beliefs about the family's central role in controlling youth were facing challenges in America.

The New World Family

American colonies outside New England developed different traditions toward youth and their own exemplary texts. Chesapeake colonists, for example, faced radically unstable conditions because of high mortality and the predominance of young, single, male immigrants. This produced a society "more highly stratified . . . more rural, more agrarian, less highly skilled, and less literate." In families of the Chesapeake great houses, young people were raised in a fashion that seemed permissive by New England standards. "Age-specific issues . . . took a backseat to problems related to labor, class, and . . . race." While the father still ruled, his influence was moderated by greater freedom given to children. Growing up emphasized "the development of self-confidence, autonomy, and the reciprocal obligations of fathers and sons." The power ceded to planters' sons did not mean that they were independent of parental authority; to the contrary, there seemed to be an expectation of grateful appreciation for what parents could give to children. Virginia's inheritance statutes allowed fathers to share wealth with their sons, creating the potential for intergenerational comity. [16] As planters developed a culture of gentility, it became more important for their sons to learn rules of proper conduct and behavior; the Chesapeake gentry often used imported courtesy books to teach decorum. The polite tradition was not exclusively Virginian, but it seemed to find its warmest reception in plantation mansions. Indeed, one English work, Francis Hawkins's *Youths Behaviour or Decency in Conversation Among Men,* was important in the life of young George Washington. [17]

Emigrants to Massachusetts, by contrast, traveled in families and for the most part were literate and urban. [18] They developed their own distinctive views. Ministers shared a rough consensus on youth's capacities.

"Truly, young people are but Novices; whatever good they have or do, they are but newly come to it; it will be a wonder if the Devil do not break them," said Cotton Mather. Eliphalet Adams told a young men's religious society in New London, Connecticut, that "young persons need direction for their conduct . . . having no Principle naturally in them which will assuredly guide them."[19] The significance of the "rising generation" in the colony's future was linked to a concern for individual youths and their families.[20]

The New England family was bound together by traditions of shared responsibility. As in early-modern Europe, youth represented a recognized stage of life, and as in Europe, a youth entered adulthood after passing through the gates of marriage and into an independent home. But the path to independence could be slow.

When Lynn's Thomas Cobbett wrote that "under the notion of children . . . are understood, all such as are in the relation of children, whether Adult persons, or children in Age," he described a broad population.[21] The calls for the young to remember their duty to the Lord occurred in a context of intense, if submerged, social conflict. Many struggles in rural New England towns revolved around too many sons coming of age with neither available land nor a likely means of escape.[22] Such conflicts were almost always individual. Historians find little evidence that such struggles provided the basis for group action. One scholar went so far as to call New England "an age-relations utopia." "Youth" probably described unmarried, landless individuals who might be more advanced in years but had not passed the significant landmarks of adulthood.[23] Ministers inspected their progress.

Most in the pulpit agreed that "Childhood and Youth are Vanity" and took another verse as their text: "Remember now thy creator in the days of thy Youth." One might die at anytime; if unconverted, youth faced uncounted dangers: "The Devil goes ranging, raging, roaring about the World; and young men are those whom he is most concerned for the catching of and spoiling of," said Cotton Mather in an early sermon.[24] Youth were especially exhorted in the popular literature created by sermons at the execution of criminals.[25] Despite their emphasis on inciting fear in a youthful audience, seventeenth-century sermons often reminded "You that are young ones" of their ability to make a decision. "Art thou past a Childe? dost thou begin to understand thy self? It is dangerous for thee to put off God."[26] The search for inner light in youth became swept up along with the social conflicts.

At age sixteen Cotton Mather founded a society for religious young

men, preached its first sermon, and promoted the creation of other societies. He appended a society's rules to the end of one of his publications so
that others would imitate its model. While the young men were primarily
interested in prayer, they also agreed every few months to devote an
evening to the general concern of the "Rising Generation in our land." [27]
Social institutions that organized young people's lives reinforced the values promoted by religious and moral authorities. Young men's involvement in the local militia put generational rhetoric about youth's
responsibilities into action and tested the boundaries of their participation in community life.

The Militia: Organizing Youth for Service

The facts of survival in the New World demanded military units for
defense against (and occasional assaults on) the native North American
population. Virginia instituted a militia organization in its first military
government; virtually every male citizen drilled and carried arms. The
militiamen serving in long campaigns were often poor, young freemen
attracted by adventure and a steady income. Declining military necessity,
and the social convulsion caused by Bacon's rebellion, scattered the militia's power. By the end of the seventeenth century only men with financial
means were eligible. [28] While the Virginia militia, even at its most egalitarian, had been led by gentry elites, New England town companies permitted most male citizens to join in a common endeavor.

Young men might not be considered adults before they had married
and established independent lives, but they still gathered with their elders
in the local town militia. As members, young men could enter the public
arena years before their age and position would normally permit such
involvement. They associated themselves with petitions to the General
Court, participated in elections for militia leaders, and expressed a clear
sense of their own important contribution to the town's well-being. [29]

One historian has used court records from Middlesex County in Massachusetts to claim that young men in the militia formed what he called
"an alternative youth culture," characterized by boisterous rebellion
against general authority. Officials blamed "the youth among the congregations" for "disturbances and inattention." Militiamen often faced accu-
sations of disorder or dalliance with young women. The study suggests
that the authorities' resort to "artificial terms of generations" was a
"symbolic" expression of a struggle between young and old. These were
neither artificial terms nor shadow indications of some "real" struggle,

but were integral to the larger issues facing New England. Undoubtedly some of the concern about generations reflected responses to actual social disruption.[30] But these disorders do not add up to an "alternative youth culture." If it were truly an alternative culture, why would militiamen themselves assert, "if there were any service to be done for the country it must be the young men that must do it"? Too much of the militia experience contributed to social integration, not alienation. Young people sought ways to become part of the community that cut them out of most other responsibilities.[31]

Young men's political participation in the militia did lead to conflict. In Roxbury in the 1640s "the young men of the town agreed together to choose one George Denison, a young soldier come lately out of the wars in England," as militia captain. The "ancient and chief men" chose another person, "a godly man and one of the chief in the town," according to John Winthrop's account. This led to "much discontent and murmuring. . . . The young men were over strongly bent to have their will." The crisis was ultimately resolved, though Winthrop's journal is vague on the details. Historians who have told this story often neglect to say that the young men's candidate was himself young. Denison was twenty-six years old, the youngest son of a founding member of the town. The candidate of the older members was a home owner, a leading subscriber to the new school, and a town selectman. Apparently, youth could enjoy limited participation in public affairs so long as it did not upset the essential balance of authority in the town. Had Denison been as established in town as his opponent, one wonders whether there would have been a crisis; in fact, in later years he and other members of his family held important area offices.[32]

In Connecticut, towns asked the General Assembly to reject the nomination of the candidates of younger militiamen. One petition charged that an aspirant's followers included "not a single person of sobriety and consideration[,] but [only] young and inconsiderate youth for the most part *who in no case could vote but in such an affair.*" The petitions used language from sermons about easy corruptibility to accuse successful candidates of trading votes for liquor and otherwise luring the "giddy youth."[33] That these voters could act only in "such an affair" illustrates the tensions built into offering participation to people otherwise unsettled in the town. "Youth" evidently served as an umbrella term to describe a complex sociopolitical condition as well as one of age. The militia left a lasting imprint on its members of allegiance to the colony's future.

Youth and Revival

By organizing and disciplining potentially disorderly young people and teaching important lessons about loyalty to a polity, the militia materialized society's concern for the young. If ministers had been monitoring their future for decades, and the militia had integrated them into some parts of community life, how do we interpret appeals to youth during an era that supposedly disrupted tradition?

Young people were at the center of the 1730s and 1740s religious revivals known today as the Great Awakening.[34] Historians disagree about what this involvement means, but they are sure it is significant. Some interpret the converts' youth as a reflection of stress in families and local society. Others think it embodies a reforming Awakening spirit against stodgy Old Light traditionalism. This view merges easily into claims about the Awakening as a prelude to social revolution and the inspiration for suspicion of elite power.[35] Evidence to support these ideas is not particularly clear-cut. Recent studies challenge any sweeping character to the revivals, point to their varied denominational and ethnic roots outside New England, and question their long-term impact. In fact, they may have been an expression of conservative rather than revolutionary ideals.[36] The dispute suggests that youth's role in the revivals needs reexamination.

William Williams described the stakes in a 1736 account of how he had won new converts in his Connecticut Valley congregation. "Religion is not the business of one Age only, but must be perpetuated and continued from Age to Age." Were parishioners "willing it should die with this Generation. Have you no hearty Concern, that the Generation that is rising up may praise the Lord," he asked. Williams also published a letter from his nephew Jonathan Edwards, who reported that young people flocked to join the ranks of the converted in revivals he had organized. In subsequent accounts, Edwards would return to the story of how the young in Northampton had spent too much time frolicking and going to taverns and too little watching their souls, and how he organized them into groups to pray together. "Many seemed to be very greatly and most agreeably affected with those views which excited humility, self-condemnation," he reported.[37] The Northampton experience was repeated throughout New England, and in many towns young people's societies carried out the work of revival.[38] Whether this gave an unmistakably youthful cast to the entire experience is another issue.

Social historians, brandishing statistical models of varying levels of sophistication, have analyzed revivals in Massachusetts and Connecticut. Their findings yield a divided picture. Most converts were young, much younger than converts during nonrevival periods.[39] After agreeing on this point, however, scholars part company. Some share the view, presented in a study of Jonathan Edwards's Northampton congregation, that because so many ministers talked about the significance of young people, "there was a crisis of adolescence" exemplified by a breakdown in "family government." The advocates of crisis relate the age of conversion to men's unsettled social location and dim prospects for gaining independent, landholding status. Chafing under parental restraints, it is suggested, they looked to a higher authority for relief. The revival's direct appeal to converts supposedly exacerbated the erosion of the traditional family structure.[40]

By contrast, other scholars argue that "historians have exaggerated adolescent crises in explaining conversion patterns" and that "childhood and youth were not periods of stress and crisis in the lives of" townspeople.[41] There may have been stresses, but "there were no revolutions, overt or silent . . . in which the younger generation overturned the elder or attempted to assert its numerical power." Rather than a rebellion against parents, their conversions drew them closer to their families.[42]

These conflicting findings demonstrate the difficulties in reading psychosocial significance across centuries. Although young people seemed to be drifting farther away from adult supervision, there seems to be no clear correlation between this experience and the large numbers of young men and women answering the revival's call.[43] There was nothing spectacularly new about the conversion appeals directed at young people. They were played in the register of traditional sermons about youth's personal spiritual life and thus reflected a certain continuity in the midst of social change. The significant difference was the scant reference to youth's responsibilities for the community's survival. Yet, even while local ministers focused on personal issues and complained about decline in parental government, others sought to link the individual congregations to significant metaphorical fathers from New England's past.

The revivals illuminate the discourse of youth and generations, not in the process of youthful conversion but in the contemporary debate over the revival itself. The story of *The Christian History,* one publication responsible for spreading news of the revival, opens a window on an eighteenth-century argument about the revival's effects on the young and who was the truest heir to the Puritan Fathers' traditions. In a battle waged through Boston magazines, pamphlets, and newspapers, we see the power of print to define positions and simultaneously create a canon of crucial texts and a historical record. Writers did not simply apply the Puritan past as a commonly accepted "foundation myth."[44] The heritage itself represented contested terrain, even if opponents offered similar reasons for invoking it.

Thomas Prince, Jr., of Boston began publishing *The Christian History* in March 1743. This first religious magazine in America recorded revivals in the colonies and Great Britain.[45] The publisher argued that readers could understand such momentous events only if they knew the story of the rise and fall of religion in New England. He offered "authentick Testimonies . . . of the most venerable Fathers of New England" to "prepare our minds the more to receive Accounts of its surprizing Revival." Religion was not the only thing being revived in *The Christian History*. The magazine breathed new life into a collection of seemingly archaic texts and gave them a coherence they had not possessed originally: election sermons by William Stoughton, Samuel Danforth, and Thomas Prince, Sr., and jeremiads by John Norton, John Higginson, and Increase Mather. These pulpit "greatest hits" enshrined the language of generational responsibility as a dominant discourse for understanding the past as they demonstrated the piety of the founders and revealed "the great and lamentable Decay of Religion in the Succeeding Generation."[46]

The Christian History offered an epic of colonial scope in its accounts of preaching tours by George Whitefield and other itinerant ministers. Most stories were local; Jonathan Edwards's letter from Northampton was only one in a flood of accounts by pastors that described young people embracing conversion in their church or in the town next door. This celebration of youthful piety was almost inevitably presented as evidence of a renewal of the old spirit of New England.[47]

One Boston minister, though, used tradition to fight the revival. Charles Chauncy called for "due Attendance . . . to the Means and Methods used by our Fathers, when the Churches in their Day were in Danger." Chauncy's Fathers were not those of *The Christian History*, however; he leapt over Mather and Stoughton to the first founders of New England and the 1630s Antinomian crisis. The current revivals were nothing more than a reprise of disobedience: "Our Fathers, under the like Difficulties with those we now complain of, have set us an Example." He hoped that "we their Posterity" would follow it. The revival's focus on the young preyed on their traditional weaknesses, Chauncy said. Like many ministers, he had preached standard sermons urging early piety. But, "When ministers particularly address themselves to children and young persons it looks very improper to discover violent Emotions or Passions. . . . first care should be to Inform the Judgment. . . . But, sure I am, this is very different from the method that hath been taken by those preachers and Exhorters." Such actions had led to more serious difficulties: "there never was a time, since the settlement of New-England, wherein there was so much bitter and rash Judging; Parents condemning their children, and children their parents."[48] He saw this "spirit of bitterness" perpetuated in *The Christian History.*

Both *The Christian History* and Chauncy claimed to be true followers of New England's heritage. This was not a case of a "progressive" faction urging rebellion while "conservatives" proclaimed themselves heirs to the Puritan Fathers. *The Christian History* said the revivals simply continued a long-standing battle with decay; ministers had reinvigorated a discourse grown frayed by the time of the elder Prince's 1730 election sermon. By grounding revivals in this revered tradition, the magazine answered Chauncy and other critics who said they were exceptional, excessive, and inappropriate. Of course, the assertions of continuity also sought to normalize the potentially disruptive activities of itinerant ministers who were Chauncy's major target.[49] Yet each focused its appeal by linking the concern for the young with the heritage of New England's founders.

While he published his objections to the revival in a series of pamphlets, Chauncy expressed concern about *The Christian History* privately.[50] Boston newspapers would not be so circumspect in the battle over religious enthusiasm. *The Christian History*'s publishers, Kneeland and Green, also printed pro-revival stories in their *Boston Gazette.* They had long been associated with Old South Church pastor Thomas Prince, Sr., a leading revival advocate. *The Boston Evening Post* and its publisher, Thomas Fleet, led the opposition.[51] Fleet was already a celebrated controversialist when he began a public campaign against *The Christian History.* The *Post*'s sarcastic attack revealed fissures along the lines of age and class: "the Publisher is a young man and by no means capable of a thing of that Nature [i.e., producing the magazine]. . . . it is a pity such a promising young Gentleman should not engage in some business that will secure him a maintenance in the World." The article asserted what many Bostonians seemed to believe; the magazine was actually managed by Prince's father. The younger Prince demanded that Fleet prove his assertions. The same week a different author challenged an *Evening Post* story that attacked the Georgia Orphan House, revival minister George Whitefield's best-known New World project.[52]

The *Evening Post* snapped back; Fleet's targets were apparently *two* sons of eminent Boston ministers. He wrote first to "Master Tommy" about "a few scraps" which the *Boston Gazette* "represent as wrote by T. Prince Jun." He did not believe it, "but nevertheless . . . I'll take for granted what is very improbable and suppose that the undertaker of *The Christian History* was the Author of them, and that you are the Person." Prince was a pampered son, the "Little Master" who embarked on "Children's Play, and it is High Time for you to think of Behaving like a Man, since you are set up for an Historian." Fleet repeated that the "many suspicions" about the actual publisher of *The Christian History* were proved by "your incapacity of performing a thing even of so trifling a Nature." He offered ironic life lessons: "You and I, Master Tommy, must take the world rough as it runs and make the best of it."[53]

Meanwhile, another article addressed to "Master Billy" dealt with that author's claim that his visit to Georgia contradicted the *Evening Post*'s account of Whitefield's orphan asylum. In this case, the object of editorial scorn was William Cooper, Jr., son of another Boston minister: "The chief end of your writing was to let the world know that you had traveled as far as Georgia and you are qualified for an Author, as well as T. Prince, Jun. A.B. tho I confess you set out upon different views, viz. he for Bread and you for Fame."[54]

Prince responded that he and "no other person was the Author of the Challenge or this piece." As if to emphasize his control of *The Christian History*, the younger Prince announced on the front page of the next *Boston Gazette* that ministers gathering for a convention should provide him with "authentick accounts of the number of Men, Women, Children, Indians, and Negroes . . . that have appeared to be under the late remarkable work." The *Evening Post*'s editor addressed another article to the "young master" and his "darling and lucrative History." Was the younger Prince merely a front for a father who could not openly claim management of the magazine because of his ministerial duties? Clearly, Rev. Thomas Prince provided much of the material for the magazine. Most historians' claims to his unquestionable management of the publication, however, are based on Chauncy's assertion in a letter and the allegations of the *Evening Post*.[55]

Perhaps we should think of Prince as one of those New England sons on a prolonged path to adulthood. He had graduated from Harvard a few years before, and had long been "in a feeble, declining state of health." His name appeared as publisher, but he also told readers to contact him at his father's house. Nonetheless, when he "thought best to discontinue" the magazine after its second year, he referred to "My Weekly Paper."[56] Are the younger Prince and Cooper simply two obedient sons following their fathers' path? The pages of *The Christian History* further underscored the significance of the generational responsibility themes we saw in Chapter 1. Prince died only a few years later at the age of twenty-seven, his final vocation and relation to his father a mystery.

The magazine, and the debate over it, made the revival an important social force: "It is here in *The Christian History* where the Awakenings were made Great," said one historian. Harry S. Stout has suggested that the Awakening established a place in public for oratorical persuasion. *The Christian History* disseminated that rhetoric and provided a vocabulary for ministers to explain their experience. It created a broad public sphere for debate over the issues of the revival.[57] How else are we to account for the remarkable similarities in ministers' descriptions of revivals across the colonies? The magazine also affirmed a particular version of New England's history to legitimize the revival against its critics.

Fleet's response rings with a deep cultural resonance. First, his objections to young Prince and Cooper echo the suspicion of youthful participation in the militia election disputes, a sense that the young should wait their turn before participating in public affairs. There is a strong hint of class tension as well; the self-made immigrant Fleet had no patience for the Master Tommys and Master Billys of his world, who seemed to be playing at occupations meant for hard-working adults.

This fight indicates a growing frustration with the terms of debate being used by both sides in the dispute. The decaying establishment that the Princes represented as well as the equally elite opponents of the revival wanted to shape the interpretation of the revival to fit their particular preconceptions. Evidently, Fleet was bored by this historical debate over who was the true heir to the founders' legacy. For Fleet, *The Christian History* was merely "reprinting Books that have been answered and exposed." His position, to reject or ignore this particular fight, represented an attitude closer to modern newspaper practice. However, it in no way makes his claims more "authentic." This is not an issue of a disjuncture between rhetoric and "reality." It is more interesting to observe that Fleet had the option to participate in the discourse shared by Chauncy and his elite opposition, and he apparently found it irrelevant. In the short run, the elites still had the power. Under pressure, Fleet recanted his opposition and argued he was merely publishing the material given to his press.[58] Although the ministers' power declined, their language would reach a wider audience. Colonial newspapers were doing more than taking sides in religious controversies. News of the Awakening and other events throughout the colonies shifted the papers' focus from London and the empire to the local scene, and promoted "an even greater willingness to refer to Americans as a single group."[59] These new conditions helped spread the discourse in an emerging revolutionary environment.

Rivals in the Great Awakening were on the same side during the next social explosion that depended on the language of youth: the American Revolution. Thirty years after his staunch opposition to the revival, Charles Chauncy, according to his biographer, compared patriots "with the Israelites of old, true heirs of the Puritan Fathers . . . justified—if not sanctified—in throwing off tyranny and oppression." Chauncy was closely allied in the patriot cause with revival supporters like William Cooper, Jr. Thomas Fleet's newspaper publishing sons opposed British impositions even as they followed their father's later policy of maintaining neutrality in major disputes. One historian celebrated "the inheritance of tradition, from one generation of newspaperman to another."[60] The complex heritage of the Awakening influenced the development of the Revolution's stance toward youth and generations. How do we interpret celebrated claims about an antitraditional and antipatriarchal Revolution?

Youth and Revolution

The Awakening's supposed transformation of young people's religious experience has been linked to the American Revolution. Whatever the extent of actual social changes resulting from the revivals in New England, it was certainly true that eighteenth-century youth's socialization and indoctrination began moving outside the home. Scholars eager to trace the rise of a modern youth identity have found a "gradual erosion" of patriarchal authority prompted by new opportunities, increasing population, and expanding available land. One concluded that by the middle of the century, "the traditional pattern of prolonged filial subordination and dependence would appear to have been broken." Although the transition to adulthood remained a prolonged process, according to this modernizing interpretation, "the tasks of youth were . . . similar to those of twentieth-century adolescents."[61] Even if we do not rush eighteenth-century young people into modern identity crises, it does seem that the possibilities for youth began to expand.

Eighteenth-century sermons had articulated a sense of increased gradation in youth's development: "In Childhood you are put to School, in the beginning of your Youth you are put to Trades; what is there to be done for you in these early Years but to instruct you," explained Benjamin Colman.[62] The young people with perhaps the greatest freedom to develop their own ideas and futures were those young men who attended college. The small collegiate population in colonial America—three thousand graduates from the 1740s to the 1770s—was still "more than twice the number of the previous hundred years." In the years immediately prior to the Revolution, young men at colonial colleges, especially Princeton, read books and participated in extracurricular activities knit together by Commonwealth ideology and the republican writings of classical Greece and Rome. These texts taught particular lessons about corruption, virtue, the past as a model for the future, the significance of exemplary ancestors, and the importance of maintaining republics for successors. A high proportion of the Revolution's leaders came from these colleges.[63]

The collegians' curriculum of independence was one instance in a larger rhetorical struggle with Great Britain. Even as the patriarchal model faded, the analogy between family and state rose in prominence. Colonists "coming of age in the 1750's and 1760's were thinking more highly of their personal worth and ability than earlier generations and had correspondingly less tolerance for an inferior and dependent status within the empire," argue Edwin Burrows and Michael Wallace. England was a bad parent. Figured as the father, it had refused to release its maturing colonial child from enforced dependence. Because of this offense, the colonies were no longer required to be loyal children.[64]

Revolutionaries did not embrace a language of parental rebellion easily. They shaped a stance out of the Puritan and classical republican traditions that treated their revolt as a kind of higher obedience: "The fathers were not English. They were New English, the English-speaking founders of a new kind of community, and what they initiated, the Revolutionary sons fulfilled." Ministers and others claimed they were upholding the integrity of the Puritan heritage. The classical tradition offered models of republics shaking off cruel and corrupt rulers: "The American Revolution was a paradox: a revolution fueled by tradition." Patriots employed a rhetoric to " 'summon obedience' and empower 'vigorous action.' "[65] America, often described as an infant, became associated with youth and growth; patriots described themselves as young men coming of age ready to stand alone against the old, tired, father England. Youth became a powerful image for the Revolution.

Boston patriots such as Samuel Adams and Charles Chauncy who emphasized past obligation came from the cohort Pauline Maier has called the "Old Revolutionaries." The colonial past dominated their responses to the conflict with England. For others, many of them college-educated "young men of the Revolution," the revolutionary experience itself shaped views of history and tradition.[66] Many came from Virginia.

In the Virginians' pantheon of the past, the classical republican heritage exerted far greater influence than Puritanism. Republicanism shared the Puritan concern with paternal models, reverence and remembrance of worthy ancestors, and a fear of decay. In republics, such values "bind a generation to those who have preceded it. . . . the patriot participates in . . . a relationship with predecessors—his 'fathers.' "[67] The younger cohort of revolutionaries may have synthesized the Puritan and republican traditions. "The eclecticism of the young revolutionaries . . . was the sign of their capacity to build their own world from portions of old and new experience," argues historian Peter Hoffer. They were forging a new conception of time that may have begun as being good "sons of the fathers." But in that revolutionary moment it seemed that the patriots themselves became founders.[68] Soon, the Revolution would represent the benchmark against which future national actions were measured. The fate of the promise and sentiments of the revolutionary situation bore certain similarities to the crises in seventeenth-century New England.[69]

The youth image endured, describing the possibilities and prospects of the country. "The young plant in America had become a tree. The child had grown up to a man's estate. Indeed, it was time to emancipate ourselves," a New Jersey minister wrote in 1791. In contrast to the vision of youth endangered on all sides by sin and temptation in the sermon literature, this was a youth full of hope.[70]

America emerged from the Revolution imagined in terms of age. The United States was "young." Writers in the colonial period had occasionally used metaphors of aging and youth to describe their states or localities; either retrospectively, as in a 1690 comment about early New England as "a Babe in the Cradle," or to characterize a new colony.[71]

The nation seemed to follow a cyclical model of growth; this perspective saw political bodies in organic terms, with an infancy, youth, maturity, and death. Whatever the significance of the colonial founders in Puritan and patriotic rhetoric, the past now seemed meaningless and the

Revolution established a new historical epoch. "Is America . . . like Jacob, the youngest, yet the most favoured child of an indulgent Providence," asked the optimistic New Jersey minister Oliver Hart.[72] Despite expansive expressions of youthful possibility, actual young persons in society still often represented disruptive forces whose energy needed to be controlled.

Many of the insurgents who joined Daniel Shays's challenge to authority in western Massachusetts during 1786 and 1787 were young men in their twenties and early thirties. One recent study interpreted their participation as "an attempt to confront directly" the frustration over diminished opportunities that had plagued rural New England's youth for most of the century. Perhaps. More intriguing is the fact that many insurgents wore particular insignia and made statements that tried to associate them with the spirit of the American Revolution. The war had been over about four years and remained a constant companion. For example, as the *Worcester Magazine* tracked Shays's rebels and published proclamations by both sides, the first story in each issue told the saga of the Revolution in a continuing serial. When one historian noted that "the tender ages of many rebels refuted their claim to represent the Revolution," this was certainly accurate in the factual sense that few of Shays's followers had served in the Continental Army themselves. The wish for the young to ally themselves with this tradition, though, represented a viewpoint that would endure.[73] Disorderly youth had other meanings in an urban setting.

Youth, Education, and Gender

Philadelphia's mayor Matthew Clarkson complained publicly that youth rioting, committing crimes, and causing disorder posed a special problem for his city. He worried about everything from young delinquent burglary rings to the seemingly trivial act of groups "wantonly knocking at doors for the express purpose of deceiving and discomposing families." All were cause for alarm: "If the morals and manners of our youth are neglected and become corrupt, society is poisoned at the fountain, and all its channels and branches will soon become infected with the deadly taint." The mayor expected an array of authorities and institutions to address the problem: clergy, magistrates, educators, parents, guardians and masters, and finally, citizens in general.[74] Education emerged as the critical solution.

Moral guardians argued that education offered the possibility that "the rising generation . . . would prove very different from their fathers."[75] Philadelphia intellectual Benjamin Rush boiled down the benefits of education to basic fears of public disorder that would appeal to even the most skeptical interests:

> The bachelor will save his tax for this purpose by being able to sleep with fewer bolts and locks to his doors, the estates of orphans will in time be benefited by being protected from the ravages of unprincipled and idle boys, and the children of wealthy parents, will be less tempted, by bad company to extravagance. Fewer pillories, and whipping posts, and smaller jails . . . will be necessary when our youth are properly educated.[76]

While Philadelphia authorities wrestled with issues of education and local peace, other citizens joined Rush in examining the implications of education for national order. Corruption and decay, the dark side of the young republic's sunny prospects, lurked in conceptions about youth harbored by traditional moralists and republican ideologues. Education, many argued, was the most important way to ensure the nation's great future. Indeed, writers acknowledged the wide acceptance of education's significance, so much so that Samuel Knox observed in the 1790s that "To have dwelt on the national advantages of national education in the present enlightened age of the world, would appear like an eulogium on the benefits of the light of the sun to the solar system." The republican consensus on education asserted that "the success—nay the salvation—of the Republic lay in education." The "Revolutionary Enlightenment" linked education with notions of progress.[77] From the 1780s to the end of the century, a series of thinkers published treatises devoted to describing how a national educational system in America would advance revolutionary ideas. Rush wrote, "Next to the duty which young men owe to their creator, I wish to see a Supreme Regard To Their Country inculcated upon them."[78]

A powerful suspicion of older traditions endured. Noah Webster warned: "The minds of youth are perpetually led by the history of Greece and Rome or . . . Great Britain; boys are constantly repeating the declamations of Demosthenes and Cicero." He wanted a different past to dominate: "every child in America should be acquainted with his own country. . . . As soon as he opens his lips, he should rehearse the history of his own country; he should lisp the praise of liberty and of those illustrious heroes and statesmen who have wrought a revolution in her favor."[79]

American plans for education emphasized the importance of egalitarian impulses and the resulting "uniformity" that would ensure their success. David Tyack argues that the educational thinkers "saw conformity as the price of liberty." This notion was summarized in Rush's oft-quoted wish for an educational system that could create "republican machines."[80] Conformity and uniformity seem to have been synonyms for assuring continuity with the revolutionary endeavor and predictability for future generations through the education of youth.

The rhetoric attached to the dramatic expansion in educational opportunities had concrete implications for the development of ideas about gender and the family in the years after the Revolution. We have seen how a language of "generations" had long been linked to an ideal of fatherhood, through the notion of a generative seed and the biblical language of generations passing down through a father's loins. Being a father proved that a man had become an adult. The fathers' importance in Puritan tradition as both honored figures and significant ancestors meshed comfortably with the republican respect for elders like Cincinnatus and the notion of government ruled by the people. George Washington, of course, became known as *the* father of his country some years later, leading Melvin Yazawa to argue that Washington's title represented the end of an old ideology of family order: "All Americans were now children of the republic." Others have noted that "the point is not that he is described as America's father, but rather what kind of father he is described as being." It was more important that he was a good father who symbolically recognized young men's need to go out on their own.[81]

The notion of being a father to one's country holds greater significance in view of the fact that virtue, a central notion in descriptions of the republican ideal, "was derived from the Latin word for *man,* with its connotations of virility. Political action seemed somehow inherently masculine." This is evident in Samuel Stanhope Smith's description of a "young and growing country not yet enervated by luxury, nor sunk into effeminacy and sloth." In this context, educational thinkers addressed the question of young women and created a rhetoric that expressed their pivotal role as preservers of generational continuity. Women had been ignored in both the accepted understandings of language and the most explicit political discourse about the republic's future. Yet some leaders invested women's roles as mothers with supreme importance for guiding, shaping, and nurturing the generations to come. As Ruth Bloch has argued, "They relegated the production and maintenance of public virtue to a new realm, one presided over largely by women." Linda Kerber has described the Republican Mother, a figure "dedicated to the service of civic virtue: she educated her sons for it, she condemned and corrected her husband's lapses from it."[82]

Jan Lewis, in contrast, responding to evidence of "anti-patriarchal" revolutionary and early national rhetoric, argues for the significance of a shift "from the parent-child nexus to the husband-wife bond." The wife, rather than the mother, represented "the indispensable half of the conjugal union" in a republican household and increased the importance of women in public life. "When the key relationship in a society is that between father and son . . . women may conveniently be ignored."[83] It seems, however, that the language of generational continuity, with its male implications, connected to concerns about youth, may have tipped the balance toward mothers over wives.

The ideology of republican wife and mother along with a belief that women might also benefit from the opportunities offered by the new nation led to the founding of educational institutions for women. While many female "academies" scraped by on limited support, in Philadelphia, as with other things educational, the new institutions enjoyed the patronage of leading citizens. These schools taught young women writing, history, and geography, as well as some "ornamental" subjects such as music, dancing, and needlework. Still, despite claims by trustees and supporters about dramatic advances in education, graduates were not expected to disrupt traditional women's relationships to family and domesticity. Even when a woman author, Hannah Foster, dedicated a work "To the Young Ladies of America," she gave no indication that these women represented anything more than persons whose individual natures and "deportment" could be improved.[84]

Two Philadelphia female academies, each supported by the same elite leaders, delineated the horizons and boundaries of republican women's education. On May 10, 1786, the *Pennsylvania Gazette* announced "An Academy Instituted for the sole purpose of Educating Young Ladies." Educational innovation was clearly in the air. The same day's edition printed an abstract of Benjamin Rush's plan for the establishment of public schools.[85] Addresses by trustees to the graduates of the Young Ladies' Academy in Philadelphia, although couched in some of the rhetoric familiar to male education, show very different expectations for women. Some speakers emphasized the cultivation of sweetness, joy, and light in women's education. Others, however, spoke of "the foundations of future greatness" that were being "laid on the exertions which may be used to cultivate the minds of the younger branches of the community, on whose virtue, wisdom, and activity, the labours of the present age must rest for their final success," adding that "successive generations" would probably depend on their efforts as well. "I see before me so large an assemblage of young ladies, destined to occupy, in all probability, so many various and important stations of life," said the merchant John Swanwick.[86]

Even an advocate for women's education was quick to emphasize, however, that women's most important role would be in "the influence which you will necessarily have in society, and over the hearts and manners of your countrymen." Swanwick described how women would benefit and ennoble men. The merchant seemed to think of education as a way to increase the value of a polished female commodity for those who would soon come to possess it:

> The numerous avocations of our sex, the labour and fatigue that are expected from us, and the little time many of us have for cultivating the finer and more delicate branches of education, all have a tendency to make us look forward with delight, to the prospect of the *acquisition* we shall make, when united to ladies who add to the useful, the ornamental endowments of the mind.

At the same time, though, Swanwick had some rough notion of education providing a measure of independence. In defending the teaching of drawing at the academy, he argued that "it will form one other shield to guard a lady, in case of unexpected misfortunes, from the horrors of dependence." But in the normal run of events—"a happy marriage"—it would allow her "to prove the best instructress of her children."[87]

Benjamin Rush's address on female education described its particular characteristics in terms of marriage and family responsibilities: "The equal share that every citizen has in liberty, and the possible share he may have in the government of our country, make it necessary that our ladies should be qualified to a certain degree by a peculiar and suitable education, to concur in instructing their sons in the principles of liberty and government." Not surprisingly, "every citizen" implied every male. Rush emphasized the cultivation metaphor. If male "seed" made generations, the young women in the academy, "our daughters, like pleasant plants shall sweetly grow," but there needed to be a "friendly hand" from the tutor/gardener to stop the growth of "noxious weeds." The young women had a "charming" opportunity, Rush argued, "of furnishing the succeeding generation with the most noble plants, and extending virtue, religion, and happiness, to ages yet unborn." The rhetoric in the addresses to both young ladies' academies reveals a conception of two "rising generations," one of men and the other of "the fair sex." "The rising fair" would use their "academical improvements . . . to mollify the temper, refine the manners."[88]

The women themselves had conflicting feelings about the value of their education. An analysis of the annual valedictory and salutatory orations found that women could imagine possibilities for greater independence. They did not always project unqualified and easy prospects for progress. In addresses not included in that study, conflict sometimes emerged in adjacent paragraphs. The salutatory orator at a graduation in 1794 celebrated the distinct accomplishments of female heroes: "In opposition to your immortal Paine, we will exalt our Wollstonecraft." She emphasized, however, that "the fatigue and the toils of war . . . the thorny paths of politics . . . belong to men," and that the "domestic cares, connected with the rearing of the tender offspring, is the arduous task of our sex. The education which we receive, should be calculated to render us capable of the employment."[89] Score one for republican motherhood.

It appears that for women, gender played a more determining role than categories of youth or generation. There was little of the rhetoric attached to young women, even when education was concerned, that there had been to young men, unless it was connected to the specific task of preparing the rising generation of males to take up their responsibilities on the stage of action.

Youth, then, remained a subordinate position, even as the spokesmen of the older generation invested it with great significance for the national future. With greater independence, urban young men and women in the nineteenth century took the claims of their elders seriously and established particular identities and institutions for themselves that made their youth the basis for a claim to participate in public.

CHAPTER THREE

Youth Organized:
The Language of Association

After two hundred years as familiar subjects in American moral rhetoric, young people began to speak for themselves in the first half of the nineteenth century. Consider these two scenes. First, at the Massachusetts convention of Whig Young Men in 1839, keynote speaker Robert C. Winthrop told delegates they were all "true-hearted children" of founding fathers and would "never falter or fail" in supporting their principles. In 1840, Henry Highland Garnet, "a colored young man of this city," reminded the American Anti-Slavery Society's annual meeting that "our fathers" stood by "your fathers" in the Revolutionary War: "We would not question the sincerity . . . which seemed to wield the swords of most of the fathers of the Revolution. But we complain . . . of the base conduct of their degenerate sons."[1] How did a loyal son of the Massachusetts Winthrops—who spent most of the 1830s as spokesman for "young men" in the Whig party—and a leader of young New York African Americans—who challenged both their own community's establishment and white reformers—share similar language in talking about themselves as young men? In the manuscript records of that 1839 Whig convention there is a stray page, unlabeled, unsigned; it might be notes for a speech, or the scribbling of one delegate. It is a list of phrases and descriptions the writer found significant:

—Fine looking men—genuine New England character;
—manly . . .
—eternal war. . . .[2]

How did young people develop a public rhetoric that gave them a meaningful place in the world? They did not weave a new language out of whole cloth. Instead, they drew on traditions of thinking about youth and generations. Young men's organizations articulated the significance they attached to their own youth and how they imagined themselves as men. While jeremiads and other addresses had often appealed to the young, young people in the nineteenth century established their own perspective that embraced and endorsed their place in national life.

Transformations in postrevolutionary America expanded commercial and political horizons as they raised new challenges for the nation's identity. It was "a time rapidly drifting away from the beliefs and purposes of the revolutionary era . . . when traditions seemed under fire," writes historian Lewis Perry.[3] Just as the declension crisis of the mid-eighteenth century led to a revision of the Puritan errand, so the first four decades of the nineteenth century witnessed the creation of a new pantheon of founding heroes and a growing emphasis on a special responsibility for the nation's young people.

Americans born after the Revolution certainly felt they fashioned an identity in the shadow of colossal fathers. The signers of the Declaration of Independence and heroes of the revolutionary struggle represented much more than worthy ancestors deserving deference—they connected the nation to Providence itself. American young men coming of age between 1820 and 1840 faced a particular problem: the Founding Fathers were old and dying. This would be the first generation to face the future in the *absence* of the founders' guiding force. As a Massachusetts young men's temperance convention put it in 1834, "Our fathers will soon fall asleep for ever! and when we have closed their eyes in death, we must enter into their places. . . . we must, unaided, work out our own character, our own condition, our own destiny."[4] They would feel bound by loyalty to their fathers even as they asserted their own vision.

American young men in towns and cities across the Northeast and in the new settlements of the Northwest formed voluntary associations whose distinctive rhetoric linked youth to the founders. They promoted issues more vigorously and emphatically than older politicians who controlled the party machinery. William Seward remembered an episode at the beginning of his long career, an 1828 convention of New York young National Republicans; of all the political meetings he ever attended, he had never "seen any assembly which exhibited a greater fervor of sentiment, or more *pure and elevated conviction of public duty.*"[5] Young men asserted their moral authority to participate in a society that some observers believed was losing direction. Their expression of "public duty" was based on the absence of the Fathers and their feeling of responsibility *as young people* to fulfill the founders' promise. The most conservative among them explicitly rejected patricidal notions; even those in direct conflict with elders still explained their role in public in terms of maintaining continuity with the fathers.

Ideas about manhood also underwent powerful transformations in the nineteenth century.[6] One recent interpretation has argued that youth offered a brief moment that permitted the expression of emotions inappropriate for adult men. Adult male institutions "offered their members a viable emotional compromise between connection and autonomy," but the tenderness of feeling would never retain the same intensity it had in youth.[7] In fact, institutions young men used to enter public life sometimes aggressively expressed masculine ideals, but they also created complex, multiple bonds between young men and across generations.

The Transformation of Youth and the Rise of Association

In the early decades of the nineteenth century, young people poured into cities in the Northeast. They came not only to the evolving metropolis but to commercial centers along canal routes and industrial towns in the interior. Like the young men in early-modern London or colonial American cities, migrants became targets for advice-book authors and moral guardians concerned about those separated from traditional family authority.[8] But the new residents of New York City, or Rochester, or Cincinnati came in far larger numbers and represented a greater proportion of the nation than had earlier young urbanites. The entire U.S. population grew at an average rate of about 35 percent (compared with a growth rate of about 19 percent during the baby boom of the post–World War II era). People between the ages of twenty and twenty-nine comprised about one-fourth of the white population in rapidly growing cities in the 1820s to 1840s.[9] The young began to notice each other as well. Only when they lived in large enough numbers and removed from family constraints did they begin to look to each other for support and to conceive of an identity based on their age.

The years of departure came to define "youth" in the antebellum North. Just as had been the case in medieval and early-modern Europe, youth was defined by social status as much as age. In the nineteenth century young people followed an irregular path of "binding transformations" on the way to adulthood: leaving school, if any; entering a regular job; leaving home; marrying; establishing one's own household. It could take decades to complete them all, and individuals did not always follow the path in precise order. As one historian notes, "There was no rite of passage to help him through, society left him largely on his own to find his way to an adult identity." [10] The "young men" in nineteenth-century cities ranged in age anywhere from late teens to early thirties. Some had even completed all these stages and still participated in young men's organizations.

Transformations in family life under way since the eighteenth century promoted young men's mobility. The previous century's tensions over available land in rural areas had gotten no better; the "erosion" of patriarchal authority continued. The declining size of families meant that the gaps between older and younger generations became more noticeable. Although the actual social power of fathers declined in daily life, the rhetorical significance of Fathers and fatherhood simultaneously increased. Motherhood, meanwhile, became more closely allied with a domestic sphere and childhood a more easily recognized stage of life. This shift was reflected in new kinds of reading material circulating throughout the nation directed at particular age groups, especially the young. In this new world, "it became increasingly difficult to believe that the experience of the older generation would directly prefigure the life of the younger one," John Demos has written. The young men who went to the cities thus completed a process of separation from domestic ties already strained in the society at large. [11]

Social historians describe an antebellum metropolis numerically dominated by young people. The young single men and women of the working class created a vibrant world that appeared to resemble modern youth counterculture. But, this complex network of associations—formed by fire companies, sports teams, trade groups, theater and leisure, and the male camaraderie of barrooms [12]—was not defined by age. Though these men and women were predominantly young, it was not their *youth,* as such, that brought them together. They gathered as butchers, volunteer firemen, or residents of the Sixth Ward. Occupational or neighborhood ties formed the basis for working-class culture. [13]

Many men enjoyed their most important association outside the home in fraternal orders. These organizations had roots in early-modern European apprenticeship and trade groups. By the nineteenth century their significance lay in the power of the rituals practiced by Masons or Odd Fellows to reinforce the hierarchical, male-dominated structure of society. The lodge provided an all-male preserve outside the home, even as

temperance reformers were making inroads into the saloon. Recent studies of fraternal orders point out, however, that the organization moved
men away from the public sphere, effacing social action as it emphasized
a universal brotherhood that submerged social divisions.[14] When young
men appeared in public, they did so under the aegis of a young men's
organization.

These groups emerged amid an explosion of associations. The predominance of young people could not be missed. James Fenimore Cooper's
1838 novel *Homeward Bound* took a dim view of the trend, personified
in the character Steadfast Dodge:

> from his tenth year up to his twenty-fifth, this gentleman had been either a
> president, vice-president, manager, or committee-man of some philosophi-
> cal, political or religious expedient to fortify human wisdom, make men
> better, and resist error and despotism. His experience had rendered him
> expert in what may well enough be termed the language of association.

Cooper's protagonists did not like what they saw. In the sequel, *Home
as Found,* one complained that "you will see young men of the country
hardily invited to meet by themselves to consult concerning public affairs,
as if they were impatient of the counsel and experience of their fathers." [15]
Young men did indeed meet by themselves. Rather than showing impatience with their fathers, however, many groups embraced them.

The language of young men's associations emerged with the new nation. Some basic images and appeals developed in a seemingly standard
form of political rhetoric, the Fourth of July oration. The first July Fourth
speeches were delivered in Boston to replace the annual orations that
memorialized the Boston Massacre. The Massacre addresses themselves
had been designed to "imprint on the mind of the rising youth" the
sacrifices of those who had died there and of those who had come before
them. As Dr. Joseph Warren, who delivered two of the best-known Massacre orations, had declared in 1772, "The voice of your fathers' blood
cries to you from the ground, 'my sons scorn to be slaves.' " Young men
continued to invoke his words and example, which took on added force
after Warren died in the Battle of Bunker Hill.[16]

The early Boston Fourth of July addresses focused on continuity, the
language of following in the fathers' footsteps. The men delivering these
speeches, and the ones who organized many celebrations, were often
young. A speaker in 1808 commented that "it has become fashionable
for the fathers . . . of the Revolution to take their seats, and for some
young genius (who has learned the grand events . . . from history alone)"
to speak.[17] The Fourth was not a neutral holiday; both Federalists and

Republicans fought to control its meaning during those early years. Beginning in 1805, the Young Democratic Republicans of Boston, despite Federalist opposition, organized and published July Fourth orations, some of which were popular enough to go into second editions. The initiative in Boston was soon repeated throughout the nation, and young men were in the center of the action. Although one scholar argues that the Federalists treated the Fourth "as a commemoration of a historical moment in time," while Republicans saw it as a moment in a "dynamic process still unfolding," the evidence from the young men's speeches suggests a different picture.[18]

Fourth of July speeches organized by young men's organizations shared some themes that were as old as New England itself, even if the words were not delivered in that region: remember the fathers, they are dying; youth has fallen from the ways of the righteous. "It shall never be said that the YOUTH OF AMERICA are so far sunk in slothful degeneracy, as to be indifferent to the fate of their country," said a speaker in New York City. The Revolution offered a new beginning that suggested youth's place in the national future. They were too young, speakers said, to be revolutionaries themselves; it was their deepest wish to have been able to fight at their fathers' side. But the fathers "have now grown old, and to us devolves the sacred trust of maintaining . . . Independence." That trust demanded that young men defend the nation from its enemies.[19]

Time and again, orations raised the specter of invasion; during the War of 1812, of course, the threat was real. Whether soldiers were landing or not, however, young men were called to the nation's defense. The consequences of inaction were dire. "Should we, who have been rocked in the 'cradle of freedom' and nursed at the bosom of liberty . . . suffer monarchy to raise its baleful head . . . the injured shades of those fallen martyrs, who sacrificed their lives for their country's Independence, would rise from their sepulchres, and even haunt us in our midnight slumbers," said an orator in 1809. As Cotton Mather had said about a century earlier, "Being Dead, they yet speak." The legacy of the fathers' blood demanded that all young men protect helpless dependents. One War of 1812 oration asked, "Can you see the dying mother, the violated daughter, the bleeding infant and the burning cottage, and not relent?" "On us (the rising generation) will fall the pleasing, yet difficult task to transmit, unimpaired, to future generations, the precious patrimony of our departed worthies," said a speaker in 1814.[20] Images and ideals articulated in these addresses mingled with a discourse drawn from religious roots to build the foundation for the language of young men's organizations in the next few decades.

The American Protestant tradition that paid close attention to youth—beginning with the Puritans and continuing in the revivals of the 1740s—formed another bridge to nineteenth-century groups. Leaders of the religious revivals known as the Second Great Awakening called for organizations to promote public benevolence. A flock of voluntary associations based in local societies raised funds to provide Bibles and educated ministers for the frontiers of western New York and beyond. Evangelical and missionary publications gave publicity and a national scope to the new societies.[21] One recurring message was that young men led the benevolent charge.

Young men merged the national appeals of Fourth of July addresses with the language of past revivals. They honored evangelical predecessors and recognized that "the young men of New-England are not now embodied for any specific or immediate object." Nonetheless, they concluded that the contemporary challenge was even greater: "To us belong . . . far higher responsibilities than rested upon our fathers." The young men's wing of the American Education Society went to the root of its "parent" body's origins, echoing the tones of Puritan exhortations to youth that had been ringing through Boston churches for almost two hundred years. Speakers reminded members that the West was yet another wilderness awaiting civilization. Young men were called to familiar responsibilities: "Will they look idly on and see their country's ruin consummated? It is in their power to make a mighty effort."[22] They often invoked an older language to explain their role. "Every sentiment of honor . . . calls upon us to be 'up and doing,' " wrote one supporter of a local Pennsylvania young men's missionary society. Another publication noted that in the past there was less "systematic attention bestowed on childhood . . . but there was much more attemped and done for Youth who had past the sense of childhood." Its evidence, and subsequent columns of material, came directly from *The Christian History*. Headlines read "Footsteps of the Flock," "A Voice From the Grave," and "They Being Dead Yet Speak." With these explicit references, the association of youth's importance to the revivals and to the missionary effort echoed the connection drawn in the revivals of the eighteenth century.[23] Later organizations also used Puritan sources of the rhetoric but would be more specific in describing the characteristics of their special responsibility for public action.

Although some urban missionary organizations looked to the welfare of their own citizens, their primary goal was to raise money. The young men's groups were particularly effective fundraisers. As the network of benevolent associations grew, so too did a consciousness of the importance of the young men. A reader in Virginia might know as much about the activities of the Young Men's Missionary Society of New York as it did of local groups.[24] These societies, along with the July Fourth groups, were the first in wave after wave of young men's organizations that emerged in the cities.

They formed associations of all kinds. Some supported education and self-improvement for newly arrived urban residents, but those groups were not "the core of male youth culture," as one historian suggested recently.[25] They represented only one avenue for young men. "Youth" became a category for division between classes and genders. Formal voluntary associations had different class bases. Benevolent societies drew their leadership from wealthy and rising businessmen, financiers, lawyers, their wives, sons, and daughters. Reform societies might include the more "middling" reaches of the city. Those for self-improvement might be filled with aspirants to middle-class status.

Participation in voluntary associations revealed that a "young man" was not just any male who happened to be young. The Apprentice's Temperance Society explained: "Young Men also possess many advantages for carrying on the work, not enjoyed by any other class . . . they have a better opportunity than apprentices, in consequence of being their own masters, and not so confined to their various callings, or occupations." A "young man" in the city was a man rising into the professional or managerial middle class.[26]

The Second Great Awakening and the move into the cities had particular consequences for young women. In the first place, they comprised the majority of new converts in the revivals themselves. "Conversion could provide young women with ideological ballast useful to stabilize their ideas and identities," argues Nancy Cott. Women's extensive involvement in voluntary associations stemmed from participation in the Awakening.[27] But their voluntary associations rarely included groups divided by age. A "young women's" group might suggest transgression of accepted boundaries of social action. As one hastened to explain, "we encroach not upon the prerogatives" of ministers. Another "Young Ladies' " society emphasized, lest there be any confusion, that they would not be young and single for long: "Every young lady is conscious that she intends . . . to form that connection which will probably give her the endearing relation of *mother*."[28] Motherhood defined adulthood for young women, while fatherhood seemed to serve as more of a metaphor, less materially connected to the actual role of being a father, for the men. Young men would grow up to become leaders in the public sphere in addition to being fathers, while young women could only look forward to becoming wives and mothers—influencing public life through private nurture. Women's reform societies formed in the 1830s and 1840s challenged assumptions that women's public actions had to derive directly from a maternal-domestic role. Reform women tended to be younger than members of women's benevolent societies, but still rarely organized young women's groups.[29] Both benevolent organizations' emphasis on women's special role in raising the next generation and the growing feminist "sisterhood" in some reform groups suggested that women's public presence was much more likely to be based on gender identification than age.[30] Men's and women's groups each made bids in a fluctuating negotiation over the terms and boundaries of participation in the public sphere. Shrill claims by young men about being heirs to fathers' traditions may have been influenced by the fact that women were also in the field.

Young men's voluntary activities exceeded the range of benevolent and reform concerns initiated by women's groups. Whether raising money to get Bibles to communities without ministers or campaigning to elect a slate of candidates, young men developed a rhetoric that gave them special qualification to participate in these realms of public life. They based this claim on their relationship to fathers, both actual parents and metaphorical ancestors.

Young Men's Societies, formed in 1831 through 1833 in New York City, Troy, Utica, Buffalo, Philadelphia, Baltimore, and other cities, merged the benevolent concerns of missionary and education societies with a strong message of self-help addressed to "young men who have come to engage in business . . . separated from all those endearing and improving influences which are associated with home." The societies recognized the danger that bad companions and a lack of "useful" ways to spend leisure time posed for lone young men in cities. In an address on the "Spirit of Association," a doctor described the dilemma facing the "inquisitive mechanic, or thrifty trader," as well as young lawyers, doctors, or ministers, "to furnish to each other incentives to diligent and active inquiry." In some cities mechanics and other skilled workers joined the young merchants and clerks, but direction of these organizations came almost exclusively from the upper reaches of the mercantile class.[31]

To join a young man's society, one had to be "of known moral character under the age of thirty-five years." These associations strictly avoided
politics. Still, they argued that young men had a higher responsibility
that demanded the moral and intellectual improvement brought by these
societies:

> We may not, nor do we, arrogate to ourselves the power or the privilege of
> directing or controlling in matters more properly within the province of our
> elders. But, as young men, we feel that we have deeply important and
> responsible duties to perform,—duties which the world acknowledge and
> declare to be peculiarly and appropriately ours.

This responsibility, while seemingly nonpartisan and "republican," supported particular class and political ideologies, as illustrated in the contrast drawn by one speaker between the good works of the American
Colonization Society and the "howlings of anarchists. . . . with them,
abolition of slavery would be accomplished by the abolition of established laws." In New York and Philadelphia, in fact, several of the same
young men managed the Young Men's Society and the Young Men's
Colonization Society. The Young Men's Society did "not aspire to revolu-
tionize or to reform the body politic or to change the present frame work
of society." Similarly the Young Men's Colonization Society believed that
slavery had to be ended "in reduction of that debt which we owe to our
ancestors—it is an incumbrance connected with our English inheritance." Their identity as young men "infused into" the Colonization
Society's "veins the inspiring virtue of youthful blood, with its impulsive
energy. As a branch of the chief establishment at Washington, it will
act upon similar views." [32] They blended their assertion of obedience—
making no special claim for themselves beyond their active, impulsive
youth—with their wish to address a problem their ancestors had preferred to avoid, by announcing a special responsibility for paying off a
debt incurred in the past. The conservative tone of their rhetoric and elite
membership reinforced the impression that the effort was appropriate
and unexceptional.

Soon, popular Young Men's Associations replaced the Young Men's
Societies' combination of elite benevolence and middle-class self-help.
The former appealed to a broader population of urban youth, departing
from strict benevolence to offer reading rooms, libraries, lectures, and
other sober and improving activities. The Associations replaced some
missing family connections and served as an island of stability in confus-
ing surroundings. Despite their more populist ethos, the Young Men's
Associations stayed squarely in the realm of professional and middle-

class youth and rarely tried to attract young working-class men. Mechanics' institutes in some cities addressed the ideal of universal education, sometimes even invoking the language of the Founding Fathers, but they did not concentrate on youth as such. The institutes and Young Men's Associations left an enduring mark on their communities when their reading-room collections formed the basis for public libraries in the post–Civil War era. Their nonpartisan character and noncontroversial useful services doubtless contributed to their popularity and persistence.[33] But Association leaders did not seem to participate in the many other young men's organizations that permeated cities, especially groups involved in reform or party politics. Benevolent and self-help organizations might refer to "peculiar responsibilities" of youth, but they left their precise nature unclear. The partisan young men's organizations that emerged in the Jacksonian political era developed a more activist rhetoric. While the benevolent groups borrowed mostly from the exhortations of ministers to youth, political and reform organizations gave young men the chance to present themselves as defenders of a founding vision.

Young Men in Politics, Temperance, and Antislavery

Property and age qualifications kept many young men from voting in the first years of the republic, but did not prevent young Federalists and Republicans from participating in popular mobbing and other political activity. Along with those organizations that planned July Fourth addresses, formal young men's organizations had their first glimmerings in the early decades of the century. The Constitutional Republican Young Men of Philadelphia met and formed a committee in 1808. While they acknowledged their youth, they explained they would "have longer to participate in" the nation's "honour or disgrace than our elder brethren. Having at least as much at stake, we speak plainly and honestly."[34]

A young men's political organization at first seemed a proper vehicle for satire. "Here politicians not yet fledg'd were seen / With scarce a bit of down to shade their chin," said one Philadelphia magazine. The account noted that at one of their meetings the young men drank more than thirty toasts; by that point, "they began to feel themselves as large as men." At other times these groups were simply an audience for a nationalized version of older exhortations to the young. A revolutionary veteran, in a July Fourth address organized by young men, reminded his audience that "the fathers of the revolution are . . . dead. . . . They leave to you, young patriots, your Independence and Liberty . . . and it is for you to improve or waste it." As the New York Democratic organization put it in 1810, "Your elder friends in this city . . . view your laudable exertions in the cause of freedom, with emotions of inexpressible pleasure." While insisting on the significance of the rising generation, the Tammany party referred to themselves as "your sincere friends and Senior Republican brethren."[35] Clearly this was a party that the young men would have little role in shaping.

Increasingly autonomous young men's political organizations emerged as part of the developing system of national political parties and the extension of suffrage to all white males over the age of twenty-one. In 1821, while a constitutional convention debated voting rights in New York state, young men held meetings calling for broader suffrage. The young men of Saratoga immediately linked their concerns to rights granted by the Revolution; they regretted the proposed constitution "should thus entrammel the privileges most propitiously lavished" by the Declaration of Independence. They expressed particular concern about any voting qualification that would leave revolutionary veterans "debarred. . . . Merely because fortune has not favoured them with her propitious smiles!"[36] Here in compact form are two key parts of young men's response to politics: a wish for greater opportunity, and a deference to the revolutionary heritage.

During New York state contests in 1825, young men's conventions and manifestos brought concrete meaning to Fourth of July rhetoric.[37] Speakers declared that if enemies landed on American shores young men would rise to defend the nation, but politicians who denied young men's rights were more dangerous than any invader. The delegates at one meeting concluded: "As young men we are emphatically called upon by duty, to unite our most active and zealous efforts to preserve those estimable political rights which we derive from the patriotic efforts of our fathers."[38] They linked this legacy to the sacrifices of the Revolution:

> Many of our fathers have long since departed to a better world, but they have transmitted a noble inheritance; and each of them has written on his last legacy in characters of blood, sentiments like these: my sons, I have toiled, I have fought for the liberties of my country. I commit that precious boon to you. Cherish it with your hearts and protect it with your fortunes and lives.[39]

Young men believed themselves the best qualified to stamp out evil; they had been given the keys to liberty, usually stained with the blood of the Founding Fathers, and had to serve as custodians of the revolutionary tradition. They brought this fervor to the leadership of contemporary reform crusades.

"Society is most healthful when the aged counsel and the youthful *act*," said a group of Albany young men. Temperance reformers pronounced a particular urgency to their cause: "the Young Men of Boston feel themselves called upon by motives of self-respect, self-preservation, patriotism, and Christianity, to maintain by moral purity that independence which our fathers purchased with their blood."[40] They compared intemperance to a foreign invasion. If young men would rise to stop an army, they would soon join together to ban liquor. Temperance was essential to preserve the founders' most precious gift: "American youth; is this the freedom which your fathers purchased and bequeathed?" Speakers proclaimed that drinking would never destroy "the *freedom to do right*."[41]

Some historians have argued that the looming presence of the founding generation in public life was too much for temperance activists. These sons struggled to match the achievements of the heroic generation and used literary surrogates in their battles. The pages of temperance fiction were filled with broken sons unable to reach their full potential and drunken old revolutionary soldiers saved by temperate sons. One study argues, "If the Fathers had won renown as formers, the Sons would win it as reformers."[42]

This problem does not seem to have troubled the members of the young men's organizations; they seemed perfectly comfortable defending the fathers' legacy. "Our fathers have originated this scheme of moral improvement: upon us devolves the duty of carrying it forward," said a young men's convention in Massachusetts. A New York convention did fear that "the rising generation, in imitation of their elders . . . commence the moderate use of strong drink," but this was not a common image, at least in speeches and addresses.[43] Even if the fathers did drink to excess, it did not seem necessary to portray this fact in public speeches in order to justify the sons' activity. Developing an identity that recognized the absence of metaphorical fathers informed young men's rhetoric. Conflict was unnecessary because a void had been created that young men felt a responsibility to fill.

The allegiance to paternal values and expression of loyalty seem appropriate for conservative benevolents and even for temperance activists. Similar tendencies, however, appear in the speeches of radical reformers. Many historians have followed David Donald in his assertion that "abolitionism was . . . a revolt of the young." Some suggest that "like most disturbers of the status quo, their enthusiasm was in large measure a function of their age." Another author asserts that young abolitionists did not "look nostalgically and romantically to an earlier day when their fathers had dominated society." Even those who find "no extraordinarily intense antagonism between father and son" in abolitionists' backgrounds, or who argue that abolition became the resolution for a young person's inevitable vocational crisis, still insist on youth's centrality. Why was age so clearly a catalyst? The young might not look back with nostalgia, yet they could still invest the past with a crucial significance.[44]

Abolitionism, in and out of young men's organizations, was "not the sectarian preserve of disgruntled and displaced New England elites," according to a study of those who joined societies and signed petitions. Rather, a majority of this "antislavery rank and file" were skilled workers or in a professional-managerial occupation, along with many members of the working class. A sizable number were young by our standards, between nineteen and twenty-nine.[45] Organizers certainly thought about young people's potential. John Greenleaf Whittier, who attended many young men's meetings in Haverhill, Massachusetts, wrote to a fellow abolitionist in 1833 that "the young men's meeting was adjourned in order to let a society of the older people take the precedence. I do not think we can make arrangements for the formation of a society for some weeks."[46] Leaders tended to be at the high end of an unofficial age level to still be a "young man," usually thirty or older. Some of them, along with other politicians and reformers, had their first taste of public life in a young men's organization.[47]

While the auxiliaries of benevolent organizations often followed their "parent" body closely, the young men's anti-slavery societies had intentions and treasuries of their own. The New York Young Men's Anti-Slavery Society seemed particularly strong financially. The regular New York City organization turned to the young men to bail them out when money got tight. Young men did not participate exclusively in young men's societies, though. Elizur Wright, Jr., for example, was twenty-nine years old and managed the headquarters for the entire American Anti-Slavery Society, and his letters to Theodore Dwight Weld about Weld's work as principal agent for the New York Young Men's Society reveal some of the tensions between the two organizations. The young men's money made Weld's salary possible. Despite the financial contribution, Wright insisted "you should still be under the marching orders of our Com. but sh'd correspond, if you pleased, with the young men for their encouragement, and it should be known that you were supported by them." Later, "Tho' I am aware that you are now considered by the young men's Society as their agent, yet I know you feel yourself the agent of the cause." When the executive committee of the American Anti-Slavery Society moved Weld to New York, Wright wrote that the committee had engineered the transfer "supposing that they have not entirely either sold you, or given you away to the Young Men." This maneuvering language stands in stark contrast to the rhetoric used by the Young Men's Society in announcing Weld's appointment as their agent; they emphasized that "He is a young man, and a young man of great power of mind"—his youth proving in some sense that he was *their* agent.[48]

Young men's antislavery associations also invoked "Revolutionary fathers" and "Pilgrim sires" in appeals to their cause. In this case, though, "those rights for which their fathers poured out their blood like water" had been denied to all those enslaved. The honor they felt for their fathers moved them, they said, to oppose such oppression and tyranny. Like their brethren in other organizations, abolitionist young men heard their fathers' voices from the grave: "Shall we go on or shall we stop? The spirits of the fathers of our liberties from their invisible dwelling places say, in audible voices, stop not, but go on, and complete the work which we began and left unfinished."[49]

Invited to attend a New Hampshire young men's anti-slavery convention, William Lloyd Garrison wrote that he hoped "to rank myself as A YOUNG MAN with the members of your convention." He made this claim simply on the basis of his age; there was more: "I am almost certain that an extraordinary share of physical endurance, intellectual endowments, moral courage, and Christian philanthropy, will be found in the convention. . . . I may therefore most appropriately adopt the language of the venerable apostle who was banished to Patmos—'I write to you, YOUNG MEN, because ye are STRONG.' " He also invoked founding fathers and spirits to justify his cause: "should you be reproached for being engaged in the work of reformation, reply in the words of Thomas Jefferson . . . 'This enterprise is for the *young*—those who can follow it up, and bear it through its consummation.' "[50] Neither abolitionist support for expanding women's sphere nor Garrison's particular promotion of female suffrage, however, prevented him from associating youth with male strength, power, and vigor.

The evangelical reform impulse that drew people to antislavery and other causes also spurred the formation of political movements such as the Antimasonic party. Antimasons combined a generational appeal with allegations of conspiratorial Freemasonry. They invoked the spirit of '76, focusing on the transfer from founders to a new generation while worrying about proving their own worth. Many of their leaders, however, were surviving founding fathers or their now aging sons, expressing concern about young people drifting from the plan. Yet some, like William Seward, not only were involved in a young men's political organization, but also were Antimasons. One leading Boston Antimason, Amasa Walker, said members included "active and respectable young men, although we have a number who are aged, wealthy respectable men." Walker had also been active in the Boston young men's temperance organization. A study of Worcester, Massachusetts, though, found its temperance constituency to be much younger than most supporters of the Antimasonic party. Young men were becoming a recognized political group, as suggested by an Antimasonic appeal for "Men who will make no truce or compromise with any men—Clay men, Jackson men, Working men, Young men, or any other party, or set of men." [51]

The officers of young men's reform organizations were generally attorneys, physicians, and members of the rising mercantile middle class. Most were settled dwellers, working in their father's business or easily identified in city directories as long-time residents. Recently arrived members of Young Men's Associations were the major exception. In politics, the young men involved in National Republican and Whig organizations were often the sons of prominent town leaders. With the populations of cities in tremendous flux, it is not surprising that an occasional few of the leaders drifted onto a membership list and then drifted off. What is more significant is that in this period of great movement, when moral guardians, advice-book writers, and established businessmen sought ways to channel and control independent urban young men, most of the people who led organizations of the young in the 1830s and 1840s were closely linked to the established order. [52]

Even as the cities of the Northeast bustled with new arrivals, the New England and Mid-Atlantic regions as a whole were losing population. The states of the Northwest, meanwhile, had tremendous population increases; much of the influx came from people aged ten to thirty. In Ohio, Michigan, and Illinois voluntary associations played a crucial role in town development. Their leaders often formed a kind of governing elite for the first few decades. Towns tended to be relatively young. In a county in Illinois, for example, in 1830, 95 percent of the population was under forty, but young men did not dominate. Participants in nonpo-

litical voluntary associations in Cincinnati were "distinguished as a relatively mature, experienced, and stable minority" of the town as a whole,
according to one study.[53] Yet there were soon young men's Whig and
Democratic clubs in Michigan and Ohio. Young men played a particular
role in political life; every party needed them. Young men's conventions
and corresponding committees played a leading role in the campaigning
in the 1836 election.

The increased importance of voluntary associations in the new towns
made them the place for a young professional on the make to launch a
career. Salmon P. Chase, for example, joined the Cincinnati Young Men's
Temperance Society, helped organize a Young Men's Bible Association,
and addressed meetings of the Young Men's Colonization Society, but
ultimately allied with a group organizing the Whig party. The Cincinnati
Whig party emerged from a young men's meeting of professionals and
small businessmen. They "represented the young, 'expectant' capitalist"
group in town.[54] Although the young men could not control Cincinnati's
Whig party for long, the more fluid state of affairs in the Northwest
appears to have made the young men's organization a clear stepping-
stone to rapid adulthood. A similar sequence occurred in Detroit, where
a young men's independent political party battled more established merchants over the issue of free schools. Again, the circumstances in the
newer towns made it easier for the young to make an immediate impact.[55]
In the Northeast's more established hierarchy for achieving political and
social power, it took more time and rhetoric to carve out a special place
for young men's organizations.

Young Men and Party Politics: The Democrats

The political activities of young men in the New York state elections of
1824 and 1825 anticipated the rise of the Democrats and the Whigs in
the Jacksonian era of politics. Young men's organizations provided the
generational component in the popular politics and partisan rhetoric of
the second American party system. A campaign plea for the party faithful
to be "up and doing" was more than the "cliché" that one historian saw.
Young people used the resources of the language of generations in ways
that went beyond the historical interpretation of youth as obsessed with
resolving a dilemma of colossal fathers.[56]

Active young men's organizations emerged across most of the Northeast in the 1828 presidential election. Young men's committees of all the
parties served as key sources of political intelligence and organization. A

palmcard for an election in this period presented a slate of "preferred" candidates for the General Committee and the Young Men's General Committee, each with an official place in the party machinery. A speaker to a group of Whig young men expressed gratitude at their "zeal and activity. . . . After all, they had the greatest interest at stake, and it was upon them that their elders relied, in the decisive warfare of the ballot boxes." [57] The martial metaphor seemed especially appropriate for this explicitly youthful, male activity. As temperance, antislavery, and suffrage advocates had said, young men were the ones to fight in wars. In the militaristic battles of partisan politics, young men's organizations appear to have been the main foot soldiers, especially during the crucial period before the election in organizing the drive to get out the vote. Young men's committees at the city and ward levels formed the core for a developing party organization in cities like New York and also provided the initial political exposure for many future leaders. [58]

The rhetoric of young men's groups after 1828 concentrated more explicitly on the absence of the Founding Fathers and the responsibilities owed to them. The Tammany General Committee of Young Men proclaimed that Jefferson "and a host of patriots who have finished their service upon earth . . . are looking down upon us, their descendants, to whom they transmitted . . . the richest legacy that man could bequeath." Andrew Jackson's teenage experiences during the war made him "one of the few remaining soldiers of the Revolution." To the young men the committee asked, "is it nothing to *you* that Jackson shed his youthful blood to purchase for you that bright inheritance?" [59]

When the Democrats talked about youth, they used assertive, masculine imagery: "these are men of action. . . . Though as yet they may not have lost their ardor of feeling and ingenuousness of character," they were "free from those prejudices which sanction abuses in the minds of those who have lived long under their operation." Although they drew a similar majority of middle-class leadership, the men in Tammany's Young Men's Democratic General Committee also included small businessmen and artisans. [60] Their youth was most significant in their wish for economic success. The young men's committee rose to center stage during one of the era's great economic controversies.

Democratic young men were more than mere cheerleaders for their party's fortunes. This was all too clear when the Young Men's General Committee in New York City helped foment the Locofoco Democratic revolt in the mid-1830s. The Locofoco or Equal Rights party was founded on the proposition that banks should be completely divorced

from the state. Locofocos favored hard currency and opposed monopo-
lies and bank credit; while they wanted the Bank of the United States
eliminated, they found the Jacksonian plan to place deposits in "pet"
state banks worse. The Democratic party split into two factions: the
bank Democrats, those "interested in banking, the timid, and the friends
of whatever is established," and the militant wing, "the Democrats of
stricter notions, the friends of reform, and the mass of young men."[61]

The Locofocos were born at a stormy Tammany Hall meeting in 1835,
made famous when party operatives turned off the lights in the hall and
the regulars slipped out, leaving everyone else in darkness; the opposition
had brought candles and matches, however, and prevailed. The matches,
known as locofocos, gave a popular name to the Equal Rights party
founded shortly after the candlelit Tammany meeting. Many Democrats
sympathetic to the Locofoco cause stayed in the party; their power base
lodged in the Young Men's Committee, which was "saturated with Equal
Rights ideas," according to one historian.[62]

While the Equal Rights party fought its battle against the organized
Democracy from the outside, the Young Men's General Committee began
several years of public skirmishes with Tammany's regular General Committee, soon dubbed by newspapers the "Old Men's Committee." The
New York Herald called the young men "the locofoco, hard-money portion of Tammany, and a fiery enthusiastic set of fellows they are." Equal
Rights papers applauded the young men for their independence: "these
resolutions are in a much better spirit than those of the seniour committee," said William Leggett's *Plaindealer* of an action taken in 1837. Leggett was the leading ideologue of the Equal Rights movement and an
influential voice for the young men. The resolutions his paper applauded
attacked "specially privileged chartered institutions," speculation, and
paper currency. The committee explained its opposition in terms of the
members' own chances for success: "as young men growing up with the
interests of this city, we feel the importance of the result of the present
crisis upon our future prospects."[63] The young men challenged the General Committee when it supported a new party newspaper; simultaneously, they tried to justify their independence: "although under ordinary
circumstances it might be foreign from the business of the Committee to
endorse the character of a political print, yet the circumstances and fashion of the times seem to require" that they did so.[64]

President Martin Van Buren, apparently responding to the militants,
proposed new hard-money financial policies in 1837 that "breathed the
sound and fury of Loco Foco distrust of banks," according to one histo-

rian, even though the measure did little actual damage to their growing power. The conflict in New York City's Democratic party came to a head when the Young Men's Committee called for a public meeting at Tammany Hall to discuss Van Buren's proposal. "We shall look to that Committee for proceedings of the most democratic character," predicted the *Plaindealer*. Again the young men felt the need to explain: "the crisis is a sufficient apology for this Committee assuming to recommend a public meeting."[65]

The "Old Men's" Committee opposed the young men's action, and a major rift split the New York party: "The Young Men's Committee . . . did what nobody else stepped forward to do; they called the meeting, and we maintain they did it wisely," said the *Evening Post*. The *Plaindealer* headlined its account of the Young Men's Committee action "Up and Doing": "They speak a language clear, explicit and manly, and prove that . . . hereafter we may count upon the body from which they issue being, in fact as well as in name, a representative of the principles and sentiments of the democracy." Ward committees met to debate the controversy; most supported the young men's right to call the meeting. Even the *New York Herald*, which had previously used the Locofocos for political comic relief, urged concerned citizens to attend.[66] The meeting itself was a great success. "The older order was gradually set aside by the younger element in Tammany," the Locofocos rejoined the party, and the rebellion faded. Young Men's Committee chairman Fernando Wood, who had helped broker the compromise, linked the group to young men's traditional duties: "We are now upon the high road of a vast financial civil revolution. We are contending against a tyranny far more absolute . . . than that so nobly opposed by our fathers." It would be up to "the young and vigorous" to beat back the enemy.[67] The young men's committee continued to support equal rights principles, as in an 1840 address that emphasized that young men were not yet "irretrievably involved in the meshes of an iniquitous and delusive system" of credit and speculation.[68]

Throughout the controversy, the young men themselves did not invoke their connection to the past to justify their actions; the crisis itself seemed reason enough. As we have seen, though, it was often the claim that young men were the natural ones to come to the rescue in time of trouble. Perhaps that was all that needed to be said. The *Plaindealer*'s "Up and Doing" headline, never explained in the text of its article on the Young Men's Committee, almost seems a non sequitur. We might speculate that the lionizing of the young men as the true defenders of democratic principle emerged from some deeply rooted assumption about what young people are supposed to be like, with the Puritan origins of this belief not even visible. William Leggett, the *Plaindealer*'s editor and principle writer, whose literary allusions usually came from Shakespeare, was no Puritan, but perhaps a Puritan legacy endured nonetheless. When Leggett died suddenly in 1839, at the age of thirty-seven, a monument was built in his honor in New York, sponsored and financed by the Young Men's Committee.[69]

Young Men and Party Politics: The Whigs

National Republicans and Whigs were much more emphatic on the importance of passing on the trust of the Founding Fathers untouched. Democrats might refer generally to those "who have imbibed" the spirit and principles of a founder, usually Jefferson, and "followed in his footsteps," while Whigs more often spoke of a holy responsibility that had been transmitted to the young generation, which it was their obligation to "hand down to posterity unimpaired, the gift of freedom bequeathed by our fathers."[70] If the Democratic young men merely mentioned the Founding Fathers and called on the young to recognize their responsibilities to them, anti-Jacksonians exclaimed fervent prayers to the fathers' memory. They felt it was youth's holy mission to rescue the Constitution from lawless abuse.

The young National Republicans expressed profound fears about the excesses of the Jackson administration. They felt the president was capricious and greedy. In effect, he ignored the laws set down by the founders. "It is particularly the duty of the Young Men of the Nation, in this time of their country's peril," to preserve their fathers' acts, said Worcester National Republicans in a broadside appropriately titled "For the Constitution and the Laws." Anti-Jacksonians were also more interested in discussing the novelty of youth organizing themselves in political associations. Conventions in the early 1830s hammered home the point that young men had never before organized on a mass basis and were doing so "to preserve from desecration and ruin the holy and beautiful temple of constitutional liberty."[71]

The preservationist message rang clearly at the national convention of the National Republican Young Men in 1832. The convention was recognized at the time as "novel in its kind. . . . the first instance in which young men of a whole nation . . . have assembled in solemn convention." One participant remembered it was popularly called "Clay's Infant

School." The resolutions approved there have been identified as the first national party platform ever decided at a convention. After concurring in the nomination of Henry Clay, the young men visited shrines and survivors of the founding era. They paid special attention to Charles Carroll, the last living signer of the Declaration of Independence, who they visited after a pilgrimage to George Washington's tomb at Mount Vernon. Clay then told the convention what it had already told itself: "Gentlemen, it belongs to you, and the young men of your age, to decide whether these great blessings of Liberty and Union shall be defended and preserved. The responsibility which attaches to you is immense." [72]

The Whig party arose from the National Republicans and retained its special concern with preserving past policies and plans. Yet it balanced this seeming nostalgia with a spirited advocacy of strong governmental action in support of progress. Several historians have noted what one called "a sense of responsibility to contemporary and future generations" in Whig ideas. [73] None felt this responsibility or articulated it with greater fervor than did the young Whigs. They had the available language and clearly carved-out position to advocate such a view. They expressed their beliefs against the backdrop of Jackson and Van Buren monetary policy. "We live in a virgin land—with bones and muscles and spirit abounding, but we are poor in money. . . . Loco-Focoism answers, 'stand still.' The Whig cry is 'On,' 'Go On!' " said young New York Whigs. There was more to it than money though: "There are some Deposits more sacred than public Funds—Deposits which money cannot pay, which Gold cannot redeem," said Robert C. Winthrop to fellow Boston young Whigs. These were "precious Deposits entrusted to our keeping by our Fathers." [74] Daniel Walker Howe's study of Whig political culture argues that party members were most likely to be those "who for one reason or another, expected to do well out of economic development. . . . They poured the new wine of commerce and industrialization into the old bottles of deference, patriarchalism." Young Whigs, like other "young men," were the ones who expected to rise and succeed in a generally expanding economy. Labor activists made scornful note of this fact, calling a young Whig's convention in New York a collection of "Aristocrats of all sorts" who had "never performed a day's useful labor in their lives." The characterization may depend on the observer's perspective. Patrician politician Philip Hone wrote in his diary about "a call signed by a large number of merchants' clerks for a meeting . . . of 'the young men of the city of New York' " who supported his election. [75]

It is significant that the young men with the strongest sentiments were the "outs" in the political struggle of their time—young men in the early 1820s attacking the entrenched Albany Regency, the young National Republicans and Whigs in the next decade battling the power of the Jacksonians. In this they were appropriating the political conflict of the time and using an interpretive frame that permitted dissent while enshrining continuity; responsibility to the Founding Fathers and the duty to carry on their plan formed an organizational identity. The language persisted as the most appropriate form for young people. Let us return to Robert C. Winthrop, professional young Whig in a state dominated by Whigs. It would be hard to imagine more of an insider. The Whig party in Boston was strongly supported by wealthy and well-known native-born members of what could almost be called an aristocracy; these elites also sent many of their number to public office.[76] Winthrop's prestige, based in part on his heritage, led him to become an exemplar during his career as a young man.

Winthrop was perhaps not the most common Whig; Salmon P. Chase, who joined young men's temperance and Whig organizations in Cincinnati, might represent the expansive young Whig spirit more accurately. Still, Winthrop did spend the better part of the 1830s as the leading spokesman for young men in the Massachusetts Whig party. Winthrop clearly had advantages: after graduating from Harvard, he read law with Daniel Webster, was appointed to the governor's staff, was elected to the state legislature, and became its Speaker before he was thirty. When Winthrop spoke of "our fathers" there was nothing metaphorical about his reference. After attending a Bunker Hill anniversary and seeing various relics of the martyr Joseph Warren, the twenty-seven-year-old heard personal anecdotes about Warren's Bible from his father. Winthrop wrote in his diary: "a beautiful illustration of the mingled piety and patriotism of our Fathers—if it were true." Of the rumors that Warren may not have been as devout as reputed, Winthrop wrote, "Perhaps both are true —but let us only remember" the pious legend.[77]

Winthrop led young men's committees in Boston from the time he was in his early twenties. When Henry Clay visited, Winthrop chaired the committee of young men that welcomed him; when Andrew Jackson removed deposits from the United States Bank in 1833, the twenty-four-year-old Winthrop and the Young Men of Boston protested: "Our Fathers . . . paid once, their sons if need be will pay for their Freedom, not only in their substance . . . but in the coinage of their hearts and the currency of their blood." Again and again in speeches to young men's gatherings Winthrop emphasized that young men would adhere to the path laid out by their fathers. "Who will undertake to point out the invisible line which separates the Young and the Old?" Winthrop asked on one occasion. His answer had as much to do with gender as age: "Vigor of bone and vigor of mind, strength of heart . . . an unflinching purpose and an unpalsied pursuit of it—these . . . entitle any man to be called young."[78]

Winthrop made his fullest statement at the Whig Young Men's state convention in 1839. He expressed surprise that young men could support Bay State Democrats. The only evidence for this belief, he said, was in "the story of certain young men of olden time," a tale in the Bible, in which "one of the Monarchs of Israel had just mounted the throne of his fathers." The citizens asked "him to abate something of the haughty and overbearing dominion which his illustrious predecessor had exercised." While the old men advised him to do as the people desired, the young men urged the new king to say, "my little finger shall be thicker than my father's loins—& whereas he only chastised you with whips, I will chastise you with scorpions." Now the Democrats, Winthrop said, expected young men "to endure and sustain the still more grievous and galling yoke" of their rule. "This convention had its origin [in the wish] to contradict the inference of assent." We may forego a Freudian reading of the Bible story and emphasize that Winthrop explicitly rejected its "patricidal" message of generational conflict. In 1840 the regular Whig party met in convention; its resolutions were fairly standard except for one, which said "that our beloved country calls aloud this day upon her sons, and with a voice hardly less imploring than that which she called five and sixty years ago on their Fathers, to rise up and rescue her from misrule and oppression." Unless Democratic tyranny was defeated, "the blood of Bunker Hill will have been shed in vain." Robert C. Winthrop was the resolution's author.[79]

Dominating Winthrop's voluminous correspondence during this period are letters to and from John Henry Clifford, Winthrop's colleague since 1835 when they both entered the state legislature. As Winthrop remembered, "There I met him for the first time; and from that association resulted a friendship and an intimacy which ended only with his life." The letters began formally but soon reflected a closer friendship, still based around political strategy. Clifford engineered Winthrop's election as president of the Whig Young Men's Convention, in fact had to convince him to come at all: "You are to be there—and you are to be the President—those two things are settled—the minor details we will arrange hereafter." Clifford's letter after the convention is filled with back-room details of various political maneuvers; names of specific delegates could be remembered only vaguely. By age thirty, the two were moving beyond the business of being professional young men.[80] The convention, and other official and unofficial activities such as hunting trips, soon became occasions for the friends to get together. Clifford named one of his children after Winthrop; when the child died, they shared their grief. Winthrop's wife died at a young age; yet when Winthrop collected his speeches for publication in 1852—he was forty-three at the time—he dedicated the book to Clifford: "I am sensible how little there is in this volume to entitle it to be made the subject of any formal dedication. But I am unwilling to forego the opportunity which it affords me, of testifying how highly I value the cordial relations of friendship and confidence which have existed between us without intermission since we first entered public life together in 1834."

What are we to make of this? Why shouldn't two men retain such a close friendship, besides the fact that we are told by some historians these friendships usually died out shortly after youth? Were the two in an intense, almost romantic kind of attachment of the kind E. Anthony Rotundo describes? The evidence does not suggest that; but there is a closeness, in the joking references Winthrop makes to his clumsiness on hunting trips, in their discussion of painful emotion on the occasion of the deaths of their children, that reveals a type of relationship we might not expect from two men of their time supposedly cut off from caring emotions by cultural expectations. But it is surely a relationship of men. Even when Winthrop's wife lived, she was rarely mentioned in their correspondence; the men lavished attention, however, on when they would next be able to see each other at a political function. Men, perhaps, had multiple bonds of loyalty, between fathers and sons, and between at least some close friends.[81]

For all of Winthrop's stature in Massachusetts and later in the nation (he soon became Speaker of the U.S. House of Representatives), he is an obscure figure today. The same cannot be said of another Whig politician, born the same year as Winthrop. *His* speech to a young men's organization is the best-known address of this kind in our century—and perhaps the only one to be remembered. When Abraham Lincoln spoke to the Young Men's Lyceum of Springfield, Illinois, in January 1838, he, like Winthrop, was a leader in his state's legislature. He spoke in terms by now familiar as the discourse of young men in politics: "we, when mounting the stage of existence found ourselves the legal inheritors" of liberty. Although "we toiled not" creating political institutions, "they are a legacy bequeathed to us, by a once hardy, brave, and patriotic, but *now* lamented and departed race of ancestors." Democratic institutions faced grave challenges, he said, from mob law, summary justice, and lynching. The legacy of the founders would be the bulwark against this rising tide of lawlessness: "Let every man remember that to violate the law is to trample on the blood of his father, and to tear the character of his own and his children's liberty." Americans were called on "to swear by the blood of the Revolution, never to violate in the least particular the laws of the country." [82] He warned against the passions of great ambition, held in check during the revolutionary era.

Authors in recent decades have dissected this speech, one of Lincoln's first major public addresses, for clues to his psychological motivations and future actions. Some see it as complex displacement; while seemingly attacking ambition, "Lincoln has projected himself into the role against which he is warning them." In this psychological vein, others suggest "Lincoln's idealization of the founders. . . . seems grounded in Lincoln's degraded image of his biological father, Thomas." Such speculations cannot be documented. It seems fruitless to wonder whether Lincoln tried to "play the loyal son," when evidence suggests a far more likely interpretation.[83] These analyses focus far too much on the man giving the speech and too little on the discourse the speaker drew from. Not only does Lincoln's address "sound very much like the effusions of a zealous Whig partisan invoking the 'standard Whig rhetoric' of the day," as one historian notes, but it fits firmly in the discourse of speeches by many other young Whigs.[84] Robert Winthrop may have lacked Lincoln's poetry, but the content of his message is quite similar to Lincoln's and most of the other speeches discussed here.

All of these young men, patrician and "railsplitter," conservative wealthy elite, or reforming middle-class modernist, could claim a share of the Founding Fathers' legacy because they were almost all native born, and all were white. A group of young African Americans revealed how the language of youth and generations could cross racial lines.

The "Colored" Young Men of New York

In the small world of free black New Yorkers, one group of young men took control of their community's politics. Most had attended the African Free School and the same high school; a few had gone to Oneida Institute, an integrated college in upstate New York. Before some had reached the age of twenty or entered the New York City Directory in an occupation of their own, they were already veteran political leaders. One of them, George T. Downing, helped organize a literary society when he was fourteen years old. The group, unlike white young men, refused to celebrate the Fourth of July because, Downing's biographer explained, "the Declaration of Independence was to the colored American, 'a perfect mockery.' "[85]

Based in two young men's literary societies, the Philomathean and the Phoenixonian, they entered virtually every public activity involving African Americans in New York, whether a benefit for the *Amistad* rebels or the honoring of a visiting black dignitary. In a "free" city in which the editors and publisher of the black community's newspaper had to make shoes and sell coal to survive, these young men were grocers, booksellers, and printers, while some of their brethren became successful restaurant owners and caterers, artists, and teachers. In Philadelphia, young black activists were more likely to be members of that city's established elite. Most of the black members of the integrated Philadelphia Young Men's Anti-Slavery Society came from this group, of whom its historian notes "none were completely unskilled or poverty stricken," but ranged occupationally from wealthy manufacturers to barbers, dentists, and tailors.[86]

An editorial in the *New York Colored American* in August 1837 called on "colored young men" to petition the state legislature for suffrage. Implicit in the appeal was the notion that young men were the appropriate group to take this action. The "colored young men of New York" agreed when they met shortly thereafter: "history is replete with evidence" that young men "are important and efficient agents" for "moral reformations" or "political revolutions." They demanded the right to vote "in consideration of the services and patriotic devotion of our fathers." This was not a heritage of rights passed down from father to son; that heritage had been denied blacks. Instead, they called for an equitable exchange relationship—services rendered, rights due. Yet sons still owed it to fathers to demand those rights.[87]

The similarity in rhetoric between blacks and whites should not be wholly surprising. Wilson Jeremiah Moses notes that for those blacks born or living in freedom, it was from "the English/American literary and intellectual traditions that the literate classes of black Americans derived their conceptions what black culture ought, ideally, to become." Black leaders in the Northern cities in the 1830s and 1840s worked for education and self-improvement of the free black population. They "held middle-class occupations and middle-class outlooks. . . . wanted to cast their lot with the middle class," notes one historian. Black literary societies, often formed in response to exclusion or discrimination against blacks in white literary societies, filled many of the same functions as the white young men's societies that offered reading rooms, discussion groups, and generally improving company for young men.[88] The crucial difference was that while the white young men's literary and self-improvement societies avoided politics, the black literary organizations in New York were the launching point for a political explosion from the city's black young men. They also suggested a heritage not included in the European tradition: "we are the offspring of that noble race of people who were once in possession of the arts and sciences, and who delivered them down to a people illiterate as many of us are at this time," said the Pittsburgh Young Men's Literary and Moral Reform Society.[89]

The calls to the young bear striking resemblance to those made by young political, temperance, antislavery, and benevolent activists: "Those philanthropic souls who have heretofore borne the burden and heat of the day in the struggle for human rights, are soon to pass off the stage of action, and to their youthful successors commit the charge of pushing forwards the great work of . . . disenthralling the enslaved from their galling chains," wrote one author. The duties of the young, however, were more than just to follow their fathers' ways but "to use every exertion to increase his own stock of knowledge. . . . If the rising generation, would, therefore . . . be not 'hewers of wood and drawers of water forever,' " they must improve their own intellect. "Knowledge has been emphatically said to be POWER . . . it will be effective in battling down the high walls of prejudice and elevating the oppressed."[90]

The major issue galvanizing the young men was the question of suffrage. The *Colored American* and its editor Samuel Cornish pushed them toward action: "The young men of New York must talk less, and DO MORE." He told them to stop "the practice of meeting and spending hours in idle speechifying." The young men formed the New York Association for the Political Elevation and Improvement of the People of Color. Its constitution embraced all people, but its rhetoric came from the young men who described the group as "Deeply sensible of our obligations to our posterity, and anxious that the rising generation of colored young men may be rescued from . . . political degradation and suffering." This new association was an important step in black self-determination, according to historians.[91] But the rapid rise to power of a group of young men caused a backlash in the older black establishment.

The Phoenixonian Literary Society, base for many of the young activists, held its anniversary celebration on July 4, 1838, the same day the new Political Association had a July Fourth event. The same young men dominated both planning committees. Letters to the *Colored American* complained about the confusion. This was not a matter of young men having too much fun—it signified a challenge to existing community authority. After the first complaining letter, the editor expressed admiration for the "talents, zeal, and enthusiasm" of the youths, but warned, "we cannot confide to their inexperience, and hasty, immature judgment, the destinies of our people nor the general management of the engines of our elevation." The next week the paper agreed that young men should participate in public life but "that the gravest and most important matters . . . such as our political rights, should not be left to a majority of inexperienced young men." [92]

"A Phoenixonian" lashed back, charging the editorials "are but the signals of a storm which has long been brooding over the devoted heads of the young men of this city—a desire to impede and crush independent thought." The young men were adamant: "in a word *we will not be put down.*" The writer continued: "Must we be 40 or 50 years of age—and of 17 or 25 years standing in the community (without taking any part in the affairs of the same), before we will be enabled to 'wield the engines of our elevation?' " [93]

Even during this quite open conflict of generations, young men sought to assert their role in the black community by standing on their fathers' shoulders:

> Let every colored young man who aspires to exercise the privileges of a freeman attend. . . . Your gray haired seniors worn out in the public service expect it of you. . . . Listen to the admonitions of HAMILTON [William Hamilton, a leader who had recently died] speaking (as it were) from the Tomb. "Youth of my people I look to you. With you rests the high responsibility of redeeming the character of our people."

This exhortation to join the Political Association was signed "Shade of Teasman." John Teasman had been a pioneer black educator in the city, principal of the African Free School and founder of the community's first benevolent societies. [94] Combined with Hamilton (his student and colleague), we see an emerging pantheon of black founding fathers whose memory was invoked to demonstrate the importance of young men in public life. At a general meeting of the Political Association the pressure continued with a resolution: "That this Association depends much for the means and ability successfully to prosecute and achieve the objects contemplated . . . upon the Young Men of this City and State." The *Colored American*'s editor denied that "the elderly men were opposed to the advancement of the young" even as he assailed a particular young man, Thomas S. Sidney. Sidney had been taken to task in April for urging violent means to gain suffrage. He wrote the resolution on the young men's significance in the Political Association. He was then accused of being the "Phoenixonian" defender of the young men who had also attacked the paper's editor.[95]

As the fight raged in the pages of the community's major newspaper, African-American young men outside the New York area watched with interest. The scrapbook of a New Haven clergyman, a contemporary of the embattled New Yorkers and the son of a longtime activist, followed key turns in the struggle.[96] After the specific conflict subsided, the young continued to lead the suffrage cause. The convention of the Colored Inhabitants of the State of New York in 1840 was dominated by the New York City group, some of them still barely into their twenties. It passed resolutions: "That this country is our country; its liberties and privileges were purchased by the exertions and blood of our fathers, as much as by the exertions and blood of other men." Like the Political Association before it, this convention insisted that blacks direct the entire convention proceedings. Henry Highland Garnet, who had grown up with the New York City activists and participated in their earliest political groups before moving to Troy, New York, shared the rhetoric in his speech before the American Anti-Slavery Society in 1840. There were parallel stories: "your fathers" and "our fathers"; each had paid the price in blood, an image that flowed freely in his address: "In consideration of the toils of our fathers in both wars we claim the rights of American citizenship. We claim it, but shall we ever enjoy it? Our ancestors fought and bled for it, but I will leave it with this assembly to decide whether they fought and bled as wise men or as fools."[97]

Historians have noted black rejection of white founding fathers and the creation of new American black heroes. Some scholars used this parallel pantheon as a way to argue "that being black was a distinctive way of being American." Thus black leaders would embrace the promise of the Declaration of Independence even as they rejected the actions of its authors in keeping blacks enslaved.[98] The young blacks had a language they shared with their white brethren to call on the memory of their own heroes and use this tradition to give themselves an important stake in the future of their community.

As with the white young men's organizations, this small group growing up together formed strong emotional bonds. We can sense some of the intensity of feeling when Thomas S. Sidney died at the age of twenty-

three. Alexander Crummell gave Sidney a lengthy eulogy at the Phoenixonian Society. Crummell recounted the first time he saw Sidney, then
only thirteen; he was impressed by his wisdom and manner: "I noticed
his keen eye, his manly good looks . . . his future greatness; and I felt my
soul grow toward him." Sidney would become a new founding hero:
"Unborn babes will yet lisp his honored name," Crummell said, echoing
the desire of many white republican educational theorists that the first
words "lisped" by babies would be "George Washington."[99]

Crummell repeated in his eulogy sentiments he had expressed in a
private letter. One sentiment he did not make public: "The loss of such a
friend completely unmans me. During my life, a difficult and struggling
one, I have had nothing that has so affected me." He could accept the
death of his sisters as God's will, he wrote, "but now I do not feel
my accustomed acquiescence." He prayed to God "who knowest the
infirmities of mortal sense and sympathy; and how tenaciously the delicate fibres of human affection cluster around earthly objects; oh . . .
recall my stray and wandering affections to thee and thine." Crummell
retained the link with his friend by naming one son after him. Forty years
after Sidney's death, Crummell, by then an internationally known leader,
was called on to deliver the eulogy of Henry Highland Garnet; discussing
their friend and classmate Sidney remained painful. One scholar called
Crummell's eulogy of Sidney "a kind of vow, a self-dedication to live
with an unswerving adherence to principle."[100] Even more than that,
Crummell located Sidney in emotional, generational, and gender terms.
Generationally, he was both founder and youth. Emotion meshed with
gender as Crummell simultaneously associated Sidney's moral and spiritual attractiveness with manly characteristics. He was "unmanned," thus
made weak, submissive, not a man, when Sidney died.

The fraternal aspects of the long association of these activists are further suggested by the fact that one of the literary associations, the Philomathean Society, became the first black Odd Fellows Lodge in America.
The head of the new lodge and many of its leaders had started their
careers in the Colored Young Men of New York.[101]

Youth and Gender

When the New York State Convention of Colored Inhabitants called for
suffrage it said, "We base our claim upon the possession of those common and yet exalted faculties of manhood. WE ARE MEN." To be a man
for the black New Yorkers went beyond bonds of gender. Given the

dominant nature of the language, to be a man was to be a person. Rhetoric from black and white organizations would dismiss actions they deemed beneath contempt as "unmanly." Conversely an action thought of as "bold" and "patriotic" was the "manly" course.[102]

Men had duties and responsibilities, a primary one of which involved warfare and the defense of those unable to defend themselves. As Connecticut Whig Young Men put it, "If the sword and torch of invasion were on our borders, and we were called to vindicate our birthright . . . on the bloody field. . . . The sacred names of wife, and sister, and mother, whose happiness is all involved in the common birthright, would move us." The young Whigs shouted "to the rescue! . . . Awake, then, the manhood, the spirit, and the strength of the North. Unfurl the Whig banner."[103] Youthful defense against invaders was a common image for Whigs, temperance advocates, and abolitionists who shared the sense of restoring the past. Democrats and others also waded in blood. This was something that only young men could do; they had always been the soldiers, and in the absence of an actual invasion, they would defend community values against all other challenges.

Along with this battlefield image was one of service to community. "But brethren, as for us, let us be up and doing. Let us quit our selves like men. Let us show that we are worthy of the gift of a great man," said Alexander Crummell in his eulogy for Sidney. As the original source for being up and doing suggested, young men were following their fathers' ways to build a society and then defend it. Interestingly, several black young men's addresses called on their fellows to be "up and doing." Like the Puritans and their biblical forebears, blacks, perhaps, especially felt the need to connect to a past and to build a strong community based on the vigor and strength of young men.[104]

This place in society was not uncontested, however. Women were also entering the public sphere and many men did not like it. "The uncertain social role of female youth" led to young men's ambivalence, one scholar has argued. Antipathy to women in public was not always automatic. An orator in the early nineteenth century offered a female parallel to young men fighting invasion: "And, should necessity now urge, they would buckle on the armor of war, and America would produce her amazons"; this was not a majority view, however.[105] A few decades later, young men's groups had designed more oblique strategies that simultaneously celebrated and marginalized women's contributions. On several occasions young men's organizations would note the work done by women, sometimes in a resolution thanking them for their crucial efforts.

Always, though, they would find a way to place young men at the forefront. They referred to "other exertions which have been excited by our success. This, we believe, we may say was the fact, with regard to the Female Society," said the Young Men's Boston Auxiliary Education Society. Temperance young men noted that "the cause of Temperance has been essentially promoted by the exertions of the females in our Country," and then in its address to the public returned to the familiar connections between fathers and sons. Women dropped out entirely. Indeed, the women may have seemed a threat if they also had societies of their young. So the young men's anti-slavery convention in New Hampshire noted, "While we highly appreciate the happy influence the abolition women of New Hampshire have exerted in behalf of bleeding humanity, we do most earnestly entreat them, by all that they hold sacred, by all that is dear to the female heart, to come to the rescue in one unbroken phalanx, and to exert that irresistible influence with which their Creator has so wisely and richly endowed them in favor of the suffering slave."[106] Why an "unbroken" phalanx? To emphasize, perhaps, that women must always be women before all else?

Rotundo has argued that "all-male clubs could provide an outlet for deep emotional needs without threatening the individual autonomy or the psychological armor that were basic parts of a man's public identity." While we have seen young men involved in youth organizations putting on armor rhetorically when they talked about going into battle, we also noted incredible expressions of emotion, both publicly in the talk about responsibilities and privately in long-term friendships like that between Robert C. Winthrop and John Henry Clifford or through tragic emotional ties, such as those between Alexander Crummell and Thomas S. Sidney. An anthropologist studying the cultural construction of manhood concludes that "manhood ideologies always include a criterion of selfless generosity. . . . Again and again we find that 'real' men are those who give more than they take; they serve others."[107] This impulse finds repeated expression among activists in young men's associations—a conception of what it is to be a real man which involves service to others, inherent in their youth, and inherent in their manhood. Crummell honored Sidney for his generosity and goodness. Young men's organizations appear to have created bonds that continued into maturity. The Colored Young Men of New York were still fighting battles for freedom decades later, even though they often fought in different wings of the struggle.

Certainly youth was no guarantee of idealism, despite the assertions by most historians of reform. The New York Young Men's Colonization

Society, for example, noted: "Colour is with us the bar. Nature has raised up the barriers between the races, which no man, with a proper sense of dignity of his species desires to see surmounted." Emancipation without colonization was "madness." Democratic attacks on banks and capitalism often meshed comfortably with a defense of chattel slavery. A Pennsylvania Young Men's Democratic Convention opposed "interference by citizens of the north with the constitutional rights of our slave holding sister states of the South," and some former Locofocos allied with John C. Calhoun in the 1840s. Whig young men could take the flip side, reserving Democratic monetary policies "for the Turks and Tartars and Huns and Hottentots, to whom only . . . they may belong."[108]

For most young men the organizations provided a means to enter the public sphere and make a mark; they claimed a special place for youth and emphasized particular male qualities of martial courage and defense of supposedly defenseless peoples. At the same time they tried to keep women from entering into the public sphere, while also providing a series of spaces for men to develop stronger emotional ties than we would expect existed in the nineteenth century. They enshrined notions of brotherhood and combined them with a rhetoric of being good and loyal sons; even their conflicts with their elders were couched in terms of obedience. This discourse of generational responsibility, based in the older language of Puritans and Founders, had its fullest expression in the young men's groups. Once established, the language migrated into wider social and political discourse, infiltrating other nationalistic movements of the nineteenth century. A rhetoric that depicted young men fighting metaphorical invaders could easily be shifted to apply to more material immigrants, and could also give substance and tradition to the calls for a new American art and literature. The next two chapters investigate how a language that youth applied to themselves began to expand to describe other parts of American life.

CHAPTER FOUR

Art and Memory

Ralph Waldo Emerson evoked more than a metaphor when he wrote in 1836, "Our age is retrospective. It builds the sepulchres of the fathers. It writes biographies, histories and criticism." Responding to commemoration ceremonies and monuments that embraced the founders of the republic—"the fathers"—he wondered, "why should we grope among the dry bones of the past, or put the living generation into masquerade out of its faded wardrobe?" Emerson was not alone in recognizing the past's command over his present; others, however, welcomed the tendency. "Among the various expressions by which the predominating spirit of the times . . . has been described, one of the happiest is that which denominates it 'the age of commemoration,' " the *North American Review* observed. It approved the inclination to "recover and record every thing." This activity was especially significant because "It will be regarded by our posterity, in all coming ages, as most fortunate for them that this commemorative propensity began to be . . . exhibited by a generation, standing so near . . . the very commencement of the country itself."[1] These opinions appeared in a review of *The National Portrait Gallery of Distinguished Americans,* a project that promised complete biographies and accurate portraits of the founding fathers.

For every Emerson worrying about a nation in thrall to its past, there was a James Fenimore Cooper complaining that in America, "the man who should resist an improvement . . . on account of his forefathers, would fare badly." Was American society as divided as Emerson had said on another occasion, between "the party of the Past and the party of the Future"? Historians celebrate Emerson's vision; they accept Cooper's diagnosis. "There is little evidence of Americans' actually preferring the past," according to one recent work; Emerson was "preaching to the converted." Those who celebrated the past supposedly ignored the dominant values of what another scholar called "the future-oriented mainstream."[2] Although forces of change eventually did triumph, and their early advocates are honored for their foresight, defenders of the past were by no means marginal figures in American culture. The Party of Hope and the Party of Memory existed in a complex relationship with one another.[3]

As young men in the cities cemented bonds with the founders and claimed a right to act in public as conservators of their tradition, so politicians and cultural authorities embraced that legacy in realms outside the political arena. Generational language was more than a passport to public legitimacy for the young; it could be a justification for cultural cohesion. To avoid being thought ungrateful to the founders and to connect future generations to the past, a general impulse toward commemoration and a more specific interest in preserving the faces of the fathers predominated. Eulogies and collections of founders' portraits expressed these feelings. With new institutions came new interests; because commemoration meshed with business and mercantile sentiments, more than political stability seemed at stake in the movement for remembrance.

The discourse of youth and generations provided the framework to explore the coexistence of past and present and to examine related cultural issues that had no explicit "youthful" content. Only some cultural archivists were young, but strong continuities existed between their impulses and those of the young men in political and reform organizations. Like the latter, the former rejected simple conservation. Meanwhile, artists and patrons promoted a unique American art. They developed institutions that incorporated their sense of responsibility to the past and suggested possible new paths for heirs to follow as they struggled to reconcile their debt to the nation's founders.

Commemoration

Acts to preserve the past were certainly not unique to the early nineteenth century. Puritans had chronicled their fathers' every move. The commemorative mode returned in force after George Washington's death in 1799. Two eulogies by young Americans demonstrate how the language of generations fit into the conservative trend. The twenty-one-year-old Joseph Story echoed Cotton Mather and others while introducing new themes as he said of America: "Too young for the luminous display of history, or the elegant fascinations of literature, she can boast a diffusion of useful knowledge coextensive with her sunbeams. Ask you her age and patrons? America is scarcely twenty; but her patron, her savior, was Washington!" The late president already headed a pantheon of sacred heroes: "We have lost a father, but we have enthroned a saint. By imitating his unsullied virtues, though dead, yet shall he live. Let us swear by the shades of Mercer, Warren, Montgomery, and Washington, that the liberties purchased by their blood and toils shall be eternal." Washington was important not only for those who now lived: "Posterity will demand it as an altar of our affection" that "we enkindle in the hearts of our youth the spirit of freedom . . . that spoke, that blazoned, that convinced, in the character of Washington."[4]

In a Fourth of July oration, Dartmouth student Daniel Webster spoke first of his contemporaries, "who were either then unborn, or not far enough advanced" to fight the Revolution. "We now most cordially unite with" the elders to celebrate the holiday. He spoke of the fathers' sacrifices; "Shall we, their descendants, now basely disgrace our lineage and pusilanimously disclaim the legacy bequeathed us?" The audience would "Swear to the God of our Fathers, To Preserve it secure, or die at its portals!"[5]

Eulogies for Washington and subsequent founders became occasions to describe the essential nature of the nation. One recent study of these addresses argues that early national eulogists tried to answer one question: "How could the state erected by revolutionary sons command the permanent loyalty of future generations?" In the context of the Revolution this meant, How could rebellious sons be turned into founding fathers? Such a transformation sought to exert control over postrevolutionary Americans, "to keep sons in their place, so to speak, and to buttress paternal authority," and, in effect, to make "the state an object of worship." This argument suggests that "filial disobedience stood for political unrest and disaffection," whether from England in the revolutionary era or from the new republic in the early national era.[6] It does not recognize, as we have seen, that the revolutionaries expressed their independence but still sought to maintain continuity with their past, insisting on their obedience to chosen colonial forebears even as they rebelled against imperial British parents they said had been forced on them. The dilemma was real enough, and its solution emerged from a tradition developed in the colonial past. Speakers' rhetorical figures resembled the colonial language that described the challenges facing New England. Just as the Puritans vested the rising generation with responsibilities that implied they would pursue new endeavors, so the eulogies for the founding fathers expressed more than a demand for blind obedience. Linked to the injunction to remember, however, was another old Puritan theme—the dangers attending the community if it forgot.

The next significant set of eulogies appeared in 1826 when apprehensions about the imminent departure of the founding fathers took on mortal shape. Thomas Jefferson and John Adams died within hours of each other on July 4, the jubilee of the Declaration of Independence's signing. Speakers agreed that it was a providential occurrence and signified approval of the nation's progress by the Highest authority.[7] One eulogy of particular interest was delivered by Samuel Lorenzo Knapp to the young men of Boston. Knapp echoed others in asserting the debt that current and future generations owed to the two eminent founding fathers, but he focused on particular aspects of their legacy: "Their reputations are now the common property of the nation, and the care of preserving them for generations is now committed to this—to the young, in a particular manner; for they have come forward since the bitterness of party distinctions have been lost." Knapp said, as had others, that the emerging young generation was unsullied by partisan conflict, but he still insisted "the youth of this age have caught the spirit of their fathers and will carry a double portion of it to transmit to the next."[8]

He called on youth to "be prepared to take the burden upon yourselves," and assured them that a path had been cleared. "Public highways are now prepared for you to travel, and mile-stones are placed along the road to guide and cheer you on the journey." Knapp clearly implied that young men must follow the road to keep the nation and its liberties secure, and said as much in suggesting that a door had closed: "We are no longer the new men of the new world. We have a noble inheritance in the fame of our ancestors. To value this possession justly, we must imitate their virtues, by raising the standard of information and purifying the currents of freedom." Knapp ended with a warning that echoed both Puritan and urban young men's rhetoric: "If darkness should gather around and shroud us, the brave defenders of their country will be enabled by its blaze [of the light shining on ancient graves] to whet their swords on the tombs of Washington and Greene, and the statesmen to read their duty in the epitaphs of Adams and Jefferson."[9]

Along with eulogies, secular icons—portraits and statues—were common means for commemoration. The images in the U.S. Capitol, for example, identified the Revolution and the colonial era as the exceptional moment of national history. A study of iconography suggests that contemporary concerns are central to the ways in which commemorative subjects are chosen. Portraits were the icons of choice during the postrevolutionary period. In the same way that religious figures brought the worshiper in touch with the sacred, an accurate portrait could link the viewer with the force and character of the person portrayed. A significant aspect of the portrait, therefore, was its power to pass important messages to succeeding generations.[10]

Washington, whose "ordinary talents and unremarkable characteristics" became heroic and embodied most every aspect of the revolutionary era that had to be preserved, was the first and central subject for early portraiture. There were so many portraits that a vigorous debate began about which was the most accurate likeness. When Rembrandt Peale began a campaign in 1824 to promote his recent portrait and wrote a pamphlet to criticize the competing images, he was making an implicit argument that he had best captured the true Washington. "These men firmly believed that the well-being of present and future generations was at stake in the discovery of Washington's authentic likeness," argued a leading analyst of Washington imagery.[11] What began with Washington soon came to include the other founders as they also began to pass away.

For about a decade, from the grand tour by the Marquis de Lafayette in 1824 until his death in 1834, the nation embarked on one major commemorative celebration after another. The jubilee of Independence, the centennial of Washington's birth, and the death of the last signers of the Declaration all hammered home the message that the original age was passing away. These events, with Lafayette's epic tour as the model, offered the nation a chance to demonstrate its debt to the past. They were used to close "a fissure between generations, between the *then* and the *now*."[12] The years of memory complemented the continuing popularity of public portraiture. Demigods would soon stand with Washington in the pantheon.[13]

Faces of the Founders

Some American artists in the new nation expected to be showered with public support for grand depictions of the country's history. They were disappointed.[14] Although government funds were not forthcoming, entrepreneurs still pursued commemorative projects. The most popular solution for preventing the past from slipping away was to preserve the faces of the founders. Even before the Revolution had ended, artists were already depicting its heroes. After the war, they began to collect these pictures in halls of the famous. "Authors persistently used a temple of fame or pantheon of worthies as a metaphor" in contemporary literature, according to a study of early portraiture. Charles Willson Peale had created a gallery of war heroes by 1782. His and similar portrait collections represented another aspect of the effort to transform the revolutionaries into founding fathers. Compared with European portrait collections, the American pantheons gave literal expression to republican ideals by including a wider range of subjects; intellectuals and "average" citizens joined military and political leaders as worthy subjects for veneration. Despite Washington's significance, the figurative image of the pantheon ensured that there would be a cohort of founding "fathers" and not a single, preeminent ruler.[15]

Peale's enterprise and the other early portrait collections came from the "initiating generation." Indeed, Peale had "a strong sense of himself as a founding father," according to his biographer. Nineteenth-century portrait collections, while based on the same impulses, included new characters and developed for slightly different reasons. Rather than representing living exemplars, the founders became more important for what they would symbolize to the next generation.[16] In this move, the creators of the portrait galleries shifted into the vocabulary of generational continuity. They also began to do more than create a stable of founders. "As the years go by, the past becomes more crowded; heroes and events accumulate and compete with one another for the present generation's attention," notes one scholar.[17]

The artists of the era struggled to capture something that would transmit the deepest truths about the virtue of their subjects. Even the most accomplished painter, however, could only offer a mediated vision. One American sculptor promoted a way to make literal contact with the faces of the founders. While many artists produced likenesses during Lafayette's tour, John H. I. Browere prepared a bust based on a life mask he had made of the general. Browere believed his method captured the living essence of a person more accurately than previous life or death mask techniques. In light of the controversy over the Washington portrait, what could have been better suited to the times than the taking of life masks? The artist thereby emphasized the *living* nature of his work. Other sculptors' casts of Lafayette were inferior, he said, because their methods gave the face "the ghostly appearance of Death!" His Lafayette would be "a perfect fac-simile of an original." After his widely praised bust of Lafayette appeared, Browere set out to take casts of other leading Americans. Adams and Jefferson sat for him, as did Charles Carroll, suddenly renowned as the last surviving signer of the Declaration. Other subjects included the men who had captured Major André, Gilbert Stuart, various military heroes from the War of 1812, and contemporary politicians DeWitt Clinton, Henry Clay, and Martin Van Buren. The press covered Browere's approach to his subjects, his arrival to take the cast, and the exhibition of the bust. Other portrait subjects and leading American artists certified the accuracy and safety of his methods. Gilbert Stuart—especially signficant because of his reputation as Washington's portraitist—hoped that his endorsement would remove any fears "that might prevent the Nation from possessing records of more important men." Browere said he wanted to erect a building in Washington, "the National Gallery of eminent personages," to house the collection.[18] The most recent study of portrait pantheons argues that Browere was "one of the last to attempt to form a gallery of living worthies who were also founders."[19] His choice of subjects seems to exemplify the feeling that the founders had to be captured and retained for later generations but also suggests that room had to be made for new heroes as well. His pursuit of one subject, James Madison, reveals that commemoration at this time began to mean more than the pure, elevated concern for history.

James Madison, a close friend of Jefferson, and architect of the Constitution as well as a former president, was perceived as a link to the founding era after the deaths of Jefferson and Adams. Browere wrote to request permission to take a cast of Madison's face; simultaneously he promoted his gallery and argued that his efforts furthered the development of American art. Along with the letter he included lists of persons he had already sculpted and the usual testimonials. He courted the former president even after Madison had agreed to sit, taking any opportunity to write, report on his progress with a statue of Thomas Jefferson, send holiday wishes, or ask permission to name one of his daughters after Dolly Madison, also a Browere subject. Always he would promote the national gallery, making veiled requests for money, describing legal complications, emphasizing repeatedly the absolute accuracy of his labors. Madison's responses were polite, encouraging, and restrained. He honored the sculptor's "professional" and "technical" accomplishments without fully endorsing his project. Browere did not explicitly say that the founders had to be captured and retained for later generations, but this idea seemed clear in a letter he sent Madison after Jefferson's death. His real purpose on that occasion was to get an endorsement for his plan to create a statue of Jefferson. The appeal was more entrepreneurial than preservationist, hagiographic, or commemorative. His entire approach suggested that both men believed these to be worthy goals in the mid-1820s, and that the sculptor saw no contradiction in his wish to promote his artistry *and* the commemorative plan, while also achieving some financial profit. Browere could not know that Madison's cautious responses may have been due in part to the fact that he received pleas from many would-be commemorators of the founders. Joseph Delaplaine, assembling a multivolume book of portraits and biographies, asked for Madison's help, as did many others. Delaplaine was one of the first pantheon creators to put his efforts between book covers.[20]

A National Gallery

Delaplaine's publishing venture failed and he next proposed a national gallery for American notables. As Peale, Browere, and others before Delaplaine had recommended, the pantheon image seemed to demand a physical location for appropriate display. In the 1830s the notion of a *published* gallery finally bore fruit. James Herring, the secretary of the American Academy of Fine Arts, asked "that the Academy support the establishment of a National Portrait Gallery." The project, like Delaplaine's, would publish biographies of great Americans with a portrait of each one. His proposal argued further that "the publication of an American Portrait Gallery would have a very important influence on the Fine Arts, by stimulating the Artists to compete with their rival foreign artists with a national ardor, and by influencing the popular taste and judgment by making of easy attainment some of the finest specimens which can be produced." He asked the academy to select subjects and artists, and to ensure that "the literary part of the work . . . shall be appropriately well written, authentic, and national."[21] The academy supported the idea, but Herring had to produce and promote it. He joined forces with James Longacre, an engraver who had been planning a similar project. They began advertising the new venture in 1833:

> The value of such a publication cannot fail to be appreciated by all who feel an interest in the preservation of the most essential ingredients in the history of their country. Taste and patriotism are equally invited to sustain an enterprise whose aims to supply the future historian with those materials, the absence of which is so often regretted in . . . the annals of our earlier times.

They promised that they would select individuals who "by common consent, are admitted to possess an interest in the minds of their fellow citizens, by their reputation for genius, acquirements, official standing, or public service." There would be no "reference to the bias or antipathies of the divisions of party." They asked for subscriptions. Three engraved portraits, "with not less than twenty-four pages of letter press," would arrive each month.[22] As Longacre explained, the project was "calculated to produce a community of feeling, most desirable at this period—It introduces the Arts as a peace offering to the angry and jealous passions that are striking at our Nation's heart."[23] This image of consensus brought about by art would be repeated in later ventures promoting artistic nationalism.

The introduction to the first volume of the *National Gallery* in 1834 linked the need to preserve the memory of the past with the creation of heroes for the next generation and connected these trends to the rise of a native school of American art. Despite earlier failures, "a more auspicious era has dawned, and the American people now display a becoming solicitude for the preservation of the relics of their own glory." A crucial aspect of the collection was its protection of the past. The gallery was "an effort at once to preserve the features, and to rescue, from the wasting hand of time, the memory of those whose noble deeds, exalted fame, or eminent virtues, have shed a lustre upon their age."[24] In the fourth and final volume, the authors explained further: "There being in our country no central repository for the preservation of the Portraits, or the important papers relating to the most distinguished individuals," they had created the gallery to "remedy . . . this peculiarity in the situation of our country," and saved from "destruction" or "oblivion" the "invaluable relics of those whose lives have most eminently contributed to the formation of our character."[25]

Perhaps these claims were canny justifications to promote sales; nonetheless, the rhetoric matched the general tone of contemporary political discourse. Indeed, the sentiment had much older roots, echoing the declension dramas in seventeenth-century New England. The use of the word *relic* shows the crucial sacralizing value of the images and demonstrates the enduring power of the argument that forgetfulness might poison the nation and lead to destruction.

The frontispiece of each volume put the founders in the center of the new pantheon. George Washington graced volume one; Benjamin Franklin, James Madison, and John Adams followed. Many contemporary figures were memorialized as well. An 1839 review summarized the contents:

We have the eight presidents and two of the vice presidents . . . a few of the signers of the declaration of independence, the principal general officers in service during the revolution and since, several naval commanders, three of the four chief justices, and some of the associate justices . . . a very liberal selection from the secretaries of the departments, and a due proportion of senators in congress, foreign ambassadors, and other public functionaries.

Also included were some doctors, ministers, and a few others. The review answered its own question about the limited range of those portrayed: "it must be recollected that the revolution was our first great theater of action."[26]

The authors never stated it so baldly, but it seemed clear that this collection was supposed to broaden the scope of founders beyond literal political fathers. The unofficial and nonmilitary figures seemed to be *representatives* from other spheres. Two artists, Trumbull and Stuart, were included, as were a few writers—Irving, Cooper, and in a later volume, Charles Brockden Brown. They became, in effect, the founding heroes for those fields; there was even Daniel Boone to represent the founding frontiersman and Lydia Huntley Sigourney as a founding woman writer. The other women, with the exception of the founder of an orphan asylum, were wives of the famous, occasionally referred to as a man's "consort."

In justifying the "somewhat remarkable absence of female biography . . . and for the little power which appears hitherto to have been exerted by individuals of that sex," the authors suggested that since women's status depended above all on their husband's position, it was a rare woman who by accident of marriage *and* talent would be able to exert influence. They argued that "the duties of the female sex may be generally expected to prove too burdensome to admit of great devotion to pursuits exclusively literary or political." The roles most appropriate for women were those of "housekeeper, a wife, and a mother," which although they "make every woman who faithfully executes them respectable in the eyes of the world, do not, when exclusively pursued, so well fit her to shine upon that brilliant theater of politics and fashion to which she may yet be called." The authors still preferred American women who "rigidly preserved the standard of our morality"; they deserved "a far more substantial claim to public gratitude" than did courtesans, who acted as "arbiters of weal or woe" in "corrupt" foreign regimes. John Quincy Adams's wife, Louisa—whose biography was prefaced by these remarks —was celebrated for her traditional women's virtues but also honored for her "strong literary taste . . . and a capacity for composition in prose and verse . . . not with a view to exhibition which renders such accomplishments too often fatal to the more delicate shades of feminine character but for . . . that of a few relations and friends."[27] The normative lesson was plain: while more virtuous than their foreign sisters, and evidently capable of outstanding artistic expression, American women's creative efforts were best left confined to the domestic arena.

Contemporary reviews applauded the series for establishing a collective memory and rescuing the nation from its inevitable doom were it to forget the sacred past. "No people can possibly be barbarous, or unintellectual, who receive from their ancestors . . . a knowledge of the men and events of their own lengthening annals," the *North American Review* commented in 1835.[28] An 1839 article noted the time of national jubilee and said the series "should remind us to examine the pages of our infant history and see if the deeds they record betoken a noble or degenerate race." Apparently, if the nation remembered, its history could only be noble. The responsibility "belongs . . . to ourselves of the present age to collect and transmit the evidence upon which the judgment" of history "must be founded. . . . We owe it to our own glory." Previous heroes in past civilization slipped into obscurity "for want of a recording pen; and ours may become alike inglorious, if we neglect to perpetuate their fame." Reviews discussed the need for histories, biographies, and monuments to the past. "We have now a glorious past, and it is time for us to value and venerate it," said the *New York Review*.[29] Another article pointed out how the portrait volumes "exhibit a specimen of the highest point of excellence to which the arts of painting, engraving and papermaking are carried in this country." The *New York Review* bemoaned the lack of support and encouragement the arts received in America, applauding the book of portraits for reversing this trend. But the volumes served a more important function: "Besides its great excellence as a work of art, it is admirably designed to cherish in our youth the principles of true American patriotism, to lead them to reflect on the generous devotedness of the men, who were ready to sacrifice every thing to resist oppression, and then crowned their labors, by securing union and strength to the country to which they had given freedom."[30] These reviews supported the sentiments of the *National Gallery*'s producers and expressed the need for commemoration, recognized the dangers of forgetting, and asserted the particular importance of maintaining values in the next generation. They tied the fear of losing the founding spirit with the need to infuse a new American art with the same values.

Advocates for the Past

The search for founders continued in other fields. Evangelical Christians in the early nineteenth century developed a lineage that began with the revivals of the 1730s and 1740s. One author compiled a record of those events; his title produced the name that still defines the period today, *The Great Awakening*. The minister Lyman Beecher, meanwhile, published a magazine, *The Spirit of the Pilgrims*, that, in essence, revived the argument of *The Christian History* by tracing a tradition from the first founders of New England through the First Awakening to contemporary revivals that could now be seen as a second Awakening. In this salvaging of the past, Jonathan Edwards became the central founding figure in the First Awakening, "regularly associated with the revered Founding Fathers of the nation," according to one historian.[31] While revivalists honored their own past and remembered glorious founders, others looked to more monumental ways to remember the nation. One vocal advocate for the past was the writer C. E. Lester.

Lester was an unlikely art critic. Trained as a Presbyterian minister, he co-authored a slave narrative in the 1830s and promoted abolition. He then traveled to England and wrote a celebrated attack on its labor system. His statement that he preferred his children grow up slaves rather than English factory workers made him infamous. This undiplomatic figure became the U.S. consul in Genoa in 1842.[32] While he was immersed in Italian culture, translating Machiavelli and others, Lester began to assert America's need to commemorate its past. Even when he had attacked England, he always celebrated the United States; later, he would compare its democracy to Roman and Renaissance republics. Although he was steeped in the Puritan tradition (Jonathan Edwards was his maternal great-grandfather), it was the republican fear that a lapse in memory would lead to oblivion that motivated his appeals.

Lester warned against ignoring the message of the founders: "And yet we profess to regard the spirit of our Fathers, whose last counsels were to train up enlightened and educated men for the service, the support, and ornament of the state." He called for monuments:

> Will the government of the United States never learn, that there is no safeguard so effectual to our liberty and our Constitution, as the patriotism of our public men? And when will they learn that patriotism can never be so inflamed among the masses of the people . . . as by covering the consecrated soil of the nation, and surrounding the Capitol with the statues and monuments of illustrious men, who have devoted themselves to the glory of their country?

He had a vision of "the young American who walked up an avenue" of the nation's capital "on either side of which stood, in colossal bronze, the great heroes of the Revolution." For the American republic to survive, he argued, it must pay homage to its past and keep that memory alive in the rising generation. Lester repeated this appeal in lectures and publications. The movements supporting monuments at Mount Vernon and Bunker Hill confirmed the interpretation that such structures were crucial objects in recalling the fathers and demonstrating continuity with their principles. As Neil Harris has commented, "the gesture was beautifully circular: the monument gave physical life to an abstraction and helped perpetuate a set of sentiments; and its own construction called forth the feelings it would symbolize in later years."[33]

Lester's *Artists of America* indulged in some hero selection of its own, presenting biographies of the nation's leading artists. The *American Whig Review*'s commentary began, as many such discussions did, with a survey of art in the nation. "Our country is the young Giant of the modern Olympiad, and we do yearn to see its large limbs informed with 'A light diviner than the common sun!' " Although the journal faulted Lester's hasty presentation of the biographies, it still hoped the work "will render the great cause of Art—the high world of ideal beauty—more familiar to the national mind."[34]

A review of Lester's *The artist, the merchant, and the statesman, of the age of the Medici, and of our own times* appeared in the *Merchant's Magazine,* squeezed between articles on foreign trade and wool tariffs. The businessmen's view of art revealed particular interests that promoted and supported commemorative activity. It included familiar observations: "The stirring incidents of our national history are fading from the minds of our people, because they have not been suitably illustrated." But the review worried that foreign immigration would close the way to the past: "our national enthusiasm grows weak, and our love and reverence for the fathers waxes cold." To breathe new life into these flickering sentiments the magazine called for monuments and works of art "illustrating our national history, and stamping in upon all minds the story of freedom, and the principles of our fathers."[35]

Businessmen would rescue the nation. A discussion of the *National Portrait Gallery* had argued that merchants must be the Medici of the modern era. The *Merchant's Magazine* agreed. While politicians "are almost utterly swallowed up in the party strifes of to-day," it argued, "our affluent and large-souled merchants alone can effectually aid in enlarging and refining the national mind, and in founding a new school and a new era in art." With suitable patrons American artists would protect the nation from dangers posed by foreign powers. Without that protection it was "back into the charnel house of despotism."[36]

Some merchants had already been leading patrons of American art, education, and high culture when Lester and others asked them to take up the challenge. Recall the mercantile support for the Philadelphia Young Ladies' Academy, especially that of John Swanwick, who included in an address on the importance of female education the "Poem on the Prospect of Seeing the Fine Arts Flourish in America."[37]

Typical of those who promoted art in Philadelphia was the lawyer, politician, and author Henry D. Gilpin, the son of a leading merchant and manufacturer. Gilpin's diary reveals a young man filled with ambition, always thinking about his place in history. At age twenty-one, on July 4, he ruminated: "as our ancestors on the anniversary of this day when surrounded by every difficulty and threatened with every danger proclaimed to the world their rights and their determination to defend them—so in the silence of my closet and in the strong conviction of my heart I pledge in their support my life my fortune and my honor." Gilpin was United States Attorney for Philadelphia by age thirty, but at thirty-five still attended a Democratic convention of young men in Pennsylvania. At age twenty-four Gilpin wrote several volumes of the *Biography of the Signers of the Declaration of Independence,* another illustrated series of the 1820s. He also made active attempts to link himself with the founders, visiting James Madison, asking permission to dedicate a portion of the biography series to him, and asking the former president for corrections to a sketch of Jefferson's life. He described himself as one "who enjoys the benefit" of the founders' efforts, although he was "too young to have in any way participated" in them. Gilpin's work confirms the affinities between biography and commemoration and maintaining continuity with the founders.[38] Such sentiments found further expression in institutions promoting the rise of American art.

New Institutions — Familiar Themes

Merchant Medicis and other leading citizens met with James Herring in early 1839 to discuss a new plan "for the promotion of Fine Arts in the United States." Just as Herring's *National Portrait Gallery* was supposed to gather the finest engravers and portraitists and commemorate American heroes old and new, his new project for a permanent art gallery in New York would allow artists to display their work to the public and prove that citizens of a republic could appreciate art.[39] The new organization, the Apollo Association for the Promotion of the Fine Arts, began in 1838 as an art gallery, but Herring soon transformed it into a cooperative art union. A few years later, the Apollo Association became the American Art-Union.

The *Knickerbocker* magazine described the art-union: "Each subscriber pays some small amount annually. This forms a fund which after defraying necessary expenses is appropriated to the production of engravings and the purchase of works of Art. The engravings are given to all subscribers, and the other works of art are distributed among them by lot." The art-union soon established a free gallery in New York to exhibit the paintings it had purchased. The union was managed by businessmen, lawyers, doctors, and brokers—dubbed "merchant amateurs" by the leading historian of the group. The commercial ethos seemed to suffuse the organization, as one contemporary account reported approvingly: "the Art-Union, in the management of its business, purchased its stock, advertised and exhibited its goods, employed its agents and clerks, just like a merchant." A network of agents nationwide promoted subscriptions. By 1851, there were one thousand of these "Honorary Secretaries." Subscription revenues purchased work by American artists, and the art-union swiftly became one of the nation's largest patrons of American art and artists. After a year it had about eight hundred members and had bought thirty-six works from twenty-four artists. Ten years later it had more than eighteen thousand members and bought as many as 460 works by about 180 different American artists.[40] The very fact of the art-union's existence and the spread of its appeal to every state in the nation provided a great boost to the development of American art, especially genre painting. The union's advocates also had an ideological program, which they promoted at the annual meeting of the association.

After the election of officers and before the heavily attended lottery— in which any subscriber might receive one of the paintings the union had purchased that year—members offered resolutions and made speeches on the course of American painting and the responsibilities of the art-union. They described nationalistic goals presented in terms of egalitarian refinement. The first principle, as President John Francis made clear at the meeting in 1840, was that "our widely extended country with its magnificent scenery and variety of population is the appropriate region for the culture of those arts which address themselves to the imaginative faculties. The organization would not "gratify the exclusive taste of a few elegant connoisseurs, but . . . aid in creating a love of Art in a whole people." It looked forward to a time in which "the poorest man in the nation will have a good picture in his parlor."[41] To sustain these edifying goals, speakers dipped into the rhetorical well of youth and generations.

The American artists the union hoped to promote were often figured as young: "it is the young artist who is struggling to plant his feet on the lowest round of the ladder of fame who most needs the helping hand of a friend to sustain him in his first step." The description of American artists' responsibilities closely resembled political speeches about the young: "A new race enters on the arena, with the ardour of youth, and strong both in talents and in numbers. I trust I labour under no undue influence of patriotic feeling . . . when I assert that present body of sculptors and painters of indigenous growth . . . need only American patronage to render additional honours to American genius." References to a "new army mustering to invade the kingdom of Renown" indicated some differences in the understanding of youth, the past, and relations with founders from those described in earlier chapters.[42] The promoters of American art echoed more of a romantic impulse that saw the past—as Emerson had suggested—as a constraining influence. To some, the past became synonymous with Europe. "Another age and spirit has come, and he that muses and dreams over the past, calling feebly on the classic age to come again, commits a folly that after years can never repair," said a speaker in 1845. Another orator that year reversed an old Puritan device when he described how "Those old painters, for whom so much veneration is professed," had "lived in sympathy with their own age. . . . Could they but rise from their graves . . . they would be the first to rebuke this false worship of the past." The "past" here referred both to old artistic styles and to nostalgia for other times. The artists'—and by implication the nation's—youth implied a swift and independent maturity: "I think this may be regarded as a patriotic Institution, that is to adorn America in her infancy, with those charms of external culture which will add lustre to her maturer age, when the star of Empire taking its westward way, having set forever in the old world . . . shall shed its full effulgence on the broad face of this great continent." The managers' mercantile-business impulses echoed the aggressive, martial rhetoric of young men's political organizations when one longtime leader said:

> Our youth as a nation is not a sufficient apology for our neglect of the cultivation of high art. . . . If we were challenged to compete with Europe in common schools, in railways. . . . If we were challenged to meet any of these nations in battle, would we plead infancy as a good defense for withdrawing from the field?

Soon the art-union itself would be described by its president as "springing as it were from infancy to vigorous manhood."[43]

This impulsive, romantic confidence was matched by gestures of continuity with the past. "On this soil, where the stern morality of our fathers has given an impress to public opinion—and religion, untrammelled as in the dark ages, sheds everywhere her pure light . . . there is little fear that our painters will ever degrade their high art, by making it pander to human passions." Union managers contributed to the creation of an art pantheon as well. Again and again the same names would be mentioned: West, Stuart, Copley, Trumbull, and Allston. The managers commissioned medals commemorating these founding artists. The practice followed the model of ancient civilizations, they explained; the medals would "perpetuate to posterity the portraits and names of their heroes, and the memory of their illustrious deeds. . . . In the transit of centuries, the heroic monument will crumble . . . but the humble medal" would survive.[44]

Creating founding fathers in their own field and promoting a new American art also advanced the preservation of national values. Many speakers joined the chorus demanding monumental art.[45] J. T. Headley began an address in 1845 by assailing Americans for "that strange infatuation about foreign art and artists, and foreign literature," and said if his fellows "dare and love to be ourselves, we should soon have an American literature, an American school of art, as well as a peculiar form of government." Art, he said, was what moved the nation: "Every great national painting of a battle-field, or great composition illustrating some event in our history—every engraving, lithograph and wood cut appealing to national feeling and rousing national sentiment—is the work of art; and who can calculate the effect of all these on the minds of our youth?" Art inspired patriotism: "Could a man be a coward fighting in the shadow of a monument of Washington." Art would inculcate the rising generation: "The youth of every land are educated more by art than by speeches." Americans were ungrateful to the founding fathers if they did not support appropriate art and monuments. The *New York Herald* reported that the address "called forth from the immense crowd reiterated plaudits." While only identified by his initials in the art-union's publication, the speaker is almost surely the author Joel Tyler Headley. His remarks follow Lester's sentiments closely; in some cases they seem word-for-word repetitions of Lester's work published earlier in 1845. Headley himself contributed to the commemorative cause by writing biographies of Washington and other historical figures.[46]

Art-union meetings adapted familiar generational themes to a compati-
ble purpose, promoting the rise of American art. They used the language
not to explain the presence of young men in public life, as young men's
organizations had, but to demand support for the young artists who
would bring America the unique art it deserved. Commemoration of
national values and the construction of founding artistic fathers had
supported these interests. At the same time, this rhetoric buttressed the
art-union managers' belief that artistic nationalist goals would further
the cause of general cultural stability.

"No political, commercial, or sectarian interests have brought us together. . . . We have deserted the caucus and the exchange, for the stu-
dio," said Unitarian minister Henry W. Bellows at the annual art-union
meeting in 1844. A movement for national artistic elevation and refinement, it seemed, not only was separated from politics and markets, but
stood above those pursuits. Indeed, Bellows suggested that art offered an
alternative to more mundane conflicts:

> Our institutions keep us politically and socially in a state of perpetual
> excitement and competition. President-making, and money-getting together,
> stir up all that is bitter, sectional and personal in us.
>
> No nation needs its exalting, purifying, calming influences more than ours.
> We need it to supplant the mean, utilitarian tastes, which threaten to make
> us a nation of shopkeepers.

The managers made larger and bolder claims for their institution's role in
society: "officers have higher duties to perform than to procure agreeable
prizes and to superintend a raffle. . . . it is fast becoming one of those
great institutions which influence the character and manners of the whole
nation."[47] The celebration and creation of institutions meshed with a
worldview that crossed lines of party affiliation. Prosper Wetmore,
a close friend of Democratic leader William Marcy, and Philip Hone, a
longtime Whig, both had been union founders; Wetmore served as president for several years.

For the managers, art patronage and artistic nationalism preserved
institutional stability; they believed that artistic refinement and its diffusion helped support conservative, preservationist goals while also damp-
ening the fires of party and market strife. Art-union publications
suggested that managers wanted "subjects illustrating national character,
or history, or scenery," as well as "the literature and manners of the
country." The types of scenes reflecting national life apparently had to
meet additional criteria, as the selection committee's dealings with

George Caleb Bingham concerning his painting *Stump Orator* suggest. The art-union refused to pay the price Bingham had asked, although they were happy to exhibit it at the art-union gallery once a price had been agreed on. The committee said it did not view the "subject and color . . . as favorably as some of your other works."[48] *Stump Orator* bore little resemblance to Bingham's *Jolly Flatboat Men* (which was a membership print for 1847) or *Raftsmen Playing Cards,* both welcomed by the union. Perhaps the view of politics illustrated in the painting offended the merchants' sensibilities as being too "rough," too close to the political world that they wanted to purify by promoting art.

The engravings and other items distributed to subscribers each year confirmed the art-union's commemorative aims as well as the group's wish to avoid controversy. Annual premium prints included some works best described as a "grand style" depiction of classical themes, but most were of Revolutionary War history, classic genre (Mount's *Farmers Nooning,* Edmonds's *Sparking,* Bingham's *Jolly Flatboat Men*), illustrations from works by James Fenimore Cooper and Washington Irving, or the medals commemorating American artists. Of the thirty-seven quantity distributions of prints, medals, and miscellaneous items, all but six of the premiums that every member of the art-union received embodied the rhetoric of its managers: Revolutionary War history (five, plus an equestrian statue of Washington, to total six); grand style/classical (six); genre (seventeen); commemorative medals (three); miscellaneous (two).[49] The themes in any year also offered "a balanced political menu, with a nod to each sectional faction and an appeal to national pride," according to one analysis.[50] Several of the artists favored by the American Art-Union embraced generational and commemorative issues, and their work provides further insight into the connections between art and memory.

Art and Memory

The rise of popular political parties, public education, territorial expansion, and the advent of mass-circulation newspapers all promoted the introduction of politics in American genre painting. Genre painters used the new American form to depict the new politics. George Caleb Bingham more than any other artist of this era was associated with capturing the spirit of popular democracy, and few artists were as actively involved in politics themselves. The scholarly commentary on Bingham's series of political paintings is extensive and is primarily concerned with identifying his political opinions relative to the paintings and politics of the

1850s; the earliest part of Bingham's political and artistic career, how-ever, demands closer examination.

By the time he was in his late twenties, Bingham had already worked as a portrait artist in Washington and in his native Missouri. Writing to an old friend in 1840, Bingham suggested that the new state capitol should have portraits of "some two or three great men whose names are identified with the history of the country." Washington, Jefferson, and Lafayette, he said, "are held sacred by all parties, and in ordering their portraits, the State would not only evince a laudable regard for the arts, but a disposition to perpetuate the remembrance of these great benefactors of the human race." Like commemorators and patrons in the East, Bingham had linked a rising art with appropriate remembrance. He also accepted as a simple fact the sacred nature of the founding fathers and their pictures. Despite their "frontier" locale, Missouri towns had young men's education and debating societies. School oratory exhibitions and July Fourth speeches used the blood of fathers, the veneration of Washington, and other familiar rhetorical devices. At the same time, westerners seemed less concerned with strict adherence to the entire pantheon of heroes; one orator was ridiculed when he invoked Joseph Warren and other heroes who seemed less connected to Missouri's experience.[51]

Missouri's Whig party tended to be wealthier, more professional, mer-cantile, and nonagricultural than the state's Democrats. As in Ohio and Michigan, young men organized as one of the first steps in the party's formation. The first major Missouri Whig convention in 1840 lasted three days. "The last day was the Young Men's day. Their convention was held for the purposes of forming some sort of permanent organization," according to a historical account. Bingham was a delegate for his county on the young men's day.[52] He painted a large banner for a parade, would paint banners again for the 1844 election, and created several more for young men's political organizations. His imagery gave little indication of generational concerns. The 1840 banner portrayed candidate William Henry Harrison with the log cabin and farming icons of the campaign. His later campaign work similarly depicted farmers, eagles, and such symbols. Recall that young men's participation in organizations in Cin-cinnati related more to progress and success than to their exclamation of older preservationist themes. A recent study of Bingham finds direct evocations of the progressive Whig program of Henry Clay in these banners. "What had formerly been prairie filled with buffalo" became "a landscape dotted with prosperous farms and factories, traversed by railroads" and other signs of progress. Many of Bingham's landscapes were similarly suffused with Whig implications and imagery.[53]

Bingham's election series, painted between 1847 and 1855, has been described by some critics as an attempt "simply to report what he saw in the world around him," and by others as elitist Whig disgust with the outbreak of popular politics. Throughout the series there is potential for finding commentary on events and personalities close to Bingham's continued participation in Missouri politics.[54] What seems clear is that Bingham's representations of politics sought to rise above partisanship. Ironically, his view of the intelligence of the people and the importance of open democracy had close affinities with Whig beliefs, even if its egalitarian portrayal may have bothered the art-union's primarily Whig managers. As some critics have noted, the "Jacksonian" character of these images could be overstated; the people depicted in the election paintings are not primarily "pioneer figures" but well-to-do citizens. Despite his western focus on progress, Bingham's Whig allegiances linked him to some preservationist themes. In the center of one painting in the series, *County Election,* an aged man returns from casting his vote. In Bingham's first sketches, "this figure proudly sported an unmistakable '76 on the crown of his hat." He can be interpreted as a recognition of the enduring significance of the revolutionary past.[55] Thus themes of continuity still persisted even in paintings addressing other issues.

Bingham's preliminary use of " '76" illustrated the endurance of the Revolutionary War and the issues raised by it as a symbol in antebellum art. Greenough's statue of Washington and Rembrandt Peale's lectures on Washington were still recent events in the late 1840s. While art continued to capture the events of the Revolution, the way it dealt with its legacy is of greater interest. How did artists address the themes we have seen explored in other cultural arenas?

Scholars' assessments of the generational content in American genre paintings fall into two by-now familiar categories, conflict or continuity. Many paintings of the era depict family scenes and seem to focus on interactions between the young and old. Some follow the traditional script of the older generation passing on knowledge of the revolutionary past to the young. In a work by art-union manager Francis William Edmonds, the "Image Pedlar" offers busts of Caesar, Napoleon, and Andrew Jackson to a sturdy American family. The family chooses instead another figure; the grandfather explains the significance of this bust of George Washington to a group of children. One little boy wears a Revolutionary War uniform.[56] The work of another artist, Richard Caton

Woodville, provokes greater debate. Woodville was avidly supported by the American Art-Union and addressed central generational themes in several of his best-known pieces. The paintings suggest expressions of "intergenerational connectedness" to some and "disquieting images of confrontation" to others.[57]

Woodville's expatriate life in Düsseldorf, Germany, may have cut him off from the developments in America that led other genre painters to deal with contemporary political issues. Woodville was left to mull over themes of earlier years. Given his family background, some of these themes might have been more suggestive than others. He was born of a famous Maryland family; one of his relations was Charles Carroll of Carrollton, the last surviving signer of the Declaration of the Independence.

An early Woodville watercolor, *Soldier's Experience,* painted in 1844, shows a soldier relating his story to other members of the family. He sits on a chair, leaning forward, directing his comments to a much older man, also sitting, who supports himself with a cane. The young man wears a military uniform. The older man wears knee breeches and other clothes suggesting the colonial era. A picture behind the old man has the date "1776" written above the frame. A colonial musket and minuteman's tricorner hat hang above the painting. As the younger man speaks, he gestures with his right hand toward the wall, his finger pointing at the musket and hat. The visual images link the soldier's experience with the revolutionary era and suggest continuity between the younger man's generation and the implements of the last war.

The generational theme continues in *Politics in an Oyster House.* Two men sit across a table from one another. An eager younger man addresses the older, who looks somewhat bored and stares toward the viewer. Their dress reveals no discontinuity of era, but youth is vital, active; age is weary, perhaps a little weak, more prone to the elements and the passing of time, as suggested by the glasses he holds in his hand, his cocked head to hear better, the umbrella that stands beside him. The robust youngster, we assume, does not need such protection. One analysis of this work finds it an "apparently nonpartisan scene," in contrast to the "tendentiously political genre paintings which advanced the causes of nationalism, democracy" that were being painted by Woodville's friends in Düsseldorf during that revolutionary year of 1848.[58] The most revolutionary aspect of this image has more to do with the passage of generations than a particular political idea.

George Caleb Bingham, *County Election*, 1851–52. *Courtesy, Saint Louis Art Museum.*

Richard Caton Woodville, *Soldier's Experience*, 1844. *Courtesy, Walters Art Gallery, Baltimore, Maryland.*

Richard Caton Woodville, *Politics in an Oyster House*, 1848. *Courtesy, Walters Art Gallery, Baltimore, Maryland.*

Richard Caton Woodville, Old '76 and Young '48, 1849. Courtesy, Walters Art Gallery, Baltimore, Maryland.

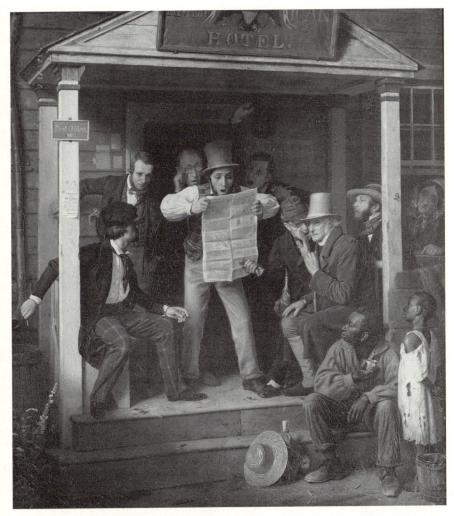

Richard Caton Woodville, *War News from Mexico*, 1848. *Courtesy, Manoogian Foundation.*

Freedom's Holy Cause, 1846 (?). Engraving after T. H. Matteson, *The Spirit of 1776*, 1845.

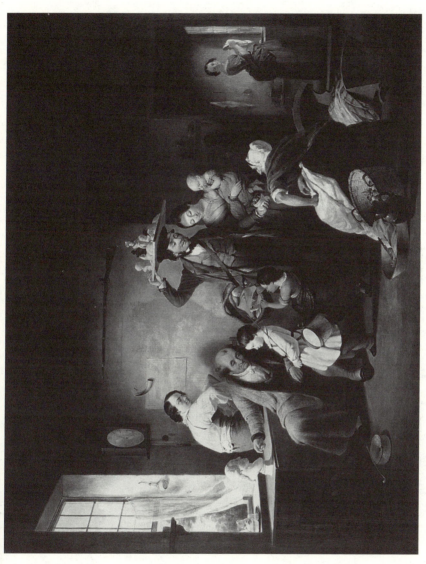

Francis William Edmonds, *The Image Peddler*, 1844. Collection of The New-York Historical Society.

John L. Magee, *Reading of an Official Dispatch (Mexican War News)*, c. 1849. *Photograph courtesy of Hirschl & Adler Galleries.*

Old '76 and Young '48, painted in 1849, deals with the same theme as *Soldier's Experience,* but the scene has changed considerably. What was a modest room with wood floor and woodburning stove is now a finely appointed house with marble fireplace and richly carpeted floors. Black servants stand in the doorframe. The two key figures, the soldier and the old man, are in essentially the same position; the younger leans forward and gestures with one hand, the older is supported by a cane and listens, his eyes not meeting the speaker's. The younger man is considerably younger in this second work. The pictures on the wall have changed, as well—one is a figure in Revolutionary War costume, usually identified as the old man in earlier days. This is the picture that Young '48 points to. Above the fireplace mantle is another painting, which appears to be Trumbull's painting of the Declaration of Independence. Next to that painting is the tricorner hat seen in *Soldier's Experience.*[59] The title, the images, and the relationship between the subjects all serve to link the time of the Mexican War with the American Revolution. Interestingly, a review in 1850 seemed to find a formulaic quality about this image: "All the accessories of the picture are purely American, and help to carry out the story; the portrait of the old man . . . the bust of Washington, the ornaments on the mantle, are all in strict keeping." The review made clear which of the two historical moments took primacy: "the old fellow seems to be just at the point of saying 'O yes my boy . . . you fought bravely no doubt, and General Taylor was a good soldier; but it's nothing to old '76 and General Taylor aint Washington.' " Yet this distinction does little to suggest that the efforts of '48 are felt to be any less, nor is there much evidence to support the "disillusionment in the face of the old man" that some critics have seen.[60]

Another painting of about the same time by John L. Magee, *Reading of an Official Dispatch (Mexican War News),* presents a similar setting of a family crowded around to hear news of the war. One recent critic has noted the "theatrical attitude" of the figures.[61] It is surely much more sentimentalized than Woodville's painting, but prominently displayed on the wall is a *Signing of the Declaration of Independence* and a portrait of Washington.[62] And a child in drummer boy regalia in the righthand corner sends a similar message of continuity in martial, patriotic spirit as the uniformed boy in the prewar *Image Pedlar.* The Mexican War inspired many comparisons with the Revolution; the relationship between these wars suggests connections between the vocabulary of generational responsibility and historical memory.

Securing the Past

The young men's organizations had reveled in martial imagery when they described their responsibility to the nation. The language seemed only natural when America entered actual combat with Mexico in 1846. Publicists and writers looked for an appropriate heritage in the nation's earlier military contests. The War of 1812, whose heroes entered illustrated biographies by the 1830s, became available as one source. Joel Tyler Headley wrote biographies of Winfield Scott, a leader in both wars, and Andrew Jackson, the hero of New Orleans before his presidency. The Revolutionary War, however, remained the dominant connection. A flood of new books on the Revolution appeared during the Mexican conflict. At ceremonies during the war, military and civic leaders drew the parallel. One soldier wrote, "I am very anxious to have a chance to try my spunk . . . I think I have the grit of '76." A history of popular images of the war finds consistent comparisons between the two. "At the first call, young men were urged to 'show the world' that they were 'chips of the old revolutionary block.' " [63] The war's links to the Revolution appeared in many other contemporary paintings and engravings. The battlefield death of Col. Henry Clay, Jr., as engraved in the *Union Magazine*, for example, resembled Trumbull's *Death of General Warren.* Woodville's *War News From Mexico,* and *Old '76 and Young '48* had been prints distributed to all members of the American Art-Union. Bryan Jay Wolf has argued that through the identifications in art, "the Mexican War is given revolutionary credentials and validated as an extension of rather than a deviation from" the original plan of the founders.[64]

The rhetoric and representations in art may have done more than provide "credentials" for the new conflict. This military adventure, occurring almost seventy years after the beginning of the Revolution, could have been a final legitimation for men who had come of age since the passing of the founders. The martial rhetoric of young men's organizations and artistic nationalists demonstrated the enduring significance of battle for proving *generational* credentials. Steven Watts has argued that the War of 1812 offered an opportunity for the sons of the founders to resolve their relationship to the past, to "escape paternal domination of the past and ascend to prominence in their own right."[65] In fact, the language Watts identified fits into the larger frame of generational responsibility that we have been tracing. By the 1840s, the War of 1812 was simply another episode for those who were still trying to answer the question of responsibility to the past: young men's organizations in northern cities had asserted the importance of youth's participation in public; the advocates of artistic nationalism had linked monuments and commemoration to generational responsibility.

The war with Mexico was touted as the first test the nation faced since the death of all the founders. The new country was achieving glory without them, but still acted in their spirit. The revolutionary symbols and characters in the paintings made clear that the older generation approved. The time of the Founding Fathers, and the concern over living up to their principles, had become incorporated into the habits of commemoration. The tradition of heroes and loyalty to their ideals that had developed in response to the original challenge in the 1820s and 1830s became standard practice by the late 1840s.

In 1850, C. E. Lester was editing a new gallery of illustrious Americans with lithographs from original daguerrotypes by Matthew Brady. It was sold monthly by subscription, just as the *National Portrait Gallery* had been almost twenty years before. In the first number Lester explained why the gallery did not begin, as virtually all predecessors had, with Washington: "We are not insensible to the claims of the men of the Revolution on the gratitude of the nation." But, Lester said of Washington and by implication the other founders, "we feel that they are removed beyond the reach even of our respect." Since the founders had become too holy for human contact, Lester continued, "We embrace, therefore, in this Gallery those men only who may be called the *second* Fathers of the Republic." In his opening "Salutation" to the collection, Lester continued to distance himself and the new heroes from the past:

> The first half of the century has now drifted by . . . we contemplate the past with gratitude and exultation, *because it is secure*. And we wish before those great men who have made it illustrious are gone, to catch their departing forms, that through this monument to their genius and patriotism, they become familiar to those whom they will never see.

As in earlier galleries, Lester promised that "there is nothing sectional in the scope of this work," but emphasized that these heroes had served the nation "since the death of the Father of the Republic."[66] With the past "secured" in commemorative portrait volumes, historical paintings, and monuments, a tradition of American heroes that began with the founders could continue to the next generation. Now it was *their* passing that needed to be captured in portraiture. Life masks had become unnecessary; there were daguerrotypes. Lester's work, however, was not one in a flurry of commemorative projects; there was no general outcry at the passing of these second founding fathers. Alan Trachtenberg has argued that the collection had other cultural work to do—to relieve a conflict in the present rather than one with the past. Politics was moving in divisive directions that captured all of the nation's attention. The gallery attempted to project onto a nation torn by the slavery crisis an "illusion of unity . . . founded on values represented by white male leaders and achievers." The figures then made "the negotiated resolution seem a natural emanation from the spirit of the Father incarnated in his 'leading' sons: the 'second Fathers.' "[67] This attempt to sacralize the recent past was possible only because of the comfortably established relationship to the now distant revolutionary era.

Also in 1850, the fraternal organization of Odd Fellows published its gift book for the year 1851, which included an engraving titled *Freedom's Holy Cause*. The original painting by T. H. Matteson, called *The Spirit of '76*, had been purchased by the American Art-Union in 1845 and "was greatly relished by the people," according to a nineteenth-century history. The engraving had first appeared in a magazine in 1846. Matteson was a genre painter and prolific illustrator of Mexican War scenes (including the death of Henry Clay, Jr.) and images of George Washington.[68] The engraving shows a modest room filled with minutemen preparing to meet the British. A woman with a baby on her knee holds a newspaper which has "July 4 1776" written at the top. In an article accompanying the engraving, *Knickerbocker* editor Lewis Gaylord Clark wrote that Matteson's work revealed "the secret impulse that led our patriot fathers, with such undying zeal and enthusiasm to the battle-fields of our revolution." It called on citizens to "hold their memory most dear in our recollection," but concluded: "now that we have grown to be a mighty nation, sitting beneath the shade of the tree of liberty which our forefathers planted, let us not forget the blessed boon for which they fought and suffered, bled and died."[69] The focus had shifted. No longer must the memory of the founders be retained in order to ensure the survival of the country. The people must not be ungrateful, but their remembrance no longer had an immediate connection to national ends.

Even as one aspect of the relationship to the past was coming to an end, another impulse, represented by the Emerson observation that opened this chapter, was still unresolved. The romantic relationship to the past, introduced from Europe, was also exerting a powerful influence. Many artistic representations of youth and age had been connected not to American history and the resolution of relations between founders and their sons, but to the timeless stages of the life cycle. Thomas Cole's *Voyage of Life* was only the most prominent example of work "shaped by . . . patterns of influence drawn from Western and Northern Europe." Michael Kammen finds this influence ironic during the part of the nineteenth century "when Americans were most anxious to establish their cultural independence." Europe brought romanticism and its rejection of the past in independent, youthful self-expression. Europe also represented a source of backlash for nationalists and nativists. The *Democratic Review*'s commentary on C. E. Lester's *Artist, Merchant, and Statesman* found most compelling not his call for merchant Medicis but his demand for reform of the American consular system. Lester had warned against hiring foreigners to U.S. consulships; his message, the *Democratic Review* said, was clear. "We owe it to ourselves to make the star-spangled banner respected in every corner of the globe, and every citizen of the republic feel, under whatever sky he may walk, that the wings of his country's eagle are over him."[70] Lester himself felt that the European revolutions, "The tide of battle . . . between Liberty and Despotism—between the Old and the New age—between the past and the future," represented the mark of progress. Yet he still took every opportunity to celebrate and venerate America's past.[71] A complex new understanding of youth and its relation to generations that incorporated many of these contradictions would be expressed in a literary and political nationalist upsurge known as Young America.

CHAPTER FIVE

Young America

"We have all heard of Young America," Abraham Lincoln told a lecture audience in 1859. "He is the most *current* youth of the age. Some think him conceited, and arrogant; but has he not reason to entertain a rather extensive opinion of himself? Is he not the inventor and owner of the present and sole hope of the *future*?" Lincoln drew on broadly accepted images to introduce his lecture on invention and discovery. Young America "has a great passion—a perfect rage—for the 'new,' particularly new men for office." Moreover, "He knows all that can possibly be known . . . and is the unquestioned inventor of 'Manifest Destiny.' His horror is for all that is old, particularly 'Old Fogy.'" Once Lincoln addressed the lecture topic, he rarely referred again to Young America,[1] but by 1859 the mere mention of the phrase was enough to suggest a boundless, even impudent, confidence about the future and an arrogant feeling of superiority toward the past and its representative, the old fogy. Lincoln did not endorse this image; he merely repeated conventional wisdom that could be found in any magazine of the time. The formulation persists in most historical interpretations of the 1840s and 1850s.

Everyone probably had heard of Young America in 1859, but *which* Young America did they know? It had already undergone several transformations, its banner taken up and discarded by different champions who had each used the words to promote varied causes. In numerous brief treatments "Young America" appears as an illustrative example for some other historical story. It is a colorful instance in the march of national expansion or, less commonly, of literary nationalism. The phrase's intrinsic significance is rarely addressed.

Its core images of youth and the arrogant rejection of the past make Young America seem like a counter-example to the themes of generational continuity described in this study. But in the quest for the new, the idea of Young America embraced older ideas even as it effaced them. While intellectuals or cultural leaders deployed the language studied in previous chapters, "Young America" came to be used by a broader range of people. It became widely accepted, perhaps because its specifics were rarely articulated. Young America synthesized older traditions with new materials, some imported from Europe and some occurring locally, to create a rhetoric about youth that implied responsibility to the past while permitting an exploration of progressive change. Young America's multiple manifestations in the 1840s and 1850s, the people who popularized the phrase, and the jagged course of its use and reception all reveal the persistence and growth of the discourse of youth and generations.

Young people had been significant figures in communities across America since the 1600s, either as a problem posed by ministers in the pulpit or as important actors in their own right as proclaimed by young men's organizations. While speakers might invoke the image of a vast polity in their addresses, the focus for their activities remained local. Young America became a truly national idea, announced, advertised, and disseminated by a new network of newspapers, magazines, and popular lectures. The penny press that first emerged in the 1830s had by the 1850s taken a firm hold in cities around the country. These papers proclaimed themselves nonpartisan guardians of the public will and the public good, thus better able to imagine a national interest. The number of newspapers in each city increased, and new information and transportation technologies transformed the ways they assimilated and dispersed their product. A debate in the United States Congress was a front-page telegraphic dispatch in New York the next day. A revolution in Europe could be a topic of conversation within weeks.[2] Meanwhile, the metropolis was reaching out to smaller communities through popular public lectures. Nationally known personages crisscrossed the country, appearing before audiences at lyceums and other local gatherings, creating what one scholar called a "national public" and a "national culture."[3] Abraham Lincoln, who had made his first important public address before a young men's lyceum, was speaking in such a popular forum when he discussed Young America.

The phrase's life in a world of widely distributed publications also made it more easily recovered by scholars. The historian who first introduced the phrase as a significant issue emphasized Young America's association with a magazine, the *Democratic Review*, its promotion of Stephen A. Douglas's candidacy for president in 1852, and its attack on the party "Old Fogies." George Sanders, the *Review*'s editor, was represented as the primary exponent of an expansionist vision that included fomenting revolution in Europe and acquiring more territory for the United States in places such as Cuba.[4] A circle of editors and writers in the 1840s who sought to extend Jacksonian democracy to American authorship and called for a national literature had also called themselves Young America. The literary nationalist New Yorkers were remembered primarily because of their close association with and influence on the writers Herman Melville and Edgar Allan Poe.[5] This shared slogan raises questions about its cultural sources, which can be found in the publicity surrounding the European movements that gave the American impulse its name, and in the discourse of youth and generations.

Europe and the "Young" Movements

Young men leaped onto Europe's main stage during the 1820s and 1830s in the first youth movements of the modern era. Students and young nationalists reacted to the defeat of Napoleon and the resulting cultural upheaval by forming associations for the reform and regeneration of their society. German university students formed unions to unify the nation, while others looked toward a cultural reawakening. French young men in the 1830s led a revolution against their political order. In Italy, Giuseppe Mazzini formed an organization that gave a name to many movements that followed him: Young Italy.[6] While historians properly associate many European youth movements with the surge in European romanticism, specific social transformations also led to youth unrest. In Germany and France, for example, the growing numbers of educated young men created greater pressure for a limited share of professional jobs. European youth organized in part to ensure a place for themselves in society.[7]

Mazzini's Young Italy proclaimed "a brotherhood of . . . men of progress, of the future, and of independence." The young embodied change, said the manifesto of Young Italy: "new circumstances call for new men —men untrammeled by old habits." The opposition could only be called one name: "Old Italy, for they are men of the past, and intellectually dangerous."[8]

Forced into exile after a failed revolution in Italy, Mazzini and others met in Switzerland in 1835 and 1836 to form a unified revolutionary movement named Young Europe. Significantly, Mazzini and the nationalists promoted their ideas through newspapers: *La giovine Italia* and *La jeune Suisse*. A Parisian newspaper, *La jeune France*, had preceded Mazzini's projects. Soon there were "Young" parties in every European nation. Mazzini's rhetoric grew more specific:

> Europe . . . is at the threshold of an entirely new development. . . . the young Generation knows how to rid itself of the past and enter freely upon the road toward the future. . . . That is the *Young Europe* of the Peoples, which will superimpose itself on the *Old Europe* of the Kings.
>
> Everywhere it is the same war, the one . . . which feeds the efforts of the young generations against the old.[9]

"When in the presence of the Young Europe now arising," Mazzini said, "all the altars of the old world shall be overthrown."[10] No American organization of young men had stated a dispute with the older generation in these stark terms. Consequently, initial American reports treated European movements and a vision of generational war with skepticism.

The always suspicious James Fenimore Cooper compared "la jeune France" and "young America" in his 1838 novel *Home as Found*. "I believe an American has little to learn from any nation but his own," says one character. Readers of the September 1841 *United States Magazine and Democratic Review* learned much more about Young Italy in "The Revolutionary Secret Societies of Modern Italy." The article referred to an insurrection "accomplished solely by the young Italians" and honored the movement's "pure and lofty patriotism," but said little about the movement's celebration of youth and its association of backward ideas with obsolete age.[11] Politics met literature more explicitly than it had in Cooper's book in 1842 when Henry Wadsworth Longfellow identified the German poet Heinrich Heine as the leader of the literary movement known as Young Germany. Longfellow himself had first achieved national acclaim in 1838 with a poem on youth, "A Psalm of Life." He had concluded this poem, subtitled "What the heart of the Young Man Said to the Psalmist," with this verse:

> Let us, then, be up and doing,
> With a heart for any fate;
> Still achieving, still pursuing,
> Learn to labor and to wait.

The directive to be up and doing had moved from Mather to Benjamin Franklin, who had used the call in his "Way to Wealth," to the young men's organizations. Longfellow now urged the young, but not to take action, rather to learn to wait. He retained a skepticism of youthful idealism in his review of German literature when he noted that "the old and oft-repeated follies of mankind come up and are lived over again by young men, who despise the wisdom of the Past, and imagine themselves wiser than their own generation." Unfortunately, in Longfellow's view, Europe was not alone. He sounded like Cooper when he said, "In this country, there are certain persons, who seem disposed to enact the same tragic farce; for we, too, have our Young America, which mocks the elder prophets." [12] Longfellow never identified his Young America, but literate, elite journals shared his grim view of "Young" movements when they noticed stirring in America's closest European cultural neighbor, England.

Newspapers had discussed a small faction in Parliament known as Young England in 1843; the phrase was originally used as a slur. Although they were first recognized more as "amiable, elegant and accomplished private gentlemen, than as statesmen; but 'Young England' . . . is a type, an indication of something that is working in the public mind." [13] Benjamin Disraeli was acknowledged as the group's leader. Although he spoke of a "party of the youth of England," it hardly resembled youth movements on the European continent. Young England emerged from a small group of aristocrats troubled by industrialization; they decided that salvation could be found in retreating from modernity and recovering traditions of an older social order and a stronger religious authority. [14]

Young England became a celebrated catchphrase when Disraeli published the novel *Coningsby, or The New Generation,* which quickly became identified as a manifesto. The *Times* shared Disraeli's description of a "movement of the young" and applauded its attempt to rescue the nation, reminding readers that "Even on the stage of public life youth has its advantages as well as age." Others were unreceptive: "Being for the most part young men, their historian, Mr. D'Israeli, declares war against age, and proclaims that England is alone to be saved by its youth," the *Edinburgh Review* commented. A speaker addressing a working-class audience, meanwhile, assailed Young England as the only "Young" movement to "look to the past; all the others look to the future. The golden age of Young England is nowhere to be found," its "heart" was "in what has gone by." [15]

Most American discussions of Young England were, if anything, more strident. "The principal characteristics of 'Young England' are arrogance, vanity, inexperience and a thorough contempt for their fathers, whose *wisdom* is, to them, the consummation of folly," said the *Southern Literary Messenger*. Young England got no credit for its traditionalism; instead, Disraeli's observation that youth had little need of experience became the springboard for lengthy criticism: "To maintain that youth, even when blessed with experience, is the only or even the most common season of great deeds, is willfully to shut the eyes to the lights of history. But to hold that youth, merely because it is youth, without the smallest ray of experience, should be entrusted with matters of gravest importance . . . is a deadly sin against the dictates of common sense." The *Messenger* dismissed Disraeli and his colleagues' potential influence in America: "There is just as little probability that the English nation will become converted to the peculiar faith of 'Young England,' as there is that the silly and mischievious book . . . will be popular with any but the more sublimated portion of the transcendentalists." [16]

In Boston, home to the transcendentalists but also to a modernizing, individualist Whig orthodoxy, the *North American Review* ridiculed Young England, not for its supposed challenge to traditional age relations but for its nostalgia for olden times: "The Reformation to Young England . . . is a terrible stumbling-block. Freedom of individual conscience they think the source of unbounded mischief and an absurdity. . . . Feudalism, with its reciprocal duties and obligations, seems to them the ideal of a wise and sound civil polity." The "oppression of the serfs," the "rude organization of society," religious persecution, and "the seigniorial rights not only over property, but over persons in their most sacred relations," were all characteristic of past epochs, according to the *North American,* and all ignored by "this retrospective party." Reversing its own earlier claims, the magazine said that Young England had it wrong. "Our age is progressive, not retrospective," and one only looked back in order "to learn from the ages of suffering" and avoid repeating past errors. "We have reached the period of manhood; and the baubles which charmed our infancy and youth can never resume their ancient power." Even neutral reviews of Disraeli's book found the name Young England "fanciful." [17]

"Young England, like Young America, has never been famous for logical consistency," the *North American Review* had noted. A reader in 1845, at the moment this statement appeared, might by the year's end have noticed a half-dozen heralds announcing the arrival of Young America.

Young America

In February 1844, Ralph Waldo Emerson addressed the Mercantile Library Association of Boston on "The Young American." He considered the effect of railroad and commercial expansion on the preeminence of New England. To discuss a young America he talked about young men and seemed to invoke the sentiments expressed since Puritan times of those who had demanded that the rising generation take responsibility for the future of the community. The call was now secularized and focused on new concerns. "How can our young men complain of the poverty of things in New England, and not feel that poverty as a demand on their charity to make New England rich?" he asked.[18]

In fact, older generational language was transformed. The young were important not because of their connection to their forebears but because they were different from them: "Here are we, men of English blood, planted now for five, six, or seven generations . . . and so planted at such a conjuncture of time and events, that we have left behind us whatever old and odious establishments the mind of men had outgrown." Emerson emphasized the importance of indigenous American creative expression: "It is remarkable that our people have their intellectual culture from one country, and their duties from another. Our books are European. . . . A gulf yawns for the young American between his education and his work." Young men still had work to do, but for Emerson it was to escape the past and take the nation into the future:

> I call upon you, young men, to obey your heart and be the nobility of this land. In every age of the world, there has been a leading nation. . . . Which should be that nation but these States? Which should lead that movement, if not New England? who should lead the leaders, but the Young American?[19]

The image of escape from the old and the importance of native culture persisted in later manifestations of Young America. After Emerson, however, Young America had little to do with New England.

The land and labor reformer George Henry Evans also saw great possibilities in national expansion, although he was most concerned about assuring the rights of all Americans to independent land ownership. In December 1844, the thirty-nine-year-old English émigré published an appreciation of Young England in his New York radical paper, the *Workingman's Advocate,* arguing that the aristocrats were "working to the same great end, the restoration of the land to the people." He applauded Disraeli for giving "go-ahead advice" to a meeting of young men in

England.[20] Two weeks later, the lead story of the *Workingman's Advocate* was headlined "Young America": "Wake up, then, men of all parties and sects! Arouse YOUNG AMERICA! and consign LandLordism to the fate of other lordly isms that are numbered among the things of the past." For the next few months every issue of the *Workingman's Advocate* had a headline in the first column of the front page reading "Young America." The slogan seemed to embody the spread of Evans's ideas to the rest of the nation. An article from another reform publication echoed the sentiment and revealed continuity with the past in its celebration of youth: "There is a general breaking up of old parties, and on every hand, an uncompromising demand for general reform. . . . The working men of New England, and the National Reformers and Agrarians of New York, and of the great West, are in the field. . . . The age waits for its Man— who will be the Washington of the YOUNG AMERICA." Evans would repeat the call for a "Washington of Young America." Later in 1845, he changed his paper's name to *Young America*.[21]

The continental "Young" movements received greater publicity in 1844 when the *Democratic Review* published a three-part interview with the European "persecuted patriot and poet" Paul Harro Harring. The author, Alexander H. Everett, reported that Harring, a former associate of Mazzini, was attempting to "establish in other parts of the world the political principles which form the basis of our institutions." The article included descriptions of Young Italy and Young Europe and reprinted Young Europe's manifesto. Everett reported that the Italian movement originated "the phraseology, which has since become familiar to us, under the forms of Young France and Young England." Perhaps inspired by meeting Harring, Everett published a short poem in the *Democratic Review* the next year, "The Young American." It included these stanzas:

> Scion of a mighty stock:
> Hands of iron,—hearts of oak,—
> Follow with unflinching tread
> Where the noble fathers led!
>
> Prudent in the council train,
> Dauntless on the battle plain,—
> Ready at the country's need
> For her glorious cause to bleed.[22]

As these selected lines suggest, Europe's influence had not completely overshadowed the power of older themes of continuity. The young American emerged as a powerful if inconsistently expressed force. The areas of life that his youthful energy could command expanded. Although

Emerson had mentioned the importance of a unique American culture, he and the other advocates had emphasized the triumph of America in politics or commerce. Now literature entered the Young America field.

The southern novelist William Gilmore Simms opened the January 1845 issue of his new magazine dedicated to the interests of the South and West with an essay on national literature. He followed a familiar biblical verse closely as he imagined breaking free from European, especially English, literary influences: "Generations must pass away, and other generations take their places . . . before they shall begin to look around them, and within themselves, for those characteristics which are peculiar to their condition." The time had passed for Europe "to taunt us because of our prolonged servility to the imperious genius of the Old World. . . . We have our own national mission to perform." He applauded the brave exceptions who ignored English influence, about whom it could be said "here stands a true scion of young America,—this is a plant of our own raising—true to the spirit of the country."[23] Thus John Cotton's warning about the degeneracy of the vine planted in the New World was reversed to become a statement of independence, and Cotton Mather's vision of ceaseless generational renewal became a search for freedom from past restrictions.

"Americanism," Cornelius Mathews's June 1845 address to a New York University literary society, continued the synthesis of the traditional approach to generations as it proposed a new direction for ideas about youth. The twenty-eight-year-old lawyer and litterateur recognized "those, loved and honored in our boyhood, ascending from the dull level of the earth we dwell on, and one by one, taking their seats in the calm heaven of fame." More significantly, "They depart—but we remain." A generation had responsibilities, but they changed over time: "The task our fathers had to do, they did well, but it was not our task. . . . The hour of their greatness has passed: and it is sacred." Whatever the great abilities and deeds of the founders, "Our duty and our destiny is another from theirs," and thus "We form a new generation."[24]

He did not like "its borrowed sound," but Mathews named the new generation "the Young America of this people . . . and it is for us now to inquire, what we may have it in our power to accomplish." Mathews, "in behalf of this young America of ours," called for "nationality and true Americanism in the books this country furnishes to itself and to the world"; his address was subtitled "Home-Writers, Home-Writings, Home Criticism." Public landmarks were unnecessary: "It need not speak of the Revolution—nor Washington—nor the declaration of independence—nor Plymouth Rock—nor Bunker Hill—nor Bunker Hill Monuments," but could still be "full of a hearty, spontaneous, genuine home feeling."

"The business of Young America," Mathews said, was to sustain "by a harmonious combination of all the true young influences, the manly young writers of the country." Indeed, writers and artists, "the unelected, but self-justified and self-sustained governors of a free people, will be the noblest body, the manliest phalanx that walks the earth." He described the power and possibility of a native literature that used America's natural beauty and unique character for its themes.[25]

The *Broadway Journal* agreed the "phrase . . . is not only borrowed, but redolent of affectation"; nonetheless this New York literary weekly, written and edited by Poe, endorsed Young America. The journal excerpted Mathews's speech, commenting that it "embodies all that there is any necessity for saying" on the subject of literary nationalism.[26]

Later in 1845 Simms congratulated a young writer on his selection as the annual orator before literary societies at South Carolina College. "You will do them justice. Give us something honorably and fearlessly American," he told Edwin DeLeon, whose address was titled "The Positions and Duties of Young America." DeLeon echoed Simms's rhetoric when he asked the students "to regard me, not as a pompous utterer of solemn saws, but even as one of yourselves,—a scion of this Young America of ours." DeLeon also apologized for the "quaint and affected" quality of the phrase, but said: "it is the only one that will convey my meaning; there is a 'Young Germany,' a 'Young France,' a 'Young England'—and why not a 'Young America'? for assuredly he is towering above his continental brethren in stature, even as his wide domain, with its majestic mountains, boundless forests . . . surpasses their old and exhausted inheritance." Young America represented, quite simply, "the men of to-day, it consists of the generations now coming on the stage."

Young America, however, was not synonymous with change. DeLeon cast suspicion on the "unsettled" nature of socialists, Fourierites, Mormons, and others "dissatisfied with the present state of things and thirsting after change of any kind." If anything, a strong national feeling would reduce differences between Americans born in many nations. He echoed Mathews and Simms in calling for "native literature" and "native authorship" to end "this literary vassalage to Great Britain." Young America's power and potential extended beyond literature: "Nations, like men, have their seasons of infancy, manly vigor, and decrepitude; our young Giant of the West stands now in the full flush of exulting manhood, and the worn-out Powers of the Old World may not hope either to restrain or impede his onward progress," a mission to bring freedom to the world. The *Southern Quarterly Review*, which only a few months before had found Young England "fanciful," called DeLeon's address "beautiful" and its "doctrines . . . in keeping with the spirit of the age." Although he did not use the phrase, Philip Hone, writing in 1845, also sensed similar feelings in the air, though he saw a much darker implication: "Overturn, overturn, overturn! is the maxim of New York . . . one generation of men seem studious to remove all relics of those which preceded them." [27]

These essays, orations, and lectures delineated the features of Young America: escape from foreign aesthetic models, a special responsibility for the nation's young people, the nation itself as young and powerful, the necessity for American literature to sustain a unified nationalism, and America's responsibility to extend its ideals throughout the world. These concepts did not capture public attention simultaneously; rather, there were two great movements of Young America interest. First the sometimes strident advocates of a national literature adopted the phrase, often expressing the tradition of youth as champion of the fathers and protector of the nation from foreign invasion. Then, after popularizing their cause, some literary men entered more traditional political arenas and formed a bridge to a Young America that became the property of political adventurers of various sorts. Eventually transformed into a popular catchphrase, Young America spread to a broader assortment of groups. We begin with the literary nationalists.

Literary Young America

There was nothing revolutionary about the call for a unique American literature, but some men specified conditions for its emergence with a stringent, strident insistence absent in the past. Cornelius Mathews, the editor Evert Duyckinck, William Gilmore Simms, and others insisted that a national literature had to be free of all European influences and derive its materials from purely American sources. Mathews and Duyckinck first gained attention through the magazine *Arcturus*, which they edited in 1841. Later they and their colleagues wrote often in the *Democratic Review*, a political magazine that also advanced their literary agenda. Mathews and Duyckinck moved like gypsies through New York's publishing world in the 1840s, founding and folding magazines within months, finding another platform, peddling their literary nationalist message, and moving on. Duyckinck had the steadier employment; as an editor at publishing houses and magazines he was a crucial conduit for aspiring writers. While highly respected, he stayed in the background. Cornelius Mathews, by contrast, became the focus of public attention and ridicule.[28] Mathews had a precocious career. He was still in his late twenties when he published a collection of writings that included several novels, a play, and numerous poems and political essays. His literary production and celebrity ended only a few years later.

His first publication, a series of poems called "Our Forefathers," for which he used the pen name "A Young American," appeared in the *American Monthly Magazine* in 1836. Mathews wrote a brief preface similar in style and sentiment to speeches by contemporary young men's organizations. The lives, "the perils . . . the hopes defeated, the hopes accomplished, of the Old Band of Colonial Fathers" provided worthy literary themes "calculated to arouse the national heart." He reminded readers: "The Republic will cease to be, when it ceases to remember, to revere, and to imitate the virtues of its founders." As yet, he argued, "None of our noted poets have hitherto walked this field." Although he expressed reverence, Mathews suggested that he had something "to teach those elder spirits who already occupy the pinnacles of Renown. . . . I would say that *their* error has been . . . that they have failed to express . . . sentiments which go home to the national spirit."[29] These poems, he implied, would begin to fill that artistic void.

Mathews portrayed American Indians, natural wonders, and New York political and city life; his fiction illustrated the need to touch "the national spirit" using local materials. His twentieth-century biographer has argued that Mathews sought to describe "the past for a new generation in order that there might be established a continuity of national purpose." Such a goal certainly seemed to be expressed in the poems on the forefathers. Mathews was not consistently reverent, however; in his 1840 play "The Politicians," he poked fun at political language favored by young men's political organizations. While a political hack invoked posterity and cried that "Freedom's temple" was "Begirt with peril," endangering what had been created by "the blood of all our grandsires and their wives," ordinary citizens mocked the clichéd rhetoric.[30] Mathews's public activities in defense of national literature, rather than the literary works he produced as examples of it, provide better clues to his faith in Young America.

A unique American literature would never develop, Mathews believed, until the publishing market was protected from cheap overseas imports.

He helped organize a campaign for international copyright only a few years before the Young America manifestos appeared.[31] This cause responded to similarly nationalist interests. "We live aside from the great Old World, we are in a new country, with a new history—give us books conforming, and a literature that shall purge off our errors," Mathews wrote in an address sponsored by the American Copyright Club. He asked whether England, "old and knit by years and wisdom into strength, or America, roused to new duties in its youth," would rule the national mind. Mathews had first introduced himself to William Gilmore Simms in letters about the copyright issue; Simms later wrote a series of articles on the question in the *Southern Literary Messenger.* For a nation to be civilized it must have its own literature, he said. "A people who receive their Literature exclusively from a foreign land, are . . . governed from abroad." Edwin DeLeon, in turn, first came to Simms's notice because of articles he wrote that argued foreign literature corrupted the young and narrowed the field for "wholesome and manly" native works.[32]

The rhetoric of these copyright proponents bears striking similarity to the heated cries of "to the rescue" by contemporary young men's organizations. Those addresses posed hypothetical threats of foreign invaders that surely would be met by the awakened youth of the land. In literature, the invaders were palpable and the damage they committed could be counted in dollars and cents. A literary nationalist movement called "Young America" that pledged to create a strong local literature protected from outside influence and embodying youthful, manly virtues provided a perfect synthesis of American cultural ideals about youth's responsibilities. The figuring of the young American as a defender against foreign invasion, however, would have grim implications a decade later.

Many literary critics who supported American authors had no patience for the strident rhetoric of literary Young America. James Russell Lowell "laughed when I saw the advertisement" for Mathews's collected works "with the effervescence about 'Young America.' " *Knickerbocker* editor Lewis Gaylord Clark noted in his "Editor's Table" that "there may be . . . readers who do not know that a new dynasty has been established in the American Republic of Letters," and then attacked Mathews, "the Corypheus of 'Young America.' "[33] The anthologist Rufus W. Griswold continued the assault in *Prose Writers of America,* calling the idea "absurd . . . that we are to create an entirely new literature. . . . All nations are indebted to each other and to preceding ages." Young America "had not the wit enough to coin for itself a name, but must parody one used in England," he said; Mathews's creative work was unoriginal and showed none of the qualities that were proclaimed as prerequisites for American literature.[34] Even some friends shared this view; Simms wrote a long essay that honored Mathews's nationalist intentions but expressed skepticism about his literary merit.[35]

Young America soon became a code name for Cornelius Mathews, and satirical newspapers and novels took full advantage of the identification. In 1846 an early issue of *Yankee Doodle* offered a story on "Young America": "Since our last issue, the fall meeting of this numerous association has been held. . . . The members, we observe, all took their seats in white cravats, but with the bows turned behind, to be as much unlike Young England as possible." A debate about the merits of *Yankee Doodle* satirized the high-flown, convoluted style apparently common in Mathews's declarations on true American literature. One speaker felt *Yankee Doodle* had

> far too much intellectual alcohol. . . . What we wanted was a work redolent of the pure and unadulterated element, if he might so express himself, the virgin rock springs of intellect, from which a young, a new and simple family of the human race might delight to drink, and might in so drinking become braced and toned up as it were for the high duties, and the severe duties—the duties high and severe, but still pleasurable . . . which pressed upon all of us who feel, as we should feel, the destinies of Young America lying near to our hearts.[36]

In Charles F. Briggs's novel, *Trippings of Tom Pepper*, Mathews appeared as a lawyer, "Mr. Ferocious," who interrupts conversation with calls for "fresh, home-born" literature free of foreign influence. When Tom Pepper gets bored reading one of Ferocious's novels, the outraged writer says, "Young America, sir, must keep his eyes open, he must study deep, dive down into the mysteries of his author." Another comic weekly, the *John-Donkey*, continued the satire with an article titled "The Mutual Admiration Society" (the *Knickerbocker*'s name for the literary nationalists), which lampooned a character called Young America (intended to be Mathews) and made fun of the copyright law movement and most of the other ideals of Young America.[37]

Some humorous commentaries revealed other meanings. The youth component to the slogan was evident; in fact, *Yankee Doodle* once presented it as somehow equivalent to a young men's political organization. Daniel Webster was portrayed warning the meeting of Young America that they would become laughingstocks if the group followed the example of the Whig Young Men's General Committee in trying "to read *Yankee Doodle* and the *Courier and Enquirer* out of 'the party.' "[38]

Other satires appeared in cartoons of a "Boy-Man," or "Old Young People," or "Young America." In each case, young people, really juveniles, dressed in elaborate adult clothes and conversed with false sophistication. These were not uniquely American jokes; a similar series of cartoons was appearing in *Punch* at the same time.[39] Jokes about premature precocity also had domestic inspiration; a list of candidates for the 1848 election included "A Young American, who witholds his name for the present and says he will be of the legally-required age in '48, and promises to make himself known before that time. He wishes a place reserved for him."[40]

The literary nationalists did have some friends, including authors now renowned as leaders of the American Renaissance. Margaret Fuller linked the New York writers and the New England transcendentalists to the European revolutionary sources of the "Young" idea. Fuller brought an intense interest in European revolutions to her work as literary critic at the *New York Tribune* from 1844 to 1846. She spent evenings in spirited discussion with Cornelius Mathews, borrowed books from him, and promoted his literary work. She also knew the exile Harro Harring, and when he was involved in a dispute with American publishers Fuller looked to Ralph Waldo Emerson and others for help. Emerson contributed no more rhetoric for Young America, but used whimsical variations on the phrase in letters—the "admired epistles of the Young Staten Island," in reference to Harro Harring, or "*young* Concord," in a description of activities during a Fourth of July weekend. We cannot determine the extent of Fuller's influence on the initial use of the "young" description in the New York literati's nationalist campaign or in Emerson's "Young American." Evidence of Fuller's involvement began some years after the first statements.[41] Her influence may have been felt after some literary nationalists became involved in world affairs.

The literary Young Americans had more direct involvement with Poe and Melville. Poe's *Broadway Journal* articles promoted Mathews's address on Young America. But shortly thereafter, Poe withdrew that support. One study suggests he had been sympathetic primarily to win favor from Duyckinck, who served as an advisory editor to several publishers.[42] Melville, however, knew Mathews and Duyckinck better; his discord with the two was more dramatic.

Melville's friendship with Duyckinck and use of the editor's library is well known. The two attended cultural events, such as the opening of the American Art-Union's new gallery, and spent evenings with Mathews discussing a newspaper to promote literary nationalism.[43] Was Melville committed to the cause of a national literature? Naturally, scholars disagree. Part of the problem is the conflation of ideas that all fall under the rubric "Young America." Some literary historians argue Melville wanted his own work to draw on the rougher "linguistic fire of the Young America *political* movement," instead of the "kind of smoothness and gentility" favored by the literary nationalists. "As Young America achieved prominence in the later 1840s," according to this view, "its literary and political tendencies divided." In fact, no political movement using the name Young America existed at the time of these literary disputes. Whether Melville's allegiance was briefly "misplaced enthusiasm," as one critic argues, or a deeply felt belief, Melville did not have to look far to find someone opposed to smooth gentility; there was Cornelius Mathews.[44]

Melville's major critical statement on these topics was described by one recent scholar as "rebellious" and "nationalist," but "Hawthorne and His Mosses" is gentle by comparison with anything in Mathews's Young America.[45] Without invoking the phrase itself, Melville asks Americans to "prize and cherish her writers," to "let America first praise mediocrity in her own children," before applauding foreign achievements. He asserts that it was "better to fail in originality than to succeed in imitation." This general appeal could almost be read as a defense of Cornelius Mathews's literary productions, although Melville's warning that he did not mean "that all American writers should studiously cleave to nationality in their writings" suggested he did not follow Mathews all the way. Hawthorne, the main subject of his essay, was hardly mediocre; Melville called him "one of the new, and far better generation" of American writers.[46] Melville made a clean break with Young America in his novel *Pierre,* but the evidence in that work suggests literary rather than political reasons for his disenchantment.

In a chapter of *Pierre* entitled "Young America in Literature," Melville satirized the publicity machinery that puffed up the author of the moment. The title character, Pierre, has written only a few verses and occasional essays, but wins critical acclaim and receives offers to have his complete works collected in book form. Scholars have suggested that this chapter is based on Melville's own experiences as a young author and on specific actions of Evert Duyckinck's. But some of Melville's descriptions suggest a satiric debt to the career of Cornelius Mathews. The title page of Mathews's *Various Writings* strongly resembles the title page of "The Complete Works of Glendinning" proposed by Pierre's would-be publishers. Pierre meets the editor of a magazine, *Captain Kidd's Monthly,* identified by critics as Duyckinck, but there is a possible nod to Mathews here as well. In Mathews's early novel *The Career of Puffer Hopkins*, the publisher of a new journal must negotiate with newsboys to get his magazine distributed. The chief newsboy asks whether the paper will "go Captain Kidd or the moral code?" The answer: "Captain Kidd decidedly. . . . We shall pirate all foreign tales regularly . . . shall in all cases employ third-rate native writers at journeyman cobbler's wages, and swear to their genius as a matter of business." That scene articulated Mathews's belief that copyright protected authors from pirated editions; Melville retained the image in a book written ten years later to attack a publishing world that had not changed. The clothing images remained consistent; the book publishers who tempt Pierre are former tailors and constantly confuse the making of books and coats.[47] Melville may well have retained literary nationalist sentiments even as he grew disenchanted with some of its advocates.[48]

Was there no political component to this literary campaign? Certainly some Young Americans had strong sympathies with the radical wing in New York City Democratic politics; William Leggett's *Plaindealer* has long been identified as a significant influence. Another important writer associated with the New York literary nationalists, William Gilmore Simms, started a political movement that called itself "Young," but he fought his battles far south of New York.

Simms joined the opposition to John C. Calhoun's control over South Carolina politics. "Our leaders have been blundering too frequently not to make the people very doubtful of them, and not to make it incumbent on young Carolina to take a little of the business into their own hands," he wrote to a friend. Simms urged another friend, former governor James Henry Hammond, to create a political journal: "Call it 'Young Carolina' and use that party which is destined to grow, for it has a truth to build on." From 1846 to 1848 Simms was giving speeches and writing articles supporting Young Carolina, a movement of the young politicians against the "Old Hunkers," a term from New York politics borrowed to describe the office-holding Calhoun coalition. The sooner Calhoun could be moved out, perhaps into the presidency, the sooner a "shadow" that "falls heavily upon our young men and darkens all their pathways" could be removed. In 1848, the Democrat Simms and Young Carolina crossed party lines to support Zachary Taylor's candidacy for president. Although Taylor won, the attempt to create an independent movement had failed and sectional concerns began to take precedence; by 1849, Simms "dropped the word 'young' from his political vocabulary" and became more concerned with southern issues.[49] Ironically, the man identified as the ultimate "Old Hunker" in South Carolina, John C. Calhoun, became a figurehead for radical New York Democrats who wanted to break the power of the original Hunkers.[50]

One New York Calhoun supporter in the battle against the Hunkers was Mike Walsh, a radical politician who used the language of youth and masculinity to mobilize working-class young men more at home in fire companies and barrooms than in the regular party young men's political organizations. Walsh proclaimed his support of what he called the "Young Democracy." His connection to youth and political rough-and-tumble seemed clear to contemporary humorists; *Yankee Doodle* reported that Joel Tyler Headley, author of *Washington and His Generals,* was "about to put to press a new work . . . 'Mike Walsh and his Cronies,' in which the various battles of the b'hoys" would be portrayed. The purpose of the book was "to warn the rising generation against the horrors of black eyes and bloody noses."[51] Walsh also played a supporting role in New York's great social drama about drama, the Astor Place riot.

The riot resulted from an 1849 feud between supporters of the British actor William Macready and the American actor Edwin Forrest, and turned into a conflict between Forrest's supporters and the New York City police and militia in which more than twenty people were killed. Walsh addressed the large crowd that gathered at a public meeting after the police battle and assailed the elite cultural leaders who supported Macready. The crowd then marched on the Opera House and fought bayonet-wielding soldiers. A few days earlier, when Forrest partisans had shouted down a Macready performance, a public statement appeared in the city's newspapers from leading cultural figures urging the actor to continue his performances. Headed by Washington Irving, the group included literary Young Americans and fellow travelers Evert Duyckinck, Cornelius Mathews, Herman Melville, and Henry J. Raymond.

Peter Buckley's comprehensive study of the riot concludes that the Young Americans were not supporting the British actor so much as they were standing "in defense of 'higher conceptions of art' against the trajectory of commercial popular culture." To Buckley, the Macready petition "mark[ed] the end of Young America's strenuous version of nationalism," and signaled its replacement by a belief in "culture as an absolute value."[52] Duyckinck seemed to be affected the most. He eschewed the old terms in his critical work and was the heartiest Macready supporter.[53] Perhaps the riot did not signify an end to literary nationalism so much as a shift in attention. Even as some cultural Young Americans gave up the attempt to democratize literature, several others began to support efforts to democratize the world.

Three months after the Astor Place riots, New Yorkers held a mass demonstration in support of the Hungarian revolution. Mike Walsh delivered a rousing oration about the struggle of the Hungarian people. A few days later a meeting of young men met in "consideration of the recent struggle for liberty in Hungary and the obligations of the young men of New-York touching the same." They resolved that it was "proper and natural" for young men "to express our admiration for" the Hungarian revolutionaries' struggle. The young men appointed a committee to prepare a statement; its members included Mike Walsh and Henry J. Raymond—on opposite sides at Astor Place, now comrades for freedom.

If the action by a group of young men and their expression of responsibility seem familiar, they were tragicomic to *New York Tribune* editor Horace Greeley: "Some rather young gentlemen of our city would seem to consider the Hungarians performers in some magnificent melo-drama. . . . They talk of drafting addresses and sending flags. . . . We cannot agree with them." The resistance needed money, not speeches, Greeley said. A letter to the *Tribune* headlined "The Young Men's Movement for Hungary" responded that Greeley's emphasis on money "exclude[d] the poor . . . from the only luxury they can afford, the right to proclaim their belief in the rights of the people." The Hungarian revolt collapsed several weeks later and the young men moved on to other pursuits. Youth continued to carry rhetorical weight in discussions of America's role in the European revolutions.[54]

In 1851 a headline in the *Herald* on a Tammany Hall meeting that ratified the Democratic platform for the 1852 elections read in part:

> No More Neutrality
> Active Alliance with Republicanism
> Throughout the World
> Young America in the Field

William Corry of Ohio, associated by modern historians with the political Young America movement, made a fiery speech about extending American political ideals and institutions abroad. With the exception of the headline, however, there was no mention of Young America.[55]

The Hungarian exile Louis Kossuth's visit to the United States in 1851–52 has also been linked to the expansionist political Young America movement. Kossuth himself used the phrase after a delegation from Yale College had "As young men . . . claiming affinity with the men who pledged their 'lives, their fortunes and their sacred honor' " vowed to support the exile. Kossuth in turn recognized the "fact that Young America sympathizes with the struggles" for freedom.[56] The Yale group was only one of many who addressed Kossuth. Sumptuous banquets celebrated the revolutionary leader every evening during his visit to New York City in December 1851.

Little attention has been paid to one banquet sponsored by the New York press. Charles F. Briggs, Parke Godwin, and Cornelius Mathews comprised the committee of arrangements. Godwin was a literary Young America stalwart who had also been associated with George Henry Evans and the land reform Young America. Briggs and Mathews had been antagonists in the literary nationalist debate, yet could find common ground on this issue. Henry J. Raymond, who had joined Mathews and the others in signing the Macready petition and had been on the young men's committee supporting the Hungarian revolution, was a featured speaker.

Mathews rose toward the evening's end to propose a toast. As the *New York Tribune* reported it, he "was so cheered, groaned, hissed, laughed at, ridiculed, abused, jeered, flouted, reviled, and in every way badgered, that no idea of what he was saying could be guessed at. Mr. M. persisted in standing on a chair and reading unintelligible sentences for about five minutes, when he subsided amid laughter." The *New York Times,* founded months before by Raymond, gave a full account of Mathews's toast, which included a statement about "People of various origins brought together and acting in harmony. . . . blending of the colors of all nations in our vast army of citizen soldiery. . . . German blue, French tri-color, the Old Continental yellow, the Italian and the Irish green—yes, sir the Irish green too, which altogether form a glorious rainbow arch, which spans the American continent."[57] This curious image of a rainbow coalition did not seem especially relevant to the celebration of the Hungarian but showed that even as a celebrant of European democracy, Mathews thought first about the strengths of his country. Literary Young America, or some of its officers, retained their initial beliefs while moving their theater of operations. Electoral politics became the new arena for the phrase they had popularized. The *Herald* editorialized after Kossuth addressed Tammany Hall: "The Whigs have had their chance at Kossuth. Now is the chance of the democrats, who appear to slumber, but are evidently now awake. 'Young America' is up, and asserts his prior right to the intervention platform."[58] The political activists who next waved the Young America banner had little in common with the literati.

Political Young America

A major change had occurred in conceptions about youth's responsibilities to the community and the nation. Earlier in the century, the young man symbolized the defender of the fathers' vision; now he represented a vanguard determined to wipe away ideas imported from Europe and held by entrenched conservatives. This sentiment expressed by the literary nationalists grew more boisterous in the hands of political Young America.

"You see that a new era is opened in our foreign relations. Young America has taken the field and will soon make her mark," William Corry wrote to a friend in November 1851. Corry, who had addressed the Tammany Hall meeting, was associated with George Sanders, a Kentucky Democrat who had been planning for some time to promote the presidential candidacy of Illinois senator Stephen A. Douglas.[59] Sanders bought the *Democratic Review* as his campaign vehicle. From its opening pages in January 1852, the magazine decried the deteriorated state of the nation and the need for a regenerating force:

> The statesmen of a previous generation, with their personal antipathies, and their personal claims . . . must get out of the way. A new generation of American statesmen . . . who have fitted to the external principles of democratic right, the exigencies of the time, the circumstances of the nation, the requirements of the future have sprung up.

Meanwhile, the people of Europe "dream in gladsome ecstasy of the day when our flag shall be unfurled or even our nod, earthshaking as the nod of Jove, shall be given for the liberation of nations."[60]

The *Review* left no doubt that this was a conflict between youth and age and between a past era and a new one: "While the fathers of the people personally lived, it was an easy task to elect the candidate most worthy of success." But while "Age is to honored . . . senility is pitiable." The nominee in 1852 had to be "a statesman who can bring young blood, young ideas, and young hearts" to the presidency. So long as the candidate came from "the young generation of America," the *Democratic Review* would not complain.[61]

That January issue had a portrait of Mazzini for its frontispiece. An admiring article on Young Europe proclaimed that Mazzini understood the necessity of "trusting political movements with young" leaders and "new men." There were no specific comparisons between Europe and America; there did not have to be. Virtually every article bespoke the theme of an end to the past and promotion of the future. Even a book review denounced a history of the Pilgrims as symptomatic of a "disease" of commemorative rituals.[62]

Being young was no guarantee of an expansive imagination—one might be an "old fogy." Despite the journal's claim to the term's "parentage," it did not begin with the *Democratic Review*. The English magazine *Blackwood's* published a short satirical piece in 1846 proposing a new association called the "Fogie Club." It identified the word's origins in Scottish slang for an old soldier, which soon came to mean an old-fashioned individual. Members of the proposed club were expected to exhibit a "certain pleasing irrelevancy, an interesting tendency to parenthesis, a longing, lingering look cast back on the events of former times." The first American use I have found appeared in 1848 in the comic periodical *John-Donkey*. In "A Treatise on Old Fogyism," the magazine said that "Old Fogy's ideas on politics, religion, society. . . . may be characterized as the very galvanism of dead commonplaces and defunct truisms." Significantly, the old fogy "can never consent, while he is able to protest against it, that young men should rise up and take the place of old and respectable citizens." The "political Old Fogy" was simply a variation on the theme of a party hack who "changes his principles as easily as a weathercock." Early in 1852, another New York comic weekly, the *Lantern,* ran an almost word-for-word reprint of the 1848 article.[63] The Old Fogy still symbolized outmoded ideals and an unwillingness to accept the new Young America.

The *Democratic Review*'s February issue continued to call for "young men" to step forward, although it argued "we are not for all the young men before the country, but only for the bold, active honor and talent of Young America." Circulation jumped from three thousand to thirty thousand. Its campaign for Young America gained further national attention when Rep. John Breckinridge, age thirty-one, rose for his first speech in Congress in March 1852 to defend the party establishment. He assailed the *Review*'s attacks on "statesmen of a past generation; their principles are denounced, in the cant language of the day as 'old fogyism.' " Sanders and his ill-disguised candidate, Douglas, were to blame. The freshman congressman insisted that he was no conservative:

> I am in favor of progress. I like young blood, and I like young ideas, too, (at a certain time of life), but I do not like this course. . . . I want no wild and visionary progress that would sweep away all the immortal principles

of our forefathers—hunt up some imaginary genius, place him on a new policy, give him "Young America" for a fulcrum, and let him turn the world upside down. . . . I want to progress in the line of the principles of our fathers.

Already, he warned, "the cant and slang of 'death to the fogies' " was proclaimed by "political loafers on the streets . . . with parrot-like facility."[64] Breckinridge's speech drew immediate acclaim and wide distribution. Sanders helped orchestrate a response. His wife's journal noted "the Young Men's party . . . are in high spirits and full of action." An Illinois representative defended Douglas with evidence that he had no control over the *Review*; this included a letter Sanders had written Douglas in February that said, "The fogie atmosphere of Washington makes cowards of you all." Another Douglas supporter sarcastically claimed victory for Young America because the fogies chose a young man, Breckinridge, to defend their interests.[65]

Sanders and the *Review* ignored public and private pleas for moderation. They ridiculed opponents and made even wilder claims. Breckinridge was a "young fogy": "old fogyism, ever deficient in originality . . . has nothing for liberty or progress . . . but to mumble over 'the immortal principles of our forefathers.' And where did our forefathers get their principles? . . . Were they imitators, inheritors of servility," the *Review* asked. Even as it rejected adherence to the immediate past, it claimed to be true heirs:

> Young America is the inheritor of their only principle, to throw aside hereditary servility, old-fogy fears . . . and live by their manhoods, by mastering the necessities and wants of the time. . . . *They* did not sit idly on the grave of their fathers, rattling old bones and saying, "they did well—we can do no more!" They did more—they justified their existence on earth by reclaiming the earth to freedom.[66]

Since the late 1820s, young men had been claiming affinity with the founders to justify their responsibility for taking action to protect the nation or the community. Even conservative young men, who often claimed intense adherence to the fathers' principles, had used that assertion to support plans for new endeavors. Political Young America shifted the terms of debate; the heritage of the fathers was to throw over the past. To be obedient to the founders' ideals was to reject those saying "they did well—we can do no more," a position rarely taken by young men in the past. Now, the elders appeared to be standing in the way of advancement. "Let us cooperate and catch hold of the Federal govt. We are over 40. It's high time," William Corry wrote to Joseph Holt.[67] And the *Review* participated in something almost unprecedented: explicit, lurid, rhetorical patricide. No recent historian, with all the contemporary concern for the patricidal theme, has discussed this remarkable text.

The *Review* "would be up and stirring, stirring as our fathers taught us, in manly industry, and like them pioneering for liberty, axe or gun in hand." They would "not be the first generation of American democrats left far in the rearward of time." They had been thwarted by "the vile and contemptible arts and subterfuges by which old fogydom has so long imposed itself upon the public and upon the country, pressing like a horrid nightmare upon the young and surging bosom of the American democracy." This "hideous phantasm . . . did not permit us to raise a hand or use a muscle." Whenever a

> new and ever fresh idea . . . would burst our heart and rise to our lips . . . it would press us down . . . and mumble in our ears, with a ghostly wink, "the immortal principles of your ancestors!" Thus have we, in common with all the young democracy of America, been held down for years by fogydom, in agony, in torture, in silence, in inefficiency.

The Old Fogies had fooled the nation into believing "that Washington and Jefferson lived, and fought, and conquered, merely to make it the owner of this generation and of posterity."[68]

The *Review* presented itself rising like a mythic hero: "having studied and knowing well the real strength of Young America . . . determined for our own and its sake, to hurl down this phantasm, and give the young folks breath to live, to fulfil for their generation, the grand destiny of the land of the Revolutionary fathers." And as in all myths, they

> determined to approach the hoary monster in his very stronghold, to take him by the throat, turn his own guns, and webs, and wires, against him, and by one bold word crush him. And we have done it. We seized him by the throat, in his own ancient castle; and said. . . . Base and false representatives of our illustrious sires, whose names you have so long blasphemed and the latchet of whose shoes you are unworthy to tie, begone.

The *Review* rejoiced in its liberation of "Young America—the young demigod of our future history—from the chains and the tortures, and the grinning intolerance of a fogy nightmare." They would put any of past generations who could not keep up in "old fogy hospitals." Young America would be sent there, too, if it was "not competent in the 19th century to carry out the work begun by its ancestors in the 18th."[69]

This effusion of hostility had no recognizable contemporary American antecedent; not since the most extreme rhetoric of the American Revolution against the controlling English parent had anything reached such emotional heights. The closest comparison was in the language of contemporary European revolutionary youth. Sanders merged their hatred of a gerontocracy that blocked political advancement with the American tradition of young men claiming the heritage of founding values. The *Review* thus created a new perjorative category: those who believed "they did well, we can do no more." Sanders was from Kentucky, far removed from the New England roots of a generational tradition that embraced continuity as part of a search for new challenges. The book review that had attacked the history of the Pilgrims hoped that some day there would be histories of founders outside New England. A new generation may have had a different significance for Sanders. Modern historical interpretations have incorporated the *Review*'s definition of a new generation and obscured the rich American tradition of youth as both defenders of generational continuity and beacons for new accomplishment. After the *Democratic Review*, who could imagine the young in any other way?

The *Review* had "descended upon the dead weeds of old fogydom like a whirlwind in a cane-brake," according to the *New York Herald*. In a rare expression of offended sensibility, the *Herald* said *Democratic Review* "articles savor too strongly of the Five Points and gin and water to be palatable to the sober reader." The *Review* did not apologize, although it made faint gestures at moderation—it hated old ideas, it said, not old people. Far more often it crowed in self-congratulation for introducing the term *old fogy* and for saving the Democratic party from disaster. It repeated its message in every issue before the Democratic convention: "we maintain that a young President is indispensable. Young men draw the sword on the battlefield, and young America asks that in the civil contest . . . a young champion shall lead on to victory." [70]

The pervasive message even insinuated itself into the few articles that had nothing to do with the election. One piece dismissed a book of criticism by W. A. Jones (known today as part of literary Young America) as "Fogy Literature." The "representative of a land which God has fashioned in a moment of gigantic thought, must discountenance such pigmy provender." Jones's book displayed "the multiform hues of sycophancy, toadyism, weakness, and unmanliness" in its "obsequious" imitation of English models. "Give us ungrammatical manhood, before the most polished meanness." The fact that the general attack on English models had originated in large measure from Jones and his colleagues—and in one case from Jones himself in the *Democratic Review*, under its earlier suspect management—was an irony apparently unnoticed by the reviewer. [71]

The embrace of the "ungrammatical" as a synonym for truly American, and references in other articles to Young America clearing frontiers with axes and guns, represented the introduction of regional concerns outside the urban Northeast to the call for a national literature. The persistent equation of youth and manhood, the linking of young men and the battlefield, illustrated that the search for the new had roots in older conceptions of youth and generations. The *Democratic Review*'s assault on the past raised another problem: where to draw the line in the attack on tradition. It appeared that one line of continuity the *Review* left untouched was the one dividing genders into male public and female domestic spheres. We have already noted in Chapter 3 that women rarely appeared in visions of young manhood. During the campaign against the old fogies, the *Democratic Review* treated attempts by women to participate in society with an aggressiveness that bordered on hostility. While trumpeting the call to arms against old fogy traditions in politics, the *Review* worried about the decline of women's traditional roles and duties. It expressed amazement that

> the men of the present generation are so unmindful of what is due to her as a sex, that woman must leave the cradle side and the nursery primer, and all the sacred household altars, to go forth into a gladitorial arena, to wrestle in defiant combat with her ordained guardian and guide, to subdue him to her will, to an acknowledgement of her rights, based not upon gospel authority, for that is to be thrown away, but upon her weak, human declaration.

It was likely that "the next generation of men growing up under this wilful abandonment" would "graduate through street companionship to vicious manhood."[72]

The barrage against women's independence culminated in an essay on Margaret Fuller, who "should have been by nature a woman among men, but by intellect she was a man among women." Fuller "would turn our wives, sisters, and daughters into husbands, brothers and sons." Her quest for equality would only lead to results the *Review* found absurd:

> Just imagine your daughter, reader, swinging a hod of "bricks and mortar" up a sixty-foot ladder on a day in July, lounging about the cafés in evenings; having whiskey-toddy matches and champagne bouts at Jones's or Delmonico's; giving Michael Phelan forty odds and beating him at the *carom* game, and flourishing in an indisputable right of the night-key.[73]

Seemingly increasing the outrage, this equal daughter was a member of the working class, thus contradicting the celebration of "ungrammatical" manhood. But then, women were expected to be grammatical—and at home.

"The gentlemen left for the Baltimore convention. . . . Young America in high spirits," Anna J. Sanders wrote in her journal in May 1852. Now everyone knew the phrase. Operatives for presidential hopeful William Marcy had been discussing Young America since Breckinridge's debate in the Congress. They did not think it meant that much, just another "shake of the Presidential kaleidoscope," as Marcy put it in a letter. They concluded that the *Review* had gone too far—"even Young 'America' staggered under the load."[74] Marcy did not get the nomination, nor did Stephen Douglas, the big loser in all of this. Douglas was unable to control the outpourings of Sanders, his vocal, infamous supporter, against the entire Democratic establishment. The manager planning the surprise victory of the eventual nominee, Franklin Pierce, recognized the power of the *Democratic Review*'s vision of Young America, and he used its image in discussions with the candidate and other party leaders.[75] Some members of the party were relieved after Pierce's nomination: "we shall have, if not a great man, at least a true one. . . . especially no Young America to pull down everything we have heretofore esteemed." The *Democratic Review* claimed victory anyway: "We have swept the track and enabled the young generation of this century to take command." After writing this, Sanders went to New Hampshire to meet with the candidate.[76]

During the general election campaign, there were still some scant references to Young America. C. Edwards Lester emerged to write a biography of the Democratic nominee and provide a more benign meaning to the phrase: "He has aided many a penniless youth of talent in the early struggle to gain education, and under his auspices, many an indigent young man has been encouraged to go forward nobly in the battle of life. Men talk about 'Young America.' It means this or it means nothing. Men talk about the wisdom of age. It means this or it means nothing. In Frank Pierce they are both united." The biography celebrated Pierce as "an experienced statesmen without being an 'Old Fogy.' " As the phrases moved into popular usage, they began to mean less and suggest more.[77]

The *Democratic Review* said little about Young America for the rest of 1852, turning its attention to Italy, Central Europe, Cuba, South America, and the strengths of the U.S. Navy, in apparent preparation for a newly aggressive American foreign policy. Meanwhile, Douglas continued to deny any connection to Young America. Months after the election, in a Senate debate he suggested that Lewis Cass was making just such an accusation. Cass denied it and, after some sparring, offered: "If from this time the honorable gentleman will call himself Young America, I will allow myself to be called the Old Fogy." Douglas declined, doubtless still wounded by his close association with the phrase during the election: "The penalty is too great for the privilege conferred."[78] The phrase had moved beyond the grasp of the *Democratic Review*.

A powerful and suggestive slogan, "Young America" came to mean different things to all who used it. Several New York newspapers created their own definitions. The *Herald*'s meditation, "State of the Parties— Old Fogydom and Young America—The Wants of the New Age," insisted that "Harum scarum youngsters such as Mike Walsh . . . Saunders [sic], and Douglas" had no monopoly on new ideas or Young America; rather, it was "the elastic, vigorous, active, progressive spirit of the American people, which looks forward . . . and goes onward with the progress of the age." The *New York Times* made Young America the emblem of an impulse that justified casting aside the original American inhabitants: "the population found here did not contribute to the general partnership of mankind their equal proportion of knowledge, industry, or useful capacity." An opposition to progress, then, was primitive. "Some there are who typify the aborigines, with their eyes always fixed upon the past . . . constantly feeding regret with the memory of things that will not return again." Young America's "true characteristics" were revealed in "the progressive sentiment of the people and the age. . . . Enterprising in design, energetic in action."[79] Although they celebrated an abstract Young America, the newspapers expressed growing skepticism about political acts by actual young people.

When young men organized for purposes the papers did not appreciate, the phrase could be used to ridicule their efforts. The *Herald* offered this derisive headline: "The Pronunciamento of Young Africa Against Old Africa." The story described a statement of African-American New Yorkers opposed to the governor's call for blacks to be removed to Africa. The "Young" appellation was never explained, although it was certainly accurate. The authors were the same men who had led the black young men's political associations a decade earlier. They were still in their early thirties, but no mention of their age or previous history appeared.[80] For more mainstream members of societies, the papers were slightly more understanding.

We have already noted the *Tribune*'s negative response to the young men's committee formed in 1849 to support the Hungarian revolution.

The *New York Herald* had agreed that "windy addresses . . . and frothy speeches delivered by old broken-down party hacks, or aspiring youths, fresh from some debating club in University Place or the Bowery," would not be of much help. The *New York Times* gave a similar, if more receptive, response when a group of young men in 1852 formed a group to support the presidential candidacy of Daniel Webster. "The young, fresh from colleges, academies, or schools, have been accustomed to declaim his sonorous and freighted sentences." These young men, "less accustomed to travel the cart-ruts of party . . . with noble generosity, seek out the highest models." The *New York Tribune* dismissed the group: "the persons present were by no means remarkable for juvenile appearance and did not seem to differ from the usual middle-aged class which forms such meetings."[81] There was no mention of Young America or the existing young men's organizations. Young men in the city no longer represented a recognized force; they were simply aspiring persons linked to a preparatory institution, either college or the working-class streets. Significantly, several of the original Young America manifestos of the 1840s had been delivered to college societies by recent alumni.

It is difficult to tell how young men themselves reacted to the rise of Young America in politics. The congressmen who debated the question were young, but they did not call attention to that fact. The meetings of young men's groups did not often invoke the magical phrase. That the concept resonated with some young people is suggested by an address in 1852 to a group at Marshall College in Pennsylvania. Entitled "Young Americanism," the speech recognized young men "attaining an unusual prominence . . . in literature, science, philosophy and art," as well as in politics. It noted that "much account was made a few years ago of Young Men's Conventions." The phrase "Young Americanism" denoted "an open warfare, a proclaimed battle against old principles in politics; and a zealous devotion to that which is new, and fast, and dauntless." The author saluted the *Democratic Review* and quoted liberally from its pages. This movement, however, was not unique; Young America was "but an imitation and namesake of the burly young giant who for some years has been shaking Europe to its centre." Youth, not nationality, represented the unifying theme. The author offered an alternative— " 'Young Humanity' "—and asserted "that it has started a wave upon the surface of history." The speech warned that America would rise to its potential only "if we are true to the principles of our fathers and of history. . . . But if we are untrue to the past . . . the star of our hopes must go down in darkness and in blood."[82]

These familiar themes in the rhetoric of young men's organizations appeared as a counterweight to a seemingly dominant ideal. Youth had become firmly associated with the assault on the past. After the election, Young America persisted. As the 1850s drew to a close, the phrase became less associated with a specific group and more of an umbrella concept available to all.

Young America for All

Scholars have long associated manifest destiny with Young America. In 1845, one reference to the United States' continental intentions said, "it is Young America, awakened to a sense of her own intellectual greatness. . . . It demands the immediate annexation of Texas at any and every hazard. It will plant its right foot upon the northern verge of Oregon and its left upon the Atlantic crag."[83] John L. O'Sullivan, the creator of the phrase "manifest destiny" in 1845, knew the literary and political Young Americans, but it was not until 1852 that the *Democratic Review* edited by George Sanders made expansion and foreign intervention synonymous with the phrase. After the election Sanders wrote that he would "gladly pass the reins into the hands of Frank Pierce, satisfied that young America . . . will find in him" a worthy leader. He and his cohorts received appointments to embassies around Europe, while O'Sullivan and others organized groups to annex Cuba. The filibusters even created a new group called, characteristically, Young Cuba.[84] While the expansionists sought to extend Young America throughout the world, others took the ideology of literary and political Young America to defend the nation from a supposed threat from beyond its shores.

Nativist political parties arose at the same time as literary and political Young America. The Know-Nothing movement came to a brief period of dominance during the politically chaotic mid-1850s. Although the surface issues did not seem related, nativists and Young Americans shared certain core beliefs. Early nativist parties in the 1830s and 1840s regularly based their appeals for ridding the political arena of Catholics, immigrants, and others on the responsibility to maintain the pure ideals of the founders. A series of nativist newspapers all had the title *Spirit of '76*. Like young men's political and reform organizations, the nativists tried to combine a defense of the past with a progressive vision. The campaign of the literary Young Americans to free authors from the oppressive control of foreign influence meshed comfortably with nativist ideas; thus the newspaper of the Order of United Americans included appeals for "purely national," homegrown literature, theater, and art. The belief in cultural unification and in the complete assimilation of immigrants was also shared by antislavery activists and the new Republican party.[85] It is not entirely surprising that "Young America" soon became a key symbol in the Know-Nothing movement of the mid-1850s and that some Young Americans became active in nativist causes.

In 1854 and 1855 sheet music illustrations, cartoons, and other works of popular culture presented a character who became known as "Young America" or "Uncle Sam's Youngest Son." These images depicted a pure American defending the nation against foreign invaders. This new Young America continued the traditional themes of youth as defender of the nation from invasion and as obedient son of the founding fathers. The Know-Nothing party itself, originally the Order of the Star Spangled Banner, was also known as the "Order of the Sons of the Sires of '76." In a scene from an allegorical drama entitled *Young America's Dream*, a character said, "we will join brothers, join as did our fathers bold. . . . We'll protect institutions for which our sires bled." In stage directions, a shield bearing the symbol of a nativist organization "arises from the waters." A tract, *The Sons of the Sires*, concluded: "May no enemy at home or from afar ever gain power to undo the work of our Fathers; and may their sons never want hearts to love, and arms to defend the altars of this nation."[86] Expansionist Young America also had certain affinities with the nativist program. There had always been an implicit notion of American—and by association white, Anglo-Saxon—superiority in the demand that the United States assist foreign revolutions and annex nearby territories such as Cuba.[87] The literary Young Americans also plunged into political nativism.

Joel Tyler Headley, who had lectured the American Art-Union on the "strange infatuation about foreign arts and artists, and foreign literature," was a charter member of the literary Young America circle. His distaste for foreign involvement in art and literature carried over to a fear of immigrants and an opposition to naturalization. In 1855 he was elected New York's secretary of state on the Know-Nothing ticket after a brief time as a nativist party state legislator.[88]

Another artistic nationalist who made the odyssey to literary and political Young Americanism and then to nativism was C. Edwards Lester. He had been noticed early as a well-meaning, but incompetent, literary nationalist in Mathews's and Duyckinck's *Arcturus:* "American literature has outlived its early poverty. . . . When Joel Barlow was thought an epic poet, Mr. Lester might have passed for a patriotic tourist." After the publication of his book *The Artist, The Merchant and the Statesman,* he was a recognized champion of American artistic nationalism. He also associated with the New York literary Young Americans. Margaret Fuller thought it appropriate to solicit his help during her campaign to help the exile Harro Harring. Lester's campaign biography for Pierce did not win him a government post; he took revenge in a series of reports for the *Times* of London.[89]

The *New York Tribune* identified Lester as the author of *Stanhope Burleigh,* a novel published anonymously in 1855 that accused leading New York politicians of conspiring with the Catholic bishop of New York in support of a Jesuit plot to take control of the United States. The *Tribune* reported that it had been offered the same material by Lester several years previously. The novel is now believed to have been written by Lester's wife, but Lester's involvement in the Know-Nothing movement seems likely as well.[90] Not only minor satellites in literary nationalism's orbit became involved in nativism. The foremost Young American also entered the fray.

The headline in the *New York Herald* showed distaste for the proceedings and also demonstrated that old labels died hard:

> Another Know Nothing Manifestation
> Mutual Admiration Humbug Meeting

The use of the phrase "Mutual Admiration" linked the meeting's organizer, Cornelius Mathews, to his literary past. While a national Know-Nothing convention met secretly in Philadelphia, Mathews had called for a public meeting in New York City to express true American sentiment free from the Know-Nothings' mysteries and ritual. He read a lengthy statement, noting that "Americans should be paramount, filling all the offices of honor." He called for an end to the "popular use" of foreign languages, and favored the mandatory use of English in all public documents and in state-supported education. Of course he insisted on "the necessity of cultivating a national literature." He continued in terms consistent with his career, but curious for a nativist:

> Though we speak the English tongue alone, and are clothed from head to foot in the most unmistakable fabrics of American make, we are not therefore Americans. This is at best a negative nationality. . . . It extirpates, but it substitutes nothing. It condemns foreigners but it does not create Americans. . . . While we are exhausting our strength to guard the door . . . we should beware. . . . It is what we think, what we feel, what we aspire to— not what we eat, drink or clothe ourselves withal—that makes us a nation.

The *Herald* sneered that Mathews's statement was "purporting to be a declaration of National American principle"; to them it was "an essay of a gentleman addicted to literature, we do not consider its publication by us at all necessary. It sounds bogus." Mathews's reputation for self-promotion haunted him, "the whole thing being got up to give prominence to some little men," the *Herald* added in an editorial.[91]

Mathews appears a sad, almost pathetic figure in 1855, clinging to the belief that American nationality could arrive only through the use of literature to bind all Americans together, and feeling the need to go before the only group that would still give him an audience. Despite its popularity with nativists, the language of Young America did not appear in Mathews's address (or the excerpts available in local newspapers). Perhaps he had something else in mind.

Not all Young Americans embraced the nativists or attempted to create a special rapprochement. Some tried to continue the literary mission. *Putnam's Magazine,* founded by Parke Godwin, George W. Curtis, and Charles F. Briggs, has been described as Young America without Cornelius Mathews. Godwin had been associating himself with causes calling themselves Young America since he proposed founding a journal of that name in the early 1840s. With *Putnam's,* the editors wrote that their contributors to a unique American literature "would come from Young America, whose name had not yet been announced on Magazine covers."[92]

These authors imagined Young America as a pure idea that could be powerfully misused. Godwin described an advocate of foreign intervention as "one of the rabidest disciples of Young America." George Curtis gave a lecture in 1854 called "Gold and Gilt in Young America," in which he argued, "What is popularly called 'Young America' . . . reads Burke on the French Revolution and seeing the tide of immigrants here, fears for the assimilation." This was a "gilt counterfeit." The real, the "Golden Young America," was more ephemeral: "Shakespeare uses the word 'man' to express all the best qualities of a man, and so patriotism should intend by 'Young America' all the best qualities of American spirit. . . . self reliance and reverence." *Putnam's* also wrote strong articles opposing the Know-Nothings.[93] Any attempt to define a "true" Young America by the mid-1850s, though, was buried by all the other uses of the phrase.

What a concise and handy label for international observers! To *London Times* writers, it meant a pushy child who got on a steamship to Saint Louis by himself or who accosted the president and asked him to repair his hatband. Young England or Young Italy are "but the bright hallucinations of old or middle age. There is only one really new nationality in the world. It is Young America." These ruminations in 1858 were inspired by a Fourth of July celebration in London where a visiting American had spoken in the strongest expansionist terms.[94] That speaker, the adventurer and entrepreneur George F. Train, took Young America as an identity and a pen name. "Each age improves upon that which went before. The 'Young American' of our time may well astonish his grandfather," he wrote in a book called *Young America in Wall-Street*. Train published a series of books all using the phrase "Young America" in the title. He boiled down the rhetoric of the previous decade into a statement about progress. "Young America is the vanguard of change— the coming age. His watchword is Reform." On progress and technology: "Steam, gas, and electricity are the 'Liberty, Equality, and Fraternity' that mark the Anglo-American mind." There was little specificity; it was almost a civil religion: "Young America considers the Declaration of Independence, the Constitution, Washington's farewell address, Yankee Doodle, and the Bible, divine institutions. Life, liberty, and happiness are the words of his Book of Life."[95] This was the Young America that Abraham Lincoln said everyone knew.

As Young America was diffused through the new information media, the catchphrase's implications seemed more appropriately applied to individuals. In an article in the *Harper's* "Editor's Table" of January 1860, Young America and a young man were synonymous. "Our Young America is . . . not wholly young; and in spite of his frequent disposition to set up for himself, he has never been able to conceal the fact that he comes of ancient parentage, and is not wholly self-existent." In tones that resemble a twentieth-century plea for a juvenile delinquent, *Harper's* said that there was good in this sometimes rambunctious boy. Young America "is at times a most affectionate son; and in spite of his efforts to talk himself into a false manliness, that affects independence at the cost of filial reverence, he is by no means a hard-hearted or ill-mannered youth."[96]

Harper's opposed those "constantly trying to abolish history, and inaugurate the new times over the annihilation of the old." The magazine could not "agree with the flaming patriots who think that we can do without the old world's literature, arts, and religion, and that we are to make every thing anew for ourselves," an especially ironic comment considering *Harper's* early role as a pirate of European works. Still, there were unique American lessons to be learned, and the magazine asked,

"Young America, take off your hat and sit down a while, if you can curb your impatient nerves." Young America must remember that the fathers worked hard; "many a young prodigal squanders like water the costly earnings of his father's sweat, and even of his father's blood."

National problems had been domesticated. The dilemmas faced by the young were problems of abundance, of a youth emerging from school unprepared for the real world: "It may not be easy . . . to find employment for every school-boy that shall allow him kid-gloves, broadcloth, and champagne." But if he would only work hard and remember old-fashioned virtues, all would be well: "Our Manifest Destiny man is not a filibuster, nor an anarchist, but a far-seeing, firm-minded, large-hearted thinker and worker, carrying intelligence, law, liberty, and religion wherever he goes."

Thus Young America's adherence to older values in support of advancement had been transformed into a sappy nostalgia, the many varieties of Young America homogenized into the platitudes of self-made success stories. The Civil War seared a rough finish onto the sentimental surface. After the war, the elements in Young America were not forgotten; as years passed they were recombined, variously recovered, and continue to form the basis for some of our modern ideas about youth and generational responsibility. That theme of responsibility and consciousness of the past has remained.

The Discourse of Youth and Generations Since 1860: A Sketch

"In the baptism of fire and blood through which our politics are passing to their purification, who can fitly estimate our indebtedness to the young men who are now making American history the history of so much ardent patriotism and heroic achievement," asked an 1865 *Atlantic* article titled "Young Men in History." Some historians suggest the Civil War was, in part, a struggle to protect the legacy of the Revolution; others argue it "released Americans from merely preservative filio-piety." By now, we have ample evidence that the impulse to remember and honor the fathers was much more complex than "mere" preservation. The war certainly ruptured ideas about youth and generations, as it did most other aspects of national life. It seemed to close the door on those earlier traditions. Oliver Wendell Holmes saw the chasm the war caused along with a solidarity formed in the struggle for union: "the generation that carried on the war has been set apart by its experience. Through our great good fortune, in our youth our hearts were touched with fire." The Civil War replaced the nation's founding as the focal point for remembrance. Rather than establishing themselves as new founders, however, young veterans "had become a generation that was committed to working in useful ways in a dynamic activist society," said the historian George Fredrickson. The intellectuals he chronicled returned from war committed to "a life of service" in occupations that demanded "professional skills and professional objectives."[1] In this climate, demands made on youth were fundamentally transformed.

Although the war represented an essential break with the past, and social observers applied the language of generations to new events and models, older concepts persisted, albeit in weaker forms. The article in the *Atlantic* argued that young men in war "proved themselves worthy of the great continent they inhabit by showing themselves capable of upholding" ideals of the revolutionary era. The author retained the belief that "forces which propel society in the direction of improvement . . . are the forces and ideas of youth." Young America, meanwhile, became associated only with aspects of its final incarnation. "He is slangy, unprincipled, selfish and of bad form all together. . . . He is just suited to his own country," said an 1872 English magazine article. "Young America" became a title for juvenile publications. Its older meanings were lost. The "old fogy" occasionally made an appearance. Ironically, in a conservative era known less for ideology than expediency, he was someone who lacked beliefs: "I call that politician an old fogy who believes more in his party than in the principles which should inspire his party." Significantly, the "antidote" for the old fogy was not to replace him, but to involve all those without ideals "in lofty commerce with the True, the Beautiful, and the Good."[2]

Young people's participation in public life through age-defined organizations faded to virtual nonexistence. In 1892, the *Christian Union*, a self-described "Family Paper," asked leaders of the two major political parties to discuss "The Duty of Young Men in Politics." The Republican leader asserted that youth had always been crucial. He celebrated the abolitionists as *young* activists and identified several people discussed in earlier chapters—Parke Godwin, George W. Curtis, William Seward, and Salmon Chase—as young men active in the party's founding in the 1850s. Seward and Chase *had* been active in young men's organizations, but decades before; Godwin and Curtis were barely young in the 1850s by antebellum standards.[3]

To a party of professional politicians that tended to elect older people, these founding heroes merged to form a generalized "youth" who represented enthusiasm, idealism, and moral fervor. The party leader seemed unconcerned that his own time's political life existed in diminished circumstances: "Young men were prominent workers in the early days of our political history because the questions that were then up for discussion were of more importance, at least from the ethical point of view." In the 1890s, "young men generally do not take as much interest in politics . . . because the questions at issue are not of a moral nature." Institutions had changed as well; "the platform, and not the magazine or the newspaper, was . . . the great educator" when young men had been more active. Neither party leader urged young men to run for elective office. "Why should a young man make office-getting his goal in politics," asked the Democratic spokesman. "Let young men keep their ideals, keep clean . . . and forge ahead." He urged them not to "make politics a trade; follow it as a way of justifying existence in a happy and free republic."[4] Except as dimly recalled symbols, the young men's organizations of the antebellum era and the rhetorical role of the young as heirs to the founders' vision had no place in Gilded Age politics.

By century's end, young people had few chances to participate in public. Since the 1840s, the lives of youth had grown increasingly regulated and routinized in state-run and adult-led institutions. Age-grading in education compressed the time of schooling and the years in which it occurred. While antebellum young people might drift in and out of school or even finish college at a "precocious" age, by the turn of the century a middle-class young person participated in school or in an organization such as the YMCA. Founded in the 1850s, the Y was related to the young men's self-help and educational associations in many cities; though its membership was young, it gave little attention to that fact.[5]

The discourse of youth and generations, developed and refined by young men as they identified a place for themselves in the public world of affairs, now emerged as part of a peer culture defined by the years spent in high school or college. Students at a Massachusetts high school at the turn of the century had a "romanticized" and "idealized" view of Civil War participants, "who appeared as distant figures in legendary times," a dramatic departure from the central presence of the founding fathers in the rhetoric of antebellum young men's groups. The students "invoked the achievements of the Civil War generation to show how history had prepared the way for the new generation they were destined to lead. . . . The generation coming of age . . . would guide a wholly united nation." Apparently they looked to the past for reassurance rather than as historical support for new activity. High school became almost universal in the twentieth century, serving as an important link in the maintenance of middle-class status.[6]

The concept of adolescence emerged in this age-graded environment; educators and social scientists identified a specific period in life as one of "storm and stress" that would be followed by appropriate socialization in a conformist adult world. Youth became associated with ideas about nature, and professional educators and new organizations emerged to promote young people's enjoyment of their "natural" environment. In cities, youth and adolescence took on new significance as schooling became a crucial part of the development of both Yankee and immigrant youth's future and their relationship to the family economy.[7] The idea of generations and generational responsibility did not fade away; in fact, the most influential sociological ideas about generations emerged in the first part of the twentieth century.[8] Despite youth's path to adulthood more firmly secured in schools, elders still expressed muted concern about their children's future. When youth spoke in its own defense, however, it introduced psychological notions of care and understanding to intergenerational relations.

"A Letter to the Rising Generation" in a 1911 *Atlantic* issue worried that new educational schemes, Sunday color newspaper sections, and "continuous vaudeville and . . . moving-picture shows" had changed the young. "I think the long generations of your fathers hold their breath to see if you do less with certainty"—the rationalism that came with psychology—"than they have done with faith," wrote Cornelia A. P. Comer. Columbia undergraduate Randolph Bourne responded: "The two generations misunderstand each other as they never did before." He blamed his elders: "Pastors, teachers, and parents flutter aimlessly about with their ready-made formulas . . . I doubt if any generation was ever thrown quite so completely on its own resources as ours is." Like the Gilded Age politicos and his worried, older opponent, Bourne also recognized the significance of new media in the diffusion of ideas to young people, but believed the flood of information justified youth's disenchantment with tradition: "In an age of newspapers, free libraries, and cheap magazines, we necessarily get a broader horizon than the passing generation had. . . . We cannot be blamed for acquiring a suspicion of ideals which, however powerful their appeal once was, seem singularly impotent now."[9]

A young life led in age-graded schools and peer communities produced the dilemma that Emerson raised in the 1840s, the "gulf between" a person's "education and his work." Jane Addams called it the "snare of preparation," an increasing alienation of youth from the "real" world outside school. As Bourne described it, "We have an eagerness to understand the world in which we live that amounts almost to a passion. We want to get behind the scenes, to see how the machinery of the world actually works. An unpleasantly large proportion of our energy is now drained off in fighting the fetishes which you of the elder generation have passed along to us." He called on the older generation to help the younger or "at least to strive to understand just what those aspirations and endeavors are."[10]

Bourne and other radical intellectuals continued to demand a signifi-

cant social role for youth. Van Wyck Brooks recalled the "Young" movements in Europe, a "revolutionary protest against whatever incubus of
crabbed age, paralysis, tyranny, stupidity . . . commercialism, lay most
heavily upon the people's life." America, Brooks said, had no such past.
"Who does not remember 'Young America,' " he asked, "a touchstone of
American juvenility." Brooks's Young America "blossomed out originally
on the covers of innumerable magazines and storybooks. . . . He was the
typical farmer's boy of our national epos, who sought adventure and
found success." This was the Young America of the postbellum era.
When Brooks put his essay "Young America" into a book, he dropped
the references to the nineteenth century but retained Bourne's sentiment
that "we of the younger generation . . . find ourselves in a grave predica-
ment. For having, unlike Europeans of any class, no fund of spiritual
experience in our blood . . . we are all but incapable of coordinating
ourselves in a free world." Literary nationalists of the past became figures
best understood in the context of school: "Since the day of Emerson's
address on 'The American Scholar' the whole of American literature
has had the semblance of one vast, all-embracing baccalaureate sermon,
addressed to the private virtues of young men." In this stifling environment of intensive preparation, "the highest ambition of Young America
is to be . . . the owner of a shoe factory." [11]

Bourne might make a passing reference to the younger generation's
"gigantic task of putting into practice its ideals and revolutionary points
of view as wholeheartedly and successfully as our great-grandfathers
applied theirs," but the Young Intellectuals' essential message was their
separation from both parents and past. Even as they asserted their alienation, however, they insisted that their identity as young people gave
them special responsibilities for change, even if that transformation was
on personal and emotional rather than national or political levels. They
thus reflected older forms of thinking about youth and generations.
Bourne, Brooks, and their colleagues left perhaps their most enduring
legacy to youth by linking the personal with the political. In doing so, as
Christopher Lasch has noted, they "set a pattern which has been followed
with variations only of detail by each subsequent generation of youthful
rebels" for most of the twentieth century. [12]

Journalists, psychological and educational experts, and creative artists
perfected the culturewide concern with youth during the 1920s. Students
and young professionals completed the picture of a seemingly autonomous peer society. "A tangle of work and play, career preparation, and
mating games, the practice of youth became . . . a fully structured, di-

rected, and effective social act," said historian Paula Fass. In the years after the twenties an author might lament, as Pearl Buck did in 1935, "Where Are the Young Rebels," and attribute the passivity of youth to the fact that they were "shielded, praised, coaxed, indulged. . . . Then suddenly, heartlessly, cruelly, we push them out of this careless sunshine into life as it is." In fact, some young college students became immersed in political activity, particularly in communist and other radical left organizations; their significance has only recently been recognized.[13]

Once twenties youth had been named the Lost Generation, magazines made occasional stabs at calling later youth cohorts a "generation." The terms of the argument were readily accepted, though often on scant evidence: "It's an old story—the conflict of the older and younger generations. . . . Old story or new story: the question is what are you going to do about it?" asked a 1940 article in *Parents' Magazine*, "When Youth Goes Radical." The radicalism was not political; it involved the need for attention and penchant for thrill-seeking that had become associated with adolescence. This period of life had speeded up, but "there is nothing at the other end of the line to accelerate their emergence from adolescence to adult life, and adolescence therefore tends to be prolonged indefinitely." The magazine's readers, increasingly expert in their role as parents, learned that "it is your job to fill this gap, to help your offspring through adolescence by taking them as early as possible . . . into the everyday, workaday world."[14]

By the middle of the century, parent-youth conflict was a recognized sociological concept resulting "from the interaction of certain universals of the parent-child relation and certain variables the nature of which are peculiar to modern culture." "Rapid social change," Kingsley Davis explained, had "given the offspring a different social context from that which the parent acquired."[15] Experts diminished youth's relation to the nation and elevated individual relations within specific families. Conflict became an accepted norm of behavior; a stage or phase that would eventually pass with the arrival of adulthood.

World War II mobilized a nation and its youth against the Axis, but after the war, tendencies of the prewar period remained. A student "born too late to fight" was dubbed part of a "lost generation," who "asks only for the chance to belong." *Time* concluded in 1951 that the "most startling fact about the younger generation is its silence. . . . It does not issue manifestoes, make speeches, or carry posters," as had the radical students of the 1930s who were now, curiously, remembered with nostalgia. The pace of mass-media diagnosis and labeling accelerated.[16]

Time's "younger generation" of 1951 had been born between 1923 and 1933. A significant postwar "generation" composed of that cohort announced itself in the *New York Times Magazine:* "this generation . . . lacks that eloquent air of bereavement" and disillusionment of the post–World War I Lost Generation, said the writer John Clellon Holmes. He offered a label attributed to his friend "John Kerouac": "beat generation." Like earlier twentieth-century youth, the beat generation was said to search for "a feeling of somewhereness. . . . The failure of most orthodox moral and social concepts to reflect fully the life they have known. . . . is what is responsible for this generation's reluctance to discuss itself as a group."[17] The media-generated beat craze of the mid-1950s was a dry run for the unrelenting national attention fixed on Americans born after World War II.

The baby boom generation's life and conflicts fill shelves of libraries and bookstores. In the 1950s, movies, books, and other popular media began to dramatize the life of teenagers and linked them to the word *generation.* More significantly, the baby boomers grew up at the same time social scientists irrevocably enshrined youth as the stage of psychological life defined by a quest for identity and understanding. Peer groups in schools and delinquent gangs on street corners became identified as youth "cultures" or subcultures.[18] This splitting into subgroups further removed youth from any national responsibilities. A few prescient sociologists were suggesting by the end of the decade that youth felt a growing sense of contradiction between their socialization and uniquely youthful ideals.[19] As years passed, all attention fell on the massive cohort born after the war that began entering the universities.

It came as a great surprise to most Americans when journalists began identifying young people as an "Explosive Generation." *Look* magazine devoted its January 1961 edition to the problems of youth. One article surveyed youth uprisings around the world and said, "Young Americans want the fruit of material prosperity. They also want something more. . . . They fear, not change, but stagnation." The contrast between material prosperity and a personal quest for identity typified the first major statement by the student new left:

> We are people of this generation bred in at least modest comfort, housed now in universities, looking uncomfortably to the world we inherit.

The Port Huron Statement of Students for a Democratic Society (SDS), released in 1962, titled its introduction "Agenda for a Generation." The students felt moved to speak "by the sense that we may be the last

generation in the experiment with living." The potential for nuclear annihilation injected an immediacy in youth's sense of responsibility for national ideals, but also fed the "paradox" they saw: "we ourselves are
imbued with urgency, yet the message of our society is that there is
no viable alternative to the present." The American tradition that *they*
imagined seemed barren: "Unlike youth in other countries we are used
to moral leadership being exercised and moral dimensions being clarified
by our elders. But today, for us, not even the liberal and socialist preach-
ments of the past seem adequate to the forms of the present." Technology
meant more than destruction; it signified "depersonalization that reduces
human beings to the status of things." Youthful energies, clearly marked
as male, were threatened by the university's potential for "emasculation
of what creative spirit there is in the individual." [20]

The SDS concluded its detailed catalogue of national problems: "A
new left must consist of younger people who mature in the post-war
world." [21] The statement never explained why this was self-evident.
Youth was synonymous with the "new"; hence, a new left had to be
young. Besides, youth seemed the only ones who insisted that things
needed to change. Heirs to nothing that they would acknowledge, they
preserved the notion that youth had the primary responsibility for saving
the nation from itself.

In a sharp departure from the nineteenth century, white activists drew
powerful inspiration from African-American youth. Throughout the
twentieth century, black organizations had included youth auxiliaries;
students at historically black universities initiated the sit-in movement.
It was at a conference of youth leaders that the Student Nonviolent
Coordinating Committee (SNCC)was formed. White organizations often
followed the SNCC's lead; ironically, when the mainstream media talked
about "youth" they focused primarily on middle-class white people.
Young people from other races usually appeared as elements in another
story of the 1960s, the saga of urban unrest. Memoirs such as Claude
Brown's *Manchild in the Promised Land* and Piri Thomas's *Down These
Mean Streets* provided evidence for social commentators who saw the
ghetto as the essential fact of life for urban youth. [22]

In 1966 *Look* called youth "the Open Generation" and asked: "Who
listens to the 25 million young Americans straining to take over? Too
few adults; it is time all did. . . . This generation is Open. . . . pushes out
for discovery everywhere. It pursues self-identity." While youth became
an increasingly national concern, the connection with psychological
strivings continued. When the phrase "generation gap" first appeared in

the *Reader's Guide to Periodical Literature,* readers were referred to the subject heading "youth-adult relationship." The gap, with its allusive connection to missile and credibility gaps, became the shorthand in the mid-1960s to describe alienation between parents and their children. The dilemmas of affluence, the rise of new technologies, and the search for personal identity hovered in the center of this social problem.[23]

The naming and identifying of a generation seemed an integral part of competition between various magazines; each one had to have its own name for youth and to associate fashions and consumption with their growing "revolt." Advertisers recognized this substantial new market. The appeal to the "Pepsi Generation" began in 1964.[24] Television and mass paperback publishing, meanwhile, permitted the almost instantaneous chronicling of the "generation" by its own members. Participant accounts of the civil rights movement, the escalation of the Vietnam War, and the conflict on college campuses all contributed to the sense that an entire generation was indeed in revolt. Thoughtful works of journalism still had sensational titles such as *We Are the People Our Parents Warned Us Against* and *Don't Shoot — We Are Your Children!* The sea of commentary washed away distinctions between careful appraisals and lockstep trend-followers; all connected national and family politics, and made it seem quite plausible that age groups were at war.[25]

Even as contemporary authors reported that a "new generation of radicals has been spawned from the chrome womb of affluent America," they began to look for historical parallels. The historian Howard Zinn suggested that "for the first time in our history a major social movement . . . is being led by youngsters." Nonetheless, he subtitled his study of the Student Nonviolent Coordinating Committee "The New Abolitionists" and compared the students to their predecessors. The American Revolution became a potent historical model. SDS president Carl Oglesby sounded like a young men's organization speaker from the 1830s when he asked what would happen if Thomas Jefferson and Thomas Paine "could sit down now for a chat with President Johnson and McGeorge Bundy" about U.S. policy in Vietnam. "Our dead revolutionaries would soon wonder why their country was fighting against what appeared to be a revolution." When Vietnam War protesters were called before the House Committee on Un-American Activities, one witness, Jerry Rubin, appeared wearing a Revolutionary War uniform. A few years later he explained he had used "the *language* of the American Revolution." Abbie Hoffman, who less deservedly than Rubin became solely associated with opportunistic media-driven antics, charged that the nation's leaders had "destroyed what I consider to be the destiny of this country and the aims of the founding fathers of the revolution, the American Revolution."[26] The claim of allegiance to the founding fathers linked SDS intellectual and Yippie strolling player to the language of youth and generations that had developed from 1630 to the 1850s.

It would take another full-length study to investigate the implications of these transformations in the twentieth century. It is interesting to observe that as members of the "sixties generation" grow older they continue to chronicle themselves and make claims for their generation's enduring significance. Optimists promised "The Second Coming of the Sixties Generation," the subtitle of a book that recalled "the 'war of values' most of us fought at home—against our parents, our government, our whole cultural heritage," and provided anecdotal evidence suggesting that an entire generation shared these characteristics and would spread this consciousness throughout society in years to come. Others argued that it had been a "Destructive Generation" that had perverted all who had lived through it except those few able to reject its vaguely described tenets.[27]

The *Utne Reader,* a digest self-consciously chronicling the lives of the baby boomers, tried to recognize the fact of aging but still asserted that its readers retained supposedly universally held youthful ideals. A special section in one issue titled "What's to Worry about Growing Older?" suggested that "the 'youth' generation is not aging gracefully," but offered the possibility of satisfaction and "opportunity" in "starting over at midlife." Several issues later, another special section reported that "The Baby Boom Yearns to Settle Down." The *Utne Reader's* topics— environmentalism, spirituality, mild skepticism about technology and U.S. foreign adventures—were familiar 1960s "youth" issues (with an emphasis on concerns of the personal development tradition). Articles about the magazine repeated the message: baby boomers had grown up and become successful. Founding editor Eric Utne was described by *People* magazine as "an archetype of the baby boom generation" who had "tried everything from antiwar protests to managing a natural foods warehouse to studying Eastern philosophy and macrobiotics." In the memory of the mainstream press the decade had simply been a smorgasbord of possible life choices to be sampled and discarded before moving on to a safer adulthood.[28]

Contemporary youth continue to provoke widespread puzzlement in social observers. Cultural critics treat 1960s protest as a normative standard for assessing the young, even though the particular context and content of that activism had in fact been exceptional. Increasingly, though, youth became important less for any particular actions than as a useful symbol for journalists charting social trends. This illuminates a recurring dilemma in American culture: the young have proclaimed their unique place in national life only infrequently, but their observers remain on constant alert to pronounce and define their significance.[29] And thus we return to Generation X.

The craze gained a theoretical apparatus at the same time it got its name. A book entitled *Generations* appeared in 1991 promising a complete generational history of America. The authors argued they had identified "a recurring dynamic of generational behavior" in eighteen distinct generations from the Puritans to the twenty-first century. In a "Theory of Generations" they noted that generations had long been used in understanding history but argued that "the first Westerners to attach a modern significance to generations were the propagandists supporting the French Revolution in the 1780s and 1790s." The key phrase is "modern significance." The authors simply applied today's categories and conceptions to the nation's past. Historical sections offered brief, homogenized, capsule profiles of the kind popular in newspapers such as *USA Today* to describe each generation's "peer personality." In the "Glorious Generation" (born 1648 to 1673) "energetic young men began elbowing aside their seniors," while in the "Enlightenment Generation" (born 1674 to 1700) those coming of age made "tepid isolated gestures" that "amounted to the closest the Enlighteners ever came" to what in the authors' view must have been an all but inevitable "generational rebellion."[30] The problem is not that the many inaccuracies and inconsistencies in this account could be resolved and the "true" generations in the past discovered by adjusting the chronology. Rather, the search for recurring cycles leads the authors away from the transformations in the discourse of generations that stand at the foundation of all this talk.

The authors of *Generations* believed they had the key to understanding the current scene and made a bid for catchphrase supremacy with a sequel that focused on the "13th Generation." Their assertions prevailed, although their label lost out to the snappier-sounding Generation X. *Generations* still plays an important role as historical ballast in subsequent works; it is invoked, usually in an introduction, then tossed aside to make room for what young people are "really" like. Accounts of Generation X are intensely self-conscious. They simultaneously seek to analyze a social reality allegedly mirrored by the term *Generation X*, and to chart the concept's promotion and diffusion through media and advertising outlets. For all their canny cynicism, these works still assume a generation is a natural occurrence, like the Old Faithful geyser or Halley's Comet.[31] In the long run, Generation X may be most significant for specialists in market segmentation, the deeper meaning of the phrase buried in a social scientific definition connected to birth cohorts and lived social experience.[32] The continuing sense of unease about the young remains isolated from its rich historical context.

In articles keyed to the anniversary of the shootings at Kent State University, the *Utne Reader* surveyed "Life on Campus in the '90s." As aging sixties veterans looked at the generation following them, they concluded that "the overall political and social climate on college campuses have taken a giant step backward." The qualities of students and youth in the 1960s seemed so apparent there was no need for further explanation.[33] Yet the study of the campuses assumed that the succeeding generation would follow in its predecessors' footsteps. The irony was that by anticipating continuity from generation to generation, the sixties vets expected their successors to embrace an attitude exemplified by protest *against* tradition and the past. What are the sources for such a contradictory belief? This text is not particularly plain, nor is the excitement about Generation X. In both cases, as Cotton Mather suggested, "We our selves are the commentary." We continue to provide the commentary on this old American text, despite our claims that we have gone beyond it all.

NOTES

Introduction

1. Douglas Coupland, *Generation X* (New York: St. Martin's Press, 1991). The phrase was also the name of a 1970s British punk rock group and of a 1964 sociological study of British youth (Charles Hamblett and Jane Deverson, *Generation X* [London: Tandem Books, 1964]). The NEXIS database revealed more than two thousand articles using the phrase since 1991.

2. "Proceeding With Caution," *Time*, July 16, 1990, 62 (emphasis added). Also see "A Generation Adrift," *Boston Globe Magazine*, September 3, 1989; *New York Times*, June 28, 1990, A1, D21.

3. Amy Wu, "Media X'd Generation X," *Editor and Publisher*, January 14, 1995, 52. For a sampling of stories about the term's decline or skepticism about its accuracy: "The Short Shelf Life of Generation X," *New York Times*, June 18, 1995; Jeff Giles, "Generalizations X," *Newsweek*, June 6, 1994, 62–72; Martin Kihn, "The Gen X Hucksters," *New York*, August 29, 1994, 94–107; Heather R. McLeod, "The Sale of a Generation," *American Prospect*, no. 21 (Spring 1995): 93–99. *New Republic* editor Andrew Sullivan, quoted in the *Washington Post*, February 22, 1994, D3.

4. Library of Congress, on-line catalogue, SH94–3506: "Here are entered works on members of the generation born between 1965 and 1976."

5. Benedict Anderson, *Imagined Communities: Reflections on the Origin and Spread of Nationalism* (London: Verso, 1983), 28, 39, 37, 44, 49, quotation on 77–78.

6. J. G. A. Pocock, "The Concept of a Language and the *métier d'historien*: Some Considerations on Practice," in *The Languages of Political Theory in Early-Modern Europe*, ed. Anthony Pagden (Cambridge: Cambridge University Press, 1987), 21; James Tully, "The Pen Is a Mighty Sword: Quentin Skinner's Analysis of Politics," in *Meaning and Context: Quentin Skinner and His Critics* (Cam-

bridge: Polity Press, 1988), 9; also, see Quentin Skinner, "Meaning and Understanding in the History of Ideas," in Tully, *Meaning and Context*, 67.

7. The first sentences in this paragraph quote from, and are indebted to, Daniel Wickberg's introduction to "The Sense of Humor in American Culture, 1850–1960" (Ph.D. diss., Yale University, 1993), 4 and passim.

8. Leading examples in the extensive historical literature on youth and the family include Joseph Kett, *Rites of Passage: Adolescence in America, 1790 to the Present* (New York: Basic Books, 1977); John R. Gillis, *Youth and History*, expanded student ed. (New York: Academic Press, 1981); John Demos, "The Rise and Fall of Adolescence," in *Past, Present, and Personal* (New York: Oxford University Press, 1986); for a survey, see the articles in Joseph M. Hawes and N. Ray Hiner, eds., *American Childhood: A Research Guide and Historical Handbook* (Westport, CT: Greenwood Press, 1985).

9. Barbara A. Hanwalt, "Historical Descriptions and Prescriptions for Adolescence," Journal of Family History 17, 4 (1992): 344.

10. For two perspectives see Alan B. Spitzer, "The Historical Problem of Generations," *American Historical Review* 78 (December 1973): 1353–85, and Anthony Esler, *Generations in History: An Introduction to the Concept* (published by the author, 1982).

11. Thomas Bender, *Toward an Urban Vision* (Baltimore: Johns Hopkins University Press, 1975), viii. For a different perspective, note Michel Foucault's reconsideration of his study of madness: "We are not trying to find out who was mad at a particular period or in what his madness consisted." Foucault, *The Archaeology of Knowledge*, trans. A. M. Sheridan Smith (New York: Harper Torchbooks, 1972), 47–48.

12. Foucault, *Archaeology of Knowledge*, 45; Skinner, "Meaning and Understanding in the History of Ideas," 55.

13. Some of the literature on familial rhetoric includes: Edwin G. Burrows and Michael Wallace, "The American Revolution: The Ideology and Psychology of National Liberation," *Perspectives in American History* 6 (1972): 167–306; Jay Fliegelman, *Prodigals and Pilgrims: The American Revolution against Patriarchal Authority, 1750–1800* (New York: Cambridge University Press, 1982); Melvin Yazawa, *From Colonies to Commonwealth: Familial Ideology and the Beginnings of the American Republic* (Baltimore: Johns Hopkins University Press, 1985).

14. Emory Elliott, *Power and the Pulpit in Puritan New England* (Princeton: Princeton University Press, 1975); Steven Novak, *The Rights of Youth: American Colleges and Student Revolt, 1798–1815* (Cambridge, MA: Harvard University Press, 1977); Michael Kammen, *A Season of Youth: The American Revolution and the Historical Imagination* (New York: Alfred A. Knopf, 1978); George Forgie, *Patricide in the House Divided* (New York: W. W. Norton, 1979).

15. Forgie, *Patricide in the House Divided*, 50–53; Paul Nagel, *This Sacred Trust* (New York: Oxford University Press, 1971); Rush Welter, *The Mind of America, 1820–1860* (New York: Columbia University Press, 1975), 25–31; and Kammen, *Season of Youth*, 31–32, are only some of the authors who address this theme.

16. David Brion Davis discusses the dilemma in "Some Themes of Counter-Subversion: An Analysis of Anti-Masonic, Anti-Catholic, and Anti-Mormon Literature," in *From Homicide to Slavery* (New York: Oxford University Press, 1986), 140. John Higham's essay *From Boundlessness to Consolidation: The Transformation of American Culture 1848–1860* (Ann Arbor: William L. Clements Library, 1969, Indianapolis: Bobbs-Merrill Reprint) is an influential interpretive framework for discussions of this period; quotation on 17, see also 16–20, 26.

17. Charles Francis Adams, Jr., *Massachusetts: Its Historians and Its History* (1893; reprint Freeport, NY: Books for Libraries Press, 1971), 31, also see 12, 41; Edward C. Kirkland, "Charles Francis Adams, Jr.: The Making of an Historian," *Proceedings of the Massachusetts Historical Society* 75 (1963): 39–51. Fliegelman, *Prodigals and Pilgrims*, 169, 267; Joanna Bowen Gillespie, "Filiopietism as Citizenship, 1810 Letters from Martha Laurens Ramsay to David Ramsay Jr.," *Early American Literature* 29, 2 (1994): 143.

18. Forgie, *Patricide in the House Divided;* idem, "Father Past and Child Nation: The Romantic Imagination and the Origins of the American Civil War" (Ph.D. diss., Stanford University, 1972), 99, 102, 123–25, 153.

19. Forgie, *Patricide in the House Divided,* 90–91, 109–10, 104–5, 109, 190.

20. For one example, see Donald Yacovone, "Samuel Joseph May, Antebellum Reform and the Problems of Patricide," *Perspectives in American History,* new ser. 2 (1985): 99–124.

21. When I was completing final revisions of this book I became aware of a fascinating dissertation by Edward Widmer, "Young America: Democratic Cultural Nationalism in Antebellum New York" (Ph.D. diss., Harvard University, 1993), which deals with many of the themes and characters I discuss here in Chapter 5, We come to different conclusions.

22. Tully, "The Pen Is a Mighty Sword," 12–13.

23. The classic formulation was developed by Karl Mannheim, "The Problem of Generations" (1928), in *Essays on the Sociology of Knowledge* (New York: Oxford University Press, 1952). For a historical treatment see Robert Wohl, *The Generation of 1914* (Cambridge, MA: Harvard University Press, 1979).

1. Up and Doing

1. Cotton Mather, *Successive Generations: Remarks Upon the Changes of a Dying World, Made by One Generation Passing Off and Another Generation Coming on* (Boston: B. Green, 1715) [EAI #1765], 1 (emphasis in original). See the bibliography for a note on the abbreviation.

2. Ibid., 5, 10–11, 19.

3. Ibid., 32, 34–35, 36, 38–39.

4. Ernest Klein, *A Comprehensive Dictionary of the Hebrew Language for Readers of English* (Carta Jerusalem: University of Haifa, 1987), 1991; Francis Brown, ed., *A Hebrew and English Lexicon of the Old Testament* (Oxford: Clarendon Press, 1906; reissued with corrections, 1951), 189–90.

5. Graham S. Ogden, "The Interpretation of דּוֹר in Ecclesiastes 1.4," *Journal*

for the Study of the Old Testament 34 (February 1986): 92; P. R. Ackroyd, "The Meaning of the Hebrew דוֹר Considered," *Journal of Semitic Studies* 13 (Spring 1968): 9.

6. Thanks to David B. Davis for pointing out the implications of this double meaning.

7. Brevard S. Childs, *Memory and Tradition in Israel* (Naperville, IL: Alec R. Allenson, 1962), 55, 74, 83.

8. Mason I. Lowance, Jr., *The Language of Canaan* (Cambridge, MA: Harvard University Press, 1980), vii–viii, 4, 59–60. D. De Sola Pool, "Hebrew Learning among the Puritans of New England Prior to 1700," *Publications of the American Jewish Historical Society* 20 (1911): 78–82, emphasizes the significance of Puritan knowledge of Hebrew and the Puritans' association with a "Hebrew Old Testament spirit."

9. See, for example, Thomas Thacher's reprinting in 1677 of a sermon given by John Wilson twelve years earlier; the sermon attacked the Quakers and was titled *A Seasonable Watch-Word Unto Christians Against the Dreams and Dreamers of This Generation* (Cambridge: S. Green, 1677) [EAI #243], [3–4], and was meant to "shew also how inexcusable those among us are, who against all such warnings are still flocking after such filthy dreamers," as Thacher explained.

10. Increase Mather, *David Serving His Generation* (Boston: B. Green and J. Allen, 1698) [EAI #831], 4; also see William Stoughton, *New England's True Interest; Not to Lie* (Cambridge: S. G. and M. T., 1670) [EAI #156], 19.

11. Dennis Baron, *Grammar and Gender* (New Haven: Yale University Press, 1986), 52, 93, 98.

12. Eleazar Mather, "A Word to the Present and Succeeding Generation," in *A Serious Exhortation to the Present and Succeeding Generation in New England* (Cambridge: S. G. and M. T., 1671) [EAI #162], 3.

13. Perry Miller, "Errand into the Wilderness," in *Errand into the Wilderness* (Cambridge, MA: Belknap Press, Harvard University Press, 1956; New York: Harper Torchbook, 1964), 1–15. Andrew Delbanco, "The Puritan Errand Reviewed," *Journal of American Studies* 18 (December 1984): 352. Also see Harry S. Stout, *The New England Soul* (New York: Oxford University Press, 1986), 54.

14. Virginia DeJohn Anderson, *New England's Generation* (New York: Cambridge University Press, 1991), 179, 182, 191–92.

15. Peter Gay, *A Loss of Mastery: Puritan Historians in Colonial America* (Berkeley: University of California Press, 1966), 111; John Demos, "Old Age in Early New England," in *Past, Present, and Personal* (New York: Oxford University Press, 1986), 180: Robert Middlekauff, *The Mathers: Three Generations of Puritan Intellectuals, 1596–1728* (New York: Oxford University Press, 1971), 98. Also see Sacvan Bercovitch, *The Puritan Origins of the American Self* (New Haven: Yale University Press, 1975), 122; David M. Scobey, "Revising the Errand: New England's Ways and the Puritan Sense of the Past," *William and Mary Quarterly*, 3d ser. 41 (January 1984): 23; Andrew Delbanco, *The Puritan Ordeal* (Cambridge, MA: Harvard University Press, 1989), 225; Theodore Dwight Bozeman, *To Live Ancient Lives* (Chapel Hill: University of North Carolina Press for the Institute of Early American History and Culture, 1988), 311, 329–30.

16. Perry Miller identified its significance in *The New England Mind: From Colony to Province* (Cambridge, MA: Harvard University Press, 1953; Boston: Beacon, 1961). Also see Sacvan Bercovitch, *The American Jeremiad* (Madison: University of Wisconsin Press, 1978).

17. Michael McGiffert, "God's Controversy with Jacobean England," *American Historical Review* 88 (December 1983): 1161; Sacvan Bercovitch, *The Rites of Assent* (New York: Routledge, 1993), 80; David L. Minter, *The Interpreted Design as a Structural Principle in American Prose* (New Haven: Yale University Press, 1969), 63, 66. Also see David D. Hall, *The Faithful Shepherd: A History of the New England Ministry in the Seventeenth Century* (Chapel Hill: University of North Carolina Press for the Institute of Early American History and Culture, 1972). 176–77.

18. Harry S. Stout, *The New England Soul* (New York: Oxford University Press, 1986), 4, 6, 85, 91–93; Bercovitch, *Rites of Assent,* 70, 86. Also see Michael Warner, *The Letters of the Republic* (Cambridge, MA: Harvard University Press, 1990), 22–23.

19. I read more than a hundred published sermons, both of the occasional kind and those expressing traditional salvation themes.

20. Robert Pope, in *The Half-Way Covenant* (Princeton: Princeton University Press, 1969), is one of the leading critics of the "reality" of declension. Emory Elliott, in *Power and the Pulpit in Puritan New England* (Princeton: Princeton University Press, 1975), has made the major argument about generational conflict; the quotation is on 7.

21. David D. Hall, *Faithful Shepherd,* 176, is a notable exception—he emphasized the *uses* of generational language; Elliott, *Power and the Pulpit,* 60–61; Werner Sollors, *Beyond Ethnicity* (New York: Oxford University Press, 1986), 220 and chap. 7 generally.

22. Sollors, *Beyond Ethnicity,* 235.

23. Increase Mather, "A Discourse Concerning the Danger of Apostasy," in *A Call From Heaven to the Present and Succeeding Generations* (Boston: John Foster, 1679) [EAI #274], 60 (emphasis added).

24. Increase Mather, *David Serving His Generation,* 18; also see Cotton Mather, "The Old Man's Honour," in *Addresses to Old Men, and Young Men, and Little Children* (Boston: R. Pierce, 1690) [EAI #534], 18, and *Successive Generations,* 27. Thomas Prince, in an election sermon, described magistrates in terms similar to those used for ministers and founders in the seventeenth century, in *The People of New England Put in Mind of the Righteous Acts of the Lord to Them and Their Fathers and Reasoned With Concerning Them* (Boston: B. Green, 1730) [EAI #3343], 40.

25. George Williamson, "Mutability, Decay, and Seventeenth-Century Melancholy," *ELH* 2 (September 1935): 132, 135; David Lowenthal, *The Past Is a Foreign Country* (Cambridge: Cambridge University Press, 1985), 87, 136, 141.

26. John Cotton, *God's Promise To His Plantations* (London: William Jones, 1630; reprinted in *Old South Leaflets,* no. 53, Boston: Old South Meeting House, n.d.), 14.

27. John Cotton, *A Brief Exposition with Practical Observations Upon the Whole Book of Ecclesiastes* (orig. 1654; reprint, Edinburgh: James Nichols,

1868), 11. Bozeman, *To Live Ancient Lives,* 11, 114, 301, analyzes other Cotton tracts to show that the founders assumed the colony would degenerate.

28. For optimistic views see, for example, "Governor Bradford's Dialogue between Old Men and Young Men, concerning 'The Church and Government Thereof,'" *Massachusetts Historical Society Proceedings* 11 (October 1870): 407, 464; Charles Chauncey, *God's Mercy, Shewed to His People in Giving Them a Faithful Ministry and Schooles of Learning for the Continual Supplyes Thereof* (Cambridge: Samuel Green, 1655) [EAI #40], 13.

29. Perry Miller, *The New England Mind: The Seventeenth Century* (New York: Macmillan, 1939; Boston: Beacon, 1961), 471–72.

30. "Verses by Governor Bradford," *Massachusetts Historical Society Proceedings* 11 (October 1870): 477.

31. Thomas Cobbet[t], *A Fruitfull and Usefull Discourse touching the Honour due from Children to Parents, and the Duty of Parents towards their children* (London: S. G. for John Rothwell, 1656), [3], 184–85, 188–91, 195, 207. Cobbett's time in Lynn is described in Alonzo Lewis, *The History Of Lynn* (Boston: Samuel N. Dickinson, 1844, 2d ed.), 101, 140–43.

32. John Norton, *The Heart of N– England Rent at the Blasphemies of the Present Generation* (Cambridge: Samuel Green, 1659)) [EAI #56], 45, 57–58. Norton's book was actually an anti-Quaker tract.

33. Charles Chauncey, "The Preface to the Reader," in Richard Mather, *A Farewel Exhortation* (Cambridge: Samuel Green, 1657) [EAI #47], [3–4].

34. Karen Ordahl Kupperman, "Errand to the Indies: Puritan Colonization from Providence Island through the Western Design," *William and Mary Quarterly,* 3d ser. 45 (January 1988): 72–73; she quotes the New Englander Robert Sedgwick on 97.

35. Anderson, *New England's Generation,* 198.

36. Samuel Danforth, "To the Christian Reader," in *A Brief Recognition of New England's Errand Into the Wilderness* (Cambridge: S. G. and M. T., 1671) [EAI #160], [5]. Also see Increase Mather, "Discourse . . . Apostasy," 60, 55; Samuel Arnold, *David Serving His Generation* (Cambridge: Samuel Green, 1674) [EAI #185], 12; and John Oxenbridge, *New-England Freemen Warned and Warmed* (Boston, 1673) [EAI #181], 22, 28. Bercovitch suggests such fears were "a Reformed commonplace, "in *Puritan Origins of the American Self,* 230 n.8.

37. Ministers were not uniformly pessimistic. To sense the tension in the writings of the Mathers, see Increase Mather, "To the Reader," in "Call to the Rising Generation," in *Call from Heaven,* [3–4]; Richard Mather and Jonathan Mitchel, *A Defence of the Answer and Arguments of the Synod Met at Boston in the Year 1662* (Cambridge: S. Green and M. Johnson, 1664) [EAI #89], 59–60; Increase Mather, *The Happiness of a People,* 52–53; idem, "Discourse . . . Apostasy," 65. Cotton Mather occasionally expressed optimism about youth, as in *The Way to Prosperity,* in *The Wonderful Works of God Commemorated* (Boston: S. Green 1690) [EAI #540], 34; also see idem, *Youth in its Brightest Glory* (Boston: T. Green, 1709) [EAI #1410], and *The Best Ornaments of Youth* (Boston: Timothy Green, 1707) [EAI #1308], 30; idem, "Duty of Children, whose Parents have Pray'd for Them," in Increase Mather, *The Duty of Parent to Pray for Their Children* (Boston: B. Green and J. Allen, 1703) [EAI #1133], [4–5].

38. Eleazar Mather, "A Word to the Present and Succeeding Generation," in *Serious Exhortation*, 28–29.

39. The sermons by Samuel Arnold and Increase Mather are two important examples.

40. Cotton Mather, *Early Religion Urged* (Boston, 1694) [EAI #698], 42. Mather was combining at least two passages about constructing the Temple: 1 Chronicles 22.16: "Arise therefore, and be doing"; and Nehemiah 6.3: "And I sent Messengers unto them, saying, 'I am doing a great work.' "

41. Thomas Shepard, Jr., *Eye-Salve* (Cambridge: Samuel Green, 1673) [EAI #182], 24. For a secular example, Joshua Scottow, *Old Mens Tears For Their Own Declensions* (Boston: Benjamin Harris and John Allen, 1691) [EAI #576], 3. In biblical chronology the time between the first and second temples was much longer than that between the colony's founding and these statements. The generational perspective was the same.

42. Arnold, *David Serving His Generation*, 2–4; Eleazar Mather, *Exhortation to the Present and Succeeding Generation*, 14–15.

43. James Allen, *New England's Choicest Blessing* (Boston: John Foster, 1679) [EAI #260], 2–3; Cotton Mather, "Old Man's Honour," 4.

44. W. J., [Evans identifies as William Jameson], *A Remembrance of Former Times for This Generation; and Our Degeneracy Lamented* (Boston: B. Green and J. Allen, 1697) [EAI #784], 4; John Higginson, *The Cause of God and His People in New England* (1663), reprinted in *Elijah's Mantle* (Boston: S. Kneeland, 1722), 7; Norton, *Heart of N– England*, 58; Increase Mather, *Call to the Rising Generation*, 29; idem, *The Necessity of Reformation* (Boston: John Foster, 1679) [EAI #263], 10

45. Shepard, *Eye-Salve*, 27; Increase Mather, "Discourse . . . Apostasy," 62; idem, *Pray for the Rising Generation* (Cambridge: Samuel Green, 1678) [EAI #255], 14.

46. Allen, *New England's Choicest Blessing*, 1.

47. Proclamation quoted in W. DeLoss Love, Jr., *The Fast and Thanksgiving Days of New England* (Boston: Houghton, Mifflin, Riverside Press, 1895), 217. Also note reference in Cotton Mather, *The Serviceable Man* (Boston: Samuel Green, 1690) [EAI #538], 31.

48. [Jameson], *Remembrance of Former Times*, 26, 24. Also note Oxenbridge, *New England Freemen Warned*, 21; Increase Mather, "Discourse . . . Apostasy," 65; Cotton Mather, *The Way to Prosperity*, 22–23.

49. Stout, *New England Soul*, 122; also see Miller, *Colony to Province*, 185.

50. Cobbett, *Fruitfull Discourse*, 187; Increase Mather, "Discourse . . . Apostasy," 78; Shepard, *Eye-Salve*, 18; Cotton Mather, *The Way to Prosperity*, 23.

51. Scottow, *Old Mens Tears*, 10, 1, [4, 6], 3. See also Thomas Prince, "A Short Account of the Author and His Family," in Roger Clap, *Memoirs of Capt. Roger Clap* (Boston: B. Green, 1731) [EAI #3403], 10, and John Hovey, *The Duty and Privilege of Aged Saints to Leave Their Dying Testimony Behind Them to Posterity* (Boston: S. Kneeland, 1749) [EAI #6333] for eighteenth-century examples of old men's testimonies, although these sources emphasize a more familial generational concern.

52. Gay, *Loss of Mastery*, 54–56, discusses the importance of detail and treats

Morton briefly; Nathaniel Morton, *New England's Memoriall* (Cambridge: S. G. and M. T., 1669) [EAI #144], [3], [5–6], 197–98. Also see Stoughton, *New England's True Interest*, 26.

53. Increase Mather, "Discourse . . . Apostasy," 70–71; Cotton Mather, *Serviceable Man*, 42.

54. Increase Mather, "To the Reader," and Cotton Mather, "Introduction," in *Johannes in Eremo* (Boston: Michael Perry, 1695) [EAI #724], 6, 15, 18; see Bercovitch, *Puritan Origins*, 130, 133, 230 n.28, on Cotton Mather and the *Magnalia Christi Americana*.

55. William Williams, *The Duty and Interest of a People, Among Whom Religion is Planted to Continue . . . From Generation to Generation* (Boston: S. Kneeland and T. Green, 1736) [EAI #4103], 79; Stoughton, *New England's True Interest*, 25–26; Increase Mather, *The Happiness of a People*, [6]; Oxenbridge, *New-England Freeman Warned*, 44; Increase Mather, "Discourse . . . Apostasy," 83; Allen, *New England's Choicest Blessing*, 14.

56. Arnold, *David Serving His Generation*, 3; Shepard, *Eye-Salve*, 1; Increase Mather, *Necessity of Reformation*, 9–10; idem, "Discourse . . . Apostasy," 61; Shepard, *Eye-Salve*, 25–26; Arnold, *David Serving His Generation*, 5; Samuel Wakeman, *A Young Man's Legacy to the Rising Generation* (Cambridge, 1673) [EAI #183], 14; Increase Mather, *Renewal of Covenant the Great Duty Incumbent on Decaying or Distressed Churches* (Boston: J. F. for Henry Phillips, 1677) [EAI #239], 16; idem, "Epistle Dedicatory," in *Necessity of Reformation*, [4].

57. Cobbett, *Fruitfull Discourse*, 187; Increase Mather, *Solemn Advice to Young Men* (Boston, 1695) [EAI #728], 53; Peter Thacher, "To the Christian Reader," *Unbelief Detected and Condemned* (Boston: B. Green, 1708) [EAI #1375], [3], shows the continuation of this rhetoric into the next century.

58. Edmund S. Morgan, *The Puritan Family* (New York: Harper and Row, 1966, new ed., rev.), 177–78, 182–83. Morgan notes the "accepted tradition that the founders of New England had left the old world for the sake of their children" (168).

59. Urian Oakes, *An Elegie Upon the Death of the Reverend Mr. Thomas Shepard* (Cambridge: Samuel Green, 1677) [EAI #240], 9.

60. Stoughton, *New England's True Interest*, 30. Also see Cotton Mather, "Duty of Children," 5; Benjamin Colman, *Early Piety Again Inculcated* (Boston: S. Kneeland, 1720) [EAI #2102], 36; Increase Mather, "Remember Now thy Creator in the Days of Thy Youth," in *A Call From Heaven*, 103–4. Other sermons by both Mathers on this theme include, Increase: *Renewal of Covenant;* "A Call to the Rising Generation" and "A Discourse concerning the Danger of Apostasy," both in *A Call From Heaven;* Cotton: "Young Man's Glory," in *Addresses to Old Men*. John Williams, *A Serious Word to the Posterity of Holy Men* (Boston: B. Green, 1729) [EAI #3238], 12. Peter Thacher, "Children Must Seek the Presence . . . ," in *Unbelief Detected*, and William Cooper, "God's Concern for a Godly Seed," in Benjamin Colman and William Cooper, *Two Sermons Preached in Boston* (Boston: S. Kneeland, 1723) [EAI #2425], are eighteenth-century examples that continue the theme.

61. Morgan, *Puritan Family*, 185; John Murrin, "Review Essay," *History and Theory* 11, 2 (1972): 239.

62. Increase Mather, *Duty of Parents*, 32.

63. Michael G. Hall, *Last American Puritan: The Life of Increase Mather* (Middletown, CT: Wesleyan University Press, 1988), 142; James Axtell, *School upon a Hill* (New Haven: Yale University Press, 1974; New York: W. W. Norton, 1976), 4; Ronald A. Bosco, "Introduction," in *Lessons For the Children of Godly Ancestors: Sermons For and About New England's Rising Generations, 1670–1750*, ed. Bosco (Delmar, NY: Scholars' Facsimiles and Reprints, 1982), 13.

64. Charles E. Hambrick-Stowe, *The Practice of Piety* (Chapel Hill: University of North Carolina Press, 1982), 242, 248–51, 276.

65. Bosco, "Introduction," in *Lessons For the Children of Godly Ancestors*, 13; Stout, *New England Soul*, 28.

66. Increase Mather, "Discourse . . . Apostasy," 93; idem, *Pray for the Rising Generation*; idem, "To the Reader," in *Duty of Parents*, [5].

67. Stoughton, *New England's True Interest*, 26–32.

68. Mather refers to the "Third Generation" in the "Epistle Dedicatory" to *Wonderful Works of God*, [5]; other generational responsibility pleas appeared in *Serviceable Man*, 56–58. In *Early Religion Urged*, 2, he said he was ready "to conclude my own youth." He was thirty years old.

69. Hall, *Last American Puritan*, 136–37, 140; Kenneth Silverman, *The Life and Times of Cotton Mather* (New York: Harper and Row, 1984), 157, 423.

70. Pope, *Half-way Covenant*, 7.

71. Richard Mather and Jonathan Mitchel, *Defence of the Answer*, 32; see also Shepard, *The Church Membership of Children and Their Right to Baptism* (Cambridge: Samuel Green, 1663, reprinted in *Elijah's Mantle*); Pope, *Half-way Covenant*, 51–52; Miller, *Colony to Province*, 95.

72. Increase Mather, "To the Church and Inhabitants of Northampton in N.E.," in *Serious Exhortation* [3]; Hall, *Last American Puritan*, 88; Eleazar Mather, "A Word to the Present and Succeeding Generation," 16–17. Philip Gura, in "Preparing the Way for Stoddard: Eleazar Mather's Serious Exhortation to Northampton," *New England Quarterly* 57 (June 1984): 244, suggests that this sentiment reveals "Eleazar's anger at his people's presumption in blaming the splintered condition of the church on his" opposition to the Halfway Covenant.

73. See for example, Increase, *Call to the Rising Generation*, 21; Cotton, *Help for Distressed Parents* (Boston: John Allen, 1695) [EAI #723], 20–22.

74. Increase Mather, "To the Reader," in *The First Principles of New England* (Cambridge: Samuel Green, 1675) [EAI #208], [7]; he declares himself ready to die in "To the Reader," in *The Wicked Man's Portion* (Boston: John Foster, 1675) [EAI #210], [4]; Bosco, "Introduction," in *Lessons For the Children of Godly Ancestors*, 36; Hall, *Last American Puritan*, 146; Increase Mather, *Renewal of Covenant*, 17; idem, "To the Reader," in *Call to the Rising Generation*, [7], 1; Hall, *Last American Puritan*, 85. John Murrin's discussion of the controversy in his "Review Essay" suggests that Increase perhaps "resent[ed] the idea that something less should be expected from the younger generation so long as he was part of it," and was able to change his view only after his father's death (237). What is most important for this study is Increase's persistent return to that death.

75. Hall, *Last American Puritan*, 140, 136–37.

76. Increase Mather, *Solemn Advice*, [3]; Miller, *Colony to Province*, 184–85.

77. Increase Mather, *An Earnest Exhortation to the Children of New England To Exalt the God of Their Fathers* (Boston, 1711) [EAI #1515], 29; idem, *David Serving His Generation,* 22; idem, "Advice to the Children of Godly Ancestors," in Cotton Mather, et al., *A Course of Sermons on Early Piety* (Boston: S. Kneeland, 1721) [EAI #2256], 12–13, and in the same volume, "Mantissa" and "A Preface of Dr. Increase Mather," i. The reference to Mather not using notes is interesting in that entire paragraphs seem lifted almost verbatim from many of his earlier discourses on the subject.

78. Shepard, *Eye-Salve,* 43.

79. "A Defense of Evangelical Churches," in John Quick, *The Young Man's Claim Unto the Sacrament of the Lords Supper,* 2d impression (Boston: B. Green and J. Allen, 1700) [EAI #949], 3, 20, 59, and "The Preface," 68. Conflict between the Mathers and others is described in Miller, *Colony to Province,* chap. 15, and more specifically in Silverman, *Life and Times of Cotton Mather,* 151–53.

80. Solomon Stoddard, "An Examination of the Power of the Fraternity," in *The Presence of Christ With the Ministers of the Gospel* (Boston: B. Green, 1718) [EAI #1999], 1–2; idem, "Young Men & Maids," in *Three Sermons Lately Preached at Boston . . . To Which a Fourth is added, to stir up Young Men and Maidens . . .* (Boston: B. Green, 1717) [EAI #1930], 114. *Philip Gura,* in "Solomon Stoddard's Irreverent Way," *Early American Literature* 21 (Spring 1986): 35, 39, has argued that Stoddard revealed that the New England Way —protected by the Mathers and unchallenged by everyone else—had changed dramatically.

81. Benjamin Colman, *A Brief Enquiry into the Reasons Why the People of God have been wont to bring into their Penitential Confessions, the sins of their Fathers and Ancestors* (Boston: T. Fleet and T. Crump, 1716) [EAI #1801], 14, 20–27, 30.

82. Jonathan Mayhew, "The Dedication," in *Christian Sobriety* (Boston: Richard and Samuel Draper, 1763) [EAI #9440], iv, viii, xi–xii.

83. Prince, *People of New England,* 36. Also see Williams, *Serious Word to the Posterity of Holy Men,* 47; William Cooper, "God's Concern for a Godly Seed," in Colman and Cooper, *Two Sermons Preached in Boston,* 36. Virginia DeJohn Anderson recently reached a similar conclusion; see *New England's Generation,* 216–19.

84. Daniel Lewis, *Good Rulers the Fathers of Their People, and the Marks of Honour Due to Them* (Boston: John Draper, 1748) [EAI #6175], 6; also see Benjamin Colman, *David's Dying Charge to the Rulers and People of Israel* (Boston: B. Green, 1723) [EAI #2419]; Bercovitch, *American Jeremiad,* 61, described an election-day speaker noting how "This Exhortation has been many times urged from this Place," which demonstrated the way such addresses cloaked themselves in the past.

85. [Nicholas Boone], *The Constable's Pocket Book* (Boston, 1710) [EAI #1445], 1; also note the title of the children's book *Be Merry and Wise: or, a Guide to the Present and Future Generation* (Boston, 1762) [EAI #9285].

86. Ebenezer Pemberton, *A True Servant of His Generation Characterized* (Boston: Bartholomew Green, 1712) EAI #1577], 29; on the state of sermons see Stout, *New England Soul,* 181. Some examples of the more remote connection

between generation and community responsibility are: William Cooper, "Jabez's Character," in *How and Why Young People Should Cleanse Their Way,* in *Two Sermons* (Boston: B. Green, 1716) [EAI #1820], and idem, *Serious Exhortations Address'd to Young Men* (Boston: S. Kneeland and T. Green, 1732) [EAI #3525]; Jonathan Todd, *The Young People Warned* (New London, CT: T. Green 1741) [EAI #4829]; *The Poor Orphans Legacy: Being a Short Collection of Godly Counsels and Exhortations to a Young Arising Generation* (Philadelphia: B. Franklin, 1734) [EAI #3828], 10.

87. Samuel Dexter, *Our Father's God, the Hope of Posterity* (Boston: S. Kneeland and T. Green, 1738) [EAI #4236], i, 24–26, 31, 37–38.

88. The account of the Plymouth celebration drawn from the "Records of the Old Colony Club," reprinted in *Proceedings of the Massachusetts Historical Society* 2 (October 1887): 382–444; the first Plymouth anniversary speech on 416–17; the communication between minister and club, 421–23; minister's sermon, 434.

89. Not surprisingly, the club records downplay the Loyalist leanings of many of its members. The *Boston Gazette* article quoted in Albert Matthews, "The Term Pilgrim Fathers and Early Celebrations of Forefathers' Day," *Publications of the Colonial Society of Massachusetts* 17 (November 1914): 305.

90. Judah Champion, *A Brief View of Distresses, Hardship, and Dangers Our Ancestors Encounter'd, in Settling New-England* (Hartford: Green and Watson, 1770) [EAI #11595], "To the Reader," and 11–14, 29, 31, 43–44; Stout has noted the tendency of New England ministers to synthesize "resistance to tyranny and covenant keeping" throughout the revolutionary era, in *New England Soul,* 273–74. Also note Nicholas Street's aptly titled *American States Acting Over the Part of the Children of Israel in the Wilderness, and Thereby Impending their Entrance into Canaan's Rest* (New Haven: Thomas and Samuel Green, 1777) [EAI #15604], 18.

91. Adams quoted in Pauline Maier, *The Old Revolutionaries* (New York: Alfred A. Knopf, 1980), 42; Boston Committee of Correspondence, June 22, 1773, Broadside [EAI #12690]; Boston Town Meeting, 1773 [EAI #12692]; Boston Committee of Correspondence, November 23, 1773, Broadside [EAI #12693].

92. Jonathan Homer, *The Succession of Generations Among Mankind* (Boston: Belknap and Young, 1792) [EAI #24406], 6, 10, 15, 17, 21, 23, 27; Thaddeus Mason Harris, *A Discourse Addressed to the Religious Society of Young Men in Dorchester* (Charlestown, MA: Samuel Etheridge, 1799) [EAI #35590], 15–16.

93. "Directions for the improvement of the rising generation," *American Museum* 6 (September 1789): 241; the article could well have been satirical. See Frank Luther Mott, *A History of American Magazines, 1741–1850* (Cambridge, MA: Harvard University Press, 1930; Belknap Press, 1957), 51, on the magazine's extensive coverage of the constitutional debate; also see 100–103. Richard Bushman suggests a tension between republicanism and gentility in *The Refinement of America* (New York: Vintage Books, 1993).

94. Jesse Edson, *A Discourse Delivered to the Young People* (Greenfield, MA: Thomas Dickman, 1799) [EAI #35436], 20–21, 5, 22.

95. *Independent Chronicle,* January 7, 1799 quoted in Matthews, "The Term Pilgrim Fathers," 311; also see 361. Two recent studies have shown how various groups used Plymouth Rock as a bulwark of conservatism, basing their claim on fidelity to the fathers' vision. Mark L. Sargent, "Plymouth Rock and the Great Awakening," *Journal of American Studies* 22 (August 1988): 249–62; idem, "The Conservative Covenant: The Rise of the Mayflower Compact in American Myth," *New England Quarterly* 61 (June 1988): 233–51.

2. Youth Imagined in Revival and Revolution

1. Philippe Ariès, *Centuries of Childhood: A Social History of Family Life,* trans. Robert Baldick (New York: Alfred A. Knopf, 1962; Vintage, 1965); for a critique see Adrian Wilson, "The Infancy of the History of Childhood: An Appraisal of Philippe Ariès," *History and Theory* 19, 2 (1980): 139, 142–43. Barbara A. Hanawalt, *Growing Up in Medieval London* (New York: Oxford University Press, 1993); Samuel C. Chew, *The Pilgrimage of Life* (New Haven: Yale University Press, 1962), esp. 144–73; Anthony Burton, "Looking Forward from Ariès? Pictorial and Material Evidence for the History of Childhood and Family Life," *Continuity and Change* 4 (August 1989): 207–9.

2. Creighton Gilbert, "When Did a Man in the Renaissance Grow Old?" *Studies in the Renaissance* 14 (1967): 23 n.39, 12; Steven R. Smith, "Religion and the Conception of Youth in Seventeenth-Century England," *History of Childhood Quarterly* 2 (Spring 1975): 495–96; John Gillis, *Youth and History* (New York: Academic Press, expanded student ed., 1981), 5; Georges Duby, *The Chivalrous Society,* trans. Cynthia Postan (London: Edward Arnold, 1977), 112–13; Susan Brigden, "Youth and the English Reformation," *Past and Present* 95 (May 1982): 37.

3. Gordon J. Schochet, "Patriarchalism, Politics, and Mass Attitudes in Stuart England," *Historical Journal* 12, 3 (1969): 436; Steven Ozment, *When Fathers Ruled: Family Life in Reformation Europe* (Cambridge, MA: Harvard University Press, 1983), 132; Keith Thomas, "Age and Authority in Early Modern England," *Proceedings of the British Academy* 62 (1976): 207–9.

4. Duby describes the pressures in medieval France, in *Chivalrous Society,* 115–22; Richard C. Trexler, *Public Life in Renaissance Florence* (New York: Academic Press, 1980); idem, *Dependence in Context in Renaissance Florence* (Binghamton, NY: Medieval and Renaissance Texts and Studies, 1994); Stanley Chojnacki, "Political Adulthood in Fifteenth-Century Venice," *American Historical Review* 91 (October 1986): 791–810; Thomas, "Age and Authority in Early Modern England," 214, 228–32.

5. Gillis, *Youth and History,* 8, 22; Richard Wall, "The Age at Leaving Home," *Journal of Family History* 3 (Summer 1978): 200, 182; Susan Brigden, *London and the Reformation* (Oxford: Clarendon Press, Oxford University Press, 1989), 134 and passim; also see Smith, "Religion and the Conception of Youth," 496–97.

6. John Cotton, *A Brief Exposition with Practical Observations Upon the Whole Book of Ecclesiastes* (orig. 1654; reprint, Edinburgh: James Nichol, 1868), 121–22. Larzer Ziff, *The Career of John Cotton: Puritanism and the*

American Experience (Princeton: Princeton University Press, 1962), 262, dates the composition of the analysis. For a contemporary and roughly similar catalogue of youth's sins, which is ultimately gentler than Cotton's, see Thomas Brooks, "Apples of Gold for Young Men and Women" (1657), in *The Complete Works of Thomas Brooks*, vol. 1 (Edinburgh: James Nichol, 1866), 199–203.

7. Carmen Luke, *Pedagogy, Printing, and Protestantism: The Discourse on Children* (Albany: State University of New York Press, 1989), 1–2; John E. Mason, *Gentlefolk in the Making* (Philadelphia: University of Pennsylvania Press, 1935); W. Lee Ustick, "Advice to a Son: A Type of Seventeenth-Century Conduct Book," *Studies in Philology* 29 (July 1932): 409–41; Michael V. Belok, "The Courtesy Tradition and Early Schoolbooks," *History of Education Quarterly* 8 (Fall 1968): 307.

8. Francis Lenton, *The Young Gallants Whirligigg* (London, 1629), See *Dictionary of National Biography* (1909), s.v. "Lenton, Francis."

9. Ilana Krausman Ben-Amos, *Adolescence and Youth in Early Modern England* (New Haven: Yale University Press, 1994), 24–25, 35–37, 183, 205.

10. Thomas Gouge, *Young Man's Guide Through the Wilderness of This World* (London, 1680); Richard Baxter, *Compassionate Counsel to all Young Men* (London, 1681), 159–60. On these ministers see C. John Sommerville, *The Discovery of Childhood in Puritan England* (Athens: University of Georgia Press, 1992), 33, 35.

11. For a few examples, in addition to those listed in the adjacent notes, see Samuel Crossman, *The Young Man's Calling* (London, 1678); Thomas Doolittle, *The Young Man's Instructor and the Old Man's Remembrancer* (London, 1673); Henry Hesketh, *The Importance of Religion to Young Persons* (London, 1683); Thomas Vincent, *Words of Advice to Young Men* (London, 1668).

12. Selmer Neville Westby described the traditional form, in "The Puritan Funeral Sermon in Seventeenth-Century England" (Ph.D. diss., University of Southern California, 1970), 101–4.

13. Gouge, "Epistle Dedicatory," in *Young Man's Guide,* [iv–v]; Baxter, *Compassionate Counsel,* 15. [John How[e] and Vincent Alsop], "To the Reader," in John Shower, *An Exhortation to Youth to Prepare for Judgment* (London, 1681), [x, xiv–xv].

14. *Dictionary of National Biography,* s.v. "John Shower," "John Howe," "Increase Mather," "Thomas Gouge." Francis J. Bremer, "Increase Mather's Friends: The Trans-Atlantic Congregational Network of the Seventeenth Century," *Proceedings of the American Antiquarian Society* 94, pt. 1 (1984): 60, 74, 92. Also note Perry Miller, *The New England Mind: From Colony to Province* (Cambridge, MA: Harvard University Press, 1953; Boston: Beacon, 1961), 216–17, on Mather's connection to these ministers.

15. Julius Herbert Tuttle, "The Libraries of the Mathers," *Proceedings of the American Antiquarian Society,* new ser. 20 (April 1910): 288; Worthington Chauncey Ford, "Appendices," in *The Boston Book Market, 1679–1700* (Boston: The Club of Odd Volumes, 1917), 88–136.

16. Jack P. Greene, *Pursuits of Happiness* (Chapel Hill: University of North Carolina Press, 1988), 165; Gerald F. Moran and Maris A. Vinovskis, "Troubled

Youth: Children at Risk in Early Modern New England, Colonial America, and Nineteenth-Century America," in *Religion, Family, and the Life Course* (Ann Arbor: University of Michigan Press, 1992), 150; David Hackett Fischer, *Albion's Seed: Four British Folkways in America* (New York: Oxford University Press, 1989), 231, 316, 323–24; Daniel Blake Smith, *Inside the Great House* (Ithaca: Cornell University Press, 1980), 82 and passim; Martin H. Quitt, "Immigrant Origins of the Virginia Gentry: A Study of Cultural Transmission and Innovation," *William and Mary Quarterly*, 3d ser. 45 (October 1988): 648, 653–54.

17. Jan Lewis, *The Pursuit of Happiness: Family and Values in Jefferson's Virginia* (Cambridge: Cambridge University Press, 1983), 30–32; also Ross W. Beales, "The Child in Seventeenth-Century America," in *American Childhood: A Research Guide and Historical Handbook*, ed. Joseph M. Hawes and N. Ray Hiner (Westport, CT: Greenwood Press, 1985), 21–22; Richard L. Bushman, "American High-Style and Vernacular Cultures," in *Colonial British America*, ed. Jack P. Greene and J. R. Pole (Baltimore: Johns Hopkins University Press, 1984), 356–59; Mason, *Gentlefolk in the Making*, 258–60.

18. Fischer, *Albion's Seed*, 31; Beales, "The Child in Seventeenth-Century America," 22; also see Virginia DeJohn Anderson, *New England's Generation* (New York: Cambridge University Press, 1991).

19. Cotton Mather, "The Young Man's Glory," in *Addresses to Old Men, and Young Men, and Little Children* (Boston: R. Pierce, 1690) [EAI #534], 76; Eliphalet Adams, "The Duty of Young Men to Cleanse Their Way," in *A Brief Discourse as it Was Delivered February 6, 1726, to a Society of Young Men* (New London, CT, 1727) [EAI #2830], 7. Also see Cotton Mather, "The Way to Prosperity," in *The Wonderful Works of God Commemorated* (Boston: S. Green, 1690) [EAI #540], 34, and N. Ray Hiner, "Adolescence in Eighteenth-Century America," *History of Childhood Quarterly* 3 (Fall 1975): 260–61, 267.

20. Richard Gildrie recently noted the persistent Puritan concern with young people in *The Profane, the Civil, and the Godly: The Reformation of Manners in Orthodox New England* (University Park: Pennsylvania State University Press, 1994), 97–98, 104–9.

21. Thomas Cobbett, "Epistle to the Reader," in *A Fruitfull and Usefull Discourse Touching the Honour Due From Children to Parents* (London: S. G. for John Rothwell, 1656), [4].

22. Daniel Scott Smith, "Old Age and the 'Great Transformation': A New England Case Study," in *Aging and the Elderly: Humanistic Perspectives in Gerontology*, ed. Stuart F. Spicker, Kathleen M. Woodward and David D. Van Tasse (Atlantic Highlands, NJ: Humanities Press, 1978), 297, 294, 290–91; Maris A. Vinovskis, " 'Aged Servants of the Lord': Changes in the Status and Treatment of Elderly Ministers in Colonial America," in *Aging from Birth to Death*, vol. 2, ed. Matilda White Riley, Ronald P. Abeles, and Michael S. Teitelbaum (Boulder, Co: Westview Press, 1982), 111, 114. Many of the studies of New England towns produced in the early 1970s make similar conclusions, notably Philip Greven's *Four Generations: Population, Land and Family in Colonial Andover, Massachusetts* (Ithaca: Cornell University Press, 1970).

23. Moran and Vinovskis, "Troubled Youth," 151; also note Thaddeus Mason Harris, "Introduction," in *A discourse, addressed to the Religious Society of*

Young Men in Dorchester (Charlestown, MA: Samuel Etheridge, 1799) [EAI #35590], iii.

24. Samuel Wakeman, *A Young Man's Legacy To the Rising Generation* (Cambridge, 1673) [EAI #183], 41, 12, 44; Cotton Mather, "Young Man's Glory," 57.

25. Daniel A. Cohen, *Pillars of Salt, Monuments of Grace: New England Crime Literature and the Origins of American Popular Culture, 1674–1860* (New York: Oxford University Press, 1993), 5, 7, 58.

26. Wakeman, *Young Man's Legacy*, 12, 44.

27. David Levin, *Cotton Mather: The Young Life of the Lord's Remembrancer* (Cambridge, MA: Harvard University Press, 1978), 74, 273; Cotton Mather, "Dedication," in "Young Man's Glory," 47; idem, *Early Religion Urged* (Boston, 1694) [EAI #698], 31, 115–17; Albert Matthews, "A Dorchester Religious Society of Young Men," *New England Historical and Genealogical Register* 60 (January 1906): 30–40.

28. William L. Shea, *The Virginia Militia in the Seventeenth Century* (Baton Rouge: Louisiana State University Press, 1983), 24, 66, 130; Albert H. Tillson, Jr., "The Militia and Popular Political Culture in the Upper Valley of Virginia, 1740–1775," *Virginia Magazine of History and Biography* 94 (July 1986): 285–306, describes local conflicts with gentry authority over the militia.

29. T. H. Breen, "The Covenanted Militia of Massachusetts Bay: English Background and New World Development," in *Puritans and Adventurers* (New York: Oxford University Press, 1980), 34; Fred Anderson, *A People's Army: Massachusetts Soldiers and Society in the Seven Years' War* (Chapel Hill: University of North Carolina Press for the Institute of Early American History and Culture, 1984), 34–39, 53, describes how militia or army service provided outlets for young men not yet established in communities; Roger Thompson, "Adolescent Culture in Colonial Massachusetts," *Journal of Family History* 9 (Summer 1984): 127–44.

30. Thompson, "Adolescent Culture in Colonial Massachusetts," 133; most of the material in his article is expanded in *Sex in Middlesex* (Amherst: University of Massachusetts Press, 1986), 84, quotation on 88–89; also see 94–95.

31. On a special form of sermon developed for the militia, see Marie L. Ahearn, *The Rhetoric of War: Training Day, the Militia, and the Military Sermon* (Westport, CT: Greenwood Press, 1898), 54, 64–67, and passim.

32. John Winthrop, *Winthrop's Journal, "History of New England," 1630–1649,* ed. James K. Hosmer, vol. 2 (New York: Barnes and Noble, 1908; reprint 1953), 232–34; look, for example, at Breen's account in "Covenanted Militia," 39–40; Charles M. Ellis, *The History of Roxbury Town* (Boston: Samuel G. Drake, 1847), 37, 61, 95, provides biographical information on the principals in the dispute; Francis S. Drake, *The Town of Roxbury: Its Memorable Persons and Places* (Roxbury, MA: by the author, 1878), 107, called the insurgents "Young America" in his version of the story.

33. Breen, "Covenanted Militia," 42–43; petition quoted in Stewart Lewis Gates, "Disorder and Social Organization: The Militia in Connecticut Public Life, 1660–1860" (Ph.D. diss., University of Connecticut, 1975), 95–98 (his emphasis).

34. Cushing Strout, "Young People of the Great Awakening: The Dynamics of a Social Movement," in *Encounter with Erikson: Historical Interpretation and Religious Biography,* ed. Donald Capps, Walter H. Capps, and M. Gerald Bradford (Missoula, MT: Scholars Press, 1977), 199–201; Gerald F. Moran, " 'Sinners Are Turned into Saints in Numbers': Puritanism and Revivalism in Colonial Connecticut," in *Belief and Behavior,* ed. Philip R. Vandermeer and Robert P. Swierenga (New Brunswick: Rutgers University Press, 1991), 56.

35. Cushing Strout, *The New Heavens and New Earth* (New York: Harper Torchbooks, 1974). Also see William G. McLoughlin, *Revivals, Awakenings, and Reform* (Chicago: University of Chicago Press, 1978), 45–97; Patricia J. Tracy, *Jonathan Edwards, Pastor* (New York: Hill and Wang, 1980); Mark Sargent, "Plymouth Rock and the Great Awakening," *Journal of American Studies* 22 (August 1988): 249–62.

36. Jon Butler, "Enthusiasm Described and Decried: The Great Awakening as Interpretive Fiction," *Journal of American History* 69 (September 1982): 305–25; idem, *Awash in a Sea of Faith: Christianizing the American People* (Cambridge, MA: Harvard University Press, 1990), 179–80; W. R. Ward, *The Protestant Evangelical Awakening* (Cambridge: Cambridge University Press, 1992), 273, 294–98.

37. William Williams, *The Duty and Interest of a People* (Boston: S. Kneeland and T. Green, 1736) [EAI #4103], 49, 89; also note in ibid., Jonathan Edwards, "The Late Wonderful Work of God." Edwards's writings on this subject are collected in *The Works of Jonathan Edwards,* vol. 4, *The Great Awakening,* ed. C. C. Goen (New Haven: Yale University Press, 1972), 100, 114, 147–48, 547–48.

38. The diary of Ebenezer Parkman offers an example of pastoral interaction with young men's societies. Ebenezer Parkman, *The Diary of Ebenezer Parkman,* ed. Francis G. Walett (Worcester, MA: American Antiquarian Society, 1974), 90, 95. Also see Joseph Tracy, *The Great Awakening* (Boston: Charles Tappan, 1845; reprint, New York: Arno Press, 1969), 204–12.

39. Philip J. Greven, "Youth, Maturity and Religious Conversion: A Note on the Ages of Converts in Andover, Massachusetts, 1711–1749," *Essex Institute Historical Collections* 108 (April 1972): 129; Stephen R. Grossbart, "Seeking the Divine Favor: Conversion and Church Admission in Eastern Connecticut, 1711–1832," *William and Mary Quarterly,* 3d ser. 46 (October 1989): 730.

40. Tracy, *Jonathan Edwards, Pastor,* 87–88, 102–3, 111; J. M. Bumstead, "Religion, Finance, and Democracy in Massachusetts: The Town of Norton as a Case Study," *Journal of American History* 57 (March 1971): 828–29.

41. Grossbart, "Seeking the Divine Favor," 735, 724; Greven, "Youth, Maturity, Conversion," 128; Susan M. Juster and Maris A. Vinovskis, "Changing Perspectives on the American Family in the Past," *Annual Review of Sociology* 13 (1987): 205; Gerald F. Moran, "Religious Renewal, Puritan Tribalism, and the Family in Seventeenth-Century Milford, Connecticut," *William and Mary Quarterly,* 3d ser. 36 (April 1979): 249.

42. Bumstead, "Religion, Finance, Democracy," 829; Ross W. Beales, Jr., "Harvard and Yale in the Great Awakening," *Historical Journal of Massachusetts* 14 (January 1986): 2, 7–8; Grossbart, "Seeking the Divine Favor," 731; James

Walsh, "The Great Awakening in the First Congregational Church of Woodbury, Connecticut," *William and Mary Quarterly*, 3d ser. 28 (October 1971): 549–51, 562.

43. See Tracy, *Jonathan Edwards, Pastor,* and Cornelia Hughes Dayton, "Taking the Trade: Abortion and Gender Relations in an Eighteenth-Century New England Village," *William and Mary Quarterly*, 3d ser. 48 (January 1991): 19–49, on young people leading increasingly separate lives. Also see Harry S. Stout and Catherine A. Brekus, "Declension, Gender, and the 'New Religious History,' " in *Belief and Behavior,* 15–37, for a critique of social historians and an argument about the significance of female conversion.

44. Anderson, *New England's Generation,* 219; Sacvan Bercovitch, *The Rites of Assent* (New York: Routledge, 1993), 160.

45. Lyon N. Richardson, *A History of Early American Magazines, 1741–1789* (New York: Thomas Nelson and Sons, 1931), 58 and generally 58–73.

46. *The Christian History* 8 (April 23, 1743)—14 (June 14, 1743); note, for example, 57, 77, 93–106; quotations, 105–6. Charles E. Hambrick-Stowe makes a similar point in "The Spirit of the Old Writers" in *Puritanism,* ed. Francis J. Bremer (Boston: Massachusetts Historical Society, 1993), 277–82.

47. *The Christian History,* vol. 1: 90, 105–16, 183, 188, 191, 196; vol. 2: no. 99 (January 19, 1744/45), 375, no. 101 (February 2, 1744/45), 392. The magazine is the main source for many historians' accounts; see Strout, *New Heavens,* 41, 352 n.23, and "Young People of the Great Awakening," in *Encounter with Erikson.*

48. Charles Chauncy, *Seasonable Thoughts on the State of Religion in New-England* (Boston: Rogers and Fowle, 1743) [EAI #5151], xxvi–xxvii, 423, 105, 169 n; [William Rand], *The Late Religious Commotions in New-England Considered, An Answer to the Reverend Mr. Jonathan Edwards's Sermon* (Boston: Green, Bushell, and Allen, for T. Fleet, 1743) [EAI #5150], 25; Some scholars attribute this last work to Chauncy, others, to Rand. For Chauncy's earlier sermon, See *Early Piety Recommended and Exemplified* (Boston: S. Kneeland and T. Green, 1732) [EAI #3518].

49. For another interpretation of Chauncy's opposition, which emphasizes the gender dimension of the Antinomian controversy, see Amy Schrager Lang, " 'A Flood of Errors': Chauncy and Edwards in the Great Awakening," in *Jonathan Edwards and the American Experience,* ed. Nathan O. Hatch and Harry S. Stout (New York: Oxford University Press, 1988), 171.

50. Charles Chauncy to Nathaniel Chauncy, March 16, 1743, in William Chauncy Fowler, "President Charles Chauncy, His Ancestors and Descendants," *New England Historical and Genealogical Register* 10 (October 1856): 332–33.

51. Charles E. Clark, *The Public Prints: The Newspaper in Anglo-American Culture, 1665–1740* (New York: Oxford University Press, 1994), 144–46, 154–57; Sidney Kobre, *The Development of the Colonial Newspaper* (1944; reprint, Gloucester, MA: Peter Smith, 1960), 46–50; M. A. Yodelis, "Boston's First Major Newspaper War: A 'Great Awakening' of Freedom," *Journalism Quarterly* 51 (Summer 1974): 208–9.

52. *Boston Evening Post,* March 14, 1743; *Boston Gazette,* May 24, 1743; *Boston Newsletter,* May 26, 1743.

53. *Boston Evening Post,* May 30, 1743.

54. For corroboration of "Master Billy's" identity, see the letter to the *Boston Gazette,* July 5, 1743, that refers to a letter to Rev. William Cooper which "your son wrote you" from the Georgia orphan asylum; see also Frederick Tuckerman, "Thomas Cooper, of Boston, and his Descendants," *New-England Historical and Genealogical Register* 44 (January 1890): 56.

55. *Boston Gazette,* June 21, 1743, and June 28, 1743; *Boston Evening Post,* July 4, 1743. John E. Van De Wetering, "The *Christian History* of the Great Awakening," *Journal of Presbyterian History* 44 (June 1966): 123. For a similar assertion see Richardson, *Early American Magazines,* 60. Clifford Shipton, in *Sibley's Harvard Graduates* (Boston: Massachusetts Historical Society, 1937, 1958), ascribes control to the son in his entry, vol. 10, 533; to both in the entry for the father, vol. 5, 356; also see n.6 on 356.

56. Thomas Prince, Jr., wrote two letters describing his publication to a Glasgow minister; *Christian Monthly History* 8 (November 1745): 227–29, 229–33.

57. James West Davidson, *The Logic of Millennial Thought* (New Haven: Yale University Press, 1977), 124, 29; Frank Lambert, *"Pedlar in Divinity": George Whitefield and the Transatlantic Revival* (Princeton: Princeton University Press, 1994), 132–33. Harry S. Stout, "Religion, Communications, and the Ideological Origins of the American Revolution," *William and Mary Quarterly,* 3d ser. 34 (October 1977): 524–25.

58. Stephen Botein, " 'Meer Mechanics' and an Open Press: The Business and Political Strategies of Colonial American Printers," *Perspectives in American History* 9 (1975): 181, 188–89; Wm. David Sloan and Julie Hedgepath Williams, *The Early American Press, 1690–1783* (Westport, CT: Greenwood Press, 1994), 110–11.

59. Richard L. Merritt, *Symbols of American Community, 1735–1775* (New Haven: Yale University Press, 1966), 180.

60. Edward M. Griffin, *Old Brick: Charles Chauncy of Boston, 1705–1787* (Minneapolis: University of Minnesota Press, 1980), 149; Kobre, *Development of Colonial Newspaper,* 118; also see Arthur M. Schlesinger, *Prelude to Independence* (New York, 1958; reprint, Boston: Northeastern University Press, 1980), 71, 236, 285. James L. Moses continues to celebrate the sons' supposed fidelity to their father's ways, in "Journalistic Impartiality on the Eve of the Revolution: The Boston Evening Post, 1770–1775," *Journalism History* 20 (Autumn-Winter 1994): 129.

61. Jay Fliegelman, *Prodigals and Pilgrims* (Cambridge: Cambridge University Press, 1982), 186; Lawrence A. Cremin, *American Education: The Colonial Experience, 1607–1783* (New York: Harper and Row, 1970), 192–93, 519; Edwin G. Burrows and Michael Wallace, "The American Revolution: The Ideology and Psychology of National Liberation," *Perspectives in American History* 6 (1972): 256, 265. Beales, "The Child in Seventeenth-Century America," 36.

62. Benjamin Colman, *Early Piety Again Inculcated* (Boston: S. Kneeland, 1720) [EAI #2102], 32.

63. James Axtell, *The School Upon a Hill* (New Haven: Yale University Press, 1974; New York: W. W. Norton, 1976), 213 and generally the chapter "The Collegiate Way," 201–44; David W. Robson, *Educating Republicans* (Westport,

CT: Greenwood Press, 1985), 12–13, 57–93, 133; John F. Roche, *The Colonial Colleges in the War for American Independence* (Millwood, NY: Associated Faculty Press, 1986), 47–48.

64. See Ozment, *When Fathers Ruled*, 174, and Christopher Hill, *The World Turned Upside Down* (London: Temple and Smith, 1972), 151–52, for Reformation and English Revolution antecedents for rejecting the fathers. Burrows and Wallace, "American Revolution," 286, 273–74, 190–209; Fliegelman, *Prodigals and Pilgrims*, 99–100. David Lowenthal, *The Past Is a Foreign Country* (Cambridge: Cambridge University Press, 1985), 105, 108. On the use of the father image, see Winthrop Jordan, "Familial Politics: Thomas Paine and the Killing of the King, 1776," *Journal of American History* 60 (September 1973): 299–300, 304–5, 308.

65. Bercovitch, *Rites of Assent*, 177; Alan Heimert, *Religion and the American Mind* (Cambridge, MA: Harvard University Press, 1966), 470 and n., 244–46, 358; Carl J. Richard, *The Founders and the Classics* (Cambridge, MA: Harvard University Press, 1994), 233; Donald Weber, *Rhetoric and History in Revolutionary New England* (New York: Oxford University Press, 1988), 39, 43.

66. Pauline Maier, *The Old Revolutionaries* (Alfred A. Knopf, 1980), esp. last chapter; Eric McKitrick and Stanley Elkins, "The Founding Fathers, Young Men of the Revolution," *Political Science Quarterly* 76 (June 1961): 182–83, 203–6; Peter C. Hoffer, *Revolution and Regeneration: Life Cycle and the Historical Vision of the Generation of 1776* (Athens: University of Georgia Press, 1983), 5; Axtell, *School Upon a Hill*, 201–44, sketches the prerevolutionary school experience.

67. Bruce James Smith, *Politics and Remembrance* (Princeton: Princeton University Press, 1985), 9–11, 18, 49. Also see Edwin S. Gaustad, "Restitution, Revolution, and the American Dream," *Journal of the American Academy of Religion* 44 (March 1976): 78, 80.

68. Hoffer, *Revolution and Regeneration*, 32, 34; Burrows and Wallace, "American Revolution"; Werner Sollors, *Beyond Ethnicity* (New York: Oxford University Press, 1986), 227; Maier, *Old Revolutionaries*, 293; Catherine L. Albanese, *Sons of the Fathers* (Philadelphia: Temple University Press, 1976), 45, 9.

69. David Brion Davis describes this problem and identifies efforts by antislavery activists to "reanimate the sense of collective peril generated by the Revolution" in the section "The Perishability of Revolutionary Time," in *The Problem of Slavery in the Age of Revolution, 1770–1823* (Ithaca: Cornell University Press, 1975), 306–26, without comparing the situation to early New England.

70. Oliver Hart, *America's Remembrancer* (Philadelphia: T. Dobson, 1791) [EAI #23428], 8. Melvin Yazawa, *From Colonies to Commonwealth: Familial Ideology and the Beginnings of the America Republic* (Baltimore: Johns Hopkins University Press, 1985), 95, 98–101, discusses the hopeful youth imagery.

71. Joshua Scottow, *Old Mens Tears For Their Own Declensions* (Boston: Benjamin Harris and John Allen, 1691) [EAI #576], 15; Cotton Mather had done the same in *The Wonderful Works of God*, [6]. Also note *An Account, Shewing The Progress of the Colony of Georgia in America From Its First Establishment* (Annapolis, MD: James Green, 1742) [EAI #4961].

72. Stow Persons, "The Cyclical Theory of History in Eighteenth Century America," *American Quarterly* 6 (Summer 1954): 147–63; Hart, *America's Remembrancer,* 19.

73. Gregory H. Nobles, "The Politics of Patriarchy in Shays's Rebellion: The Case of Henry McCulloch," *Dublin Seminar for New England Folklife Annual Proceedings* 10 (1985): 42–43, 45; William Pencak, " 'The Fine Theoretic Government of Massachusetts is Prostrated to the Earth': The Response to Shays's Rebellion Reconsidered," in *In Debt to Shays,* ed. Robert A. Gross (Charlottesville: University Press of Virginia, 1993), 129, 131–32; *Worcester Magazine,* November 1786–April 1787.

74. Matthew Clarkson, *An Address to the Citizens of Philadelphia, Respecting the Better Government of Youth* (Philadelphia, Ormrod and Conrad, 1795) [EAI #28424], 5, 7, 12.

75. John K. Alexander, *Render Them Submissive: Responses to Poverty in Philadelphia, 1760–1800* (Amherst: University of Massachusetts Press, 1980), 81, 152–56; the quotation on the rising generation is on 155; Alexander also noted Mayor Clarkson's speech, 82. Anne M. Boylan, *Sunday School: The Formation of an American Institution 1790–1880* (New Haven: Yale University Press, 1988), 6.

76. Benjamin Rush, "A Plan for the Establishment of Public Schools" (1786), in *Essays on Education in the Early Republic,* ed. Frederick Rudolph (Cambridge, MA: Belknap Press, Harvard University Press, 1965), 6.

77. Samuel Knox, "An Essay on the Best System of Liberal Education," in Rudolph, *Essays on Education,* 296; note the similar sentiments by Anthony Benezet (attributed author) in *Some Necessary Remarks on the Education of Youth* (Philadelphia, 1778?) [EAI #15739], [1]. Also see David Tyack, "Forming the National Character: Paradox in the Educational Thought of the Revolutionary Generation," *Harvard Educational Review* 36 (Winter 1966): 29–30; Lawrence Cremin, *American Education: The National Experience* (New York: Harper and Row, 1980), 124; Allen Oscar Hansen, *Liberalism and American Education* (New York: Macmillan, 1926), 256. Also see Henry F. May, *The Enlightenment in America,* (New York: Oxford University Press, 1976), 210, 235–36.

78. Knox, "Essay on the Best System of Liberal Education," 276; Benjamin Rush, "Address to the People of the United States," *American Museum* 1 (January 1787): 11; idem, "A Plan for the Establishment of Public Schools" (1786), and "Thoughts Upon the Mode of Education Proper in a Republic" (1786), in Rudolph, *Essays on Education,* 6, 13–14, 19.

79. Noah Webster, "On the Education of Youth in America" (1790), in Rudolph, *Essays on Education,* 59–60 n., 65. Also see Tyack, "Forming the National Character," 31, and Jonathan Messerli, "The Columbian Complex: The Impulse to National Consolidation," *History of Education Quarterly* 7 (Winter 1967): 422.

80. Messerli, "The Columbian Complex," 417; Tyack, "Forming the National Character," 31, 41; Donald J. D'Elia, "Benjamin Rush: Philosopher of the American Revolution," *Transactions of the American Philosophical Society,* new ser.,

pt. 5, 64 (September 1974): 73. Yazawa, *Colonies to Commonwealth*, 165–87, also summarizes much of this material, though I am less convinced by his conclusion that a "world of order and affection, of filial fear and paternal faithfulness" was replaced by a regime emphasizing "autonomy and personal independence" (194).

81. Jürgen Gebhardt, *Americanism: Revolutionary Order and Societal Self-Interpretation in the American Republic*, trans. Ruth Hein (Baton Rouge: Louisiana State University Press, 1993), 45–49; Yazawa, *Colonies to Commonwealth*, 198; Fliegelman, *Prodigals and Pilgrims*, 199, 194. For a prerevolutionary example of a call to be a father to one's country, see *The Countryman's Lamentation, on the Neglect of a Proper Education of Children* (Philadelphia: W. Dunlap, 1762) [EAI #9097], 42.

82. Linda K. Kerber, *Women of the Republic* (Chapel Hill: University of North Carolina Press, 1980), 229; Smith quoted by Persons, "The Cyclical Theory of History in Eighteenth Century America," 156; Ruth Bloch, "The Gendered Meanings of Virtue in Revolutionary America," *Signs* 13 (Autumn 1987): 56 and passim; also see idem, "American Feminine Ideals in Transition: The Rise of the Moral Mother," *Feminist Studies* 4 (June 1978): 113–15, 119–20, Kerber, *Women of the Republic*, 199–200.

83. Jan Lewis, "The Republic Wife: Virtue and Seduction in the Early Republic," *William and Mary Quarterly*, 3d ser. 44 (October 1987): 690, 699, 702–3. Maris A. Vinovskis, "Family and Schooling in Colonial and Nineteenth-Century America," *Journal of Family History* 12, 1–3 (1987): 23; Gerald F. Moran and Maris A. Vinovskis, "The Great Care of Godly Parents: Early Childhood in Puritan New England," in *History and Research in Child Development*, ed. Alice Boardman Smuts and John W. Hagen (*Monographs of the Society for Research in Child Development* no. 4–5, 1985), 35–36.

84. Thomas Woody, *A History of Women's Education in the United States*, vol. 1 (New York: Science Press, 1929), 339. Mary Beth Norton, *Liberty's Daughters* (Boston: Little, Brown, 1980), 276 and passim; Ann D. Gordon, "The Young Ladies Academy of Philadelphia," in *Women of America: A History*, ed. Carol Ruth Berkin and Mary Beth Norton (Boston: Houghton Mifflin, 1979), 69–91; Kerber, *Women of the Republic*, 213, 227. Sarah Emily Newton, "Wise and Foolish Virgins: 'Usable Fiction' and the Early American Conduct Tradition," *Early American Literature* 25, 2 (1990): 148, quoted Foster's dedication to different purposes in a discussion of themes in early national fiction.

85. Historians often refer to a single academy, a conception promoted by one of the schools in *The Rise and Progress of the Young Ladies' Academy of Philadelphia* (Philadelphia: Steward and Cochran, 1794) [EAI #27514], [3]; this was in fact the second of the two schools. See *Pennsylvania Gazette*, August 25, 1784, 3; May 10, 1786, 1. Samuel Magaw, *Discourse Occasioned by the Mournful Catastrophe, Through Fire, Which Overwhelmed and Destroyed Mr. Andrew Brown* (Philadelphia, 1797) [EAI #32413], 11, and "Appendix," [29–30], on the first academy and its founder.

86. Samuel Magaw, "An address delivered in the Young Ladies' Academy at Philadelphia, on February 8th 1787, at the close of a public examination," *Amer-*

ican Museum 3 (January 1788): 25–28; John Swanwick, *Thoughts on Education Addressed to the Visitors of the Young Ladies Academy in Philadelphia* (Philadelphia: Thomas Dobson, 1787) [EAI #20736], 6, 25–26.

87. Swanwick, *Thoughts on Education*, 23, 25–26, 22 (emphasis added).

88. Benjamin Rush, *Thoughts Upon Female Education Accommodated to the Present State of Society, Manners, and Government in the United States of America* (Philadelphia: Prichard and Hall, 1787) [EAI #20691], 6–7, 8, 10–11; "Address of Rev. Sproat," in *The Rise and Progress of the Young Ladies' Academy of Philadelphia*, 26; John Poor, "Address," in James Armstrong Neal, *An Essay on the Education and Genius of the Female Sex* (Philadelphia, Jacob Johnson and Co., 1795) [EAI #29135], which included material from the commencement of December 1794, and in the same volume, John Swanwick, "Address," 23. Swanwick was one trustee of the first academy who then became part of the board of Poor's school.

89. Gordon, "The Young Ladies Academy of Philadelphia," 82–83. Ann Harker, "Salutatory Oration," and Ann Negus, "Valedictory Oration," in Neal, *An Essay on the Education and Genius of the Female Sex*, 17–18, 19, 35.

3. Youth Organized

1. Speech by Robert C. Winthrop, State Convention of Whig Young Men, Whig Party Papers, Box 6, Folder 2, Massachusetts Collection, American Antiquarian Society, Worcester; American Anti-Slavery Society, *Seventh Annual Report* (1840; Kraus Reprint Co., 1972), 4.

2. "Notes of Convention," State Convention of Whig Young Men, September 11, 1839, Whig Party Papers, Box 6, Folder 2, Massachusetts Collection, American Antiquarian Society.

3. Lewis Perry, *Boats against the Current: American Culture between Revolution and Modernity, 1820–1860* (New York: Oxford University Press, 1993), 48.

4. "To the Young Men of Massachusetts," *Proceedings of the Convention of the Young Men of Massachusetts Friendly to the Cause of Temperance* (Boston: Ford and Damrell, 1834), 15.

5. William H. Seward, *Autobiography of William H. Seward from 1801 to 1834* (New York: D. Appleton and Co., 1877), 68 (emphasis added).

6. See, for example, Phillip Andrew Gibbs, "Seasons of American Manhood, 1750–1860: Mirror of the Changing Republic" (Ph.D. diss., Mississippi State University, 1988); E. Anthony Rotundo, "Manhood in America: The Northern Middle Class, 1770–1920" (Ph.D. diss., Brandeis University, 1982).

7. E. Anthony Rotundo, "Romantic Friendship: Male Intimacy and Middle Class Youth in the Northern United States, 1800–1900," *Journal of Social History* 23 (fall 1989): 1, 13–14, 18–19. Also see idem, "Body and Soul: Changing Ideals of American Middle-Class Manhood, 1770–1920," *Journal of Social History* 16 (Summer 1983): 23–38, and idem, "Learning about Manhood: Gender Ideals and the Middle-Class Family in Nineteenth-Century America," in *Manliness and Morality*, ed. J. A. Mangan and James Walvin (Manchester: Manchester University Press, 1987).

8. Karen Halttunen, *Confidence Men and Painted Women* (New Haven: Yale University Press, 1982), 1–55.

9. Joseph Kett, *Rites of Passage: Adolescence in America 1790 to the Present* (New York: Basic Books, 1977), 93–102, 31, 43, covers the migration to cities and young people's associations. Also see Walter Nugent, *Structures of American Social History* (Bloomington: Indiana University Press, 1981), 25–30; Warren S. Thompson and P. K. Whelpton, *Population Trends in the United States* (New York: McGraw-Hill, 1933), 131.

10. John Modell, Frank Furstenberg, Jr., and Theodore Hershberg, "Social Change and Transitions to Adulthood in Historical Perspective," *Journal of Family History* 1 (Autumn 1976): 7–32; Kett, *Rites of Passage*, 13–36; E. Anthony Rotundo, *American Manhood* (New York: Basic Books, 1993), 55.

11. John Demos, "Oedipus and America: Historical Perspectives on the Reception of Psychoanalysis in the United States," *Annual of Psychoanalysis* 6 (1978): 30, 35; E. Anthony Rotundo, "American Fatherhood: A Historical Perspective," *American Behavioral Scientist* 29 (September/October 1985): 11, 13; idem, *American Manhood*, 26; Ronald P. Byars, "The Making of the Self-Made Man: The Development of Masculine Roles and Images in Antebellum America" (Ph.D. diss., Michigan State University, 1979), 34–36; William J. Gilmore, *Reading Becomes a Necessity of Life* (Knoxville: University of Tennessee Press, 1989), 216–20.

12. Richard Stott, *Workers in the Metropolis: Class, Ethnicity, and Youth in Antebellum New York City* (Ithaca: Cornell University Press, 1990), 74, 245 and passim; Christine Stansell, *City of Women: Sex and Class in New York, 1789–1860* (Urbana: University of Illinois Press, 1986), 76, 89–101; Stuart Blumin, *The Emergence of the Middle Class* (Cambridge: Cambridge University Press, 1989), 215–17.

13. Paul A. Gilje, *The Road to Mobocracy* (Chapel Hill: University of North Carolina Press, 1987), 260–64; Susan G. Davis, " 'Making Night Hideous': Christmas Revelry and Public Disorder in Nineteenth Century Philadelphia," *American Quarterly* 34 (Summer 1982): 189–90. Blumin, *Emergence of the Middle Class*, 231. Louis Mazoyer, "Categories d'âge et groupes sociaux—les jeunes générations françaises de 1830," *Annales d'histoire économique et sociale* 53 (September 30, 1938): 385–419, describes the parallel situation in France of young men coming to Paris; class and occupational divisions ensured there was no uniform attitude among the young. Parisian young men in the middle and professional classes were also the most age-conscious. See esp. 395, 418–19.

14. Mary Ann Clawson, *Constructing Brotherhood: Class, Gender, and Fraternalism* (Princeton: Princeton University Press, 1989), 47; also see Mark C. Carnes, *Secret Ritual and Manhood in Victorian America* (New Haven: Yale University Press, 1989).

15. James Fenimore Cooper, *Homeward Bound* (1838; New York: G. P. Putnam's Sons, Leatherstocking Edition, n.d.), 38–39; idem, *Home as Found* (1838; New York: Capricorn Books, 1961), 225–26.

16. Arthur M. Schlesinger cites the quotation about rising youth in *Prelude to Independence* (New York: Alfred A. Knopf, 1958; reprint, Boston: Northeastern

University Press, 1980), 30; see Richard Frothingham, *Life and Times of Joseph Warren* (Boston: Little Brown, 1865 reprint, New York: Da Capo Press, 1971), 176–77, 430–33, for excerpts from the two orations; these words are quoted on the title page of Joseph Gleason, Jr., *An Oration Pronounced on the Thirtieth Anniversary of American Independence* (Boston: Oliver and Munroe, 1806) [EAI #S10487].

17. Gerd Hurm, "The Rhetoric of Continuity in Early Boston Orations," in *The Fourth of July: Political Oratory and Literary Reactions, 1776–1876*, ed. Paul Goetsch and Gerd Hurm (Tübingen: Gunter Narr Verlag, 1992), 57–60, 67, 74, 78; John Leland, *Address to the Young Men of Cheshire* (Pittsfield, MA: Phineas Allen, 1808) [EAI #S50863], [3].

18. Len Travers, "Hurrah for the Fourth: Patriotism, Politics, and Independence Day in Federalist Boston, 1783–1818," *Essex Institute Historical Collections* 125 (April 1989): 131, 148, 160. For some orations organized by the Young Democratic Republicans, see those by Gleason, *An Oration Pounced on the Thirtieth Anniversary*; Ebenezer French, *An Oration Pronounced July 4, 1805* (Boston: J. Ball, 1805) [EAI #S8480, S8481, 2d ed.]; and Elihu Hobart, *An Oration Pronounced At Abington, July 4, 1807* (Boston: Manning and Loring, 1807) [EAI #S12762].

19. John Wells, *An Oration Delivered on the Fourth of July, 1798 . . . Before the Young Men of the City of New-York* (New York: McLean and Lang, 1798) [EAI #34998], 19–20.

20. Charles G. Haines, *An Oration Before the Young Republican Gentlemen of Concord* (Concord, NH: Isaac Hill, 1809) [EAI #S17694], 13; Jonathan B. Smith, *Oration Delivered . . . Before the Association of Democratic Young Men* (Philadelphia, 1813) [EAI #S29800], 24–25; David L. Parmalee, *An Address Delivered at Goshen . . . At the Desire of the Young Men of the Town* (Hartford, CT: Peter B. Gleason and Co., 1814) [EAI #S32439], 19.

21. Whitney R. Cross, *The Burned-Over District* (Ithaca: Cornell University Press, 1950; New York: Harper Torchbook, 1965), 19–26; William Warren Sweet, *Religion in the Development of American Culture, 1765–1840* (New York: Charles Scribner's Sons, 1952), 262, 258; Clifford S. Griffin, *Their Brothers' Keepers* (New Brunswick: Rutgers University Press, 1960).

22. "Young Men's Education Society," *Boston Recorder*, February 12, 1820; "Second Annual Report of the Board of Directors of the General Missionary Society of Young People in the Western District," *Evangelical Recorder*, February 28, 1818, 66, 67; Auxiliary Education Society of the Young Men of Boston, *Second Report of the Directors* (Boston: Crocker and Brewster, 1821), 15, and *First Report of the Directors* (Boston: U. Crocker, 1820), 11.

23. *Religious Miscellany*, August 16, 1823, 58; *Monitor*, January 1823, 18–20, and February 1823, 50; Hillel Schwartz, "Adolescence and Revivals in Ante-Bellum Boston," *Journal of Religious History* 8 (December 1974): 144–58. The appeals were not always so nationally minded; see, for example, *Religious Intelligencer*, November 16, 1816, 394, and February 1, 1817, 576.

24. On the role of New York young men's societies, see Carroll Smith Rosenberg, *Religion and the Rise of the American City* (Ithaca: Cornell University

Press, 1971), 54–60; she discusses women's and other organizations throughout the book. *Boston Recorder,* January 11, 1823; "Young Men's Missionary Society, Charleston, S.C.," *Boston Recorder,* July 27, 1822; *Virginia Evangelical and Literary Magazine* 3 (April 1820): 199–200; *Religious Miscellany,* July 25, 1823, 3–5.

25. Rotundo, *American Manhood,* 71; also see 21, 61, 64.

26. New York Apprentice's Temperance Society, *Second Annual Report* (New York, 1832), 11; Blumin, *Emergence of the Middle Class,* 201, uses other temperance materials to make an observation similar to the one made by the apprentices; also see 193–95.

27. Nancy F. Cott, "Young Women in the Second Great Awakening in New England," *Feminist Studies* 3 (Fall 1975): 16, 21; idem, *The Bonds of Womanhood* (New Haven: Yale University Press, 1977), 133–34, 140–41, 148, 158–59; Anne M. Boylan surveys the period in "Growing Up Female in Young America, 1800–1860," in *American Childhood,* ed. Joseph M. Hawes and N. Ray Hiner (Westport, CT: Greenwood Press, 1985).

28. "Young Ladies' Missionary Society of Philadelphia," *Religious Intelligencer,* December 20, 1828, 468; Young Ladies' Association for Promotion of Literature and Missions, *Second Annual Report* (Philadelphia: King and Baird, 1840), 27.

29. Anne M. Boylan notes differences in "Women in Groups: An Analysis of Women's Benevolent Organizations in New York and Boston, 1797–1840," *Journal of American History* 71 (December 1984): 502–7; she describes the relative ages of women's organization participants in "Timid Girls, Venerable Widows and Dignified Matrons: Life Cycle Patterns among Organized Women in New York and Boston, 1797–1840," *American Quarterly* 38 (Winter 1986): 784–88.

30. See Lori D. Ginzberg, *Women and the Work of Benevolence* (New Haven: Yale University Press, 1990); Jean Fagan Yellin, *Women and Sisters: The Antislavery Feminists in American Culture* (New Haven: Yale University Press, 1989); and Blanche Glassman Hersh, *The Slavery of Sex: Feminist-Abolitionists in America* (Urbana: University of Illinois Press, 1978), on feminist consciousness in antislavery organizations.

31. Philadelphia Young Men's Society, *Constitution* (Philadelphia: William F. Geddes, 1833), 6; John Bell, *An Address on the Spirit of Associations, Delivered Before the Philadelphia Young Men's Society* (Philadelphia: William Stavely, 1834), 6–7; *Journal of the National Convention of Young Men's Societies* 1 (January 1834): 12.

32. Philadelphia Young Men's Society, *Constitution,* 5; New York Young Men's Society, *Constitution* (New York: J. and J. Harper, 1831), 4–5; Bell, *Address on the Spirit of Associations,* 20; J. R. Tyson, *A Discourse Before the Young Men's Colonization Society of Pennsylvania* (Philadelphia, 1834), 7, 6.

33. Mary P. Ryan, *Cradle of the Middle Class* (Cambridge: Cambridge University Press, 1981), 105–44, esp. 128–30, discusses young men's associations; Gary J. Kornblith, "The Rise of the Mechanic Interest and the Campaign to Develop Manufacturing in Salem, 1815–1830," *Essex Institute Historical Collections* 121 (January 1985): 51–52; Wallace Kenneth Schoenberg, "The Young Men's Associ-

ation, 1833–1876: The History of a Social-Cultural Organization" (Ph.D. diss., New York University , 1962), provides careful detail on the organizations' role in founding public libraries.

34. *Proceedings of the Constitutional Republican Young Men of the City and County of Philadelphia* (Philadelphia: C. Zentler, 1808) [EAI #S14772], 8, 11.

35. "Democratic Young Men," *Tickler,* July 12, 1809; Leland, *Address to the Young Men of Cheshire,* 11, 12; "Address of the Republican General Committee of the City and County of New York, To the Republican Young Men," *Rhode Island Republican,* June 13, 1810.

36. *New York American,* February 15, 1821.

37. Dixon Ryan Fox, *The Decline of Aristocracy in the Politics of New York* (New York: Columbia University Press, 1919), 297, noted that the 1824 campaign was the first to include special appeals to young men.

38. *Republican Meeting: At a Numerous Meeting of Democratic Republican Young Men of the Town of Delhi,* October 22, 1824, Broadside.

39. "Young Men's County Convention," *Albany Daily Advertiser Extra,* October 18, 1824, Broadside.

40. Young Men's Temperance Society of the City of Albany, *Proceedings of the Annual Meeting* (Albany: Hoffman and White, 1836), 19; Boston Young Men's Temperance Society, *Address to the Young Men of Boston* (Boston: Garrison and Knapp, 1832), 11.

41. Young Men's Temperance Society of Albany, *Proceedings,* 24.

42. William Breitenbach, "Sons of the Fathers: Temperance Reformers and the Legacy of the American Revolution," *Journal of the Early Republic* 3 (Spring 1983): 69–82; also see W. J. Rorabaugh, *The Alcoholic Republic* (New York: Oxford University Press, 1979), 138–40.

43. *Convention of the Young Men of Massachusetts Friendly to the Cause of Temperance* (1834), 14; New York Young Men's Society for the Promotion of Temperance, *An Address to the Young Men of the United States on the Subject of Temperance* (New York: Jonathan Leavitt, 1830), 15.

44. David Donald, "Toward a Reconsideration of the Abolitionists," in *Lincoln Reconsidered* (New York: Alfred A. Knopf, 1956), 27, 33, 35; Jane H. Pease and William H. Pease, *Bound with Them in Chains* (Westport, CT: Greenwood Press, 1972), 313; Lawrence J. Friedman, "Pious Fellowship and Modernity: A Psychological Interpretation," in *Crusaders and Compromisers,* ed. Alan M. Kraut (Westport, CT: Greenwood Press, 1983), 236–37; Bertram Wyatt-Brown, *Yankee Saints and Southern Sinners* (Baton Rouge: Louisiana State University Press, 1985), 56; Charles A. Jarvis, "Admission to Abolition: The Case of John Greenleaf Whittier," *Journal of the Early Republic* 4 (summer 1984): 161–76.

45. Edward Magdol, *The Antislavery Rank and File* (Westport, CT: Greenwood Press, 1986), 46–47, 50, 64–65, 97.

46. John Greenleaf Whittier to Isaac Knapp, September 26, 1833, in Antislavery Collections, Rare Books and Manuscripts, Boston Public Library. The editor of Whittier's letters thinks this refers to the adult antislavery society. Also see Whittier's attendance at other young men's meetings for temperance as well as abolition, in *The Letters of John Greenleaf Whittier,* vol. 1, ed. John B. Pickard (Cambridge, MA: Belknap Press, Harvard University Press, 1975), 134, 167.

47. Occupations of leaders in notes to *Letters of William Lloyd Garrison,* vol. 2, ed. Louis Ruchames (Cambridge: Belknap Press, Harvard University Press, 1971), 183, 96, 88; the abolitionist Henry B. Stanton recalled his experience in *Random Reflections* (Johnstown, NY: Blanck and Leaming, 1885), 21. In his case, it was a Young Men's state National Republican Convention in New York.

48. Hugh Davis, *Joshua Leavitt, Evangelical Abolitionist* (Baton Rouge: Louisiana State University Press, 1990), 158, 161, describes financial dealings between groups; Lawrence B. Goodheart, *Abolitionist, Actuary, Atheist: Elizur Wright and the Reform Impulse* (Kent, OH: Kent State University Press, 1990), 61; Theodore Dwight Weld, *Letters of Theodore Dwight Weld, Angelina Grimké Weld and Sarah Grimké* ed. Gilbert H. Barnes and Dwight L. Dumond, vol. 1 (New York: D. Appleton-Century Co., 1934), 204, 221, 227–28, 232, 240; New York Young Men's Anti-Slavery Society, *First Annual Report* (New York: Coolidge and Lambert, 1835), 14.

49. New-York Young Men's Anti-Slavery Society, *First Annual Report,* 16–17; John W. Browne, speech at anniversary meeting of the New York Young Men's Anti-Slavery Society, reported in the *Liberator,* June 23, 1837, 101.

50. William Lloyd Garrison to Joseph Kimball, *Letters of William Lloyd Garrison,* vol. 2, 282, 287; also see Garrison to George W. Benson, in ibid., vol. 1, ed. Walter M. Merrill, 272.

51. Paul Goodman, *Towards a Christian Republic* (New York: Oxford University Press, 1988), is the most recent treatment of Antimasonry; see esp. 20–29; he suggests a competition with Masons over controlling the socialization of the young (89–90). Amasa Walker is quoted by Ronald P. Formisano in *The Transformation of Political Culture: Massachusetts Parties, 1790s–1840s* (New York: Oxford University Press, 1983), 439 n. 80; the appeal is quoted on 220. John L. Brooke, *The Heart of the Commonwealth: Society and Political Culture in Worcester County, Massachusetts 1713–1861* (Cambridge: Cambridge University Press, 1989), 356, describes the situation in Worcester.

52. But note that Paul Boyer argues that voluntary association leaders were "comparative newcomers" to the cities, although he agrees with their white-collar/professional character. My assertions are based on the lists of officers of numerous young men's organizations in many cities and a comparison of the lists to city directories and town histories. See, for example, the Worcester, Massachusetts, delegates to young men's temperance, National Republican, and Whig conventions, and William Lincoln, *History of Worcester, Massachusetts* (Worcester, MA: Moses D. Phillips and Co., 1837). Paul Boyer, *Urban Masses and Moral Order in America, 1820–1920* (Cambridge, MA: Harvard University Press, 1978), 15, 112.

53. Peter D. McClelland and Richard J. Zeckhauser, *Demographic Dimensions of the New Republic* (Cambridge: Cambridge University Press, 1982), 50, 138–41; Don Harrison Doyle, "The Social Functions of Voluntary Associations in a Nineteenth-Century American Town," *Social Science History* 1 (Spring 1977): 336, 338, 346–49, and discussion in his *Social Order of a Frontier Community* (Urbana: University of Illinois Press, 1978). Walter S. Glazer, "Participation and Power: Voluntary Associations and the Functional Organization of

Cincinnati in 1840," *Historical Methods Newsletter* 5 (September 1972): 155, 165, 167.

54. Homer J. Webster, "History of the Democratic Party Organization in the Northwest," *Ohio Archaeological and Historical Publications* 24 (1915): 44, 64–66, 84, 87 and passim; Frederick J. Blue, *Salmon P. Chase: A Life in Politics* (Kent, OH: Kent State University Press, 1987), 16, 28, 42; James E. Stegemoeller, "That Contemptible Bauble: The Birth of the Cincinnati Whig Party, 1834–1836," *Cincinnati Historical Society Bulletin* 39 (Fall 1981): 201, 203, 207, 219.

55. David L. Angus, "Common School Politics in a Frontier City: Detroit, 1836–1842," in *Schools in Cities,* ed. Ronald K. Goodenow and Diane Ravitch (New York: Holmes and Meier, 1983), 217–18.

56. Paul Goodman, "The Social Basis of New England Politics in Jacksonian America," *Journal of the Early Republic* 6 (spring 1986): 31, 35, argues that generation was an important political category but did not find it in political speeches; Jean Baker, "The Ceremonies of Politics: Nineteenth-Century Rituals of National Affirmation," in *A Master's Due: Essays in Honor of David Herbert Donald,* ed. William J. Cooper, Jr., Michael F. Holt, John McCardell. (Baton Rouge: Louisiana State University Press, 1985), 167, 170, characterizes the phrase as a "cliché."

57. John Julius Reed, "The Emergence of the Whig Party in the North: Massachusetts, New York, Pennsylvania, and Ohio" (Ph.D. diss., University of Pennsylvania, 1953), 150 describes communication between young men's committees and party leaders; Whig Party, *Proceedings of a Meeting of the Whig Young Men of the City of New-York* (New York: T. Snowden, 1834), 5–6; Palmcard in Whig Scrapbook, Rare Book and Manuscript Library, Columbia University .

58. On campaigning see Richard P. McCormick, *The Presidential Game* (New York: Oxford University Press, 1982), esp. 149–54, 197–201; Amy Bridges, *A City in the Republic* (Cambridge: Cambridge University Press, 1984), 82, writes that "most prominent Democratic politicians of the 1850s were already at work in Tammany's Young Men's General Committee by 1840."

59. Democratic Party, *Address of the Republican General Committee of Young men of the City and County of New-York Friendly to the Election of Gen. Andrew Jackson to the Presidency* (New York: Alexander Ming, Jr., 1828), 4, 35–36.

60. Democratic Party, *Address of the Democratic Young Men's General Committee* (New York: Peter Van Pelt, 1835), 7; occupations in Walter Hugins, *Jacksonian Democracy and the Working Class* (Stanford: Stanford University Press, 1960), 95, 102.

61. This nineteenth-century observation quoted in William Trimble, "Diverging Tendencies in the New York Democracy in the Period of the Locofocos," *American Historical Review* 24 (April 1919): 399–400. Also see Carl Degler, "The Locofocos: Urban 'Agrarians,' " *Journal of Economic History* 16 (September 1956): 322–33, for a summary of Locofoco beliefs.

62. Fitzwilliam Byrdsall, *The History of the Loco-Foco or Equal Rights Party* (New York, 1842; reprint, New York: Burt Franklin, 1967), 23–27, gives a full account of the incident (Byrdsall was the party secretary); also see James Gordon Bennett's editorial in the *New York Herald,* October 30, 1835; Gustavus

Myers, *The History of Tammany Hall* (New York: published by the author, 1901), 133.

63. *New York Herald,* September 5, 1837; "The Young Men's Resolutions," *Plaindealer,* June 17, 1837, 452–53; "Resolution of Democratic-Republican Young Men's General Committee," printed as an advertisement in the *Plaindealer* on that day.

64. Resolutions in *New York Evening Post,* September 5, 1837.

65. Bray Hammond, *Banks and Politics in America from the Revolution to the Civil War* (Princeton: Princeton University Press 1957), 496, 498, explains the Van Buren proposal; *Plaindealer,* September 9, 1837, 649; Young Men's Committee resolution printed in the *Evening Post,* September 13, 1837.

66. *Evening Post,* September 14, 1837; "Up and Doing," *Plaindealer,* September 16, 1837, 665; ward committee resolutions in the *Evening Post,* September 16–19, 1837; Byrdsall, *History of the Loco-Foco,* 162; *New York Herald,* September 21, 1837.

67. Trimble, "Diverging Tendencies," 412; also see *Plaindealer,* September 30, 1837, 689–92, for coverage of the meeting; Democratic Party, *Address of the Democratic Republican Young Men's General Committee* (New York: J. M. Marsh, 1838), 21–22; for the role of future New York mayor Wood in the compromise, see Jerome Mushkat, *Fernando Wood: A Political Biography* (Kent, OH: Kent State University Press, 1990), 8–11.

68. Democratic Party, *Address of the Democratic Republican Young Men's General Committee of the City of New York to the Republican Young Men of the State* (New York, 1840), 3.

69. Note also Leggett's review of a new edition of *Pilgrim's Progress,* in *Plaindealer,* December 24, 1836, 55; "Political Portraits with Pen and Pencil—William Leggett," a posthumous tribute in the *United States Magazine and Democratic Review* 6 (July 1839): 23, 27, discusses Leggett's influence on young men and mentions the monument.

70. "Minutes of the Young Men's Whig Association of Pittsburgh, 1834," Russell J. Ferguson, ed., *Western Pennsylvania Historical Magazine* 19 (March 1936): 215–16. Daniel Walker Howe, in *The Political Culture of the American Whigs* (Chicago: University of Chicago Press, 1979), 71, wrote that Whigs "typically turned to history," Democrats "to principle."

71. National Republican Young Men's Meeting, *For the Constitution and the Laws* (Worcester, MA, 1832), Broadside; National Republican Party, *Proceedings of the State Convention of National Republican Young Men, Holden at Hartford* (Hartford, CT: Hamner and Comstock, 1832), 7.

72. *Niles' Register,* May 26, 1832, 237; Nathan Sargent, *Public Men and Events,* vol. 1 (Philadelphia: J. B. Lippincott and Co., 1875), 195; Glyndon G. Van Deusen, "The Whig Party," in *History of U.S. Political Parties,* ed. Arthur Schlesinger, Jr., vol. 1 (New York: Chelsea House, R. R. Bowker, 1973), 336; National Republican Party, *Proceedings of the National Republican Convention of Young Men, Which Assembled in the City of Washington May 7, 1832* (Washington, DC: Gales and Seaton, 1832), 6, 11–13, 8–9; Robert P. Hay, "Charles Carroll and the Passing of the Revolutionary Generation," *Maryland Historical Magazine* 67 (Spring 1972): 54–62, describes his national appeal.

73. Elliott R. Barkan, "The Emergence of a Whig Persuasion: Conservatism, Democratism, and the New York State Whigs," *New York History* 52 (October 1971): 384–85; he cites young men's groups on several occasions without connecting them to this sense.

74. Whig Young Men of New York City, "Address to the Young Men of New York," *Jeffersonian*, October 28, 1838; Winthrop speech, October 1834, clipping in a scrapbook in the microfilm edition of the *Winthrop Family Papers* (Boston: Massachusetts Historical Society), Reel 44.

75. Howe, *Political Culture of American Whigs*, 31–32, 72; *Workingman's Advocate*, October 26, 1844, assailed the young Whigs; Philip Hone, *The Diary of Philip Hone*, ed. Bayard Tuckerman, vol. 1 (New York: Dodd, Mead and Co., 1889), 386.

76. Frederick Cople Jaher, "The Politics of the Boston Brahmins, 1800–1860," in *Boston 1700–1980: The Evolution of Urban Politics*, ed. Ronald P. Formisano and Constance K. Burns (Westport, CT: Greenwood Press, 1987), describes Winthrop's integral place in elite Boston.

77. Robert C. Winthrop Diary, 1836, Winthrop Papers, Reel 22.

78. On Winthrop's biography, see Robert C. Winthrop, Jr., *Memoir of Robert C. Winthrop* (Boston: Little, Brown, 1897), 1–23; many of Winthrop's speeches to young men's groups can be read in newspaper clippings kept in a scrapbook in the Winthrop Papers, Reel 44; the speech on divisions between old and young was made on November 21, 1834.

79. Manuscript notes of Winthrop's speech to the Young Men's Whig Convention in the Whig Party Papers at American Antiquarian Society; *Proceedings of the Whig State Convention at Worcester, Mass, June 17, 1840*, Broadside.

80. Clifford to Winthrop, July 19, 1839, and idem, September 24, 1839, Winthrop Papers. Gov. Edward Everett, Winthrop's long-time political mentor, had read Winthrop's speech to the Young Men's Convention and urged him as he revised it not to "avow so entire an ignorance of the individuals of the body." Winthrop's rhetoric, however, seems to be his own, and is consistent with his previous decade of young men's addresses. Everett to Winthrop, September 16, 1839, Winthrop Papers.

81. Robert C. Winthrop, *Memoir of the Hon. John H. Clifford* (Boston: John Wilson and Son, 1877), 8–9, 19; Robert C. Winthrop, "Dedication," *Addresses and Speeches on Various Occasions* (Boston: Little, Brown, 1852); Winthrop and Clifford's correspondence in "Miscellaneous Family Correspondence," Reel 22, and "Robert C. Winthrop Correspondence," Reel 39, Winthrop Papers. Further evidence on lifelong emotional attachments formed in youth between men of this time is presented in Donald Yacovone, "Abolitionists and the 'Language of Fraternal Love,' " in *Meanings for Manhood*, ed. Mark C. Carnes and Clyde Griffen (Chicago: University of Chicago Press, 1990), 85–95.

82. Abraham Lincoln, *The Collected Works of Abraham Lincoln*, ed. Roy P. Basler, vol. 1 (New Brunswick: Rutgers University Press, 1953), 109, 112, 113.

83. Edmund Wilson, *Patriotic Gore* (New York: Oxford University Press, 1962), 108; Charles B. Strozier, "On the Verge of Greatness: Psychological Reflections on Lincoln at the Lyceum," *Civil War History* 36 (June 1990): 146; Dwight G. Anderson, *Abraham Lincoln: The Quest for Immortality* (New York:

Alfred A. Knopf, 1982), 73; George Forgie offers another version of these arguments in *Patricide in the House Divided* (New York: W. W. Norton, 1979). These are only some of the recent studies on the Lyceum speech.

84. Major L. Wilson, "Lincoln and Van Buren in the Steps of the Fathers: Another Look at the Lyceum Address," *Civil War History* 29 (September 1983): 203. Other critical examinations of the psychological interpretation include Richard Nelson Current, "The Myth of the Jealous Son," in *Arguing with Historians* (Middletown, CT: Wesleyan University Press, 1987), and Drew R. McCoy, "Lincoln and the Founding Fathers: A Reconsideration," *Journal of the Abraham Lincoln Association* 16 (Winter 1995): 1–13; neither of these authors, nor the others just cited, assess the address as a young men's association speech. But see Thomas F. Schwartz, "The Springfield Lyceums and Lincoln's 1838 Speech," *Illinois Historical Journal* 83 (Spring 1990): 45–9.

85. S. A. M. Washington, *George Thomas Downing, Sketch of His Life and Times* (Newport, RI: Milne Printers, 1910), 6–7; for more background on the group's early education see Milton C. Serrett, *Abolition's Axe: Beriah Green, Oneida Institute, and the Black Freedom Struggle* (Syracuse: Syracuse University Press, 1986), 54–57; Robert A. Warner, "Amos Gerry Beman—1812–1874, A Memoir on a Forgotten Leader," *Journal of Negro History* 22 (April 1937): 202.

86. Rhoda G. Freeman, "The Free Negro in New York City in the Era before the Civil War" (Ph.D. diss., Columbia University , 1966; University Microfilms, Inc., 1969), 282–83, 430–34; other occupations from advertisements in the *Colored American*; Julie Winch, "The Leaders of Philadelphia's Black Community, 1787–1848" (Ph.D. diss., Bryn Mawr College, 1982), 317–18, gives more details on young men's activities than does her published version, *Philadelphia's Black Elite* (Philadelphia: Temple University Press, 1988).

87. "A Call to Colored Young Men," *Colored American*, August 19, 1837; "Important Meeting," *Colored American*, September 2, 1837.

88. Wilson Jeremiah Moses, *Alexander Crummell: A Study of Civilization and Discontent* (New York: Oxford University Press, 1989), 9; Frederick Cooper, " 'Elevating the Race': The Social Thought of Black Leaders, 1827–50," *American Quarterly* 24 (December 1972): 615–16; Dorothy B. Porter, "The Organized Educational Activities of Negro Literary Societies, 1828–1846," *Journal of Negro Education* 5 (October 1936): 555–76.

89. *Colored American*, September 2, 1837.

90. "Philomiracks," Letter to the *Colored American*, October 7, 1837.

91. "Right of Suffrage," *Colored American*, December 16, 1837; "Constitution," *Colored American*, June 23, 1838, 71; Daniel Perlman, "Organizations of the Free Negro in New York City," *Journal of Negro History* 56 (July 1971): 188–90.

92. "Publico," Letter to the Editor, and editorial response, *Colored American*, July 14, 1838; also see David Ruggles, "Anniversary Meeting of the Phoenixonian Literary Society," and "To Correspondents" (editorial), *Colored American*, July 21, 1838, 87.

93. "A Phoenixonian," Letter to the Editor, *Colored American*, August 18, 1838, 103.

94. Robert J. Swan, "John Teasman: African-American Educator and the

Emergence of Community in Early Black New York City, 1787–1815," *Journal of the Early Republic* 12 (Fall 1992): 331–56; "Shade of Teasman," *Colored American*, August 25, 1838, 107.

95. Political Association resolutions in *Colored American*, September 8, 1838; "An Absent Sufferer," an editorial in the same day's paper, accuses Sidney. For the earlier charges against him see *Colored American*, March 3 and April 12, 1838.

96. Scrapbook of Amos G. Beman, Pastor, 1838–1857, vol. 1, James Weldon Johnson Collection, Beinecke Rare Book and Manuscript Library, Yale University.

97. Resolution at convention of the Colored Inhabitants of the State of New York, in Philip S. Foner and George E. Walker, eds., *Proceedings of the Black State Conventions, 1840–1865*, vol. 1 (Philadelphia: Temple University Press, 1979), 14; Howard Holman Bell, "A Survey of the Negro Convention Movement, 1830–1861" (Ph.D. diss., Northwestern University, 1953), 61–64, 66; American Anti-Slavery Society, *Seventh Annual Report*, 5.

98. William B. Gravely, "The Dialectic of Double-Consciousness in Black American Freedom Celebrations, 1808–1863," *Journal of Negro History* 67 (Winter 1982): 311–12; Benjamin Quarles, "Antebellum Free Blacks and the 'Spirit of '76,' " *Journal of Negro History* 61 (July 1976): 236.

99. Alexander Crummell, "Eulogium on the Life and Character of Thomas Sipkins Sidney," July 4, 1840, manuscript in *Black Abolitionist Papers*, Reel 3, 7, 54.

100. Crummell to ?, June 1840, in ibid., #464; Moses, *Alexander Crummell*, 18; the son was named Sidney Garnet; Crummell, "Eulogium on Henry Highland Garnet," in *Africa and America* (Springfield, MA: Willey and Co., 1891), 278 n.; for a different reading of the eulogy see Gregory U. Rigsby, *Alexander Crummell, Pioneer in Nineteenth-Century Pan-African Thought* (Westport, CT: Greenwood Press, 1987), 30–41.

101. Porter, "Activities of Negro Literary Societies," 564; Charles H. Brooks, *The Official History and Manual of the Grand United Order of Odd Fellows in America* (Philadelphia, 1902; reprint, Freeport, NY: Books for Libraries Press, 1971), 12, 15, 24, 33, 221.

102. New York State Convention of Colored Inhabitants, 1840, in Foner and Walker, *Proceedings of Black State Conventions*, 22; New York Young Men's Anti-Slavery Society, 18; *Proceedings of Whig Young Men of New York* (1834), 4.

103. Whig Party, *Proceedings of State Convention of Whig Young Men of Connecticut* (Hartford, CT: The Courant Office, (1840), 4; "Address to the Young Men of New York," *Jeffersonian*, October 28, 1838.

104. Crummell, "Eulogium on Sidney," 55; also note usage in "Important Meeting," *Colored American*, September 2, 1837.

105. Schwartz, "Adolescence and Revivals," 150–51; French, *Oration, July 4, 1805*, 21. For variations on the female warrior image in this period, see Daniel A. Cohen, " 'The Female Marine' in an Era of Good Feelings: Cross-Dressing and the 'Genius' of Nathaniel Coverly, Jr.," *Proceedings of the American Antiquarian Society* 103, pt. 2 (1993): 389.

106. Auxiliary Education Society of Young Men of Boston, *First Report*, 4; *Proceedings of the Convention of the Young Men of Massachusetts Friendly to the Cause of Temperance* (1834), 9; Young Men's Anti-Slavery Convention in New Hampshire, reported in *Liberator*, September 1, 1837, 142.

107. Rotundo, "Romantic Friendship," 19; David D. Gilmore, *Manhood in the Making: Cultural Concepts of Masculinity* (New Haven: Yale University Press, 1990), 229–30.

108. Young Men's Colonization Society, *Constitution* (New York: W. Osborn and Co., 1832), 4; Democratic Party, *Proceedings of the Democratic Republican Convention of Young Men of the State of Pennsylvania* (Harrisburg: Office of Pennsylvania Reporter and State Journal, 1836), 15; Michael A. Bernstein, "Northern Labor Finds a Southern Champion: A Note on the Radical Democracy, 1833–1849," in *New York and the Rise of American Capitalism*, ed. Walter Pencak and Conrad Edick Wright (New York: New-York Historical Society, 1989), 147–63; "Address to the Young Men of New York," *Jeffersonian*, October 28, 1838.

4. Art and Memory

1. Ralph Waldo Emerson, "Nature," in *Essays and Lectures* (New York: Library of America, 1983), 7; "National Gallery," *North American Review* 40 (April 1835): 409–10.

2. James Fenimore Cooper, *Home as Found* (1838; New York: Capricorn Books, 1961), 24; Ralph Waldo Emerson, "Introductory Lecture on the Times," in *Essays and Lectures*, 157; Lewis Perry, *Boats against the Current* (New York: Oxford University Press, 1993), 76–77; Michael Kammen, *Mystic Chords of Memory: The Transformation of Tradition in American Culture* (New York: Alfred A. Knopf, 1991), 87–88.

3. Emerson used these labels in "The Conservative," in *Essays and Lectures*, 173; R. W. B. Lewis offered a memorable analysis of the parties in *The American Adam* (Chicago: University of Chicago Press, 1955). Also see Fred Somkin, *Unquiet Eagle: Memory and Desire in the Idea of American Freedom, 1815–1860* (Ithaca: Cornell University Press, 1967), 176–80, and Paul C. Nagel, *This Sacred Trust* (New York: Oxford University Press, 1971), 68–73.

4. Joseph Story, *An Eulogy on General George Washington* (Salem, MA: Joshua Cushing, 1800) [EAI #38568], 12, 15, 3.

5. Daniel Webster, *An Oration Pronounced at Hanover* (Hanover, NH: Moses Davis, 1800) [EAI #39035], 3, 14–15.

6. Michael T. Gilmore, "Eulogy as Symbolic Biography: The Iconography of Revolutionary Leadership, 1776–1826," in *Studies in Biography*, ed. Daniel Aaron (Cambridge, MA: Harvard University Press, 1978), 131, 143, 146–48, 153.

7. See Robert P. Hay, "The Glorious Departure of the American Patriarchs: Contemporary Reactions to the Deaths of Jefferson and Adams," *Journal of Southern History* 35 (November 1969): 543–55.

8. Samuel Lorenzo Knapp, "An Address Delivered in Chauncey Place Church, Before the Young Men of Boston, August 2, 1826, in Commemoration of the

Deaths of Adams and Jefferson," in *A Selection of Eulogies Pronounced in the Several States in Honor of Those Illustrious Patriots and Statesmen, John Adams and Thomas Jefferson* (Hartford, CT: D. F. Robinson and Co., 1826), 188.

9. Ibid., 189, 190, 192.

10. Barry Schwartz, "The Social Context of Commemoration: A Study in Collective Memory," *Social Forces* 61 (December 1982): 395–96; Eugene F. Miller and Barry Schwartz, "The Icon of the American Republic: A Study in Political Symbolism," *Review of Politics* 47 (October 1985): 533–34, 527.

11. Barry Schwartz, *George Washington: The Making of an American Symbol* (New York: Free Press, 1987), 6; Miller and Schwartz, "Icon of the American Republic," 525–26.

12. Marc H. Miller, "Lafayette's Farewell Tour of America, 1824–25: A Study of the Pageantry and Public Portraiture" (Ph.D. diss., New York University, 1979), 146; Robert P. Hay, "Charles Carroll and the Passing of the Revolutionary Generation, *Maryland Historical Magazine* 67 (Spring 1972): 54–62; idem, "The American Revolution Twice Recalled: Lafayette's Visit and the Election of 1824," *Indiana Magazine of History* 69 (March 1973): 43–62; Somkin, *Unquiet Eagle,* 170, 137.

13. Miller makes a similar point in "Lafayette's Farewell Tour," 188.

14. Wendy Greenhouse, "The Landing of the Fathers: Representing the National Past, 1770–1860," in *Picturing History, American Painting 1770–1930,* ed. William Ayres (New York: Rizzoli, 1993), 53.

15. Brandon Brame Fortune, "Portraits of Virtue and Genius: Pantheons of Worthies and Public Portraiture in the Early American Republic" (Ph.D. diss., University of North Carolina, 1987), xxi, 207, 68, 71.

16. Lillian B. Miller, "Charles Willson Peale: A Life of Harmony and Purpose," in *Charles Willson Peale and His World* (New York: Harry N. Abrams, 1983), 233.

17. Schwartz, *George Washington,* 199.

18. Advertisement for Lafayette bust, *New York American,* August 20, 1825; Stuart's endorsement, *Richmond Enquirer,* December 13, 1825; *Richmond Enquirer,* November 4, 1825; all photocopies in the clipping file, Browere Collection, New York State Historical Association, Cooperstown, New York.

19. Fortune, "Portraits of Virtue," 70. Little seems to be known about Browere. Charles Henry Hart, *Browere's Life Masks of Great Americans* (New York: Doubleday and McClure, 1899), a revision of articles the author wrote for *McClure's,* remains the main source. Miller discusses Browere's work in "Lafayette's Farewell Tour," 190. David Meschutt, *A Bold Experiment: John Henri Isaac Browere's Life Masks* (Cooperstown: New York State Historical Society, 1988), is a recent pamphlet that provides good historical background on the busts that survive from Browere's gallery.

20. For the Browere-Madison correspondence see the James Madison Papers, Microfilm, Manuscripts and Archives, Yale University Library, September 12, 17, 28, 1825; February 4, July 17, 1826; and Delaplaine to Madison, February 26, May 23, October 22, 1816. Gordon M. Marshall, "The Golden Age of Illustrated Biographies: Three Case Studies," in *American Portrait Prints,* ed.

Wendy Wick Reaves (Charlottesville: University Press of Virginia, 1984), 59, characterizes Delaplaine's book.

21. Board of Directors Meeting, October 15, 1831, American Academy of Fine Arts, Microfilm, Manuscripts and Archives, Yale University Library. Robert G. Stewart, *A Nineteenth-Century Gallery of Distinguished Americans* (Washington, DC: Smithsonian Institution Press, 1969), 2–3, gives additional background on the project's origins.

22. Advertisement reprinted in Stewart, *Nineteenth-Century Gallery,* 5.

23. Quoted by Marshall in "Golden Age of Illustrated Biographies," 59.

24. "Address," *The National Portrait Gallery of Distinguished Americans,* ed. James B. Longacre and James Herring, vol. 1 (Philadelphia: Henry Perkis; New York: Monson Bancroft, 1834).

25. "Address," in ibid., vol 4 (1839).

26. "National Portrait Gallery of Distinguished Americans," *New York Review* 4 (April 1839): 378–79, 355.

27. "Louisa C. Adams," *National Portrait Gallery of Distinguished Americans,* vol. 4.

28. "National Gallery," *North American Review* 40 (April 1835): 410.

29. "National Portrait Gallery" (1839) 352, 353.

30. "National Gallery" (1835), 411; "National Portrait Gallery" (1839), 392.

31. Joseph Tracy used *The Christian History* as his main source in *The Great Awakening* (Boston: Charles Tappan, 1845; reprint, New York: Arno Press, 1969). Joseph Conforti has traced the creation of Jonathan Edwards as a founding father of the Second Great Awakening in a series of articles; the quotation appeared in "Antebellum Evangelicals and the Cultural Revival of Jonathan Edwards," *American Presbyterians* 64 (Winter 1986): 237; also see idem, "Edwardsians, Unitarians, and the Memory of the Great Awakening, 1800–1840," in *American Unitarianism, 1805–1865,* ed. Conrad Edick Wright (Boston: Massachusetts Historical Society, 1989), and idem, "The Invention of the Great Awakening, 1795–1842," *Early American Litearture* 26, 2 (1991): 99–118. Also see Perry, *Boats against the Current* 52.

32. Marcus Cunliffe analyzes Lester's life and career (although without reference to any of the works I discuss here) in *Chattel Slavery and Wage Slavery* (Athens: University of Georgia Press, 1979); see 70–81.

33. C. Edwards Lester, *The artist, the merchant, and the statesman, of the age of the Medici, and of our own times,* vol. 2 (New York: Paine and Burgess, 1845), 118–19, 126–27, 133–34; Neil Harris, *The Artist in American Society: The Formative Years 1790–1860* (New York: George Braziller, 1966; Chicago: University of Chicago Press, Phoenix Edition, 1982), 197. Harris quotes Lester on 196 from one of Lester's other works expressing similar sentiments to those I cited earlier.

34. "Artists of America," *American Whig Review* 3 (May 1846): 517, 522.

35. "The Artist, the Merchant, and the Statesman. The Value of National Home Feeling, and the Future Influence of Influence, Commerce and the Arts on the Fortunes of America," *Merchant's Magazine* 14 (March 1846): 242.

36. Ibid., 235.

37. John Swanwick, *Thoughts on Education* (Philadelphia: Thomas Dobson, 1787) [EAI #20736].

38. Henry D. Gilpin Diary, 14 April 1822 to 30 December 1843, 19, Gilpin Papers, vol. 12, Historical Society of Pennsylvania, Philadelphia. Gilpin to Madison, October 9, 1827, and Madison's response October 25, Madison Papers. Gilpin became an art patron later in his busy life; Harris characterizes him as typical of Philadelphia, in *Artist in American Society*, 276; Marshall described Gilpin's work on the biography of the signers, in "Golden Age of Illustrated Biographies," 52–53; a contemporary assessment of Gilpin does not mention his young men's association activities or his historical efforts, but nonetheless emphasizes his surprising youth considering his accomplishments. Was generational continuity not as common a sentiment among Democrats? "Political Portraits with Pen and Pencil—Henry D. Gilpin," *United States Magazine and Democratic Review* 8 (December 1840): 512–35.

39. Charles E. Baker, "The American Art-Union," in *American Academy of Fine Arts and American Art-Union*, ed. Mary Bartlett Cowdrey, vol. 1 (New York: New-York Historical Society, 1953), 100; Lillian B. Miller, *Patrons and Patriotism* (Chicago: University of Chicago Press, 1966), 166. The latest survey of the Art-Union appears in Rachel N. Klein, "Art and Authority in Antebellum New York City: The Rise and Fall of the American Art-Union," *Journal of American History* 81 (March 1995): 1534–61.

40. "The American Art-Union," *Knickerbocker* 32 (November 1848): 443; the quotation comparing the union to a merchant in Baker, "American Art-Union," 103, also see 111–12, 148, 161.

41. *Transactions of the Apollo Association for the Promotion of the Fine Arts in the United States for the Year 1840*, 9; *Transactions of the American Art-Union* (1843), 5, 10.

42. *Transactions of the American Art-Union* (1843), 8; *Transactions of the Apollo Association* (1840), 9; *Bulletin of the American Art-Union* 2, 1 (1849): 12–13.

43. *Transactions of the American Art-Union* (1845), 17, 23; *Transactions of the American Art-Union* (1844), 15; *Transactions* (1846), 18; *Transactions* (1849), 23.

44. *Transactions* (1844), 14; *Transactions* (1847), 19; *Transactions* (1848), 44.

45. On monumental art see *Transactions* (1846), 20, and Harris, *Artist in American Society*.

46. *Transactions* (1845), 12, 14, 15–16; *New York Herald*, December 21, 1845; Headley had recently returned from Italy; perhaps he had met Lester there. Biographical data on Headley from *Dictionary of American Biography*, vol. 5 (New York: Charles Scribner's Sons, 1932), 479–80.

47. *Transactions* (1844), 10. Bellows himself became an advocate of a "doctrine of institutions" that promoted their importance in keeping society together; see George Fredrickson, *The Inner Civil War* (New York: Harper and Row, 1965; Harper Torchbooks, 1968), 26–27. Quotation about officers' "higher duties" in *Transactions* (1847), 24–25; also see Baker's discussion of the increasingly lofty aims of the union, in "American Art-Union," 164, 174.

48. Cited in John Francis McDermott, "George Caleb Bingham's 'Stump Orator,'" *Art Quarterly* 20 (Winter 1957): 390.

49. Mary Bartlett Cowdrey, "Publications of the American Art-Union," in *American Academy of Fine Arts and American Art-Union,* vol. 1, 285, 286–93; my own count and identification of types are from this list. Lucille Wrubel Grindhammer, *Art and the Public: The Democratization of the Fine Arts in the United States, 1830–1860* (Stuttgart: J. B. Metzlersche Verlagsbuchhandlung, 1975), 25, makes a similar breakdown using different categories.

50. Carol Troyen, "Retreat to Arcadia: American Landscape and the American Art-Union," *American Art Journal* 23, 1 (1991): 27, 29.

51. George Caleb Bingham, "Letters of George Caleb Bingham to James S. Rollins," ed. C. B. Rollins, *Missouri Historical Review* 32 (October 1837): 9; Francis Lea McCurdy, *Stump, Bar, and Pulpit: Speechmaking on the Missouri Frontier* (Columbia: University of Missouri Press, 1969), 43, 58, 65.

52. John Vollmer Mering, *The Whig Party in Missouri* (Columbia: University of Missouri Press, 1967), 56, 45; Leota Newhard, "The Beginnings of the Whig Party in Missouri, 1824–1840," *Missouri Historical Review* 25 (January 1931): 278; John Francis McDermott, *George Caleb Bingham: River Portraitist* (Norman: University of Oklahoma Press, 1959), 36 n.9.

53. McDermott, *Bingham: River Portraitist,* 35–36; E. Maurice Bloch, "Art in Politics," *Art in America* 33 (April 1945): 96; Nancy Rash, *The Painting and Politics of George Caleb Bingham* (New Haven: Yale University Press, 1991), 28 and passim. This is not to suggest that Democrats did not share some of these concerns, simply that Bingham was reflecting Whig ideals in his work.

54. Marshall Davidson, "Democracy Delineated," *American Heritage* 31 (October-November 1980): 11; Robert F. Westervelt, "The Whig Painter of Missouri," *American Art Journal* 2 (Spring 1970): 48, Barbara Groseclose, "Painting, Politics, and George Caleb Bingham," *American Art Journal* 10 (November 1978): 4–19. See Rash's bibliography in her book on Bingham for more references to this debate.

55. Rash, *Painting and Politics of George Caleb Bingham,* 99–100, 132; for another recent interpretation see Gail E. Husch, " 'Freedom's Holy Cause': History, Religious and Genre Painting in America, 1840–1860," in Ayres, *Picturing History,* 88; John Demos discusses the class character of the figures in the paintings in "George Caleb Bingham: The Artist as Social Historian," *American Quarterly* 17 (Summer 1965): 220.

56. H. Nichols B. Clark, *Francis W. Edmonds* (Washington, DC: Smithsonian Institution Press, 1988), 76; Elizabeth Johns, *American Genre Painting* (New Haven: Yale University Press, 1991), 54; Husch, "Freedom's Holy Cause," 81, 82; *Knickerbocker* 23 (June 1844): 597.

57. Francis S. Grubar, "Richard Caton Woodville: An American Artist, 1825 to 1855" (Ph.D. diss., Johns Hopkins University, 1966), remains the central source on the artist's work; see his discussion of the Revolution on 141. Michael Kammen sees connectedness in *Mystic Chords of Memory,* 79; Husch sees otherwise in "Freedom's Holy Cause," 93. They are both commenting on *Old '76 and Young '48.*

58. Barbara Groseclose, "Politics and American Genre Painting of the Nineteenth Century," *Antiques* 120 (November 1981): 1215.

59. Jay Cantor makes the Trumbull identification, in "Prints and the American Art-Union," in *Prints in and of America to 1850,* ed. John D. Morse (Charlottesville: University Press of Virginia, 1970), 316; Grubar, "Richard Caton Woodville," 215, makes the connection between hats.

60. "Fine Arts," *Graham's Magazine* 37 (October 1850): 260; Ron Tyler sees disillusionment in "Historic Reportage and Artistic License: Prints and Paintings of the Mexican War," in Ayres, *Picturing History,* 115.

61. Herman Warner Williams, Jr., characterizes the Magee painting in *Mirror to the American Past* (Greenwich, CT: New York Graphic Society, 1973), 80–81. Elizabeth Johns, *American Genre Painting,* 180–81, has suggested that *Old '76 and Young '48* was designed for those who held either view on the war.

62. Mark Thistlewaite also notes the Trumbull and the depiction of Washington in both paintings, in *The Image of George Washington* (New York: Garland, 1979), 28.

63. Robert W. Johannsen, *To the Halls of the Montezumas: The Mexican War in the American Imagination* (New York: Oxford University Press, 1985), 55–58, 114.

64. *Union Magazine of Literature and Art* 1 (July 1847): frontispiece; on the Trumbull painting and its roots in older images, see Gilbert Tapley Vincent, "American Artists and Their Changing Perceptions of American History, 1770–1940" (Ph.D. diss., University of Delaware, 1982), 32–34; Bryan Jay Wolf, "All the World's a Code: Art and Ideology in Nineteenth-Century American Painting," *Art Journal* 44 (Winter 1984): 332. Wolf also points out the differences in clothing in Woodville's *Mexican War News,* which I have found in *Soldier's Experience* and *Old '76 and Young '48.*

65. Steven Watts, *The Republic Reborn* (Baltimore: Johns Hopkins University Press, 1987), 210 and passim. His account joins those of other scholars who discover sons trying to escape paternal domination in various crises since the seventeenth century.

66. C.E. Lester, "Fly Leaf of Art and Criticism" and "Salutation," in *The Gallery of Illustrious Americans,* no. 1, January 1, 1850 (New York: John Wiley, G. P. Putnam, D. Appleton and Co., 1850) (emphasis added). Thanks to Prof. Alan Trachtenberg, who loaned me his microfilm copy in 1987.

67. Alan Trachtenberg, *Reading American Photographs* (New York: Hill and Wang, 1989), 45, 51, 52.

68. Matteson was an Odd Fellow, as was C. E. Lester, who contributed to several of the order's annuals. Henry T. Tuckerman, *Book of the Artists* (New York, 1867; reprint James F. Carr, 1966), 432–33; Thistlewaite dates the first appearance in a magazine and discusses Matteson's work, in *The Image of George Washington,* 230.

69. Lewis G. Clark, "Freedom's Holy Cause," in *Odd-Fellow's Offering For 1851* (New York: Edward Walker, 1851), 291–93. Husch discusses this work in "Freedom's Holy Cause," and uses similar quotations, 81–82; I read her account years after writing this.

70. Michael Kammen, "Changing Perceptions of the Life Cycle in American

Thought and Culture," *Proceedings of the Massachusetts Historical Society* 91 (1979): 36; "The Artist, Merchant, and Statesman," *United States Magazine and Democratic Review* 17 (November 1845): 344, 345.

71. C. Edwards Lester, "Dedication of Odd-Fellows' Hall, New York, Oration of C. Edwards Lester," in *Odd-Fellows' Offering for 1850* (New York: Edward Walker, 1850), 297; see Lester's essay "Washington's Marriage," in the *Odd-Fellows' Offering for 1851*, 9–15.

5. Young America

1. Abraham Lincoln, "Second Lecture on Discoveries and Inventions," in *Collected Works of Abraham Lincoln*, ed. Roy P. Basler, vol. 3 (New Brunswick: Rutgers University Press, 1953), 356–57.

2. Dan Schiller, *Objectivity and the News: The Public and the Rise of Commercial Journalism* (Philadelphia: University of Pennsylvania Press, 1981), 75, provides one of the best discussions of the newspapers' claim "to the defense of natural rights and public good." Richard Schwarzlose, *The Nation's News Brokers*, vol. 1, *The Formative Years* (Evanston: Northwestern University Press, 1989), surveys changing technology and the rise of press associations. But note the warning of Michael Schudson that "technological change was not autonomous"; see his critique in *Discovering the News: A Social History of American Newspapers* (New York: Basic Books, 1978), 31–35.

3. Donald M. Scott, "The Popular Lecture and the Creation of a Public in Mid-Nineteenth-Century America," *Journal of American History* 66 (March 1980): 808–9. Scott does not comment on it, but much of his evidence is drawn from young men's institutes and lyceums that organized many of the lecture programs. These were the broadly defined self-education young men's groups described in Chapter 3. Also see Mary Kupiec Cayton, "The Making of an American Prophet: Emerson, His Audiences, and the Rise of the Culture Industry in Nineteenth-Century America," *American Historical Review* 92 (June 1987): 597–620. She discusses young men's groups briefly.

4. Merle Curti's article is usually cited as the first serious consideration by a historian; see his " 'Young America,' " *American Historical Review* 32 (October 1926): 34–55. For years, Siert F. Riepma, " 'Young America': A Study in American Nationalism before the Civil War" (Ph.D. diss., Western Reserve University, 1939), was the only full-length study of the idea.

5. John Stafford, *The Literary Criticism of "Young America"* (Berkeley: University of California Press, 1952), and Perry Miller, *The Raven and the Whale* (New York: Harcourt, Brace, 1956), remain the two major sources.

6. Betty Jean Verbal, "Youth Movements in Modern European History, 1815–1914" (Ph.D. diss., Carnegie-Mellon University , 1971), reviews this oft-told story on 14–22. Also see William L. Langer, *Political and Social Upheaval, 1832–1852* (New York: Harper Torchbooks, 1969), 110–25; Anthony Esler gives modern parallels and the dimension of generational revolt in *Bombs Beards and Barricades: 150 Years of Youth in Revolt* (New York: Stein and Day, 1971), 43–117.

7. For Germany see F. Gunther Eyck, "The Political Theories and Activities of

the German Academic Youth between 1815 and 1819," *Journal of Modern History* 27 (March 1955): 27–38, and Gary D. Stark, "The Ideology of the German Burschenschaft Generation," *European Studies Review* 8 (July 1978): 323–48; Stark notes the occupational crowding on 326. Louis Mazoyer, "Categories d'âge et groupes sociaux—les jeunes générations françaises de 1830," *Annales d'histoire économique et sociale* 53 (September 30, 1938), is an outstanding treatment of this subject; see particularly 399, 412.

8. Giuseppe Mazzini, *Life and Writings of Joseph Mazzini*, vol. 1, *Autobiographical and Political* (London: Smith, Elder, and Co., 1864), 96, 124–25, 165.

9. Denis Mack Smith, *Mazzini* (New Haven: Yale University Press, 1994), on the importance of the press, 11–12; see *Historical Dictionary of France from the 1815 Restoration to the Second Empire*, ed. Edgar Leon Newman, vol. 1 (Westport, CT: Greenwood Press, 1987), 528, for *La jeune France*. Quotation in F. Gunther Eyck, "Mazzini's Young Europe," *Journal of Central European Affairs* 17 (January 1958): 363; see 368–69 for details on the Young Europe organizations.

10. Mazzini, *Writings*, vol. 3, 132.

11. James Fenimore Cooper, *Home as Found* (1838; New York: Capricorn Books, 1961), 173, 374, quotation on 440; "The Revolutionary Secret Societies of Modern Italy," *United States Magazine and Democratic Review* 9 (September 1841): 263, 275.

12. Henry W. Longfellow, "German Writers," *Graham's Lady's and Gentleman's Magazine* 20 (March 1842): 134; idem, "A Psalm of Life," in *The Complete Poetical Works of Longfellow* (Boston: Houghton Mifflin, 1893), 3; on Franklin's use of "up and doing" see Daniel F. Littlefield, Jr., "Longfellow's 'A Pslam of Life': A Relation of Method to Popularity," *Markham Review* 7 (Spring 1978): 50; Kenneth Hovey, " 'A Psalm of Life' Reconsidered: The Dialogue of Western Literature and Monologue of Young America," *American Transcendental Quarterly*, new ser. 1 (March 1987): 3–19, despite its title does not discuss Young America per se, but does deal with Longfellow's wish to show skepticism about youth.

13. Richard Faber, *Young England* (London: Faber and Faber, 1987), 45–46; *London Times*, September 12, 1843, 3.

14. J. T. Ward, "Young England," *History Today* 16 (February 1966): 120–27; Disraeli quotation on 123. In addition to the Faber's *Young England*, see Charles Whibley, *Lord John Manners and His Friends* (London: William Blackwood and Sons, 1925), 150–54, and discussions in Robert Blake, *Disraeli* (New York: St. Martin's Press, 1967), 167–220, and Sarah Bradford, *Disraeli* (London: Weidenfeld and Nicolson, 1982), 118–46.

15. *London Times*, May 11, May 20, 1844, 7; "Young England," *Edinburgh Review* 81 (October 1844): 518–19; "Young England" ["Mr. Fox's Lectures to the Working Classes, Reported in 'The Artizan' "], *Littell's Living Age* 2 (September 1844): 363.

16. " 'Young England,' 'Coningsby,' " *Southern Literary Messenger* 10 (December 1844): 739, 745, 747.

17. "Young England," *North American Review* 61 (July 1845): 232–33, 236–37; "Coningsby," *Southern Quarterly Review* 8 (October 1845): 514, 516; also

see, "Young England" [from the *Edinburgh Review*], *The Eclectic Magazine of Foreign Literature; Science, and Art* 9 (December 1844): 524–28.

18. Ralph Waldo Emerson, "The Young American," in *Collected Works of Ralph Waldo Emerson,* vol. 1, *Nature; Addresses and Lectures,* introduction and notes by Robert E. Spiller (Cambridge, MA: Belknap Press, Harvard University Press, 1971), 238.

19. Ibid., 242, 222, 239.

20. *Workingman's Advocate,* December 7, 1844. Evans might not have been as sanguine about Young England had he seen a letter to the *London Times* that wondered why Lord John Manners, a leading Young Englander, could celebrate the revival of ancient English sports but support a measure enforcing land enclosure: "if I were a poor man, I should prefer feeding my cow upon the common to dancing upon the high road." *London Times,* March 15, 1844, 5.

21. *Workingman's Advocate,* December 21, 1844, January 11, 1845, February 15, 1845. Riepma discusses Evans in "Young America," 59; see also Helene Sara Zahler, *Eastern Workingmen and National Land Policy, 1829–1862* (New York: Columbia University Press, 1941), 38. Sean Wilentz discusses Evans's land policy in *Chants Democratic* (New York: Oxford University Press, 1984).

22. Alexander H. Everett, "Harro Harring: A Biographical Sketch," *Democratic Review* 15 (December 1844): 568–69, 579, and the rest of the profile in the October and November issues, 337–47, 462–75; idem, "The Young American," *Democratic Review* 16 (May 1845): 495.

23. William Gilmore Simms, "Americanism in Literature," in *Views and Reviews in American Literature, History and Fiction* (New York: Wiley and Putnam, 1845), 2–4, 8–9; originally in the *Southern and Western Monthly Magazine and Review* 1 (January 1845): 1–14. David Tomlinson offers more details on Simms's efforts in "Simms's Monthly Magazine: The Southern and Western Magazine and Review," *Southern Literary Journal* 8 (Fall 1975): 95–125.

24. Cornelius Mathews, *Americanism, An Address Delivered Before the Eucleian Society of the New-York University* (New York: Paine and Burgess, 1845), 15, 17–18.

25. Ibid., 15, 18, 20, 26–27, 31–32.

26. "Young America," *Broadway Journal,* July 19 1845, 26–27.

27. Edwin DeLeon, *The Position and Duties of "Young America," An Address Delivered Before the Two Literary Societies of The South Carolina College* (Columbia, SC, 1845), 6, 14–15, 21, 24–25; *Southern Quarterly Review* 9 (January 1846): 283; Philip Hone, *The Diary of Philip Hone,* ed. Bayard Tuckerman (New York: Dodd, Mead and Co., 1889), vol. 2, 246 (April 7, 1845).

28. Benjamin T. Spencer in "A National Literature, 1837–1855," *American Literature* 8 (May 1936): 125–59; idem, *The Quest for Nationality* (Syracuse: Syracuse University Press, 1957), sketches the broader terms of the national literature debate. On the *Democratic Review*'s role see Landon Edward Fuller, "The *United States Magazine and Democratic Review,* 1837–1859: A Study of Its History, Contents and Significance" (Ph.D. diss., University of North Carolina, 1948), 267–68. Stafford and Miller both provide the details on Duyckinck and Mathews, see esp. Miller, *Raven and the Whale,* 186–219, on the editors' hopping from journal to journal in 1847.

29. A Young American [Cornelius Mathews], "Our Forefathers," *American Monthly Magazine* 7 (May, June 1836): 453, 559–61.

30. Allen F. Stein, *Cornelius Mathews* (New York: Twayne Publishers, 1974), 161; Cornelius Mathews, "The Politicians," in *The Various Writings of Cornelius Mathews* (New York: Harper and Brothers, 1843), 140–41.

31. The international copyright advocates wanted a bill passed in Congress. When the House named a special committee to investigate, it put Robert C. Winthrop in the chair. A recent history described his leadership as "apathetic," demonstrating again that Winthrop's long association with young men's organizations did not automatically make him sympathetic to other causes associated with "youth." James J. Barnes, *Authors, Publishers and Politicians* (London: Routledge and Kegan Paul, 1974), is a relevant history of international copyright; see esp. 78–84.

32. William Cullen Bryant, Francis L. Hawks, and Cornelius Mathews, *Address to the People of the United States in Behalf of the American Copyright Club* (New York, 1843), 8, 9, 17; see William Gilmore Simms, *The Letters of William Gilmore Simms,* ed. Mary C. Simms Oliphant, vol. 1 (Columbia: University of South Carolina Press, 1953), 346. William Gilmore Simms, "International Copyright Law," *Southern Literary Messenger* 10 (January 1844): 15–17; E[dwin] D[eLeon], "Cheap Literature: Its Character and Tendencies," ibid., 39. Simms and DeLeon published other articles in the *Messenger* that year on the same subject: Simms in March and two other issues, DeLeon in July ("E. D. to J. B. D.").

33. Lowell to Duyckinck, August 1843, "Letters of James Russell Lowell, 1843–54," *Bulletin of the New York Public Library* 4 (October 1900): 340; "Editor's Table," *Knickerbocker* 26 (December 1845): 580. The *Knickerbocker,* apparently, had no qualms about borrowing from England. The description of Mathews as a "Corypheus"—the leader of the chorus in Greek comedy—had appeared the previous year, using similar diction, in an attack on Young England and Disraeli, identified "as its corypheus." See "A Few Words Anent the Laboring Classes," *Fraser's Magazine* 30 (November 1844): 624.

34. Rufus Wilmot Griswold, *The Prose Writers of America,* 2d ed. rev. (Philadelphia: Carey and Hart, 1847), 49–50, 544; Joy Bayless, *Rufus Wilmot Griswold, Poe's Literary Executor* (Nashville: Vanderbilt University Press, 1943), 122–23. Another possible reason for Griswold's dislike of Mathews may have arisen from disagreements during the time that Griswold was the Washington lobbyist for the American Copyright Club; everyone connected with the organization grew to dislike Mathews, according to Barnes, *Authors, Publishers,* 78–79.

35. William Gilmore Simms, "Writings of Cornelius Mathews," *Southern Quarterly Review* 6 (October 1840): 307–42.

36. See *North American Review* (July 1845), reporting that members of Young England "have as yet executed no measures that we have heard of . . . except the wearing of white cravats," 232; "Young America," *Yankee Doodle,* vol. 1 89.

37. Harry Franco [Charles F. Briggs], *The Trippings of Tom Pepper* (New York: Burgess, Stringer and Co., 1847, 1850), 76; also see Miller, *Raven and the·*

Whale, 177–83, for description of the background of the novel; "Meeting of the Mutual Admiration Society," *John-Donkey,* April 1, 1848, 222.

38. This was an extremely topical reference; the Whig Young Men's Committee had accused the *New York Courier and Enquirer* of contributing to recent electoral defeats and said it would no longer be the party organ. *Yankee Doodle* found this so funny that it referred to the incident twice in the same issue; it seemed worthy of such attention because the *Courier and Enquirer's* editor, James Watson Webb, was credited with coining the phrase "Whig." The joke was: what if he had "taken the name with him" when he left the party. "Young America," *Yankee Doodle,* vol. 1, 89; "Nomenclature," ibid., 93. See also *New York Tribune,* November 14, 1846, for the notice from the Whig Young Men's Committee.

39. See for example, "A Twilight Scene in Broadway," *Yankee Doodle,* vol. 1, 175, "Young America," ibid., vol. 2, 63, "Old Young People," ibid., vol. 2, 88. See notice in *Literary World,* February 6, 1847, 14, on the *Punch* cartoons. Duyckinck ran the *Literary World;* Mathews edited *Yankee Doodle.* Apparently all material could not come from American sources.

40. "Yankee Doodle's List of Candidates," *Yankee Doodle,* vol. 2, 174. For more on *Yankee Doodle* and Mathews and Duyckinck's involvement, see Donald Yannella, "Yankee Doodle," in *American Literary Magazines: The Eighteenth and Nineteenth Centuries* (Westport, CT: Greenwood Press, 1986), 451–56. On *John-Donkey* see David E. E. Sloane, ed., *American Humor Magazines and Comic Periodicals* (Westport, CT: Greenwood Press, 1987), 103–5.

41. Heyward Bruce Ehrlich, "A Study of Literary Activity in New York City during the 1840-decade" (Ph.D. diss., New York University, 1963), 130, said of Fuller: "No other New York critic of the decade so successfully planted one foot on either side of the Atlantic"; Margaret Fuller, *The Letters of Margaret Fuller,* ed. Robert W. Hudspeth, vol. 4 (Ithaca: Cornell University Press, 1987), 206–7, 211–12; Ralph Waldo Emerson, *Letters of Ralph Waldo Emerson,* ed. Ralph L. Rusk, vol. 3 (New York: Columbia University Press, 1939), 381–83, 385–87, 403; also see the chapter on Fuller in Joseph Rossi, *The Image of America in Mazzini's Writings* (Madison: University of Wisconsin Press, 1954), 47–61.

42. Claude Richard, "Poe and 'Young America,' " *Studies in Bibliography* 21 (1964): 27–29, 36, 56–57.

43. On Melville and Duyckinck see Miller, *Raven and the Whale,* or F. O. Matthiessen, *American Renaissance* (New York: Oxford University Press, 1941), 122 and passim. Jay Leyda, *The Melville Log,* vol. 1 (New York: Gordian Press, 1969), 261–63, provides details on Melville's association with Mathews and Duyckinck.

44. David S. Reynolds, *Beneath the America Renaissanace* (New York: Alfred A. Knopf, 1988), 277–78, 292 ("linguistic fire"), and Michael Paul Rogin, *Subversive Genealogy* (New York: Alfred A. Knopf, 1983), 73–74 ("As Young America"), each make this argument; Reynolds confuses matters further by associating the Young America political movement with the New York Democratic activist Mike Walsh, who was involved but not in the way Reynolds imagines; P. Marc Bousquet suggests Melville's commitment was momentary, in "Mathews's Mosses," *New England Quarterly* 67 (December 1994): 649. Ehrlich, "Literary

Activity in New York City," argues for Mathews's influence on Melville, although not in the ways suggested here (see 376).

45. Rogin characterizes Melville's essay in *Subversive Genealogy,* 74.

46. Herman Melville, "Hawthorne and His Mosses," in *Writings of Herman Melville Northwestern-Newberry Edition,* vol. 9, *Piazza Tales and Other Prose Pieces* (Evanston and Chicago: Northwestern University Press and the Newberry Library, 1987), 247–49. Hawthorne's own use of the Puritan past and its relation to his nineteenth-century present needs to be explored further. John P. McWilliams, Jr., *Hawthorne, Melville, and the American Character* (Cambridge: Cambridge University Press, 1984), investigated these themes, although he views Young America as a single entity.

47. Melville, *Pierre Or, The Ambiguities,* in *Writings of Herman Melville,* vol. 7 (Evanston and Chicago: Northwestern University Press and the Newberry Library, 1971), 247, 251, 253–54; Cornelius Mathews, *The Career of Puffer Hopkins,* in *Various Writings,* 221.

48. A recent study finds satires of political Young America and other figures in Melville's *Confidence Man* (published after *Pierre*), but it also thinks it was an organized movement that "sponsored a satirical periodical to express its views," a magazine published in 1856 called *Young America.* It provides no evidence for this "sponsorship." Given such confusion it is difficult to assess the attributions of satire, especially in a complex work like *The Confidence Man.* Helen P. Trimpi, *Melville's Confidence Men and American Politics in the 1850s* (Hamden, CT: Archon Books, 1987), 196.

49. Simms, *Letters,* vol. 2, 7, 206 and n.226, 253, 295, 420 n.85. William R. Taylor described Young Carolina as part of the nationalist, expansionist Young America in *Cavalier and Yankee* (New York: George Braziller, 1961; Harper Torchbooks, 1969), 273–74, and reports Simms's discarding of "young" on 278. See also Jon L. Wakelyn, "Party Issues and Political Strategy of the Charleston Taylor Democrats of 1848," *South Carolina Historical Magazine* 73 (April 1972): 72, 75, and idem, *The Politics of a Literary Man: William Gilmore Simms* (Westport, CT: Greenwood Press, 1973), 96, 104, 138.

50. Michael A. Bernstein, "Northern Labor Finds a Southern Champion: A Note on the Radical Democracy, 1833–1849," in *New York and the Rise of American Capitalism,* ed. William Pencak and Conrad Edick Wright (New York: New-York Historical Society, 1989), 158, 162–63, discusses the campaign against the Democratic establishment.

51. Robert Ernst, "The One and Only Mike Walsh," *New-York Historical Society Quarterly* 36 (January 1952): 46–47, 55, 56; "Forthcoming Work," *Yankee Doodle,* vol 1, 107. Headley (discussed briefly in the previous chapter in relation to artistic nationalism) was the primary target of this satiric piece; his prolific output was, perhaps, a result of his willingness to chronicle anyone. Walsh provided the absurd example.

52. Peter George Buckley, "To the Opera House: Culture and Society in New York City, 1820–1860" (Ph.D. diss., State University of New York at Stony Brook, 1984), discusses Walsh on 370–76; for the petition see 62–64; on the Young Americans see 212–13, 268, 281, 291–92, 285–86.

53. Ibid., 281–84.

54. On the rally and the young men see the *New York Tribune,* August 28 and 30, September 1, 4, 5, 18, 1849.

55. *New York Herald,* October 23, 1851.

56. *New York Tribune,* December 17, 1851. On Kossuth in general, although it does not mention the examples noted here, see Donald S. Spencer, *Louis Kossuth and Young America* (Columbia: University of Missouri Press, 1977).

57. *New York Tribune,* December 16, 1851, and *New York Times,* December 16, 1851. The *Herald* complained the entire event had been organized to benefit the *Tribune* and the *Times; Herald,* December 16, 1851.

58. *New York Herald,* December 18, 1851.

59. Corry to Joseph Holt, November 29, 1851, Joseph Holt Papers, vol. 14, Library of Congress; Anna J. Sanders Journal, March 29, 1851, George N. Sanders Papers, Library of Congress, Container 1.

60. "Eighteen-Fifty-Two and the Presidency," *Democratic Review* 30 (January 1852): 9, 4.

61. Ibid., 9, 10, 12.

62. "Mazzini—Young Europe," *Democratic Review* 30 (January 1852): 41–42; "Book Notices," ibid., 93.

63. "The Nomination," *Democratic Review* 30 (April 1852): 367; "Prospectus," *Blackwood's* 59 (May 1846): 621–23; "A Tretise on Old Fogyism," *John-Donkey,* January 22, 1848, 60; "The Political Old Fogy," *John-Donkey,* February 5, 1848, 88; "An Essay on Fogyism," *Lantern,* February 14, 1852, 53. This article might even precede usage in the *Democratic Review.* Curti noted the *Lantern* article without identifying its predecessors, in "Young America," 36 n.10. The editors of *John-Donkey* were also leading contributors to the *Lantern.* Frank Luther Mott, *A History of American Magazines 1850–1865* (Cambridge, MA: Harvard University Press, 1938), 181.

64. "The Presidency and the Review," *Democratic Review* 30 (February 1852): 185. Circulation figures in Fuller, "The *United States Magazine and Democratic Review,*" 30. Appendix to *Congressional Globe,* 32nd Congress, 1st Session, March 4, 1852, 302.

65. *Congressional Globe,* 32nd Congress, 1st Session, 712, and the rest of the debate, 710–15; *Appendix to Congressional Globe,* 32nd Congress, 1st Session, 384, 385. For background on the speech see William C. Davis, *Breckinridge: Statesman, Soldier, Symbol* (Baton Rouge: Louisiana State University Press, 1974), 61–67. Anna J. Sanders Journal, March 9, 1852, Sanders Papers, Container 1.

66. "Congress, The Presidency, and the Review," *Democratic Review* 30 (March 1852): 204–5.

67. Corry to Holt, March 4, 1852, Holt Papers, vol. 14.

68. *Democratic Review* 30 (March 1852): 212.

69. Ibid., 212–13, 214.

70. *New York Herald,* May 25, 1852. Virtually any article in the first six months of 1852 illustrates the message; two articles in the April issue had the word *fogy* in them: "The Nomination—The 'Old Fogies' and Fogy Conspiracies," 366–84, is a good example. See also "Daniel—'76, '98, '44, '48, And a Fast Man," *Democratic Review* 30 (May 1852), quotation on 389.

71. "Fogy Literature," *Democratic Review* 30 (May 1852): 398; see "Nationality in Literature," ibid. 20 (March, April 1847): 264–72, 316–20, attributed to Jones.

72. "Book Notices," *Democratic Review* 30 (January 1852): 94; "Parlor Periodicals," ibid., 76–82; "Dr. Dewey on Women's Rights," ibid. (February 1852): 181.

73. "Vanity versus Philosophy," *Democratic Review* (June 1852): 513, 523, 524; also, see "Female Politicians," ibid. (April 1852): 355–59.

74. Anna J. Sanders Journal, May 28, 1852, Sanders Papers, Container 1. See B. F. Angel to W. L. Marcy, March 11, 1852; James G. Berret to Marcy, March 22, 1852; Marcy to Berret, March 23, 1852; W. W. Snow to Marcy, April 10, 1852, and April 17, 1852, William L. Marcy Papers, vol. 23, Library of Congress.

75. On Douglas's difficulties with Sanders see Robert W. Johannsen, *Stephen A. Douglas* (New York: Oxford University Press, 1973), 362, 369; on Pierce see Roy F. Nichols, *The Democratic Machine 1850–1854* (New York: Columbia University, 1923), 121–23, and idem, *Franklin Pierce* (Philadelphia: University of Pennsylvania Press, 1931). On the familiarity of Pierce's promoter, Edmund Burke, with Young America, Curti quotes a letter in "Young America," 45; also see Burke to Thomas Ritchie, March 29, 1852, Franklin Pierce Papers, Microfilm, Yale University Library, Series 2, Reel 1.

76. John F. Lee to W. L. Marcy, June 7, 1852, Marcy Papers, vol. 24; "Eighteen Fifty-two and the 'Coming Man,' " *Democratic Review* 30 (June 1852): 483, 487; see Anna J. Sanders Journal, June 12, 1852, Sanders Papers, on Sanders's schedule.

77. "Hermitage" [C. Edwards Lester], *The Life of Gen. Frank. Pierce* (New York: Cornish, Lamport and Co., 1852), 25. Roy Nichols identifies Lester as "Hermitage," in *Franklin Pierce,* 208. Nathaniel Hawthorne wrote a better-known biography of Pierce. See Scott E. Casper, "The Two Lives of Franklin Pierce," *American Literary History* 5 (Summer 1993): 203–30.

78. See *Democratic Review,* vol. 31, which ran from July to December 1852; *Appendix to the Congressional Globe,* 32nd Congress, 2nd Session, February 14, 1853, 173–75.

79. *New York Herald,* April 14, 1852; *New York Times,* April 8, 1852.

80. *New York Herald,* January 29, 1852; see *New York Tribune,* same day, for the names of the petitioners.

81. *New York Herald,* September 5, 1849; *New York Times,* April 17, 1852; *New York Tribune,* April 20, 1852.

82. Joseph Clark, *Young Americanism* (Chambersburg, PA: M. Kieffer and Co., 1852), 5, 6, 8, 10, 15, 20, 24.

83. *United States Journal,* May 3, 1845, quoted by Frederick Merk in *Manifest Destiny and Mission in American History* (New York: Alfred A. Knopf, 1963), 54; Merk's assertion of youth's essential influence on manifest destiny, "to get the nation going again, to move to new frontiers," ibid., 53, seems more influenced by the Kennedy administration than the political climate of the 1840s and 1850s.

84. *New York Herald,* February 7, 1853. See Julius W. Pratt, "The Origin of

'Manifest Destiny,' " *American Historical Review* 32 (July 1927): 795–98; in another bizarre coincidence, the first public utterance of the phrase was by Robert C. Winthrop during a debate in the House on U.S. territorial rights in Oregon. Winthrop did not seem supportive. On the equation of Young America with manifest destiny and the involvement in European politics and Cuban filibustering of Sanders and O'Sullivan, see Amos A. Ettinger, *The Mission to Spain of Pierre Soulé, 1853–1855* (New Haven: Yale University Press, 1932), 125, 77, 316–18, 189, and Basil Rauch, *American Interest in Cuba, 1848–1855* (New York: Columbia University Press, 1948), 264.

85. Louis Dow Scisco, *Political Nativism in New York State* (New York, 1901), 33–34. Riepma, "Young America," 336, refers to the parallel rise of nativism and Young America. David Brion Davis, "Some Themes of Counter-Subversion: An Analysis of Anti-Masonic, Anti-Catholic, and Anti-Mormon Literature," in *From Homicide to Slavery* (New York: Oxford University Press, 1986), discusses the combination of tradition and progress, esp. on 146 and 154. Dale Knobel identifies the literary nationalism in an Order of United Americans newspaper in " 'Native Soil': Nativists, Colonizationists, and the Rhetoric of Nationality," *Civil War History* 27 (December 1981): 328. Eric Foner, *Free Soil, Free Labor, Free Men* (New York: Oxford University Press, 1970), 229, 239, 260.

86. Bernard F. Reilly, Jr., *American Political Prints, 1766–1876* (Boston: G. K. Hall, 1991), 382–88, also see 418–19, 516; Scisco, *Political Nativism in New York*, 65–66, gives the original names of the Know-Nothings. Philip Thorp, *Young America's Dream: Or, A Discoursory Interview Between the Spirits of Liberty, Tyranny and A Citizen of the World* (New York: Abbe and Yates, 1854), 25; *The Sons of the Sires: A History of the Rise, Progress and Destiny of the American Party* (Philadelphia: Lippincott, Grambo and Co., 1855), 179.

87. Rauch, *American Interest in Cuba,* 192–93, 212; David B. Danbom, "The Young America Movement," *Journal of the Illinois State Historical Society* 67 (June 1974): 294–306, mentions the move of Sanders's ally George Law toward nativism on 305. Reginald Horsman, *Race and Manifest Destiny* (Cambridge, MA: Harvard University Press 1981), 285, describes the ideological links between political Young America and nativism.

88. Stafford calls Headley "close friends" with the literary Young Americans in *Literary Criticism of "Young America,"* 31; Thomas J. Curran, "Know Nothings of New York State" (Ph.D. diss., Columbia University, 1963), details Headley's views on immigration on 193; Scisco describes the Know-Nothing ticket in *Political Nativism in New York,* 164.

89. "Lester's Glory and Shame," *Arcturus* 13 (December 1841): 59–65; see Simms, *Letters,* vol. 2, and Fuller, *Letters,* vol. 4, 210–11, for references to Lester. Nichols discusses Lester's involvement with Pierce and Lester's revenge, in *Franklin Pierce,* 208, 276, 288.

90. *New York Tribune,* March 3, 1855, June 18, 1855. Scisco in *Political Nativism in New York,* 130, and Curran in "Know Nothings of New York," 151–53, similarly attribute the novel. *The National Union Catalog,* on the basis of an inscription in one copy of the book, attributes it to Lester's wife; perhaps he had been acting as her surrogate when he offered the material to the *Tribune.*

The National Union Catalog Pre-1956 Imprints, vol. 328 (London: Mansell, 1974), 451.

91. *New York Herald, New York Times,* and *New York Tribune,* June 5, 1855. Edward K. Spann mentions Mathews's address, in *The New Metropolis: New York City, 1840–1857* (New York: Columbia University Press, 1981), but gives the impression that it was a regular Know-Nothing speech, 498 n.53.

92. On Godwin see Stafford, *Literary Criticism of "Young America,"* 19; for his embrace of George Henry Evans's Young America see Godwin's letter "The Organization of Labor," in the *Workingman's Advocate,* March 22, 1845; "Close of the First Volume," *Putnam's* 1 (June 1853): [704]. Also see Edward K. Spann's profile of Godwin in *Ideals and Politics: New York Intellectuals and Liberal Democracy, 1820–1880* (Albany: State University of New York Press, 1972), 145–54, 174–87; Miller sketches *Putnam's* in *Raven and the Whale,* 315–23, and characterizes it as Young America without Mathews.

93. "What Impression Do We Make Abroad?" *Putnam's* 2 (October 1853): 351; Curtis's speech in *New York Tribune,* February 25, 1854; see "Secret Societies—The Know-Nothings" and "America for the Americans," in *Putnam's* 5 (January and May 1855), for anti-Know-Nothing articles.

94. *London Times,* May 25, 1853, 7; December 3, 1855, 10; July 7, 1858, 9.

95. George F. Train, *Young America in Wall-Street* (New York: Derby and Jackson, 1857), 377–78, iii–vi; idem, *Spread-Eagleism* (New York: Derby and Jackson, 1859), 107, 120. Rauch mentions Train in *American Interest in Cuba,* 219. For his varied career, see Willis Thornton, *The Nine Lives of Citizen Train* (New York: Greenberg, 1948).

96. [Samuel Osgood], "Editor's Table: Youth and Age in America," *Harper's* (January 1860): 263; subsequent quotations are from 264, 265, 267.

Epilogue

1. [E. P. Whipple], "Young Men in History," *Atlantic Monthly* (July 1865): 7–8; Reid Mitchell, *The Vacant Chair: The Northern Soldier Leaves Home* (New York: Oxford University Press, 1993); David Lowenthal, *The Past Is a Foreign County* (Cambridge: Cambridge University Press, 1985), 120–21; Holmes quoted in George Fredrickson, *The Inner Civil War* (New York: Harper and Row, 1965), 219, also see 175.

2. [Whipple], "Young Men in History," 1; "Young America," *Belgravia* 18 (July 1872): 45; C. P. Cranch, "Old Fogies," *Appleton's Journal* 19 (June 1878): 532–33, 535. See the magazines and books for juveniles that used the phrase "Young America" in the *National Union Catalog Pre-1956 Imprints,* vol. 679 (London: Mansell, 1968–81), 579–82.

3. "The Duty of Young Men in Politics," *Christian Union* 46 (October 1, 1892): 578–79.

4. Thomas L. James, "A Republican's View," and Joseph C. Hendrix, "A Democrat's View," *Christian Union* 46 (October 1, 1892): 580, 581–82.

5. Joseph F. Kett traces the rise of age-grading in *Rites of Passage* (New York: Basic Books, 1977), 127–32, and the rise of adolescence on 243–44; John Demos identifies the "codification and confinement" of youth in "The Rise and Fall of

Adolescence," in *Past, Present, and Personal* (New York: Oxford University Press, 1986), 104–6. Also see Howard P. Chudacoff, *How Old Are You? Age Consciousness in American Culture* (Princeton: Princeton University Press, 1989), 36 and chaps. 3–5. Paul Boyer discusses the YMCA in *Urban Masses and Moral Order in America, 1820–1920* (Cambridge, MA: Harvard University Press, 1978), 112–19.

6. Reed Ueda, *Avenues to Adulthood: The Origins of the High School and Social Mobility in an American Suburb* (Cambridge: Cambridge University Press, 1987), 143–44, 221–23, discusses the Massachusetts high schoolers. John Modell, *Into One's Own* (Berkeley: University of California Press, 1989), traces the changing meanings and status of the transition from youth to adulthood in the twentieth century.

7. These developments fall beyond this study's scope and are being explored by other scholars. On youth and nature see Amy Green, "Savage Childhood: The Scientific Construction of Girlhood and Boyhood in the Progressive Era" (Ph.D. diss., Yale University, 1995); on urban and immigrant youth see Stephen Lassonde, "Learning to Forget: Schooling and Family in New Haven's Working Class, 1870–1940" (Ph.D. diss., Yale University, 1994).

8. Anthony Esler sketches the history of the generation concept in *Generations in History* (n.p.: published by the author, 1982), 22–25. For the development of the generation idea and its relationship to the activities of young people in Europe see Robert Wohl, *The Generation of 1914* (Cambridge, MA: Harvard University Press, 1979).

9. Cornelia A. P. Comer, "A Letter to the Rising Generation," *Atlantic Monthly* (February 1911): 145–54; Randolph Bourne, "The Two Generations," *Atlantic Monthly* (May 1911): 592, 596.

10. Christopher Lasch, ed., *The Social Thought of Jane Addams* (Indianapolis: Bobbs-Merrill, 1965), 1–43; Bourne, "Two Generations," 598.

11. Van Wyck Brooks, "Young America" (originally in *Seven Arts,* December 1916), in *Van Wyck Brooks: The Early Years,* ed. Claire Sprague (New York: Harper and Row, 1968), 163; idem, *Letters and Leadership* (New York: B. W. Huebsch, 1918), 52–53; idem, "America's Coming of Age," in *Van Wyck Brooks: The Early Years,* 117.

12. Randolph Bourne, "This Older Generation," *Atlantic Monthly* (September 1915): 391; Lasch discusses Addams and Bourne in *The New Radicalism in America 1889–1963* (New York: Vintage Books, 1965), the quotation is on 69. Casey Nelson Blake studied the cultural criticism of the Young Intellectuals and discussed their transformations of the personal and political, but did not discuss the "youth" content to their ideas, in *Beloved Community* (Chapel Hill: University of North Carolina Press, 1990).

13. Paula S. Fass, *The Damned and the Beautiful: American Youth in the 1920s* (New York: Oxford University Press, 1977), 120; Pearl S. Buck, "Where Are the Young Rebels," *Harper's* (September 1935): 427; on 1930s student radicalism see Robert Cohen, *When the Old Left Was Young* (New York: Oxford University Press, 1993); for an earlier view, Seymour Martin Lipset and Gerald M. Schaflander, *Passion and Politics: Student Activism in America* (Boston: Little, Brown, 1971), 159–96.

14. Paul Popenoe, "When Youth Goes Radical," *Parents' Magazine* 15 (November 1940): 118.

15. Kingsley Davis, "The Sociology of Parent-Youth Conflict" (originally in *American Sociological Review,* August 1940), in *The Sociology of Youth: Evolution and Revolution,* ed. Harry Silverstein (New York: Macmillan, 1973), 98, 99.

16. "Our 'Lost Generation' Wants to Belong," *Saturday Evening Post,* August 2, 1947, 120; "The Younger Generation," *Time,* November 5, 1951, 46.

17. John Clellon Holmes, " 'This Is the Beat Generation,' " *New York Times Magazine,* November 16, 1952, 10, 19, 22.

18. For the use of the word *generation* in popular films about youth, see the listings in Alan Betrock, *The I Was a Teenage Juvenile Delinquent Rock 'N Roll Horror Beach Party Movie Book* (New York: St. Martin's Press, 1986), a nostalgic guide. The most influential psychological statement appears in Erik H. Erikson, *Childhood and Society* (1950; 2d ed., New York: W. W. Norton, 1963); also see Demos, "Rise and Fall of Adolescence," 107, and the essays in Erik H. Erikson, ed., *The Challenge of Youth* (New York: Basic Books, 1963; Doubleday Anchor Books, 1965); David Matza, "Subterranean Traditions of Youth," *Annals of the American Academy of Political and Social Science* 338 (November 1961): 103–18.

19. Kenneth Keniston's and Bennett Berger's early essays on the development of youth culture remain perceptive; Berger's are collected in *Looking for America* (Englewood Cliffs, NJ: Prentice-Hall, 1971) and Keniston's in *Youth and Dissent* (New York: Harcourt Brace Jovanovich, 1971).

20. George Leonard, "Explosive Generation," *Look,* January 3, 1961, 17–20; "The Port Huron Statement," in James Miller, *Democracy Is in the Streets* (New York: Simon and Schuster, 1987), 329–30, 330–31, 332, 334.

21. "Port Huron Statement," 373.

22. See Clayborne Carson, *In Struggle: SNCC and the Black Awakening of the 1960s* (Cambridge, MA: Harvard University Press, 1981), esp. 1–65; Claude Brown, *Manchild in the Promised Land* (New York: Signet Books, 1965); Piri Thomas, *Down These Mean Streets* (New York: Alfred A. Knopf, 1967; Vintage Books, 1974). This paragraph is drawn from my entry on youth in *A Companion to American Thought,* ed. Richard Wightman Fox and James T. Kloppenberg (Cambridge, MA: Blackwell, 1995), 759.

23. "Open Generation," *Look,* September 20, 1966, 29; *Reader's Guide to Periodical Literature, March 1967–February 1968* (New York: H. W. Wilson Co., 1968), 469; "The Generation Gap," *Look,* February 21, 1967, 26–32; also see Kenneth Crawford, "Generation Gap," *Newsweek,* March 13, 1967, 48.

24. Carol Dreyfus and Thomas Connors, "Oral History and American Advertising: How the 'Pepsi Generation' Came Alive," *International Journal of Oral History* 6 (November 1985): 196 n.3, 192; the advertising campaign was part of a process of identifying youth as a target audience that had begun in the 1920s. See Stanley C. Hollander and Richard Germain, *Was There a Pepsi Generation before Pepsi Discovered It?* (Lincolnwood, IL: NTC Business Books, 1992).

25. Jack Newfield, *A Prophetic Minority* (New York: New American Library, 1966; Signet Books, 1967); Hal Draper, *Berkeley: The New Student Revolt* (New

York: Grove Press, 1965); Paul Jacobs and Saul Landau, *The New Radicals* (New York: Vintage Books, 1966); Michael Ferber and Staughton Lynd, *The Resistance* (Boston: Beacon Press, 1971) are some notable works. Nicholas Von Hoffman, *We Are the People Our Parents Warned Us Against* (New York: Quadrangle Books, 1967; Fawcett Crest Books, 1969), J. Anthony Lukas, *Don't Shoot — We Are Your Children!* (New York: Random House, 1971; Delta Book, 1973).

26. Newfield, *A Prophetic Minority*, 19; Howard Zinn, *SNCC: The New Abolitionists* (Boston: Beacon Press, 1965), 1; Carl Oglesby, "Liberalism and the Corporate State," in Jacobs and Landau, *The New Radicals*, 258–59; Jerry Rubin, "Do It!" and Abbie Hoffman, "Freedom and License," in Abbie Hoffman et al., *The Conspiracy* (New York: Dell, 1969), 43, 211 (emphasis added). Soon historians were searching for continuities and contrasts in the past. Lewis S. Feuer wrote a massive comparative study arguing that the study of generations *was* the study of students; in America before the Civil War there was no nationwide *student* activity, and thus no generational consciousness. Lewis S. Feuer, *The Conflict of Generations* (New York: Basic Books, 1969), 33, 318–20.

27. Annie Gottlieb, *Do You Believe in Magic?* (New York: Times Books, 1987), 10; Peter Collier and David Horowitz, *Destructive Generation: Second Thoughts about the Sixties* (New York: Summit Books, 1989).

28. "What's to Worry about Growing Older," *Utne Reader* (January/February 1990): 69–93; "Eric Utne Created the Impossible: A *Reader's Digest* That Both Baby Boomers and Highbrows Can Love," *People*, September 10, 1990, 79–81; "What Tune Does the Utne Play?" *Time*, December 3, 1990, 94.

29. I have also borrowed several phrases in this paragraph from my entry on youth in *A Companion to American Thought*, 759.

30. William Strauss and Neil Howe, *Generations: The History of America's Future, 1584 to 2069* (New York: William Morrow, 1991), 8, 438, 137–50.

31. See for example, Douglas Rushkoff, ed., The GenX Reader (New York: Ballantine Books, 1994); Geoffrey T. Holtz, *Welcome to the Jungle: The Why behind "Generation X"* (New York: St. Martin's Griffin, 1995); Everett Carll Ladd offers a refreshingly sensible critique in "The Twentysomethings: 'Generation Myths' Revisited," *Public Perspective* 5 (January/February 1994): 14–18.

32. On generations and marketing, Scott Donaton, "The Media Wakes Up to Generation X," *Advertising Age*, February 1, 1993, 16–17; Karen Ritchie, *Marketing to Generation X* (New York: Lexington Books, 1995).

33. "Twenty Years after Kent State," *Utne Reader* (May/June 1990): 56. Note, for example, the attempt to link today's young people to allegedly authentic roots in Paul Rogat Loeb, *Generation at the Crossroads* (New Brunswick: Rutgers University Press, 1994).

BIBLIOGRAPHY

Note on an abbreviation: In the primary works listed in this bibliography an additional citation is added at the end of each entry that was read in microform in the *Early American Imprints* series produced by the American Antiquarian Society. I include the numbers assigned to each publication in Charles Evans, *American Bibliography: A Chronological Dictionary of All Books Pamphlets and Periodical Publications Printed in the United States of America, 1630–1800* (14 vols., 1903–59), and Ralph R. Shaw and Richard H. Shoemaker, *American Bibliography: A Preliminary Checklist* (19 vols., 1958–65). The citation reads EAI (for *Early American Imprints*) and then lists the number.

Primary Works Published 1600–1799

An Account, Shewing The Progress of the Colony of Georgia in America From Its First Establishment. Annapolis, MD: James Green, 1742. EAI #4961.

Adams, Eliphalet. *A Brief Discourse as it Was Delivered February 6, 1726,7 to a Society of Young Men.* New London, CT, 1727. EAI #2830.

Allen, James. *New England's Choicest Blessing.* Boston: John Foster, 1679. EAI #260.

Arnold, Samuel. *David Serving His Generation.* Cambridge: Samuel Green, 1674. EAI #185.

Barnard, John. *A Call to Parents, and Children.* Boston: T. Fleet, 1737. EAI #4112.

Baxter, Richard. *Compassionate Counsel to all Young Men.* London, 1681.

Belcher, Joseph. *Two Sermons Preached in Dedham N.E. The First on a Day Set Apart for Prayer With Fasting, to Implore Spiritual Blessing on the Rising Generation.* Boston: B. Green, 1710. EAI #1443.

Be Merry and Wise: or, a Guide to the Present and Future Generation. Boston, 1762. EAI #9285.

Boone, Nicholas. *The Constable's Pocket Book*. Boston, 1710. EAI #1445.

Bosco, Ronald, editor. *Lessons For the Children of Godly Ancestors: Sermons For and About New England's Rising Generations, 1670–1750*. Delmar, NY: Scholars' Facsimiles and Reprints, 1982.

Boston Committee of Correspondence. Broadside, June 22, 1773. EAI #12690.

———. Broadside, November 23, 1773. EAI #12693.

Boston Town Meeting. 1773. EAI #12692.

Bradford, William. "Governor Bradford's Dialogue between Old Men and Young Men, Concerning 'The Church and Government Thereof.' " *Massachusetts Historical Society Proceedings* 11 (October 1870): 407–64.

———. "Verses by Governor Bradford." *Massachusetts Historical Society Proceedings* 11 (October 1870): 465–82.

Brooks, Thomas. "Apples of Gold for Young Men and Women" (1657). In *The Complete Works of Thomas Brooks*. Vol. 1. Edinburgh: James Nicol, 1866.

Champion, Judah. *A Brief View of the Distresses, Hardship, and Dangers Our Ancestors Encounter'd, in Settling New-England*. Hartford: Green and Watson, 1770. EAI #11595.

Chauncey, Charles. *God's Mercy, Shewed to His People in Giving Them a Faithful Ministry and Schooles of Learning for the Continual Supplyes Thereof*. Cambridge: Samuel Green, 1655. EAI #40.

Chauncy, Charles. *Early Piety Recommended and Exemplified*. Boston: S. Kneeland and T. Green, 1732. EAI #3518.

—— [William Rand]. *The Late Religious Commotions in New-England Considered, An Answer to the Reverend Mr. Jonathan Edwards's Sermon*. Boston: Green, Bushell and Allen, for T. Fleet, 1743. EAI #5150.

———. *Seasonable Thoughts on the State of Religion in New-England*. Boston: Rogers and Fowle, 1743. EAI #5151.

Clap, Roger. *Memoirs of Capt. Roger Clap*. Boston: B. Green, 1731. EAI #3403.

Clarkson, Matthew. *An Address to the Citizens of Philadelphia, Respecting the Better Government of Youth*. Philadelphia: Ormrod and Conrad, 1795. EAI #28424.

Cobbet[t], Thomas. *A Fruitfull and Usefull Discourse touching the Honour due from Children to Parents, and the duty of parents towards their children*. London: S. G. for John Rothwell, 1656.

Colman, Benjamin. *A Brief Enquiry into the Reasons Why the People of God have been wont to bring into their Penitential Confessions, the sins of their Fathers and Ancestors*. Boston: T. Fleet and T. Crump, 1716. EAI #1801.

———. *Early Piety Again Inculcated*. Boston: S. Kneeland, 1720. EAI #2102.

———. *David's Dying Charge to the Rulers and People of Israel*. Boston: B. Green, 1723. EAI #2419.

———, and William Cooper. *Two Sermons Preached in Boston, March 5, 1723*. Boston: S. Kneeland, 1723. EAI #2425.

Cooper, William. *How and Why Young People Should Cleanse Their Way, in Two Sermons*. Boston: B. Green, 1716. EAI #1820.

———. *Serious Exhortations Address'd to Young Men*. Boston: S. Kneeland and T. Green, 1732. EAI #3525.

Cotton, John. *God's Promise To His Plantations*. London: William Jones, 1630; reprint, *Old South Leaflets*, no. 53. Boston: Old South Meeting House, n.d.

———. *A Brief Exposition with Practical Observations Upon the Whole Book of Ecclesiastes*. 1654; reprint, Edinburgh: James Nichol, 1868.

The Countryman's Lamentation, on the Neglect of a Proper Education of Children. Philadelphia: W. Dunlap, 1762. EAI #9097.

Crossman, Samuel. *The Young Man's Calling*. London, 1678.

Danforth, Samuel. *A Brief Recognition of New England's Errand Into the Wilderness*. Cambridge: S. G. and M. T., 1671. EAI #160.

Dexter, Samuel. *Our Father's God, the Hope of Posterity*. Boston: S. Kneeland and T. Green, 1738. EAI #4236.

Doolittle, Thomas. *The Young Man's Instructor and the Old Man's Remembrancer*. London, 1673.

Dunton, John. "Michael Perry's Inventory." In *Letter Written from New England A.D. 1686*. Boston: Prince Society, 1867; Burt Franklin Reprints.

Edson, Jesse. *A Discourse Delivered to the Young People*. Greenfield, MA: Thomas Dickman, 1799. EAI #35436.

Edwards, Jonathan. *Works of Jonathan Edwards*. Vol. 4, *The Great Awakening*. Edited by C. C. Goen. New Haven: Yale University Press, 1972.

Elijah's Mantle: A Faithful Testimony to the Cause and Work of God, in the Churches of New England and the Great End and Interest of These Plantations, Dropt and Left by Four Servants of God, Famous in the Service of the Churches. Boston: S. Kneeland, 1722.

Eliot, Andrew. *An Evil and Adulterous Generation*. Boston: S. Kneeland, 1753. EAI #6997.

Fitch, James. *A Holy Connexion*. Cambridge: Samuel Green, 1674. EAI #187.

Folger, Peter. *A Looking Glass for the Times, Or the Former Spirit of New England, Revived in This Generation*. Boston, 1676. EAI #211.

Ford, Paul Leicester, editor. *The New England Primer*. New York: Dodd, Mead and Co., 1897.

[Foster, Hannah]. *The Boarding School*. Boston, 1798. EAI #33748.

Gatchell, Increase. *The Young American Ephemeris*. Boston, 1715. EAI #1741.

Gouge, Thomas. *Young Man's Guide Through the Wilderness of This World*. London, 1680.

Harris, Thaddeus Mason. *A discourse, addressed to the Religious Society of Young Men in Dorchester*. Charlestown, MA: Samuel Etheridge, 1799. EAI #35590.

Hart, Oliver. *America's Remembrancer*. Philadelphia: T. Dobson, 1791. EAI #23428.

Hesketh, Henry. *The Importance of Religion to Young Persons*. London, 1683.

Homer, Jonathan. *The Succession of Generations Among Mankind*. Boston: Belknap and Young, 1792. EAI #24406.

Hovey, John. *The Duty and Privilege of Aged Saints to Leave Their Dying*

Testimony Behind Them to Posterity. Boston: S. Kneeland, 1749. EAI #6333.

Hubbard, William. *The Happiness of a People in the Wisdome of Their Rulers Directing and in the Obedience of Their Brethren Attending Unto What Israel Ought to Do.* Boston: John Foster, 1676. EAI #214.

[Jameson, William]. *A Remembrance of Former Times for This Generation; and Our Degeneracy Lamented.* Boston: B. Green and J. Allen, 1697. EAI #784.

Lenton, Francis. *The Young Gallants Whirligigg.* London, 1629.

Lewis, Daniel. *Good Rulers the Fathers of Their People, and the Marks of Honour Due to Them.* Boston: John Draper, 1748. EAI #6175.

Lingard, Richard. *A Letter of Advice to a Young Gentleman Leaving the University.* New York: W. Bradford, 1696. EAI #745.

Magaw, Samuel. *An Address Delivered in the Young Ladies Academy at Philadelphia on February 8 1787.* Philadelphia: Thomas Dobson, 1787.

———. *Discourse Occasioned by the Mournful Catastrophe, Through Fire, Which Overwhelmed and Destroyed Mr. Andrew Brown.* Philadelphia, 1797. EAI #32413.

Mather, Cotton. *Addresses to Old Men, and Young Men, and Little Children.* Boston: R. Pierce, 1690. EAI #534.

———. *The Serviceable Man.* Boston: Samuel Green, 1690. EAI #538.

———. *The Wonderful Works of God Commemorated.* Boston: S. Green, 1690. EAI #540.

———. *Unum Necessarium, Awakenings for the Unregenerate.* Boston: B. H., 1693. EAI #654.

———. *Warnings From the Dead.* Boston: Bartholomew Green, 1693. EAI #655.

———. *Early Religion Urged.* Boston, 1694. EAI #698.

———. *Help for Distressed Parents.* Boston: John Allen, 1695. EAI #723.

———. *Johannes in Eremo.* Boston: Michael Perry, 1695. EAI #724.

———. *A Family Well Ordered.* Boston: B. Green and J. Allen, 1699. EAI #875.

———. *The Best Ornaments of Youth.* Boston: Timothy Green, 1707. EAI #1308.

———. *Youth in its Brightest Glory.* Boston: T. Green, 1709. EAI #1410.

———. *The Young Man Spoken To.* Boston: T. Green, 1712. EAI #1564.

———. *Successive Generations: Remarks Upon the Changes of a Dying World, Made by One Generation Passing Off and Another Generation Coming on.* Boston: B. Green, 1715. EAI #1765.

———, et al. *A Course of Sermons on Early Piety.* Boston: S. Kneeland, 1721. EAI #2256.

Mather, Eleazar. *A Serious Exhortation to the Present and Succeeding Generation in New England.* Cambridge: S. G. and M. T., 1671. EAI #162.

Mather, Increase. *The First Principles of New England.* Cambridge: Samuel Green, 1675. EAI #208.

———. *The Wicked Man's Portion.* Boston: John Foster, 1675. EAI #210.

———. *Renewal of Covenant the Great Duty Incumbent on Decaying or Distressed Churches.* Boston: J. F. for Henry Phillips, 1677. EAI #239.

————. *Pray for the Rising Generation*. Cambridge: Samuel Green, 1678. EAI #255.

————. *The Necessity of Reformation*. Boston: John Foster, 1679. EAI #263.

————. *A Call From Heaven to the Present and Succeeding Generations*. Boston: John Foster, 1679. EAI #274.

————. *Solemn Advice to Young Men*. Boston, 1695. EAI #728.

————. *David Serving His Generation*. Boston: B. Green and J. Allen, 1698. EAI #831.

————. *The Duty of Parents to Pray for Their Children*. Boston: B. Green and J. Allen, 1703. EAI #1133.

————. *An Earnest Exhortation to the Children of New England To Exalt the God of Their Fathers*. Boston, 1711. EAI #1515.

Mather, Richard. *A Farewel Exhortation*. Cambridge: Samuel Green, 1657. EAI #47.

————, and Jonathan Mitchel. *A Defense of the Answer and Arguments of the Synod Met at Boston in the Year 1662*. Cambridge: S. Green and M. Johnson, 1664. EAI #89.

Mayhew, Jonathan. *Christian Sobriety*. Boston: Richard and Samuel Draper, 1763. EAI #9440.

Morton, Nathaniel. *New England's Memoriall*. Cambridge: S. G. and M. T., 1669. EAI #144.

Neal, James Armstrong. *An Essay on the Education and Genius of the Female Sex*. Philadelphia: Jacob Johnson and Co., 1795. EAI #29135.

Norton, John. *The Heart of N– England Rent at the Blasphemies of the Present Generation*. Cambridge: Samuel Green, 1659. EAI #56.

Oakes, Urian. *An Elegie Upon the Death of the Reverend Mr. Thomas Shepard*. Cambridge: Samuel Green, 1677. EAI #240.

Oxenbridge, John. *New-England Freemen Warned and Warmed*. Boston, 1673. EAI #181.

Parkman, Ebenezer. *The Diary of Ebenezer Parkman, First Part, 1719–1755*. Edited by Francis G. Walett. Worcester, MA: American Antiquarian Society, 1974.

Pemberton, Ebenezer. *A True Servant of His Generation Characterized*. Boston: Bartholomew Green, 1712. EAI #1577.

The Poor Orphans Legacy: Being a Short Collection of Godly Counsels and Exhortations to a Young Arising Generation. Philadelphia: B. Franklin, 1734. EAI #3828.

Prince, Thomas. *The People of New England Put in Mind of the Righteous Acts of the Lord to Them and Their Fathers and Reasoned With Concerning Them*. Boston: B. Green, 1730. EAI #3343.

Prince, Thomas, Jr. "Part of a Letter from Mr. Prince Junior to a Minister in the Neighborhood of Glasgow, dated Boston, October 8, 1744." *Christian Monthly History* 8 (November 1745): 227–29.

————. "Part of a Letter from Mr. Prince Junior to a Minister in the Neighbourhood of Glasgow, dated Boston 17th June 1745." *Christian Monthly History* 8 (November 1745): 229–33.

Quick, John. *The Young Man's claim unto the Sacrament of the Lords Supper.* 2d impression. Boston: B. Green and J. Allen, 1700. EAI #949.

"Records of the Old Colony Club." *Proceedings of the Massachusetts Historical Society* 2 (October 1887): 382–444.

The Rise and Progress of the Young Ladies' Academy of Philadelphia. Philadelphia: Stewart and Cochran, 1794. EAI #27514.

Rudolph, Frederick, editor. *Essays on Education in the Early Republic.* Cambridge, MA: Belknap Press, Harvard University Press, 1965.

Rush, Benjamin. "Address to the People of the United States." *American Museum* 1 (January 1787): 11.

———. *Thoughts Upon Female Education Accommodated to the Present State of Society, Manners, and Government in the United States of America.* Philadelphia: Prichard and Hall, 1787. EAI #20691.

———. *Letters of Benjamin Rush.* Edited by L. H. Butterfield. Vol. 1. Princeton: Princeton University Press, 1951.

Scottow, Joshua. *Old Mens Tears For Their Own Declensions.* Boston: Benjamin Harris and John Allen, 1691. EAI #576.

A Seasonable Account of the Christian and Dying-Words of Some Young-Men. Philadelphia: Renier Jansen, 1700. EAI #950.

Sewall, Joseph. *The Holy Spirit the Gift of God.* Boston: D. Henchman, 1728. EAI #3103.

Shepard, Jeremiah. *Early Offerings Best Accepted.* Boston: B. Green, 1712. EAI #1583.

Shepard, Thomas. *The Church Membership of Children and Their Right to Baptisme.* Cambridge: Samuel Green, 1663.

Shepard, Thomas, Jr. *Eye-Salve.* Cambridge: Samuel Green, 1673. EAI #182.

Shower, John. *An Exhortation to Youth to Prepare for Judgment.* London, 1681.

Stoddard, Solomon. *Three Sermons Lately Preached at Boston . . . To Which a Fourth is added, to stir up Young Men and Maidens. . . .* Boston: B. Green, 1717. EAI #1930.

———. "An Examination of the Power of the Fraternity." In *The Presence of Christ With the Ministers of the Gospel.* Boston: B. Green, 1718. EAI #1999.

Stoughton, William. *New England's True Interest; Not to Lie.* Cambridge: S. G. and M. T., 1670. EAI #156.

Street, Nicholas. *The American States Acting Over the Part of the Children of Israel in the Wilderness, and Thereby Impending their Entrance into Canaan's Rest.* New Haven: Thomas and Samuel Green, 1777. EAI #15604.

Swanwick, John. *Thoughts on Education, Addressed to the Visitors of the Young Ladies Academy in Philadelphia.* Philadelphia: Thomas Dobson, 1787. EAI #20736.

Thacher, Peter. *Unbelief Detected and Condemned.* Boston: B. Green, 1708. EAI #1375.

Todd, Jonathan. *The Young People Warned.* New London, CT: T. Green, 1741. EAI #4829.

Tulley, John. *An Almanack*. Boston: Benjamin Harris, 1695. EAI #940.

Vincent, Thomas. *Words of Advice to Young Men*. London, 1668.

Wakeman, Samuel. *A Young Man's Legacy to the Rising Generation*. Cambridge, 1673. EAI #183.

Webb, John. *The Young-Man's Duty*. Boston: S. Kneeland, 1718. EAI #2007.

Wells, John. *An Oration Delivered on the Fourth of July, 1798 at St. Paul's Church Before the Young Men of the City of New-York*. New York: McLean and Lang, 1798. EAI #34998.

Willard, Samuel. *Useful Instruction for a Professing People in Times of Great Security and Degeneracy*. Cambridge: Samuel Green, 1673. EAI #184.

———. *The Child's Portion*. Boston: Samuel Green, 1684. EAI #380.

Williams, John. *A Serious Word to the Posterity of Holy Men*. Boston: B. Green, 1729. EAI #3238.

Williams, William. *An Essay to Prove the Interest of the Children of Believers in the Covenant*. Boston, 1727. EAI #2978.

———. *The Duty and Interest of a People, Among Whom Religion is Planted to Continue . . . From Generation to Generation*. Boston: S. Kneeland and T. Green, 1736. EAI #4103.

Winthrop, John. *Winthrop's Journal, "History of New England," 1630–1649*. Edited by James K. Hosmer. 2 vols. New York: Barnes and Noble, 1908; reprint, 1953.

Primary Works Published 1800–1995

Adams, Charles Francis, Jr. *Massachusetts: Its Historians and Its History*. 1893; reprint, Freeport, NY: Books for Libraries Press, 1971.

Address of the Democratic Young Men of the City and County of Philadelphia to Their Republican Fellow Citizens. Philadelphia, 1823.

Address of the Democratic Young Men of the City and Liberties of Philadelphia. Philadelphia, 1812.

Address of the Independent Republican Young Men of the City and County of Philadelphia. Philadelphia, 1817.

"Address of the Republican General Committee of the City and County of New York, to the Republican Young Men—The Columbian Society—and the Republican Literary Debating Society." *Rhode-Island Republican*, June 13, 1810.

Address of the Republican Young Men of the Town of Galway, County of Saratoga, to Their Fellow Citizens. Ballston Spa, 1828.

Address of the Whig Young Men's Convention to the People of Massachusetts. Worcester, MA: [1838?].

Address of the Young Men of the National Republican Party of the Fifth Congressional District, to the Young Men of the State of Maryland. Baltimore, 1832.

"Address to the Young Men of New York." *Jeffersonian*, October 28, 1838.

Address to the Young Men of Worcester County by a Committee of the Young Men's Temperance Convention. Worcester, MA: S. H. Colton and Co., 1835.

Algeo, John and Adele. "Among the New Words." *American Speech* 67 (Winter 1992): 421–23.

American Anti-Slavery Society. *Seventh Annual Report of the Executive Committee of the American Anti-Slavery Society.* 1840; Kraus Reprint Co., 1972.

"The American Art-Union." *Knickerbocker* 32 (November 1848): 442–47.

"The Artist, Merchant, and Statesman." *United States Magazine and Democratic Review* 17 (November 1845): 340–45.

"The Artist, the Merchant, and the Statesman. The Value of National Home Feeling, and the Future Influence of Literature, Commerce and the Arts on the Fortunes of America." *Merchant's Magazine* 14 (March 1846): 235–43.

"Artists of America." *American Whig Review* 3 (May 1846): 517–22.

Auxiliary Education Society of Young Men of Boston. *First Report of the Directors of the Auxiliary Education Society of the Young Men of Boston.* Boston: U. Crocker, 1820.

———. *Second Report of the Directors of the Auxiliary Education Society of the Young Men of Boston.* Boston: Crocker and Brewster, 1821.

"Bad News for the Transcendental Poets." *Literary World* 1 (February 20, 1847): 53.

Beecher, Edward. *An Address, Delivered at the Eighth Anniversary of the Auxiliary Education Society of the Young Men of Boston.* Boston: T. R. Marvin, 1827.

Beecher, Lyman. "The Memory of Our Fathers." In *Beecher's Works.* Vol. 1, *Lectures on Political Atheism and Kindred Subjects.* Boston: John P. Jewett and Co., 1852.

Bell, John. *An Address on the Spirit of Associations, Delivered Before the Philadelphia Young Men's Society.* Philadelphia: William Stavely, 1834.

Beman, Nathan S. S. *The Claims of Our Country on Young Men.* Troy, NY: N. Tuttle, 1843.

Bingham, George Caleb. "Letters of George Caleb Bingham to James S. Rollins." Edited by C. B. Rollins. *Missouri Historical Review* 32 (October 1937, January 1938): 3–34, 164–202.

Boston Young Men's Benevolent Society. *The Claims of Benevolence Upon the Young Men of the Community.* Boston: Lyceum Press, 1833.

Boston Young Men's Temperance Society. *Address to the Young Men of Boston.* Boston: Garrison and Knapp, 1832.

Bourne, Randolph. "The Two Generations." *Atlantic Monthly* (May 1911): 591–98.

———. "This Older Generation," *Atlantic Monthly* (September 1915): 391.

Brooks, Van Wyck. *Letters and Leadership.* New York: B. W. Huebsch, 1918.

———. *Van Wyck Brooks: The Early Years.* Edited by Claire Sprague. New York: Harper and Row, 1968.

Bryant, William Cullen, Francis L. Hawks, Cornelius Mathews. *Address to the People of the United States in Behalf of the American Copyright Club.* New York, 1843.

Byrdsall, Fitzwilliam. *The History of the Loco-Foco or Equal Rights Party.* New York, 1842; reprint, New York: Burt Franklin, 1967.

Charlestown Young Men's Evangelical Union. *Constitution and By-laws.* Charlestown, MA, 1853.

Circular by Order of General Committee of Young Men. Albany, 1824.

Clark, Joseph. *Young Americanism.* Chambersburg, PA: M. Kieffer and Co., 1852.

Clark, Lewis G. "Freedom's Holy Cause." In *Odd-Fellow's Offering For 1851.* New York: Edward Walker, 1850.

Comer, Cornelia A. P. "A Letter to the Rising Generation." *Atlantic Monthly* (February 1911): 145–54.

Cooper, James Fenimore. *Homeward Bound.* 1838; New York: G. P. Putnam's Sons, Leatherstocking Edition, n.d.

———. *Home as Found.* 1838; New York: Capricorn Books, 1961.

Cranch, C. P. "Old Fogies." *Appleton's Journal* 19 (June 1878): 531–35.

Crummell, Alexander. *Africa and America.* Springfield, MA: Willey and Co., 1891.

DeLeon, Edwin. "Cheap Literature: Its Character and Tendencies." *Southern Literary Messenger* 10 (January 1844): 33–39.

———. *The Position and Duties of "Young America," An Address Delivered Before the Two Literary Societies of The South Carolina College.* Columbia, SC, 1845.

Democratic Party. *Address of the Democratic Republican General Committee of Young Men, to the Republican Electors of the County of Albany.* Albany, 1825.

———. *Proceedings and Address of the Republican Young Men of the State of New York Assembled at Utica.* New York: J. Seymour, 1828.

———. *Address of the Republican General Committee of Young men of the City and County of New-York Friendly to the Election of Gen. Andrew Jackson to the Presidency, to the Republican Electors of the State of New York.* New York: Alexander Ming, Jr., 1828.

———. *Address of the General Committee of Republican Young Men of the City of New York to the Republican Young Men of the State of New-York Recommending a State Convention.* New York, 1828.

———. *Proceedings of a Meeting of Republican Young Men Held in the village of Johnstown, December 13, 1831, Including an Address to the Republican Young Men of the County of Montgomery.* N.p., n.d.

———. *Address of the Democratic Young Men's General Committee, to the Democratic Young Men of New-York and Their Fellow Citizens Generally.* New York: Peter Van Pelt, 1835.

———. *Proceedings of the Democratic Republican Convention of Young Men of the State of Pennsylvania.* Harrisburg: Office of Pennsylvania Reporter and State Journal, 1836.

———. *Address of the Democratic Republican Young Men's General Committee, to the Republican Young Men of New York.* New York: J. M. Marsh, 1838.

———. *Address of the Democratic Republican Young Men's General Committee of the City of New York to the Republican Young Men of the State.* New York, 1840.

Dickinson, Austin. *Appeal to American Youth on Temperance.* New York: American Tract Society, [1830?].

Doane, George Washington. *Sons of Washington.* Burlington: E. Morris, 1847.

Drake, Francis S. *The Town of Roxbury: Its Memorable Persons and Places.* Roxbury, MA: by the author, 1878.

"The Duty of Young Men in Politics." *Christian Union* 46 (October 1, 1892): 580–82.

Eddy, Ansel D. *An Address Delivered Before the Pennsylvania Temperance Society at Their Third Anniversary.* N.p., n.d.

Ellis, Charles M. *The History of Roxbury Town.* Boston: Samuel G. Drake, 1847.

Emerson, Ralph Waldo. *Letters of Ralph Waldo Emerson.* Edited by Ralph L. Rusk. Vol. 3. New York: Columbia University Press, 1939.

———. *Collected Works of Ralph Waldo Emerson.* Introduction and notes by Robert E. Spiller. Vol. 1, *Nature; Addresses and Lectures.* Cambridge, MA: Belknap Press, Harvard University Press, 1971.

———. *Essays and Lectures.* New York: Library of America, 1983.

"Eric Utne Created the Impossible: A *Reader's Digest* That Both Baby Boomers and Highbrows Can Love." *People,* September 10, 1990, 79–81.

"Eulogies on Jefferson and Adams." *American Quarterly Review* 1 (March 1827): 54–77.

Everett, Alexander H. "Harro Harring: A Biographical Sketch." *United States Magazine and Democratic Review* 15 (October, November, December 1844): 337–47, 462–75, 561–79.

———. "The Young American." *United States Magazine and Democratic Review* 16 (May 1845): 495.

Everett, Edward. *An Address Delivered at Charlestown, August 1, 1826, in Commemoration of John Adams and Thomas Jefferson.* Boston: William L. Lewis, 1826.

"Fine Arts." *Graham's Magazine* 37 (October 1850): 260.

Foner, Philip S., and George E. Walker, editor. *Proceedings of the Black State Conventions, 1840–1865.* Vol. 1. Philadelphia: Temple University Press, 1979.

Fowler, William Chauncy. "President Charles Chauncy, His Ancestors and Descendants." *New England Historical and Genealogical Register* 10 (October 1856): 323–36.

Franco, Harry [Charles F. Briggs]. *The Trippings of Tom Pepper.* 2 vols. New York: Burgess, Stringer and Co., 1847, 1850.

French, Ebenezer. *An Oration Pronounced July 4, 1805, Before the Young Democratic Republicans of the Town of Boston.* Boston: J. Ball, 1805. EAI #S8480, S8481 (2d ed.).

Frost, Henry F. *An Address Delivered Before the Young Men's Temperance Society.* Charleston, SC, 1832.

Fuller, Margaret. *The Letters of Margaret Fuller.* Edited by Robert W. Hudspeth. Vol. 4. Ithaca: Cornell University Press, 1987.

Garrison, William Lloyd. *The Letters of William Lloyd Garrison.* Vol. 1, edited by Walter M. Merrill. Vol. 2, edited by Louis Ruchames. Cambridge, MA: Belknap Press, Harvard University Press, 1971.

Giles, Jeff. "Generalizations X." *Newsweek,* June 6, 1994, 62–72.

Gleason, Joseph, Jr. *An Oration Pronounced on the Thirtieth Anniversary of American Independence Before the Young Democratic Republicans of the Town of Boston.* Boston: Oliver and Munroe, 1806. EAI #S10487.

Gottlieb, Annie. *Do You Believe in Magic?* New York: Times Books, 1987.

"The Great Nation of Futurity." *United States Magazine and Democratic Review* 6 (November 1839): 426–30.

Griswold, Rufus Wilmot. *The Prose Writers of America.* 2d ed. rev. Philadelphia: Carey and Hart, 1847.

Haines, Charles G. *An Oration Before the Young Republican Gentlemen of Concord and its Vicinity, on the Fourth of July, 1809.* Concord, NH: Isaac Hill, 1809. EAI #S17694.

Hall, Baynard R. *Disciplined Youth Necessary for the Duties of Middle Age and the Comfort of Old Age.* Philadelphia: I. Ashmead and Co., 1838.

———. *An Address Delivered to the Young Ladies of the Spring-Villa Seminary.* Burlington: Powell and George, 1839.

Hamblett, Charles, and Jane Deverson. *Generation X.* London: Tandem Books, 1964.

History of the Young Men's Missionary Society of New York. New York: D. Fanshaw, 1817. EAI #S42992.

Hobart, Elihu. *An Oration Pronounced At Abington, July 4, 1807, In Commemoration of American Independence; at the Request of a Committee of Young Democratic Republicans.* Boston: Manning and Loring, 1807. EAI #S12762.

Hobart, John Henry. *An Address Delivered Before the New-York Protestant Episcopal Missionary Society of Young Men and Others.* New York: T. and J. Swords, 1817. EAI #S41060.

Hone, Philip. *The Diary of Philip Hone.* Edited by Bayard Tuckerman. 2 vols. New York: Dodd, Mead and Co., 1889.

Howe, Neil, and Bill Strauss. *13thGen: Abort, Retry, Ignore, Fail?* New York: Vintage Books, 1993.

Jarvis, Samuel Farmar. *A Sermon Preached Before the Auxiliary Education Society of the Young Men of Boston.* Boston: Joseph W. Ingraham, 1822.

Jefferson, Thomas. *Autobiography of Thomas Jefferson.* New York: G. P. Putnam's Sons, Capricorn Books, 1959.

Jenkins, John S. *History of Political Parties in the State of New-York.* Auburn, NY: Alden and Markham, 1846.

Jones, William A. "The Early Maturity of Genius." *United States Magazine and Democratic Review* 14 (June 1844): 634–37.

———. "Nationality in Literature." *United States Magazine and Democratic Review* 20 (March, April 1847): 264–72, 316–20.

Journal of the National Convention of Young Men's Societies 1 (January 1834).

Keith, Isaac Stockton. *National Affliction and National Consolation.* Charleston, SC: W. P. Young, 1800.

Kihn, Martin. "The Gen X Hucksters." *New York,* August 29, 1994, 94–107.

Leland, John. *Address to the Young Men of Cheshire.* Pittsfield, MA: Phinehas Allen, 1808. EAI #S50863.

Lester, C. Edwards. *The artist, the merchant, and the statesman, of the age of the Medici, and of our own times.* 2 vols. New York: Paine and Burgess, 1845.

——. *The Gallery of Illustrious Americans.* New York: John Wiley, G. P. Putnam, D. Appleton and Co., C. S. Francis and Co., 1850.

——. "Dedication of Odd-Fellows' Hall, New York, Oration of C. Edwards Lester." In *Odd-Fellows' Offering for 1850.* New York: Edward Walker, 1850.

——. "Washington's Marriage." In *Odd-Fellows' Offering for 1851.* New York: Edward Walker, 1850.

——. ["Hermitage."] *The Life of Gen. Frank. Pierce.* New York: Cornish, Lamport and Co., 1852.

Lincoln, Abraham. *Collected Works of Abraham Lincoln.* Edited by Roy P. Balser. Vols. 1, 3. New Brunswick: Rutgers University Press, 1953.

Lincoln, William. *History of Worcester, Massachusetts.* Worcester, MA: Moses D. Phillips and Co., 1837.

Longacre, James B., and James Herring, editors. *The National Portrait Gallery of Distinguished Americans.* 4 vols. Philadelphia: Henry Perkis; New York: Monson Bancroft, 1834–39.

Longfellow, Henry W. "German Writers." *Graham's Lady's and Gentleman's Magazine* 20 (March 1842): 134–37.

Lowell, James Russell. "Letters of James Russell Lowell, 1843–54." *Bulletin of the New York Public Library* 4 (October 1900): 339–45.

Mathews, Cornelius [A Young American]. "Our Forefathers." *American Monthly Magazine* 7 (May, June 1836): 453–56, 559–61.

——. *The Various Writings of Cornelius Mathews.* New York: Harper and Brothers, 1843.

——. *Americanism, An Address Delivered Before the Eucleian Society of the New-York University.* New York: Paine and Burgess, 1845.

Matza, David. "Subterranean Traditions of Youth." *Annals of the American Academy of Political and Social Science* 338 (November 1961): 103–18.

Mazzini, Giuseppe. *Life and Writings of Joseph Mazzini.* 6 vols. London: Smith, Elder, and Co., 1864–70.

Melville, Herman. *Pierre Or, The Ambiguities.* In *Writings of Herman Melville Northwestern-Newberry Edition.* Vol. 7. Evanston and Chicago: Northwestern University Press and the Newberry Library, 1971.

——. "Hawthorne and His Mosses." In *Writings of Herman Melville Northwestern-Newberry Edition.* Vol. 9, *Piazza Tales and Other Prose Pieces.* Evanston and Chicago: Northwestern University Press and the Newberry Library, 1987.

"National Gallery." *North American Review* 40 (April 1835): 409–17.

"National Portrait Gallery of Distinguished Americans." *New York Review* 4 (April 1839): 352–92.

National Republican Party. *Proceedings of the National Republican Convention of Young Men, Which Assembled in the City of Washington May 7, 1832.* Washington, DC: Gales and Seaton, 1832.

————. *Proceedings of the State Convention of National Republican Young Men, Holden at Hartford.* Hartford, CT: Hanmer and Comstock, 1832.

National Republican Young Men's Meeting. *For the Constitution and the Laws.* Worcester, MA, 1832. Broadside.

New York Apprentice's Temperance Society. *Second Annual Report of the New-York Apprentice's Temperance Society.* New York, 1832.

New York General Committee of Whig Young Men. *Proceedings of a Meeting of the Whig Young Men of the City of New York.* New York: T. Snowden Printer, 1834.

New York Young Men's Anti-Slavery Society. *First Annual Report of the New-York Young Men's Anti-Slavery Society.* New York: Coolidge and Lambert, 1835.

New York Young Men's Society. *Constitution.* New York: J. and J. Harper, 1831.

————. *First Annual Report.* New York: John T. West and Co., 1832.

New York Young Men's Society for the Promotion of Temperance. *An Address to the Young Men of the United States on the Subject of Temperance.* New York: Jonathan Leavitt, 1830.

[Osgood, Samuel]. "Editor's Table: Youth and Age in America." *Harper's* (January 1860): 263–67.

Parker, Theodore. *Works of Theodore Parker.* Edited by James K. Hosmer. Vol. 11, *The Slave Power.* Boston: American Unitarian Association, 1907.

Parmalee, David L. *An Address Delivered at Goshen, at the Anniversary Celebration of the 4th of July, 1814, At the Desire of the Young Men of the Town.* Hartford, CT: Peter B. Gleason and Co., 1814. EAI #S32439.

Philadelphia Young Men's Anti-Slavery Society. *Constitution, By-Laws, and List of Officers.* Philadelphia, 1835.

Philadelphia Young Men's Society. *The Constitution, By-Laws and Standing Rules of the Philadelphia Young Men's Society.* Philadelphia: William F. Geddes, 1833.

Pike, James S. *First Blows of the Civil War.* New York: American News Company, 1879.

"Political Portraits with Pen and Pencil—William Leggett." *United States Magazine and Democratic Review* 6 (July 1839): 17–28.

"Political Portraits with Pen and Pencil—Henry D. Gilpin." *United States Magazine and Democratic Review* 8 (December 1840): 512–35.

"The Port Huron Statement." In James Miller, *Democracy Is in the Streets.* New York: Simon and Schuster, 1987.

Proceedings of a Convention of Democratic Young Men, Delegates From the Citizens of Pennsylvania, in Favour of the Re-Election of Joseph Ritner, and Opposed to Martin Van Buren and the Sub-treasury. Reading, PA, 1838.

Proceedings of the Constitutional Republican Young Men of the City and County of Philadelphia. Philadelphia: C. Zentler, 1808. EAI #S14772.

Proceedings of the Convention of the Young Men of Massachusetts Friendly to the Cause of Temperance. Boston: Ford and Damrell, 1834.

"Proceedings of the Convention of the Young Men of Massachusetts, Friendly to the Cause of Temperance, Held at Worcester, July 1st and 2d 1834." *Christian Examiner and General Review* 18 (March 1835): 30–50.

Republican Meeting: At a Numerous Meeting of Democratic Republican Young Men of the Town of Delhi. Broadside, October 22, 1824.

"The Revolutionary Secret Societies of Modern Italy." *United States Magazine and Democratic Review* 9 (September 1841): 260–76.

Ritter, Abraham. *Philadelphia and Her Merchants.* Philadelphia: by the author, 1860.

Rocchietti, Joseph. *Why a National Literature Cannot Flourish in the United States of North America.* New York, 1845.

Rushkoff, Douglas, editor. *The GenX Reader.* New York: Ballantine Books, 1994.

Sargent, Nathan. *Public Men and Events.* 2 vols. Philadelphia: J. B. Lippincott and Co., 1875.

A Selection of Eulogies Pronounced in the Several States in Honor of Those Illustrious Patriots and Statesmen, John Adams and Thomas Jefferson. Hartford, CT: D. F. Robinson and Co., 1826.

Seward, William H. *Autobiography of William H. Seward from 1801 to 1834.* New York: D. Appleton and Co., 1877.

———. *The Works of William H. Seward.* Edited by George E. Burke. 5 vols. Boston: Houghton Mifflin, 1884.

Simms, William Gilmore. "Writings of Cornelius Mathews." *Southern Quarterly Review* 6 (October 1840): 307–42.

———. "International Copyright Law." *Southern Literary Messenger* 10 (January 1844): 7–17.

———. *Views and Reviews in American Literature, History and Fiction.* New York: Wiley and Putnam, 1845.

———. *The Letters of William Gilmore Simms.* Edited by Mary C. Simms Oliphant. 5 vols. Columbia: University of South Carolina Press, 1953.

Smith, Jonathan B. *Oration Delivered on the Fourth of March, 1813 Before the Association of Democratic Young Men of the City and Liberties of Philadelphia.* Philadelphia, 1813. EAI #S29800.

The Sons of the Sires: A History of the Rise, Progress and Destiny of the American Party. Philadelphia: Lippincott, Grambo and Co., 1855.

Stanton, Henry B. *Random Reflections.* Johnston, NY: Blanck and Leaming, 1885.

Story, Joseph. *An Eulogy on General George Washington.* Salem, MA: Joshua Cushing, 1800. EAI #38568.

Thorp, Philip. *Young America's Dream: Or, A Discoursory Interview Between the Spirits of Liberty, Tyranny and A Citizen of the World.* New York: Abbe and Yates, 1854.

Tracy, Joseph. *The Great Awakening.* Boston: Charles Tappan, 1845; reprint, New York: Arno Press, 1969.

Train, George Francis. *Young America in Wall-Street.* New York: Derby and Jackson, 1857.

———. *Spread-Eagleism.* New York: Derby and Jackson, 1859.

Tyson, J. R. *A Discourse Before the Young Men's Colonization Society of Pennsylvania.* Philadelphia, 1834.

A Voice From Old Tammany: Meeting of the People. New York: Joseph M. Marsh, 1838.

Webster, Daniel. *An Oration Pronounced at Hanover New Hampshire, 4th of July 1800.* Hanover, NH: Moses Davis, 1800. EAI #39035.

Weld, Theodore Dwight. *Letters of Theodore Dwight Weld, Angelina Grimké Weld and Sarah Grimké.* Edited by Gilbert H. Barnes and Dwight L. Dumond. Vol. 1. New York: D. Appleton-Century Co., 1934.

"What Tune Does the Utne Play?" *Time,* December 3, 1990, 94.

Whig Party. *Proceedings of a Meeting of the Whig Young Men of the City of New-York Together With the Address of the General Committee.* New York: T. Snowden, 1834.

———. *Proceedings of a State Convention of the Whig Young Men of Connecticut.* Hartford, CT: The Courant Office, 1840.

———. *Proceedings of the Whig State Convention at Worcester, Mass, June 17, 1840.* Broadside.

———. *Address to the Democratic Whig Young Men of the City and County of New York.* New York, 1841.

[Whipple, E. P.] "Young Men in History." *Atlantic Monthly* (July 1865): 1–11.

Whittier, John Greenleaf. *The Letters of John Greenleaf Whittier.* Edited by John B. Pickard. 3 vols. Cambridge, MA: Belknap Press, Harvard University Press, 1975.

Winthrop, Robert C. *Addresses and Speeches on Various Occasions.* Boston: Little, Brown, 1852.

Winthrop, Robert C., Jr. *A Memoir of Robert C. Winthrop.* Boston: Little, Brown., 1897.

Wu, Amy. "Media X'd Generation X." *Editor and Publisher,* January 14, 1995.

Young America! Principles and Objects of the National Reform Association. New York, 1845.

Young America—Extra. *Freedom of the Public Lands.* Broadside, n.d.

"Young England." *Edinburgh Review* 81 (October 1844): 517–25.

" 'Young England.' 'Coningsby.' " *Southern Literary Messenger* 10 (December 1844): 737–49.

"Young England." *North American Review* 61 (July 1845): 231–44.

Young Ladies Association for the Promotion of Literature and Missions. *First Annual Report.* Philadelphia: William F. Geddes, 1839.

———. *Second Annual Report.* Philadelphia: King and Baird, 1840.

Young Men's Colonization Society. *Constitution of the Young Men's Colonization Society.* New York: W. Osburn and Co., 1832.

Young Men's Convention. Broadside, October 15, 1825.

"Young Men's County Convention." *Albany Daily Advertiser Extra,* October 18, 1824.

Young Men's Missionary Society of New York. *Constitution of the Young Men's Missionary Society of New-York.* New York: Daniel Fanshaw, 1816. EAI #S39901.

Young Men's Missionary Society of Richmond. *Constitution.* Richmond, VA: Franklin Press, 1819. EAI #S49281.

Young Men's Temperance Society of the City of Albany. *Proceedings of the Annual Meeting.* Albany: Hoffman and White, 1836.

Young Men's Whig Association of Pittsburgh. "Minutes of the Young Men's Whig Association of Pittsburgh, 1834." Edited by Russell J. Ferguson. *Western Pennsylvania Historical Magazine* 19 (March 1936): 213–20.

Primary Works, Unpublished

American Academy of Fine Arts. Minutes of Board of Directors Meeting. Microfilm. Manuscripts and Archives, Yale University Library.

Ashhurst, Lewis R. Private Journal of Lewis R. Ashhurst A.D. 1834 to 1844. Historical Society of Pennsylvania, Philadelphia.

Beman, Amos G. Scrapbook of Amos G. Beman, Pastor, 1838–1857. Vol. 1. James Weldon Johnson Collection. Beinecke Rare Book and Manuscript Library. Yale University.

Black Abolitionist Papers 1830–1865. Edited by George E. Carter and C. Peter Ripley. Microfilm edition. Sanford, NC: Microfilming Corporation of America, 1981.

Crummell, Alexander. "Eulogium on the Life and Character of Thomas Sipkins Sidney." *Black Abolitionist Papers,* Reel 3/478–506.

Gilpin, Henry D. Diary, 14 April 1822 to 30 December 1843. Gilpin Papers, vol. 12. Historical Society of Pennsylvania, Philadelphia.

Holt, Joseph. Papers, vol. 14. Manuscript Division, Library of Congress.

Kilroe Collection. Box 29, Tammany Society photostats and newsclippings. Rare Books Library, Butler Memorial Library, Columbia University.

Madison, James. James Madison Papers. Microfilm. Manuscripts and Archives, Yale University Library.

Marcy, William L. Papers. Manuscript Division, Library of Congress.

Pierce, Franklin. Franklin Pierce Papers. Microfilm. Manuscripts and Archives, Yale University Library.

Sanders, Anna J. Journal. George N. Sanders Papers. Manuscript Division, Library of Congress.

Whig Party Papers. Box 6, Folder 2. Massachusetts Collection, American Antiquarian Society, Worcester, MA.

Whig Scrapbook. Rare Book and Manuscript Library, Columbia University.

Winthrop Family Papers. Edited by Marjorie F. Gutheim. Microfilm edition. Boston: Massachusetts Historical Society, 1976. Reel 22, Miscellaneous Family Correspondence; Reel 39, #14, Robert C. Winthrop Correspondence; Reel 44, #19, Robert C. Winthrop Scrapbook.

Reference Works

The Biographical Encyclopedia of Pennsylvania of the Nineteenth Century. Philadelphia: Galaxy Publishing Co., 1874.

Brown, Francis, ed. *A Hebrew and English Lexicon of the Old Testament.* Oxford: Clarendon Press, 1906; reissued with corrections, 1951.

Chielens, Edward E., editor. *American Literary Magazines: The Eighteenth and Nineteenth Centuries.* Westport, CT: Greenwood Press, 1986.

Dictionary of American Biography. 22 vols. New York: Charles Scribner's Sons, 1928–58.

Dictionary of National Biography. 22 vols. London: Smith, Elder and Co., 1908–9.

Klein, Ernest. *A Comprehensive Dictionary of the Hebrew Language for Readers of English.* Carta Jerusalem: University of Haifa, 1987.

Logan Rayford W., and Michael A. Winston, editors. *Dictionary of American Negro Biography.* New York: W. W. Norton, 1982.

Longworth's American Almanac, New York Register and City Directory. New York: Thomas Longworth, 1836–42.

The National Union Catalog Pre-1956 Imprints. 754 vols. London: Mansell, 1968–81.

New-York City and Co-Partnership Directory. New York: John Doggett, Jr., 1843–48.

Sloan, David E., editor. *American Humor Magazines and Comic Periodicals.* Westport, CT: Greenwood Press, 1987.

Newspapers and Periodicals

The Christian History. Boston. 1743–45.

New York Herald. October 1835; September 1837; 1851–52.

New York Evening Post. September 1837.

Plaindealer. New York. 1837.

Colored American. New York. 1837–38.

Working Man's Advocate. New York. 1844–June 1845.

London Times. September 1843; March, May 1844.

New York Tribune. August–September 1849; December 1851; January, April 1852; February 25, 1854; March 3, June 5, 18, 1855.

New York Times. December 1851; January, April 1852; June 1855.

Transactions of the Apollo Association for the Promotion of Fine Arts in the United States. New York. 1840.

Transactions of the American Art-Union. New York. 1843–49.

United States Magazine and Democratic Review. New York. Vols. 15–17, 1844–45; 30–31, 1852.

Yankee Doodle. New York. 1846–47.

John-Donkey. New York. 1848.

Secondary Works

Abramovitz, Mimi. *Regulating the Lives of Women.* Boston: South End Press, 1988.

Abrams, Philip. "Rites de Passage: The Conflict of Generations in Industrial Society." *Journal of Contemporary History* 5, 1 (1970): 175–90.

Ackroyd, P. R. "The Meaning of Hebrew דור Considered." *Journal of Semitic Studies* 13 (Spring 1968): 3–10.

Adams, William Harrison, III. "The Louisiana Whig Party." Ph.D. diss., Louisiana State University, 1960.

Ahearn, Marie L. *The Rhetoric of War: Training Day, the Militia, and the Military Sermon.* Westport, CT: Greenwood Press, 1989.

Albanese, Catherine L. *Sons of the Fathers.* Philadelphia: Temple University Press, 1976.

Alexander, John K. *Render Them Submissive: Responses to Poverty in Philadelphia, 1760–1800.* Amherst: University of Massachusetts Press, 1980.

Anderson, Benedict. *Imagined Communities: Reflections on the Origin and Spread of Nationalism.* London: Verso, 1983.

Anderson, Dwight G. *Abraham Lincoln: The Quest for Immortality.* New York: Alfred A. Knopf, 1982.

Anderson, Fred. *A People's Army: Massachusetts Soldiers and Society in the Seven Years' War.* Chapel Hill: University of North Carolina Press for the Institute of Early American History and Culture, 1984.

Anderson, Virginia DeJohn. *New England's Generation.* New York: Cambridge University Press, 1991.

Angus, David L. "Common School Politics in a Frontier City: Detroit, 1836–1842." In *Schools in Cities,* edited by Ronald K. Goodenow and Diane Ravitch. New York: Holmes and Meier, 1983.

Appleby, Joyce. "New Cultural Heroes in the Early National Period." In *The Culture of the Market: Historical Essays,* edited by Thomas L. Haskell and Richard F. Teichgraber III. New York: Cambridge University Press, 1993.

Ariès, Philippe. *Centuries of Childhood: A Social History of Family Life.* Translated by Robert Baldick. New York: Alfred A. Knopf, 1962; Vintage Books, 1965.

Axtell, James. *The School upon a Hill.* New Haven: Yale University Press, 1974; New York: W. W. Norton, 1976.

Ayres, William, editor. *Picturing History, American Painting 1770–1930.* New York: Rizzoli, 1993.

Bailyn, Bernard. *Education in the Forming of American Society, Needs and Opportunities for Study.* Chapel Hill: University of North Carolina Press for the Institute of Early American History and Culture, 1960.

Baker, Jean H. *Affairs of Party: The Political Culture of Northern Democrats in the Mid-Nineteenth Century.* Ithaca: Cornell University Press, 1983.

Bancroft, Frederic. *The Life of William H. Seward.* 2 vols. New York: Harper and Brothers, 1900.

Banner, Lois. "Religion and Reform in the Early Republic: The Role of Youth." *American Quarterly* 23 (December 1971): 677–95.

Barkan, Elliott R. "The Emergence of a Whig Persuasion: Conservatism, Democratism, and the New York State Whigs." *New York History* 52 (October 1971): 367–95.

Barnes, James J. *Authors, Publishers and Politicians.* London: Routledge and Kegan Paul, 1974.

Baron, Dennis. *Grammar and Gender.* New Haven: Yale University Press, 1986.
Baxter, P. T. W., and Uri Almagor. *Age, Generation and Time.* New York: St. Martin's Press, 1978.
Bayless, Joy. *Rufus Wilmot Griswold, Poe's Literary Executor.* Nashville: Vanderbilt University Press, 1943.
Beales, Ross W., Jr. "Cares for the Rising Generation: Youth and Religion in Colonial New England." Ph.D. diss., University of California, Davis, 1971.
———. "In Search of the Historical Child: Miniature Adulthood and Youth in Colonial New England." *American Quarterly* 27 (October 1975): 379–98.
———. "Harvard and Yale in the Great Awakening." *Historical Journal of Massachusetts* 14 (January 1986): 1–10.
Bell, Howard Holman. "A Survey of the Negro Convention Movement, 1830–1861." Ph.D. diss., Northwestern University, 1953.
Bellomy, Donald C. "Two Generations: Modernists and Progressives, 1870–1920." *Perspectives in American History,* n.s., 3 (1987): 296–306.
Belok, Michael V. "The Courtesy Tradition and Early Schoolbooks." *History of Education Quarterly* 8 (Fall 1968): 306–18.
Ben-Amos, Ilana Krausman. *Adolescence and Youth in Early Modern England.* New Haven: Yale University Press, 1994.
Benson, Mary Sumner. *Women in Eighteenth-Century America.* New York: Columbia University Press, 1935.
Bercovitch, Sacvan. *The Puritan Origins of the American Self.* New Haven: Yale University Press, 1975.
———. *The American Jeremiad.* Madison: University of Wisconsin Press, 1978.
———. *The Rites of Assent.* New York: Routledge, 1993.
Berens, John F. *Providence and Patriotism in Early America, 1640–1815.* Charlottesville: University Press of Virginia, 1978.
Berg, Barbara T. *The Remembered Gate: Origins of American Feminism.* New York: Oxford University Press, 1978.
Berger, Bennett M. *Looking for America.* Englewood Cliffs, NJ: Prentice-Hall, 1971.
Berger, Peter L. *The Sacred Canopy.* New York: Doubleday, 1967; Anchor Books, 1969.
———, and Thomas Luckmann. *The Social Construction of Reality.* New York: Doubleday, 1966; Anchor Books, 1967.
Bernstein, Iver. *The New York City Draft Riots.* New York: Oxford University Press, 1990.
Bernstein, Michael A. "Northern Labor Finds a Southern Champion: A Note on the Radical Democracy, 1833–1849." In *New York and the Rise of American Capitalism,* edited by Walter Pencak and Conrad Edick Wright. New York: New-York Historical Society, 1989.
Bloch, Ruth H. "Untangling the Roots of Modern Sex Roles: A Survey of Four Centuries of Change." *Signs* 4 (Winter 1978): 237–52.
———. "American Feminine Ideals in Transition: The Rise of the Moral Mother." *Feminist Studies* 4 (June 1978): 100–126.

———. "The Gendered Meanings of Virtue in Revolutionary America." *Signs* 13 (Autumn 1987): 37–58.

Blue, Frederick J. *Salmon P. Chase: A Life in Politics.* Kent, OH: Kent State University Press, 1987.

Blumin, Stuart M. *The Emergence of the Middle Class.* Cambridge: Cambridge University Press, 1989.

Bodge, George Madison. *Soldiers in King Philip's War.* Leominster, MA: by the author, 1896.

Botein, Stephen. " 'Meer Mechanics' and an Open Press: The Business and Political Strategies of Colonial American Printers." *Perspectives in American History* 9 (1975): 127–225.

Bousquet, P. Marc. "Mathews's Mosses: Fair Papers and Foul: A Note on the Northwestern-Newberry Edition of Melville's 'Hawthorne and his Mosses.' " *New England Quarterly* 67 (December 1994): 622–49.

Boyer, Paul. *Urban Masses and Moral Order in America, 1820–1920.* Cambridge, MA: Harvard University Press, 1978.

Boylan, Anne M. "Women in Groups: An Analysis of Women's Benevolent Organizations in New York and Boston, 1797–1840." *Journal of American History* 71 (December 1984): 497–523.

———. "Timid Girls, Venerable Widows and Dignified Matrons: Life Cycle Patterns among Organized Women in New York and Boston, 1797–1840." *American Quarterly* 38 (Winter 1986): 779–97.

———. *Sunday School: The Formation of an American Institution 1790–1880.* New Haven: Yale University Press, 1988.

Bozeman, Theodore Dwight. *To Live Ancient Lives.* Chapel Hill: University of North Carolina Press for the Institute of Early American History and Culture, 1988.

Braungart, Richard G. "Historical Generations and Generation Units: A Global Pattern of Youth Movements." *Journal of Political and Military Sociology* 12 (Spring 1984): 113–35.

Breen, T. H. *Puritans and Adventurers.* New York: Oxford University Press, 1980.

Breitenbach, William. "Sons of the Fathers: Temperance Reformers and the Legacy of the American Revolution." *Journal of the Early Republic* 3 (Spring 1983): 69–82.

Bremer, Francis J. "Increase Mather's Friends: The Trans-Atlantic Congregational Network of the Seventeenth Century." *Proceedings of the American Antiquarian Society* 94, pt. 1 (1984): 59–96.

Bridges, Amy. *A City in the Republic.* Cambridge: Cambridge University Press, 1984.

Brigden, Susan. "Youth and the English Reformation." *Past and Present* 95 (May 1982): 37–67.

———. *London and the Reformation.* Oxford: Clarendon Press, Oxford University Press, 1989.

Brooke, John L. *The Heart of the Commonwealth: Society and Political Culture in Worcester County, Massachusetts 1713–1861.* Cambridge: Cambridge University Press, 1989.

Brooks, Charles H. *The Official History and Manual of the Grand United Order of Odd Fellows in America.* Philadelphia, 1902; reprint, Freeport, NY: Books for Libraries Press, 1971.

Brown, Charles H. *William Cullen Bryant.* New York: Charles Scribner's Sons, 1971.

Brown, Thomas. *Politics and Statesmanship: Essays on the American Whig Party.* New York: Columbia University Press, 1985.

Buckley, Peter George. "To the Opera House: Culture and Society in New York City, 1820–1860." Ph.D. diss., State University of New York at Stony Brook, 1984.

Bumstead, J. M. "Religion, Finance, and Democracy in Massachusetts: The Town of Norton as a Case Study." *Journal of American History* 57 (March 1971): 817–31.

Burrows, Edwin G., and Michael Wallace. "The American Revolution: The Ideology and Psychology of National Liberation." *Perspectives in American History* 6 (1972): 167–306.

Burton, Anthony. "Looking Forward from Ariès? Pictorial and Material Evidence for the History of Childhood and Family Life." *Continuity and Change* 4 (August 1989): 203–29.

Bushman, Richard L. "American High-Style and Vernacular Cultures." In *Colonial British America,* edited by Jack P. Greene and J. R. Pole. Baltimore: Johns Hopkins University Press, 1984.

Butler, Jon. "Enthusiasm Described and Decried: The Great Awakening as Interpretive Fiction." *Journal of American History* 69 (September 1982): 305–25.

———. *Awash in a Sea of Faith: Christianizing the American People.* Cambridge, MA: Harvard University Press, 1990.

Butterfield, Herbert. *The Discontinuities between the Generations in History.* Cambridge: Cambridge University Press, 1972.

Byars, Ronald P. "The Making of the Self-Made Man: The Development of Masculine Roles and Images in Antebellum America." Ph.D. diss., Michigan State University, 1979.

Callow, James T. *Kindred Spirits: Knickerbocker Writers and American Artists, 1802–1855.* Chapel Hill: University of North Carolina Press, 1967.

Calvert, Karin. "Children in American Family Portraiture." *William and Mary Quarterly,* 3d ser. 39 (January 1982): 87–113.

Cantor, Jay. "Prints and the American Art-Union." In *Prints in and of America to 1850,* edited by John D. Morse. Charlottesville: University Press of Virginia, 1970.

Canup, John. *Out of the Wilderness: The Emergence of an American Identity in Colonial New England.* Middletown, CT: Wesleyan University Press, 1990.

Carnes, Mark C. *Secret Ritual and Manhood in Victorian America.* New Haven: Yale University Press, 1989.

———, and Clyde Griffen, editors. *Meanings for Manhood.* Chicago: University of Chicago Press, 1990.

Chew, Samuel C. *The Pilgrimage of Life.* New Haven: Yale University Press, 1962.

Childs, Brevard S. *Memory and Tradition in Israel.* Naperville, IL: Alec R. Allenson, 1962.

Chojnacki, Stanley. "Political Adulthood in Fifteenth-Century Venice." *American Historical Review* 91 (October 1986): 791–810.

Chudacoff, Howard P. *How Old Are You? Age Consciousness in American Culture.* Princeton: Princeton University Press, 1989.

Clark, Charles E. *The Public Prints: The Newspaper in Anglo-American Culture, 1665–1740.* New York: Oxford University Press, 1994.

Clark, H. Nichols B. *Francis W. Edmonds.* Washington, DC: Smithsonian Institution Press, 1988.

Clawson, Mary Ann. "Nineteenth-Century Women's Auxiliaries and Fraternal Orders." *Signs* 12 (Autumn 1986): 40–61.

———. *Constructing Brotherhood: Class, Gender, and Fraternalism.* Princeton: Princeton University Press, 1989.

Cohen, Daniel A. *Pillars of Salt, Monuments of Grace: New England Crime Literature and the Origins of American Popular Culture, 1674–1860.* New York: Oxford University Press, 1993.

———. " 'The Female Marine' in an Era of Good Feelings: Cross-Dressing and the 'Genius' of Nathaniel Coverly, Jr." *Proceedings of the American Antiquarian Society* 103, pt. 2 (1993): 359–93.

Colbourn, H. Trevor. *The Lamp of Experience.* Chapel Hill: University of North Carolina Press, 1965.

Conforti, Joseph. "Jonathan Edwards's Most Popular Work: 'The Life of David Brainerd' and 19th Century Evangelical Culture." *Church History* 54 (June 1985): 188–201.

———. "Antebellum Evangelicals and the Cultural Revival of Jonathan Edwards." *American Presbyterians* 64 (Winter 1986): 227–41.

———. "Edwardsians, Unitarians, and the Memory of the Great Awakening, 1800–1840." In *American Unitarianism, 1805–1865,* edited by Conrad Edick Wright. Boston: Massachusetts Historical Society and Northeastern University Press, 1989.

———. "The Invention of the Great Awakening, 1795–1842." *Early American Literature* 26, 2 (1991): 99–118.

Cooper, Frederick. "Elevating the Race: The Social Thought of Black Leaders, 1827–50." *American Quarterly* 24 (December 1972): 604–25.

Cooper, William J., Jr., Michael F. Holt, and John McCardell, editors. *A Master's Due: Essays in Honor of David Herbert Donald.* Baton Rouge: Louisiana State University Press, 1985.

Corcoran Gallery of Art. *Richard Caton Woodville: An Early American Genre Painter.* Washington, DC: Corcoran Gallery of Art, 1967.

Cott, Nancy F. "Young Women in the Second Great Awakening in New England." *Feminist Studies* 3 (Fall 1975): 15–29.

———. *The Bonds of Womanhood.* New Haven: Yale University Press, 1977.

Cowdrey, Mary Bartlett, editor. *American Academy of Fine Arts and American Art-Union.* 2 vols. New York: New-York Historical Society, 1953.

Craven, Wesley Frank. *The Legend of the Founding Fathers.* New York: New York University Press, 1956.

Cremin, Lawrence A. *American Education: The Colonial Experience, 1607–1783.* New York: Harper and Row, 1970.

———. *American Education: The National Experience.* New York: Harper and Row, 1980.

Cross, Whitney R. *The Burned-Over District.* Ithaca: Cornell University Press, 1950; New York: Harper Torchbook, 1965.

Cunliffe, Marcus. *Chattel Slavery and Wage Slavery.* Athens: University of Georgia Press, 1979.

Curran, Thomas J. "Know Nothings of New York State." Ph.D. diss., Columbia University, 1963.

Current, Richard Nelson. *Arguing with Historians.* Middletown, CT: Wesleyan University Press, 1987.

Curti, Merle. " 'Young America.' " *American Historical Review* 32 (October 1926): 34–55.

Danbom, David B. "The Young America Movement." *Journal of the Illinois State Historical Society* 67 (June 1974): 294–306.

Davenport, David Paul. *Population Persistence and Migration in Rural New York 1855–1860.* New York: Garland, 1989.

Davidson, James West. *The Logic of Millennial Thought.* New Haven: Yale University Press, 1977.

Davidson, Marshall B. "Democracy Delineated." *American Heritage* 31 (October-November 1980): 4–15.

Davis, David Brion. *The Problem of Slavery in the Age of Revolution, 1770–1823.* Ithaca: Cornell University Press, 1975.

———. *From Homicide to Slavery.* New York: Oxford University Press, 1986.

Davis, Susan G. " 'Making Night Hideous': Christmas Revelry and Public Disorder in Nineteenth Century Philadelphia." *American Quarterly* 34 (Summer 1982): 185–99.

Davis, William C. *Breckinridge: Statesman, Soldier, Symbol.* Baton Rouge: Louisiana State University Press, 1974.

Dawson, Jan C. *The Unusable Past: America's Puritan Tradition, 1830 to 1930.* Chico, CA: Scholars Press, 1984.

Dayton, Cornelia Hughes. "Taking the Trade: Abortion and Gender Relations in an Eighteenth-Century New England Village." *William and Mary Quarterly,* 3d ser. 48 (January 1991): 19–49.

Degler, Carl. "The Locofocos: Urban 'Agrarians.' " *Journal of Economic History* 16 (September 1956): 322–33.

Delbanco, Andrew. "The Puritan Errand Re-Viewed." *Journal of American Studies* 18 (December 1984): 343–60.

———. *The Puritan Ordeal.* Cambridge, MA: Harvard University Press, 1989.

D'Elia, Donald J. "Benjamin Rush: Philosopher of the American Revolution." *Transactions of the American Philosophical Society,* new ser., pt. 5, 64 (September 1974).

DeMartini, Joseph R. "Change Agents and Generational Relationships: A Reevaluation of Mannheim's Problem of Generations." *Social Forces* 64 (September 1985): 1–16.

Demos, John. "George Caleb Bingham: The Artist as Social Historian." *American Quarterly* 17 (Summer 1965): 218–28.

———. *A Little Commonwealth: Family Life in Plymouth Colony.* New York: Oxford University Press, 1970.

———. "Oedipus and America: Historical Perspectives on the Reception of Psychoanalysis in the United States." *Annual of Psychoanalysis* 6 (1978): 23–39.

———. *Past, Present, and Personal.* New York: Oxford University Press, 1986.

De Sola Pool, D. "Hebrew Learning among the Puritans of New England Prior to 1700." *Publications of the American Jewish Historical Society* 20 (1911): 31–83.

Donald, David. *Lincoln Reconsidered.* New York: Alfred A. Knopf, 1956.

Doyle, Don Harrison. "The Social Functions of Voluntary Associations in a Nineteenth-Century American Town." *Social Science History* 1 (Spring 1977): 333–55.

———. *The Social Order of a Frontier Community.* Urbana: University of Illinois Press, 1978.

Dreyfus, Carol, and Thomas Connors. "Oral History and American Advertising: How the 'Pepsi Generation' Came Alive." *International Journal of Oral History* 6 (November 1985): 191–97.

Duby, Georges. *The Chivalrous Society.* Translated by Cynthia Postan. London: Edward Arnold, 1977.

Eggleston, Edward. *The Transit of Civilization from England to America in the Seventeenth Century.* New York: D. Appleton and Co., 1901.

Ehrlich, Heyward Bruce. "A Study of Literary Activity in New York City during the 1840-decade." Ph.D. diss., New York University, 1963.

Elliott, Emory. *Power and the Pulpit in Puritan New England.* Princeton: Princeton University Press, 1975.

Erikson, Erik H. *Childhood and Society* (1950). 2d ed. New York: W. W. Norton, 1963.

———, editor. *The Challenge of Youth.* New York: Basic Books, 1963; Doubleday Anchor Books, 1965.

Ernst, Robert. "The One and Only Mike Walsh." *New-York Historical Society Quarterly* 36 (January 1952): 43–65.

Esler, Anthony. *Bombs Beards and Barricades: 150 Years of Youth in Revolt.* New York: Stein and Day, 1971.

———. *Generations in History: An Introduction to the Concept.* N.p.: published by the author, 1982.

———. " 'The Truest Community': Social Generations as Collective Mentalities." *Journal of Political and Military Sociology* 12 (Spring 1984): 99–112.

Ettinger, Amos A. *The Mission to Spain of Pierre Soulé, 1853–1855.* New Haven: Yale University Press, 1932.

Eyck, F. Gunther. "The Political Theories and Activities of the German Academic Youth between 1815 and 1819." *Journal of Modern History* 27 (March 1955): 27–38.

―――. "Mazzini's Young Europe." *Journal of Central European Affairs* 17 (January 1958): 356–77.

Faber, Richard. *Young England.* London: Faber and Faber, 1987.

Fass, Paula S. *The Damned and the Beautiful: American Youth in the 1920s.* New York: Oxford University Press, 1977.

Febvre, Lucien. "Générations." *Revue de synthèse historique* 47 (June 1929): 36–43.

Feuer, Lewis S. *The Conflict of Generations.* New York: Basic Books, 1969.

Fingerhut, Eugene R. "Were the Massachusetts Puritans Hebraic?" *New England Quarterly* 40 (December 1967): 521–31.

Finkelstein, Barabara, editor. *Regulated Children/Liberated Children: Education in Psychohistorical Perspective.* New York: Psychohistory Press, 1979.

Fischer, David Hackett. *Growing Old in America.* New York: Oxford University Press, 1977.

―――. *Albion's Seed: Four British Folkways in America.* New York: Oxford University Press, 1989.

Fliegelman, Jay. *Prodigals and Pilgrims: The American Revolution against Patriarchal Authority, 1750–1800.* Cambridge: Cambridge University Press, 1982.

Foner, Eric. *Free Soil, Free Labor, Free Men.* New York: Oxford University Press, 1970.

Ford, Worthington Chauncey. *The Boston Book Market, 1679–1700.* Boston: The Club of Odd Volumes, 1917.

Forgie, George. "Father Past and Child Nation: The Romantic Imagination and the Origins of the American Civil War." Ph.D. diss., Stanford University, 1972.

―――. *Patricide in the House Divided.* New York: W. W. Norton, 1979.

Formisano, Ronald P. *The Transformation of Political Culture: Massachusetts Parties, 1790s–1840s.* New York: Oxford University Press, 1983.

Fortune, Brandon Brame. "Portraits of Virtue and Genius: Pantheons of Worthies and Public Portraiture in the Early American Republic." Ph.D. diss., University of North Carolina, 1987.

Foucault, Michel. *The Archaeology of Knowledge.* Translated by A. M. Sheridan Smith. New York: Harper Torchbooks, 1972.

Fox, Dixon Ryan. *The Decline of Aristocracy in the Politics of New York.* Columbia Studies in History, Economics and Public Law. New York: Columbia University Press, 1919.

Fox, Richard Wightman, and James T. Kloppenberg, editors. *A Companion to American Thought.* Cambridge, MA: Blackwell, 1995.

Franklin, Benjamin V. *Boston Printers, Publishers, and Booksellers: 1640–1800.* Boston: G. K. Hall, 1980.

Franklin, Phyllis. *Show Thyself a Man: A Comparison of Benjamin Franklin and Cotton Mather.* The Hague: Mouton and Co., 1969.

Fredrickson, George M. *The Inner Civil War.* New York: Harper and Row, 1965; Harper Torchbooks, 1968.

Freeman, Rhoda G. "The Free Negro in New York City in the Era before the Civil War." Ph.D. diss., Columbia University, 1966.

Friedman, Lawrence J. *Inventors of the Promised Land.* New York: Alfred A. Knopf, 1975.

———. *Gregarious Saints: Self and Community in American Abolitionism, 1830–1870.* Cambridge: Cambridge University Press, 1982.

———. "Pious Fellowship and Modernity: A Psychological Interpretation." In *Crusaders and Compromisers,* edited by Alan M. Kraut. Westport, CT: Greenwood Press, 1983.

Frothingham, Richard. *Life and Times of Joseph Warren.* Boston: Little, Brown, 1865; reprint, New York: Da Capo Press, 1971.

Fuller, Landon Edward. "The *United States Magazine and Democratic Review,* 1837–1859: A Study of Its History, Contents, and Significance." Ph.D. diss., University of North Carolina, 1948.

Furtwangler, Albert. *American Silhouettes.* New Haven: Yale University Press, 1987.

Garms-Homlová, Vjenka, Erika M. Hoerning, and Doris Schaeffer, editors. *Intergenerational Relationships.* Lewiston, NY: C. J. Hogrefe, 1984.

Gates, Stewart Lewis. "Disorder and Social Organization: The Militia in Connecticut Public Life, 1660–1860." Ph.D. diss., University of Connecticut, 1975.

Gaustad, Edwin S. "Restitution, Revolution, and the American Dream." *Journal of the American Academy of Religion* 44 (March 1976): 77–86.

Gay, Peter. *A Loss of Mastery: Puritan Historians in Colonial America.* Berkeley: University of California Press, 1966.

Gebhardt, Jürgen. *Americanism: Revolutionary Order and Societal Self-Interpretation in the American Republic.* Translated by Ruth Hein. Baton Rouge: Louisiana University Press, 1993.

Gerson, Judith M., and Kathy Peiss. "Boundaries, Negotiation, Consciousness: Reconceptualizing Gender Relations." *Social Problems* 32 (April 1985): 317–31.

Gibbs, Phillip Andrew. "Seasons of American Manhood, 1750–1860: Mirror of the Changing Republic." Ph.D. diss., Mississippi State University, 1988.

Gilbert, Creighton. "When Did a Man in the Renaissance Grow Old?" *Studies in the Renaissance* 14 (1967): 7–32.

Gildrie, Richard P. *The Profane, the Civil, and the Godly: The Reformation of Manners in Orthodox New England.* University Park: Pennsylvania State University Press, 1994.

Gilje, Paul A. *The Road to Mobocracy.* Chapel Hill: University of North Carolina Press, 1987.

Gillespie, Joanna Bowen. "Filiopietism as Citizenship, 1810 Letters from Martha Laurens Ramsay to David Ramsay Jr." *Early American Literature* 29, 2 (1994): 141–65.

Gillis, John R. *Youth and History.* Expanded student ed. New York: Academic Press, 1981.

Gilmore, David D. *Manhood in the Making: Cultural Concepts of Masculinity.* New Haven: Yale University Press, 1990.

Gilmore, Michael T. "Eulogy as Symbolic Biography: The Iconography of Revolutionary Leadership, 1776–1826." In *Studies in Biography*, edited by Daniel Aaron. Cambridge, MA: Harvard University Press, 1978.

Gilmore, William J. *Reading Becomes a Necessity of Life*. Knoxville: University of Tennessee Press, 1989.

Ginzberg, Lori D. *Women and the Work of Benevolence*. New Haven: Yale University Press, 1990.

Glazer, Walter S. "Participation and Power: Voluntary Associations and the Functional Organization of Cincinnati in 1840." *Historical Methods Newsletter* 5 (September 1972): 151–68.

Goodheart, Lawrence B. *Abolitionist, Actuary, Atheist: Elizur Wright and the Reform Impulse*. Kent, OH: Kent State University Press, 1990.

Goodman, Paul. "The Social Basis of New England Politics in Jacksonian America." *Journal of the Early Republic* 6 (Spring 1986): 23–58.

———. *Towards a Christian Republic*. New York: Oxford University Press, 1988.

Gordon, Ann D. "The Young Ladies Academy of Philadelphia." In *Women of America: A History*, edited by Carol Ruth Berkin and Mary Beth Norton. Boston: Houghton Mifflin, 1979.

Gowin, Enoch Burton. *The Executive and His Control of Men*. New York: Macmillan, 1915.

Graff, Harvey J., editor. *Growing Up in America*. Detroit: Wayne State University Press, 1987.

Graubard, Stephen R., editor. *Generations*. New York: W. W. Norton, 1979.

Gravely, William B. "The Dialectic of Double-Consciousness in Black American Freedom Celebrations, 1808–1863." *Journal of Negro History* 67 (Winter 1982): 302–17.

Greene, Jack P. "Search for Identity: An Interpretation of the Meaning of Selected Patterns of Social Response in Eighteenth-Century America." *Journal of Social History* 3 (Spring 1970): 189–220.

———. *Pursuits of Happiness*. Chapel Hill: University of North Carolina Press, 1988.

Greven, Philip J. *Four Generations: Population, Land and Family in Colonial Andover, Massachusetts*. Ithaca: Cornell University Press, 1970.

———. "Youth, Maturity, and Religious Conversion: A Note on the Ages of Converts in Andover, Massachusetts, 1711–1749." *Essex Institute Historical Collections* 108 (April 1972): 119–34.

Griffin, Clifford S. *Their Brothers' Keepers*. New Brunswick: Rutgers University Press, 1960.

Griffin, Edward M. *Old Brick: Charles Chauncy of Boston, 1705–1787*. Minneapolis: University of Minnesota Press, 1980.

Grindhammer, Lucille Wrubel. *Art and the Public: The Democratization of the Fine Arts in the United States, 1830–1860*. Stuttgart: J. B. Metzlersche Verlagsbuchhandlung, 1975.

Groseclose, Barbara S. "Paintings, Politics, and George Caleb Bingham." *American Art Journal* 10 (November 1978): 4–19.

———. "Politics and American Genre Painting of the Nineteenth Century." *Antiques* 120 (November 1981): 1210–17.

Gross, Robert A., editor. *In Debt to Shays*. Charlottesville: University Press of Virginia, 1993.

Grossbart, Stephen R. "Seeking the Divine Favor: Conversion and Church Admission in Eastern Connecticut, 1711–1832." *William and Mary Quarterly*, 3d ser. 46 (October 1989): 696–740.

Grubar, Francis S. "Richard Caton Woodville: An American Artist, 1825 to 1855." Ph.D. diss., Johns Hopkins University, 1966.

Gura, Philip F. "Sowing the Harvest: William Williams and the Great Awakening." *Journal of Presbyterian History* 56 (Winter 1978): 326–41.

———. "Preparing the Way for Stoddard: Eleazar Mather's *Serious Exhortation to Northampton*." *New England Quarterly* 57 (June 1984): 240–49.

———. "Solomon Stoddard's Irreverent Way." *Early American Literature* 21 (Spring 1986): 29–43.

Hall, David D. *The Faithful Shepherd: A History of the New England Ministry in the Seventeenth Century*. Chapel Hill: University of North Carolina Press for the Institute of Early American History and Culture, 1972.

Hall, Michael G. *The Last American Puritan: The Life of Increase Mather*. Middletown, CT: Wesleyan University Press, 1988.

Halttunen, Karen. *Confidence Men and Painted Women*. New Haven: Yale University Press, 1982.

Hambrick-Stowe, Charles E. *The Practice of Piety*. Chapel Hill: University of North Carolina Press, 1982.

———. "The Spirit of the Old Writers: The Great Awakening and the Persistance of Puritan Piety." In *Puritanism*, edited by Francis J. Bremer. Boston: Massachusetts Historical Society, 1993.

Hammond, Bray. *Banks and Politics in America from the Revolution to the Civil War*. Princeton: Princeton University Press, 1957.

Hanawalt, Barbara A. "Historical Description and Prescriptions for Adolescence." *Journal of Family History* 17, 4 (1992): 341–51.

———. *Growing Up in Medieval London*. New York: Oxford University Press, 1993.

Hansen, Allen Oscar. *Liberalism and American Education*. New York: Macmillan, 1926.

Harris, Neil. *The Artist in American Society: The Formative Years 1790–1860*. New York: Geroge Braziller, 1966; Chicago: University of Chicago Press, Phoenix Edition, 1982.

Hart, Charles Henry. *Browere's Life Masks of Great Americans*. New York: Doubleday and McClure, 1899.

Hawes, Joseph M., and N. Ray Hiner, editors. *American Childhood: A Research Guide and Historical Handbook*. Westport, CT: Greenwood Press, 1985.

Hay, Robert P. "The Glorious Departure of the American Patriarchs: Contemporary Reactions to the Deaths of Jefferson and Adams." *Journal of Southern History* 35 (November 1969): 543–55.

———. "Charles Carroll and the Passing of the Revolutionary Generation." *Maryland Historical Magazine* 67 (Spring 1972): 54–62.

———. "The American Revolution Twice Recalled: Lafayette's Visit and the

Election of 1824." *Indiana Magazine of History* 69 (March 1973): 43–62.

Heimert, Alan. *Religion and the American Mind.* Cambridge, MA: Harvard University Press, 1966.

Herlihy, David. "The Generation in Medieval History." *Viator* 5 (1974): 347–64.

Hersh, Blanche Glassman. *The Slavery of Sex: Feminist-Abolitionists in America.* Urbana: University of Illinois Press, 1978.

Hewitt, John H. "Mr. Downing and His Oyster House." *New York History* 74 (July 1993): 229–52.

Higham, John. *From Boundlessness to Consolidation: The Transformation of American Culture 1848–1860.* William L. Clements Library, 1969; Indianapolis: Bobbs-Merrill Reprint, 1969.

Hill, Christopher. *The World Turned Upside Down.* London: Temple and Smith, 1972.

Hiner, N. Ray. "The Cry of Sodom Enquired Into: Educational Analysis in Seventeenth-Century New England." *History of Education Quarterly* 13 (Spring 1973): 3–22.

———. "Adolescence in Eighteenth-Century America." *History of Childhood Quarterly* 3 (Fall 1975): 253–80.

———, and Joseph M. Hawes, editors. *Growing Up in America.* Urbana: University of Illinois Press, 1985.

Hoffer, Peter C. *Revolution and Regeneration: Life Cycle and the Historical Vision of the Generation of 1776.* Athens: University of Georgia Press, 1983.

Hollander, Stanley C., and Richard Germain. *Was There a Pepsi Generation before Pepsi Discovered It?* Lincolnwood, IL: NTC Business Books, 1992.

Hollis, Daniel Walker. *University of South Carolina.* Vol. 1, *South Carolina College.* Columbia: University of South Carolina Press, 1951.

Horlick, Alan Stanley. *Country Boys and Merchant Princes: The Social Control of Young Men in New York.* Lewisburg, PA: Bucknell University Press, 1975.

Horsman, Reginald. *Race and Manifest Destiny.* Cambridge, MA: Harvard University Press, 1981.

Horton, James Oliver. "Generations of Protest: Black Families and Social Reform in Antebellum Boston." *New England Quarterly* 49 (June 1976): 242–56.

Hovey, Kenneth. " 'A Psalm of Life' Reconsidered: The Dialogue of Western Literature and Monologue of Young America." *American Transcendental Quarterly,* new ser. 1 (March 1987): 3–19.

Howe, Daniel Walker. *The Political Culture of the American Whigs.* Chicago: University of Chicago Press, 1979.

Hugins, Walter. *Jacksonian Democracy and the Working Class.* Stanford: Stanford University Press, 1960.

Hurm, Gerd. "The Rhetoric of Continuity in Early Boston Orations." In *The Fourth of July: Political Oratory and Literary Reactions, 1776–1876,* edited by Paul Goetsch and Gerd Hurm. Tübingen: Gunter Narr Verlag, 1992.

Jaeger, Hans. "Generations in History: Reflections on a Controversial Concept." *History and Theory* 24, 3 (1985): 273–92.

Jaffee, David. "The Village Enlightenment in New England, 1760–1820." *William and Mary Quarterly*, 3d ser. 47 (July 1990): 327–46.

Jaher, Frederick Cople. "The Politics of the Boston Brahmins, 1800–1860." In *Boston 1700–1980: The Evolution of Urban Politics*, edited by Ronald P. Formisano and Constance K. Burns. Westport, CT: Greenwood Press, 1987.

Jansen, Nerina. *Generation Theory*. Johannesburg: McGraw-Hill, 1975.

Jarvis, Charles A. "Admission to Abolition: The Case of John Greenleaf Whittier." *Journal of the Early Republic* 4 (Summer 1984): 161–76.

Jeffries, John W. "The Separation in the Canterbury Congregational Church: Religion, Family, and Politics in a Connecticut Town." *New England Quarterly* 52 (December 1979): 522–49.

Johannsen, Robert W. *Stephen A. Douglas*. New York: Oxford University Press, 1973.

———. *To the Halls of the Montezumas: The Mexican War in the American Imagination*. New York: Oxford University Press, 1985.

Johns, Elizabeth. *American Genre Painting*. New Haven: Yale University Press, 1991.

Jordan, Cynthia S. *Second Stories: The Politics of Language, Form and Gender in Early American Fiction*. Chapel Hill: University of North Carolina Press, 1989.

Jordan, Winthrop. "Familial Politics: Thomas Paine and the Killing of the King, 1776." *Journal of American History* 60 (September 1973): 294–308.

Juster, Susan M., and Maris A. Vinovskis. "Changing Perspectives on the American Family in the Past." *Annual Review of Sociology* 13 (1987): 193–216.

Kaestle, Carl F. *Pillars of the Republic*. New York: Hill and Wang, 1983.

Kammen, Michael. *A Season of Youth: The American Revolution and the Historical Imagination*. New York: Alfred A. Knopf, 1978.

———. "Changing Perceptions of the Life Cycle in American Thought and Culture." *Proceedings of the Massachusetts Historical Society* 91 (1979): 35–66.

———. *Mystic Chords of Memory: The Transformation of Tradition in American Culture*. New York: Alfred A. Knopf, 1991.

Kashatus, William C. III. "A Virtuous Education of Youth: The Evolution of a Republican Paradigm in the Educational Thought of Benjamin Franklin and Benjamin Rush, 1728–1798." *Valley Forge Journal* 4, 4 (1989): 307–32.

Kerber, Linda K. *Women of the Republic*. Chapel Hill: University of North Carolina Press, 1980.

Kertzer, David I. "Generation as a Sociological Problem." *Annual Review of Sociology* 9 (1983): 125–49.

Kett, Joseph F. *Rites of Passage: Adolescence in America, 1790 to the Present*. New York: Basic Books, 1977.

Kirkland, Edward C. "Charles Francis Adams, Jr.: The Making of an Historian." *Proceedings of the Massachusetts Historical Society* 75 (1963): 39–51.

Kivisto, Peter, and Dag Blanck editors. *American Immigrants and Their Generations.* Urbana: University of Illinois Press, 1990.

Klein, Rachel N. "Art and Authority in Antebellum New York City: The Rise and Fall of the American Art-Union." *Journal of American History* 81 (March 1995): 1534–61.

Knobel, Dale T. " 'Native Soil': Nativists, Colonizationists, and the Rhetoric of Nationality." *Civil War History* 27 (December 1981): 314–37.

Kohl, Lawrence Frederick. *The Politics of Individualism.* New York: Oxford University Press, 1989.

Kornblith, Gary J. "The Rise of the Mechanic Interest and the Campaign to Develop Manufacturing in Salem, 1815–1830." *Essex Institute Historical Collections* 121 (January 1985): 44–65.

Kupperman, Karen Ordahl. "Errand to the Indies: Puritan Colonization from Providence Island through the Western Design." *William and Mary Quarterly,* 3d ser. 45 (January 1988): 70–99.

Laing, Alexander. "Jefferson's Usufruct Principle." *The Nation,* July 3–10, 1976, 7–16.

Lambert, Frank. *"Pedlar in Divinity": George Whitefield and the Transatlantic Revivals.* Princeton: Princeton University Press, 1994.

Lang, Amy Schrager. " 'A Flood of Errors': Chauncy and Edwards in the Great Awakening." In *Jonathan Edwards and the American Experience,* edited by Nathan O. Hatch and Harry S. Stout. New York: Oxford University Press, 1988.

Leverenz, David. *The Language of Puritan Feeling.* New Brunswick: Rutgers University Press, 1980.

Levin, David. *Cotton Mather: The Young Life of the Lord's Remembrancer.* Cambridge, MA: Harvard University Press, 1978.

Lewis, Jan. *The Pursuit of Happiness: Family and Values in Jefferson's Virginia.* Cambridge: Cambridge University Press, 1983.

———. "The Republican Wife: Virtue and Seduction in the Early Republic." *William and Mary Quarterly,* 3d ser. 44 (October 1987): 689–721.

Littlefield, Daniel F., Jr. "Longfellow's 'A Psalm of Life': A Relation of Method to Popularity." *Markham Review* 7 (Spring 1978): 49–51.

Lockridge, Kenneth A. *Literacy in Colonial New England.* New York: W. W. Norton, 1974.

Love, W. DeLoss, Jr. *The Fast and Thanksgiving Days of New England.* Boston: Houghton Mifflin, Riverside Press, 1895.

Lovell, Margaretta M. "Reading Eighteenth-Century American Family Portraits: Social Images and Self-Images." *Winterthur Portfolio* 22 (Winter 1987): 243–67.

Lowance, Mason I., Jr. "Cotton Mather's *Magnalia* and the Metaphors of Biblical History." In *Typology and Early American Literature,* edited by Sacvan Bercovitch. Amherst: University of Massachusetts Press, 1972.

———. *The Language of Canaan.* Cambridge, MA: Harvard University Press, 1980.

Lowenthal, David. *The Past Is a Foreign Country.* Cambridge: Cambridge University Press, 1985.

Luke, Carmen. *Pedagogy, Printing, and Protestantism: The Discourse on Children.* Albany: State University of New York Press, 1989.

Lutz, Rolland Ray, Jr. "Fathers and Sons in the Vienna Revolution of 1848." *Journal of Central European Affairs* 22 (July 1962): 161–73.

McClelland, Peter D., and Richard J. Zeckhauser. *Demographic Dimensions of the New Republic.* Cambridge: Cambridge University Press, 1982.

McCormick, Richard P. *The Second American Party System.* Chapel Hill: University of North Carolina Press, 1966.

———. *The Presidential Game.* New York: Oxford University Press, 1982.

McCurdy, Francis Lea. *Stump, Bar, and Pulpit: Speechmaking on the Missouri Frontier.* Columbia: University of Missouri Press, 1969.

McDermott, John Francis. "George Caleb Bingham's 'Stump Orator.'" *Art Quarterly* 20 (Winter 1957):

———. *George Caleb Bingham: River Portraitist.* Norman, University of Oklahoma Press, 1959.

McGiffert, Michael. "The Problem of the Covenant in Puritan Thought: Peter Bulkeley's Gospel-Covenant." *New England Historical and Genealogical Register* 130 (April 1976): 107–29.

———. "God's Controversy With Jacobean England." *American Historical Review* 88 (December 1983): 1151–76.

McKitrick, Eric, and Stanley Elkins. "The Founding Fathers, Young Men of the Revolution." *Political Science Quarterly* 76 (June 1961): 181–216.

McWilliams, John P., Jr. *Hawthorne, Melville, and the American Character.* Cambridge: Cambridge University Press, 1984.

Madsen, David. *The National University, Enduring Dream of the USA.* Detroit: Wayne State University Press, 1966.

Magdol, Edward. *The Antislavery Rank and File.* Westport, CT: Greenwood Press, 1986.

Maier, Pauline. *The Old Revolutionaries.* New York: Alfred A. Knopf, 1980.

Maizlish, Stephen E., and John T. Kushma, editors. *Essays on American Antebellum Politics.* College Station: Texas A & M University Press, 1982.

Mannheim, Karl. *Essays on the Sociology of Knowledge.* New York: Oxford University Press, 1952.

Marías, Julián. *Generations: A Historical Method.* Translated by Harold C. Raley. University: University of Alabama Press, 1970.

Marshall, Gordon M. "The Golden Age of Illustrated Biographies: Three Case Studies." In *American Portrait Prints,* edited by Wendy Wick Reaves. Charlottesville: University Press of Virginia, 1984.

Mason, John E. *Gentlefolk in the Making.* Philadelphia: University of Pennsylvania Press, 1935.

Matthews, Albert. "A Dorchester Religious Society of Young Men." *New England Historical and Genealogical Register* 60 (January 1906): 30–40.

———. "The Term Pilgrim Fathers and Early Celebrations of Forefathers' Day." *Publications of the Colonial Society of Massachusetts* 17 (November 1914): 293–393.

May, Arthur James. *Contemporary American Opinion of the Mid-Century Revolutions in Central Europe.* Philadelphia, 1927.

May, Henry F. *The Enlightenment in America.* New York: Oxford University Press, 1976.

Mazoyer, Louis. "Catégories d'âge et groupes sociaux—les jeunes générations françaises de 1830." *Annales d'histoire économique et sociale* 53 (September 30, 1938): 385–419.

Mering, John Vollmer. *The Whig Party in Missouri.* Columbia: University of Missouri Press, 1967.

Merk, Frederick. *Manifest Destiny and Mission in American History.* New York: Alfred A. Knopf, 1963.

Merritt, Richard L. *Symbols of American Community, 1735–1775.* New Haven: Yale University Press, 1966.

Meschutt, David. *A Bold Experiment: John Henri Isaac Browere's Life Masks.* Cooperstown: New York State Historical Society, 1988.

Messerli, Jonathan. "The Columbian Complex: The Impulse to National Consolidation." *History of Education Quarterly* 7 (Winter 1967): 417–31.

Meyer, John W. "The Self and the Life Course: Institutionalization and Its Effects." In *Human Development and the Life Course: Multidisciplinary Perspectives,* edited by Aage B. Sørensen. Hillsdale, NJ: Lawrence Erlbaum Associates, 1986.

Middlekauff, Robert. *The Mathers: Three Generations of Puritan Intellectuals, 1596–1728.* New York: Oxford University Press, 1971.

Miller, Eugene F., and Barry Schwartz. "The Icon of the American Republic: A Study in Political Symbolism." *Review of Politics* 47 (October 1985): 516–43.

Miller, Lillian B. *Patrons and Patriotism.* Chicago: University of Chicago Press, 1966.

———. "Charles Willson Peale: A Life of Harmony and Purpose." In *Charles Willson Peale and His World.* New York: Harry N. Abrams, 1983.

Miller, Marc H. "Lafayette's Farewell Tour of America, 1824–25: A Study of the Pageantry and Public Portraiture." Ph.D. diss., New York University, 1979.

Miller, Perry. *The New England Mind: The Seventeenth Century.* New York: Macmillan, 1939; Boston: Beacon, 1961.

———. *The New England Mind: From Colony to Province.* Cambridge, MA: Harvard University Press, 1953; Boston: Beacon, 1961.

———. *The Raven and the Whale.* New York: Harcourt, Brace, 1956.

———. *Errand into the Wilderness.* Cambridge, MA: Belknap Press, Harvard University Press, 1956; New York: Harper Torchbooks, 1964.

———. *The Life of the Mind in America from the Revolution to the Civil War.* New York: Harcourt Brace and World, 1965.

Minter, David L. *The Interpreted Design as a Structural Principle in American Prose.* New Haven: Yale University Press, 1969.

Mitchell, Reid. *The Vacant Chair: The Northern Soldier Leaves Home.* New York: Oxford University Press, 1993.

Modell, John. *Into One's Own: From Youth to Adulthood in the United States, 1920–1975.* Berkeley: University of California Press, 1989.

Modell, John, Frank Furstenberg, Jr., and Theodore Hershberg. "Social Change and Transitions to Adulthood in Historical Perspective." *Journal of Family History* 1 (Autumn 1976): 7–32.

Monaghan, E. Jennifer. "Literacy Instruction and Gender in Colonial New England." *American Quarterly* 40 (March 1988): 18–41.

Mook, H. Telfer. "Training Day in New England." *New England Quarterly* 11 (December 1938): 675–97.

Moran, Gerald F. "Religious Renewal, Puritan Tribalism, and the Family in Seventeenth-Century Milford, Connecticut." *William and Mary Quarterly*, 3d ser. 36 (April 1979): 236–54.

———. " 'Sinners Are Turned into Saints in Numbers': Puritanism and Revivalism in Colonial Connecticut." In *Belief and Behavior*, edited by Philip R. Vandermeer and Robert P. Swierenga. New Brunswick: Rutgers University Press, 1991.

———, and Maris A. Vinovskis. "The Great Care of Godly Parents: Early Childhood in Puritan New England." In *History and Research in Child Development*, edited by Alice Boardman Smuts and John W. Hagen. *Monographs of the Society for Research in Child Development*, no. 4–5 (1985).

———. *Religion, Family, and the Life Course*. Ann Arbor: University of Michigan Press, 1992.

Morgan, Edmund S. *The Puritan Family*. New ed., rev. and enl. New York: Harper and Row, 1966.

Morris, Richard Joseph. "Memorializing among Americans: The Case of Lincoln's Assassination." Ph.D. diss., University of Wisconsin, 1986.

Moses, James L. "Journalistic Impartiality on the Eve of the Revolution: The *Boston Evening Post*, 1770–1775." *Journalism History* 20 (Autumn-Winter 1994): 125–30.

Moses, Wilson Jeremiah. *Alexander Crummell: A Study of Civilization and Discontent*. New York: Oxford University Press, 1989.

Moss, Sidney P. "Poe, Hiram Fuller, and the Duyckinck Circle." *American Book Collector* 18 (October 1967): 8–18.

Mott, Frank Luther. *A History of American Magazines, 1741–1850*. Cambridge, MA: Harvard University Press, 1930; Belknap Press, 1957.

Murrin, John M. "Review Essay." *History and Theory* 11, no. 2 (1972): 226–75.

Mushkat, Jerome. *Tammany: The Evolution of a Political Machine, 1789–1865*. Syracuse: Syracuse University Press, 1971.

———. *Fernando Wood: A Political Biography*. Kent, OH: Kent State University Press, 1990.

Myers, Gustavus. *The History of Tammany Hall*. New York: Published by the author, 1901.

Nagel, Paul C. *This Sacred Trust*. New York: Oxford University Press, 1971.

Naylor, Natalie A. " 'Holding High the Standard': The Influence of the American Education Society in Antebellum Education." *History of Education Quarterly* 24 (Winter 1984): 479–97.

Newhard, Leota. "The Beginnings of the Whig Party in Missouri, 1824–1840." *Missouri Historical Review* 25 (January 1931): 254–80.

Newton, Sarah Emily. "Wise and Foolish Virgins: 'Usable Fiction' and the Early American Conduct Tradition." *Early American Literature* 25, 2 (1990): 139–67.

Nichols, Roy Franklin. *The Democratic Machine 1850–1854*. Columbia Studies in History, Economics and Public Law. New York: Columbia University, 1923.

———. *Franklin Pierce*. Philadelphia: University of Pennsylvania Press, 1931.

Nobles, Gregory H. "The Politics of Patriarchy in Shays's Rebellion: The Case of Henry McCulloch." *Dublin Seminar for New England Folklife Annual Proceedings* 10 (1985): 37–47.

Norton, Mary Beth. *Liberty's Daughters*. Boston: Little, Brown, 1980.

Novak, Steven J. *The Rights of Youth: American Colleges and Student Revolt, 1798–1815*. Cambridge, MA: Harvard University Press, 1977.

Nugent, Walter. *Structures of American Social History*. Bloomington: Indiana University Press, 1981.

Ogden, Graham S. "The Interpretation of דור in Ecclesiastes 1.4." *Journal for the Study of the Old Testament* 34 (February 1986): 91–92.

Oravec, Christine. "The Democratic Critics: An Alternative American Rhetorical Tradition of the Nineteenth Century." *Rhetorica* 4 (Autumn 1986): 395–421.

Ozment, Steven. *When Fathers Ruled: Family Life in Reformation Europe*. Cambridge, MA: Harvard University Press, 1983.

Pease, Jane H., and William H. Pease. *Bound with Them in Chains*. Westport, CT: Greenwood Press, 1972.

———. "Ends, Means, and Attitudes: Black-White Conflict in the Antislavery Movement." *Civil War History* 18 (June 1972): 117–28.

Perkins, Howard C. "A Neglected Phase of the Movement for Southern Unity, 1847–1852." *Journal of Southern History* 12 (May 1946): 153–203.

Perry, Lewis. *Boats against the Current: American Culture between Revolution and Modernity, 1820–1860*. New York: Oxford University Press, 1993.

Persons, Stow. "The Cyclical Theory of History in Eighteenth Century America." *American Quarterly* 6 (Summer 1954): 147–63.

Pocock, J. G. A. "The Concept of a Language and the *métier d'historien*: Some Considerations on Practice." In *The Languages of Political Theory in Early-Modern Europe*, edited by Anthony Pagden. Cambridge: Cambridge University Press, 1987.

Pope, Robert. *The Half-way Covenant*. Princeton: Princeton University Press, 1969.

Portales, Marco. *Youth and Age in American Literature*. New York: Peter Lang, 1989.

Porter, Dorothy B. "The Organized Educational Activities of Negro Literary Societies, 1828–1846." *Journal of Negro Education* 5 (October 1936): 555–76.

Potter, David M., completed and edited by Don E. Fehrenbacher. *The Impending Crisis, 1848–1861*. New York: Harper and Row, 1976.

Pratt, Julius W. "The Origin of 'Manifest Destiny.' " *American Historical Review* 32 (July 1927): 795–98.

Quarles, Benjamin. "Antebellum Free Blacks and the 'Spirit of '76.' " *Journal of Negro History* 61 (July 1976): 229–42.

Quitt, Martin H. "Immigrant Origins of the Virginia Gentry: A Study of Cultural Transmission and Innovation." *William and Mary Quarterly*, 3d ser. 45 (October 1988): 629–55.

Rash, Nancy. *The Painting and Politics of George Caleb Bingham*. New Haven: Yale University Press, 1991.

Rauch, Basil. *American Interest in Cuba, 1848–1855*. New York: Columbia University Press, 1948.

Reed, John Julius. "The Emergence of the Whig Party in the North: Massachusetts, New York, Pennsylvania, and Ohio." PhD. diss., University of Pennsylvania, 1953.

Reilly, Bernard F., Jr. *American Political Prints, 1766–1876*. Boston: G. K. Hall, 1991.

Reynolds, David S. *Beneath the American Renaissance*. New York: Alfred A. Knopf, 1988.

Rich, Robert. " 'A Wilderness of Whigs': The Wealthy Men of Boston." *Journal of Social History* 4 (Spring 1971): 263–76.

Richard, Carl J. *The Founders and the Classics*. Cambridge, MA: Harvard University Press, 1994.

Richard, Claude. "Poe and 'Young America.' " *Studies in Bibliography* 21 (1968): 25–58.

Richardson, Lyon N. *A History of Early American Magazines, 1741–1789*. New York: Thomas Nelson and Sons, 1931.

Riepma, Siert F. " 'Young America': A Study in American Nationalism before the Civil War." Ph.D. diss., Western Reserve University, 1939.

Rigsby, Gregory U. *Alexander Crummell, Pioneer in Nineteenth-Century Pan-African Thought*. Westport, CT: Greenwood Press, 1987.

Riley, Matilda White, Ronald P. Abeles, and Michael S. Teitelbaum, editors. *Aging from Birth to Death*. Vol. 2, *Sociotemporal Perspectives*. Boulder, CO: Westview Press, 1982.

Rintala, Marvin. *The Constitution of Silence*. Westport, CT: Greenwood Press, 1979.

Ritter, Kurt, W. "Rhetoric and Ritual in the American Revolution: The Boston Massacre Commemorations, 1771–1783." Ph.D. diss., Indiana University, 1974.

Robson, David W. *Educating Republicans*. Westport, CT: Greenwood Press, 1985.

Roche, John F. *The Colonial Colleges in the War for American Independence*. Millwood, NY: Associated Faculty Press, 1986.

Rogin, Michael Paul. *Fathers and Children*. New York: Alfred A. Knopf, 1975.

———. *Subversive Genealogy*. New York: Alfred A. Knopf, 1983.

Rorabaugh, W. J. *The Alcoholic Republic.* New York: Oxford University Press, 1979.
————. *The Craft Apprentice.* New York: Oxford University Press, 1986.
Rosenberg, Carroll Smith. *Religion and the Rise of the American City.* Ithaca: Cornell University Press, 1971.
Ross, Dorothy. *The Origins of American Social Science.* Cambridge: Cambridge University Press, 1991.
Rossi, Joseph. *The Image of America in Mazzini's Writings.* Madison: University of Wisconsin Press, 1954.
Rotundo, E. Anthony. "Manhood in America: The Northern Middle Class, 1770–1920." Ph.D. diss., Brandeis University, 1982.
————. "Body and Soul: Changing Ideals of American Middle-Class Manhood, 1770–1920." *Journal of Social History* 16 (Summer 1983): 23–38.
————. "American Fatherhood: A Historical Perspective." *American Behavioral Scientist* 29 (September/October 1985): 7–23.
————. "Learning about Manhood: Gender Ideals and the Middle-Class Family in Nineteenth-Century America." In *Manliness and Morality,* edited by J. A. Mangan and James Walvin. Manchester: Manchester University Press, 1987.
————. "Romantic Friendship: Male Intimacy and Middle Class Youth in the Northern United States, 1800–1900." *Journal of Social History* 23 (Fall 1989): 1–25.
————. *American Manhood.* New York: Basic Books, 1993.
Ryan, Mary P. *Cradle of the Middle Class.* Cambridge: Cambridge University Press, 1981.
Ryder, Norman B. "The Cohort as a Concept in the Study of Social Change." *American Sociological Review* 30 (December 1965): 843–61.
Samuels, Richard J., editor. *Political Generations and Political Development.* Lexington, MA: Lexington Books, D. C. Heath, 1977.
Sargent, Mark L. "The Conservative Covenant: The Rise of the Mayflower Compact in American Myth." *New England Quarterly* 61 (June 1988): 233–51.
————. "Plymouth Rock and the Great Awakening." *Journal of American Studies* 22 (August 1988): 249–62.
Schlesinger, Arthur M. *Prelude to Independence.* New York: Alfred A. Knopf, 1958; reprint, Boston: Northeastern University Press, 1980.
Schlesinger, Arthur M., Jr. *The Age of Jackson.* Boston: Little, Brown, 1945.
Schochet, Gordon J. "Patriarchalism, Politics, and Mass Attitudes in Stuart England." *Historical Journal* 12, 3 (1969): 413–41.
Schoenberg, Wallace Kenneth. "The Young Men's Association, 1833–1876. The History of a Social-Cultural Organization." Ph.D. diss., New York University, 1962.
Schwartz, Barry. "The Social Context of Commemoration: A Study in Collective Memory." *Social Forces* 61 (December 1982): 374–402.
————. *George Washington: The Making of an American Symbol.* New York: Free Press, 1987.

————, and Eugene F. Miller. "The Icon and the Word: A Study in the Visual Depiction of Moral Character." *Semiotica* 61, 1/2 (1986): 69–99.

Schwartz, Hillel. "Adolescence and Revivals in Ante-Bellum Boston." *Journal of Religious History* 8 (December 1974): 144–58.

Schwartz, Thomas F. "The Springfield Lyceums and Lincoln's 1838 Speech." *Illinois Historical Journal* 83 (Spring 1990): 45–49.

Schwarzlose, Richard. *The Nation's News Brokers.* Vol. 1, *The Formative Years, from Pretelegraph to 1865.* Evanston: Northwestern University Press, 1989.

Scisco, Louis Dow. *Political Nativism in New York State.* New York, 1901.

Scobey, David M. "Revising the Errand: New England's Ways and the Puritan Sense of the Past." *William and Mary Quarterly,* 3d ser. 41 (January 1984): 3–31.

Scott, Donald M. "The Popular Lecture and the Creation of a Public in Mid-Nineteenth-Century America." *Journal of American History* 66 (March 1980): 791–809.

Scott, Joan W. "Gender: A Useful Category of Historical Analysis." *American Historical Review* 91 (December 1986): 1053–75.

————. "On Language, Gender, and Working-Class History." *International Labor and Working Class History* 31 (Spring 1987): 1–13.

Seilbels, Cynthia. "James Herring, American Portraitist." *Antiques* 113 (January 1978): 212–20.

Serrett, Milton C. *Abolition's Axe: Beriah Green, Oneida Institute, and the Black Freedom Struggle.* Syracuse: Syracuse University Press, 1986.

Seybolt, Robert F. *Apprenticeship and Apprenticeship Education in Colonial New England and New York.* New York: Teachers College, Columbia University, 1917.

Shea, William L. *The Virginia Militia in the Seventeenth Century.* Baton Rouge: Louisiana State University Press, 1983.

Shipton, Clifford. *Sibley's Harvard Graduates.* Vol. 5, 1701–1712. Boston: Massachusetts Historical Society, 1937. Vol. 10, 1736–1740. Boston: Massachusetts Historical Society, 1958.

Silverman, Kenneth. *The Life and Times of Cotton Mather.* New York: Harper and Row, 1984.

Sloan, Wm. David, and Julie Hedgepath Williams. *The Early American Press, 1690–1783.* Westport, CT: Greenwood Press, 1994.

Smith, Bruce James. *Politics and Remembrance.* Princeton: Princeton University Press, 1985.

Smith, Daniel Blake. *Inside the Great House.* Ithaca: Cornell University Press, 1980.

Smith, Daniel Scott. "Old Age and the 'Great Transformation': A New England Case Study." In *Aging and the Elderly: Humanistic Perspectives in Gerontology,* edited by Stuart F. Spicker, Kathleen M. Woodward, and David D. Van Tassel. Atlantic Highlands, NJ: Humanities Press, 1978.

Smith, Denis Mack. *Mazzini.* New Haven: Yale University Press, 1994.

Smith, Steven R. "Religion and the Conception of Youth in Seventeenth-Century England." *History of Childhood Quarterly* 2 (Spring 1975): 493–516.

Snyder, Charles McCool. *The Jacksonian Heritage: Pennsylvania Politics, 1833–1848.* Harrisburg: Pennsylvania Historical and Museum Commission, 1958.

Sollors, Werner. *Beyond Ethnicity.* New York: Oxford University Press, 1986.

Somkin, Fred. *Unquiet Eagle: Memory and Desire in the Idea of American Freedom, 1815–1860.* Ithaca: Cornell University Press, 1967.

Sommerville, C. John. *The Discovery of Childhood in Puritan England.* Athens: University of Georgia Press, 1992.

Spann, Edward K. *Ideals and Politics: New York Intellectuals and Liberal Democracy, 1820–1880.* Albany: State University of New York Press, 1972.

———. *The New Metropolis: New York City, 1840–1857.* New York: Columbia University Press, 1981.

Spencer, Benjamin T. "A National Literature, 1837–1855." *American Literature* 8 (May 1936): 125–59.

———. *The Quest for Nationality.* Syracuse: Syracuse University Press, 1957.

Spencer, Donald S. *Louis Kossuth and Young America.* Columbia: University of Missouri Press, 1977.

Spitzer, Alan B. "The Historical Problem of Generations." *American Historical Review* 78 (December 1973): 1353–85.

———. *The French Generation of 1820.* Princeton: Princeton University Press, 1987.

Stafford, John. *The Literary Criticism of "Young America."* Berkeley: University of California Press, 1952.

Stansell, Christine. *City of Women: Sex and Class in New York, 1789–1860.* Urbana: University of Illinois Press, 1986.

Stark, Gary D. "The Ideology of the German Burschenschaft Generation." *European Studies Review* 8 (July 1978): 323–48.

Stegemoeller, James E. "That Contemptible Bauble: The Birth of the Cincinnati Whig Party, 1834–1836." *Cincinnati Historical Society Bulletin* 39 (Fall 1981): 201–23.

Stein, Allen F. *Cornelius Mathews.* New York: Twayne Publishers, 1974.

Steinbrink, Jeffrey. "The Past as 'Cheerful Apologue': Emerson on the Proper Uses of History." *ESQ* 27 (1981): 207–21.

Stewart, Robert G. *A Nineteenth-Century Gallery of Distinguished Americans.* Washington, DC: Smithsonian Institution Press, 1969.

Stott, Richard B. *Workers in the Metropolis: Class, Ethnicity, and Youth in Antebellum New York City.* Ithaca: Cornell University Press, 1990.

Stout, Harry S. "Religion, Communications, and the Ideological Origins of the American Revolution." *William and Mary Quarterly,* 3d ser. 34 (October 1977): 519–41.

———. *The New England Soul.* New York: Oxford University Press, 1986.

Strauss, Gerald. *Luther's House of Learning: Indoctrination of the Young in the German Reformation.* Baltimore: Johns Hopkins University Press, 1978.

Strauss, William, and Neil Howe. *Generations: The History of America's Future, 1584 to 2069.* New York: William Morrow, 1991.

Strout, Cushing. *The New Heavens and New Earth.* New York: Harper Torchbooks, 1975.

————. "Young People of the Great Awakening: The Dynamics of a Social Movement." In *Encounter with Erikson: Historical Interpretation and Religious Biography,* edited by Donald Capps, Walter H. Capps, and M. Gerald Bradford. Missoula, MT: Scholars Press, 1977.

Strozier, Charles B. "On the Verge of Greatness: Psychological Reflections on Lincoln at the Lyceum." *Civil War History* 36 (June 1990): 137–48.

Swan, Robert J. "John Teasman: African-American Educator and the Emergence of Community in Early Black New York City, 1787–1815." *Journal of the Early Republic* 12 (Fall 1992): 331–56.

Sweet, William Warren. *Religion in the Development of American Culture, 1765–1840.* New York: Charles Scribner's Sons, 1952.

Taylor, William R. *Cavalier and Yankee.* New York: George Braziller, 1961; Harper Torchbooks, 1969.

Teaford, Jon. "The Transformation of Massachusetts Education, 1670–1780." *History of Education Quarterly* 10 (Fall 1970): 287–307.

Thistlewaite, Mark Edward. *The Image of George Washington.* New York: Garland, 1979.

Thomas, Keith. "Age and Authority in Early Modern England." *Proceedings of the British Academy* 62 (1976): 205–48.

Thompson, Roger. "Adolescent Culture in Colonial Massachusetts." *Journal of Family History* 9 (Summer 1984): 127–44.

————. *Sex in Middlesex.* Amherst: University of Massachusetts Press, 1986.

Thompson, Warren S., and P. K. Whelpton. *Population Trends in the United States.* New York: McGraw-Hill, 1933.

Thornton, Willis. *The Nine Lives of Citizen Train.* New York: Greenberg, 1948.

Tillson, Albert H., Jr. "The Militia and Popular Political Culture in the Upper Valley of Virginia, 1740–1785." *Virginia Magazine of History and Biography* 94 (July 1986): 285–306.

Tomlinson, David. "Simms's Monthly Magazine: The Southern and Western Magazine and Review." *Southern Literary Journal* 8 (Fall 1975): 95–125.

Towner, Lawrence W. "The Indentures of Boston's Poor Apprentices: 1734–1805." *Transactions of the Colonial Society of Massachusetts* (March 1962). In *Publications of the Colonial Society of Massachusetts* 43 (1956–63): 417–68.

Trachtenberg, Alan. *Reading American Photographs.* New York: Hill and Wang, 1989.

Tracy, Patricia J. *Jonathan Edwards, Pastor.* New York: Hill and Wang, 1980.

Trattner, Walter I. *From Poor Law to Welfare State.* 3d ed. New York: Free Press, 1984.

Travers, Len. "Hurrah for the Fourth: Patriotism, Politics, and Independence Day in Federalist Boston, 1783–1818." *Essex Institute Historical Collections* 125 (April 1989): 129–61.

Trexler, Richard C. *Public Life in Renaissance Florence.* New York: Academic Press, 1980.

————. *Dependence in Context in Renaissance Florence.* Binghamton, NY: Medieval and Renaissance Texts and Studies, 1994.

Trimble, William. "Diverging Tendencies in the New York Democracy in the

Period of the Locofocos." *American Historical Review* 24 (April 1919): 396–421.

———. "The Social Philosophy of the Loco-Foco Democracy." *American Journal of Sociology* 26 (May 1921): 705–15.

Trimpi, Helen P. *Melville's Confidence Men and American Politics in the 1850s.* Hamden, CT: Archon Books, 1987.

Troyen, Carol. "Retreat to Arcadia: American Landscape and the American Art-Union." *American Art Journal* 23, 1 (1991): 21–37.

Tucker, Bruce. "The Reinvention of New England, 1691–1770." *New England Quarterly* 59 (September 1986): 315–340.

Tuckerman, Frederick. "Thomas Cooper, of Boston, and his Descendants." *New-England Historical and Genealogical Register* 44 (January 1890): 53–61.

Tully, James, editor. *Meaning and Context: Quentin Skinner and His Critics.* Cambridge: Polity Press, 1988.

Tuttle, Julius Herbert. "The Libraries of the Mathers." *Proceedings of the American Antiquarian Society,* new ser. 20 (April 1910): 269–356.

Tyack, David. "Forming the National Character: Paradox in the Educational Thought of the Revolutionary Generation." *Harvard Educational Review* 36 (Winter 1966): 29–41.

Tyrrell, Ian R. *Sobering Up: From Temperance to Prohibition in Antebellum America, 1800–1860.* Westport, CT: Greenwood Press, 1979.

Ueda, Reed. *Avenues to Adulthood: The Origins of the High School and Social Mobility in an American Suburb.* Cambridge: Cambridge University Press, 1987.

Ustick, W. Lee. "Advice to a Son: A Type of Seventeenth-Century Conduct Book." *Studies in Philology* 29 (July 1932): 409–41.

Van Deusen, Glyndon G. "The Whig Party." In *History of U.S. Political Parties,* edited by Arthur Schlesinger, Jr. Vol. 1. New York: Chelsea House, R. R. Bowker, 1973.

Van De Wetering, John E. "The *Christian History* of the Great Awakening." *Journal of Presbyterian History* 44 (June 1966): 122–29.

Verbal, Betty Jean. "Youth Movements in Modern European History, 1815–1914." Ph.D. diss., Carnegie-Mellon University, 1971.

Vincent, Gilbert Tapley. "American Artists and Their Changing Perceptions of American History, 1770–1940." Ph.D. diss., University of Delaware, 1982.

Vinovskis, Maris A. "Family and Schooling in Colonial and Nineteenth-Century America." *Journal of Family History* 12, 1–3 (1987): 19–37.

Wakelyn, Jon L. "Party Issues and Political Strategy of the Charleston Taylor Democrats of 1848." *South Carolina Historical Magazine* 73 (April 1972): 72–86.

———. *The Politics of a Literary Man: William Gilmore Simms.* Westport, CT: Greenwood Press, 1973.

Wall, Richard. "The Age at Leaving Home." *Journal of Family History* 3 (Summer 1978): 181–202.

Wallach, Glenn Seth. "Obedient Sons: Youth and Generational Consciousness in American Culture, 1630–1850s." Ph.D. diss., Yale University, 1991.

Walsh, James. "The Great Awakening in the First Congregational Church of Woodbury, Connecticut." *William and Mary Quarterly*, 3d ser. 28 (October 1971): 543–62.

Walters, Ronald G. *American Reformers 1815–1860.* New York: Hill and Wang, 1978.

Ward, J. T. "Young England." *History Today* 16 (February 1966): 120–27.

Ward, W. R. *The Protestant Evangelical Awakening.* Cambridge: Cambridge University Press, 1992.

Warner, Michael. *The Letters of the Republic.* Cambridge, MA: Harvard University Press, 1990.

Warner, Robert A. "Amos Gerry Beman—1812–1874, A Memoir on a Forgotten Leader." *Journal of Negro History* 22 (April 1937): 200–221.

Washington, S. A. M. *George Thomas Downing, Sketch of His Life and Times.* Newport, RI: Milne Printers, 1910.

Watters, David H. " 'I Spake as a Child': Authority, Metaphor and the New-England Primer." *Early American Literature* 20 (Winter 1985/86): 193–213.

Watts, Steven. *The Republic Reborn.* Baltimore: Johns Hopkins University Press, 1987.

Weber, Donald. *Rhetoric and History in Revolutionary New England.* New York: Oxford University Press, 1988.

Webster, Homer J. "History of the Democratic Party Organization in the Northwest." *Ohio Archaeological and Historical Publications* 24 (1915): 1–120.

Welter, Rush. *Popular Education and Democratic Thought in America.* New York: Columbia University Press, 1962.

———. *The Mind of America, 1820–1860.* New York: Columbia University Press, 1975.

Westby, Selmer Neville. "The Puritan Funeral Sermon in Seventeenth-Century England." Ph.D. diss., University of Southern California, 1970.

Westervelt, Robert F. "The Whig Painter of Missouri." *American Art Journal* 2 (Spring 1970): 46–53.

Whibley, Charles. *Lord John Manners and His Friends.* London: William Blackwood and Sons, 1925.

Wickberg, Daniel. "The Sense of Humor in American Culture, 1850–1960." Ph.D. diss., Yale University, 1993.

Widmer, Edward. "Young America: Democratic Cultural Nationalism in Antebellum New York." Ph.D. diss., Harvard University, 1993.

Williams, David R. *Wilderness Lost.* Cranbury, NJ: Associated University Presses, 1987.

Williams, Herman Warner, Jr. *Mirror to the American Past.* Greenwich, CT: New York Graphic Society, 1973.

Williams, Raymond. *Culture and Society: 1780–1950.* New York: Harper and Row, 1958; reprint, New York: Columbia University Press, 1983.

Williamson, Chilton. *American Suffrage.* Princeton: Princeton University Press, 1960.

Williamson, George. "Mutability, Decay, and Seventeenth-Century Melancholy." *ELH* 2 (September 1935): 121–50.

Wilson, Adrian. "The Infancy of the History of Childhood: An Appraisal of Philippe Ariès." *History and Theory* 19, 2 (1980): 132–53.

Wilson, Edmund. *Patriotic Gore.* New York: Oxford University Press, 1962.

Wilson, Major L. "Lincoln and Van Buren in the Steps of the Fathers: Another Look at the Lyceum Address." *Civil War History* 29 (September 1983): 197–211.

Winch, Julie. "The Leaders of Philadelphia's Black Community, 1787–1848." Ph.D. diss., Bryn Mawr College, 1982.

———. *Philadelphia's Black Elite.* Philadelphia: Temple University Press, 1988.

Winterich, John T. *Early American Books and Printing.* Boston: Houghton Mifflin, 1935; reprint, Detroit: Gale Research, 1974.

Wohl, Robert. *The Generation of 1914.* Cambridge, MA: Harvard University Press, 1979.

Wolf, Bryan Jay. "All the World's a Code: Art and Ideology in Nineteenth-Century American Painting." *Art Journal* 44 (Winter 1984): 328–37.

Wolff, Hans Walter. "Problems between the Generations in the Old Testament." In *Essays in Old Testament Ethics,* edited by James L. Crenshaw and John T. Willis. New York: KTAV Publishing House, 1974.

Woody, Thomas. *A History of Women's Education in the United States.* Vol. 1. New York: Science Press, 1929.

Wyatt-Brown, Bertram. *Yankee Saints and Southern Sinners.* Baton Rouge: Louisiana State University Press, 1985.

Yacovone, Donald. "Samuel Joseph May, Antebellum Reform and the Problem of Patricide." *Perspectives in American History,* new ser. 2 (1985): 99–124.

Yannella, Donald. "Writing the 'Other Way': Melville, the Duyckinck Crowd, and Literature for the Masses." In *A Companion to Melville Studies,* edited by John Bryant. Westport, CT: Greenwood Press, 1986.

Yazawa, Melvin. *From Colonies to Commonwealth: Familial Ideology and the Beginnings of the American Republic.* Baltimore: Johns Hopkins University Press, 1985.

Yellin, Jean Fagan. *Women and Sisters: The Antislavery Feminists in American Culture.* New Haven: Yale University Press, 1989.

Yerushalmi, Yosef Hayim. *Zakhor: Jewish History and Jewish Memory.* Seattle: University of Washington Press, 1982.

Yodelis, M. A. "Boston's First Major Newspaper War: A 'Great Awakening' of Freedom." *Journalism Quarterly* 51 (Summer 1974): 207–12.

Zahler, Helene Sara. *Eastern Workingmen and National Land Policy, 1829–1862.* New York: Columbia University Press, 1941.

Zboray, Ronald J. *A Fictive People: Antebellum Economic Development and the American Reading Public.* New York: Oxford University Press, 1993.

Ziff, Larzer. *The Career of John Cotton: Puritanism and the American Experience.* Princeton: Princeton University Press, 1962.

INDEX